HABITAT Gray wolves live throughout a large part of North America.

BEHAVIOR Wolves live in family groups called packs. The pack hunts together.

COVERING Wolves have two coats of fur that keep them warm in winter. They can stay warm in temperatures as cold as −40° C.

GROOMING Wolves sometimes bathe in rivers or streams to wash mud from their fur.

Science

Gray Wolf

Harcourt
SCHOOL PUBLISHERS

Orlando   Austin   New York   San Diego   Toronto   London

Visit *The Learning Site!*
www.harcourtschool.com

ISBN 0-15-343731-6

2 3 4 5 6 7 8 9 10 032 13 12 11 10 09 08 07 06

Gray Wolf

Consulting Authors

Michael J. Bell
Assistant Professor of Early Childhood Education
College of Education
West Chester University of Pennsylvania

Michael A. DiSpezio
Curriculum Architect
JASON Academy
Cape Cod, Massachusetts

Marjorie Frank
Former Adjunct, Science Education
Hunter College
New York, New York

Gerald H. Krockover
Professor of Earth and Atmospheric Science Education
Purdue University
West Lafayette, Indiana

Joyce C. McLeod
Adjunct Professor
Rollins College
Winter Park, Florida

Barbara ten Brink
Science Specialist
Austin Independent School District
Austin, Texas

Carol J. Valenta
Senior Vice President
St. Louis Science Center
St. Louis, Missouri

Barry A. Van Deman
President and CEO
Museum of Life and Science
Durham, North Carolina

Senior Editorial Advisors

Napoleon Adebola Bryant, Jr.
Professor Emeritus of Education
Xavier University
Cincinnati, Ohio

Robert M. Jones
Professor of Educational Foundations
University of Houston-Clear Lake
Houston, Texas

Mozell P. Lang
Former Science Consultant
Michigan Department of Education
Science Consultant, Highland Park Schools
Highland Park, Michigan

PHYSICAL SCIENCE

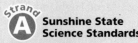

Strand A Sunshine State Science Standards
The Nature of Matter

Science Spin Weekly Reader

Technology
PB and J: A Sticky Problem, **52**

People
Building the Bridge, **54**
Career, **54**

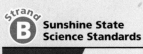

Strand B Sunshine State Science Standards
Energy

Science Spin Weekly Reader

Technology
President's Sunken Ship Discovered, **86**

People
The Mosquito Kid, **88**

Science Spin Weekly Reader

Technology
Heat from Earth, **118**

People
A Bright Idea, **120**

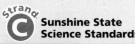

Force and Motion

Sunshine State Science Standards

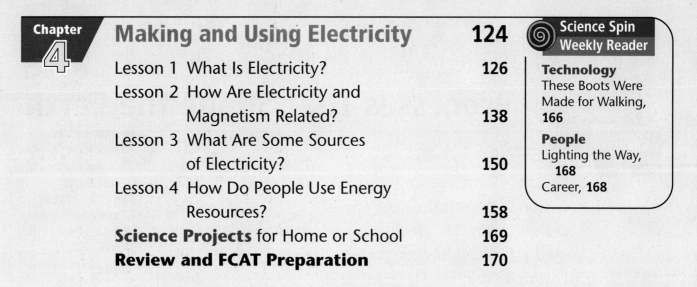

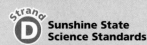

EARTH SCIENCE

Strand **D** Sunshine State Science Standards

Processes That Shape the Earth

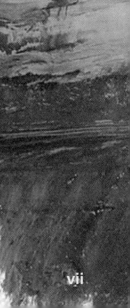

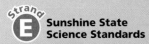
Earth and Space

Chapter 10

Planets and Other Objects in Space

 Science Spin
Weekly Reader

Technology
Water World, **378**
People
Moonstruck, **380**

LIFE SCIENCE

 Sunshine State Science Standards **Processes of Life**

How Living Things Interact with Their Environment

 Sunshine State Science Standards

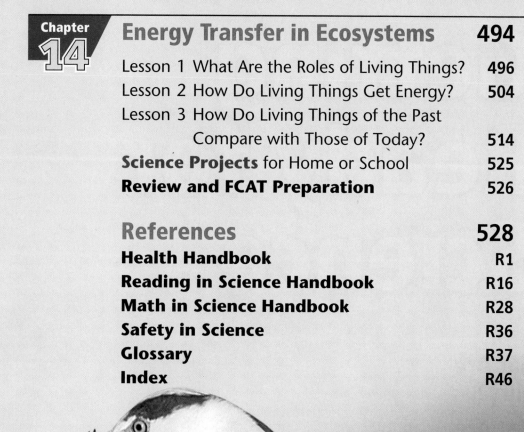

Getting Ready for Science

Lesson 1 **What Are Tools for Inquiry?**

Lesson 2 **What Are Inquiry Skills?**

Lesson 3 **What Is the Scientific Method?**

Vocabulary

FCAT-Tested
experiment
scientific method

Other Terms
standard measure
microscope
pan balance
spring scale
observation
inference
hypothesis

What do YOU wonder?

Does "doing science" require special skills? Which science skills is this young snorkeler using?

What Are Tools for Inquiry?

Fast Fact

Out-of-This-World Tools The wheels of the Mars Rovers were tools for exploration. They exposed layers of soil. Scientists used the soil data to draw conclusions about Mars. In the Investigate, you will draw conclusions about ways to measure.

Measuring with Straws

Materials
- plastic straws
- 2 cups
- classroom objects
- water
- marker

Procedure

1. Use straws to measure length and width (distance). For example, you might measure this textbook or another flat object. Record your measurements.

2. Now use straws to measure the distance around a round object (its circumference). Hint: Flatten the straws before you start. Record your measurements.

3. Next, work with a partner to find a way to use straws to measure the amount of water in a cup (its volume). Record your measurements.

Draw Conclusions

1. Compare your measurements with those of other students. What can you conclude?

2. **Inquiry Skill** Scientists measure carefully so they can record changes accurately. Why do all scientists need to use the same unit of measurement when working on the same problems?

Step 2

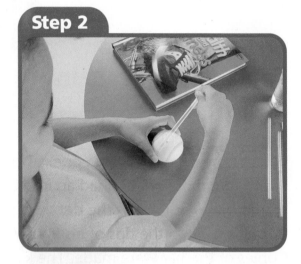

Step 3

Investigate Further

How could you mark a straw to divide it into smaller units? How would this change the way you collect data? What might be a reason to do this?

VOCABULARY

standard measure p. 4
microscope p. 6
pan balance p. 8
spring scale p. 8

SCIENCE CONCEPTS

► how scientists use tools to measure, observe, and manipulate

► how to use tools properly and safely

READING FOCUS SKILL

MAIN IDEA AND DETAILS

Look for tools that scientists use.

| Main Idea |
| detail | detail | detail |

Tools for Measuring Distance

Long ago, people sometimes used body parts to measure distance. For example, King Henry I of England had an iron bar made. It was as long as the distance from his nose to the tips of his fingers. Copies of the bar were made. The king told everyone to use the bars to measure things. This bar became the standard length for one yard. A **standard measure** is an accepted measurement.

When it was introduced, the meter, another unit of length, was not based on a body part. It was defined as 1/10,000,000 of the distance from the North Pole to the equator. Imagine measuring that distance!

These units of measurement may seem strange. Yet they helped people agree on the lengths of objects and the distances between places.

MAIN IDEA AND DETAILS Why do we have standard units of measure?

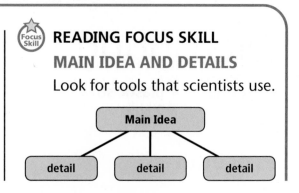

▼ A flexible measuring tape can measure circumference.

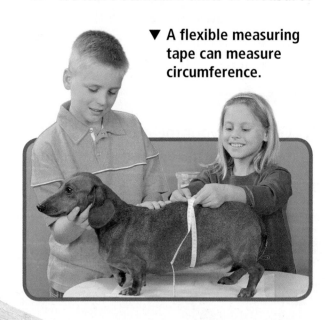

Geologists and surveyors use this tool to measure large distances.

◄ A ruler measures length. Place the first line of the ruler at one end of the object. The point on the ruler where the object ends is its length.

Tools for Measuring Volume

Cooks use cups and spoons to measure ingredients for a recipe. Scientists measure volume with tools, too. To find the volume of a liquid, you put it into a container such as a measuring cup, a beaker, or a graduate. The numbers on the side of the container show the volume of the liquid. Never use tools from your science lab for measuring food or medicine!

To measure the volume of a solid, multiply its length by its width by its height. For example, one box has a length of 4 centimeters and a width of 2 centimeters. Its height is 2 centimeters. The volume is 4 cm x 2 cm x 2 cm = 16 cubic centimeters.

 MAIN IDEA AND DETAILS How do you measure the volume of a solid? Of a liquid?

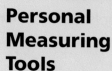

Personal Measuring Tools

Think of other ways that you could measure distance or volume, using items you have at home or in the classroom. Test your new measuring tools, and exchange ideas with other students.

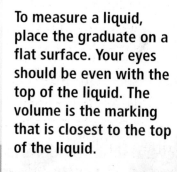

To measure a liquid, place the graduate on a flat surface. Your eyes should be even with the top of the liquid. The volume is the marking that is closest to the top of the liquid.

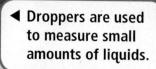

◄ Droppers are used to measure small amounts of liquids.

5

Tools for Observing and Handling

Sometimes scientists need to observe an object closely. Certain tools can help them observe details they might not be able to see using just their eyes.

A hand lens makes things look larger than they are. It magnifies them. Hold the lens a few centimeters in front of your eye. Then move the object closer to the lens until you can see it clearly. Never let the lens touch your eye. Never use it to look at the sun!

Forceps let you pick up a sharp or prickly object without getting hurt. They can also protect a delicate object from too much handling. However, you must squeeze the forceps gently.

A magnifying box is sometimes called a bug box. Students often use it to observe live insects. An insect can move around in the box while you watch.

A **microscope** makes an object look several times bigger than it is. The microscope on the next page has several lenses that can magnify a little or a lot. Two knobs help you adjust the image until you can see it clearly.

(Focus Skill) **MAIN IDEA AND DETAILS** How do the tools on these pages help scientists?

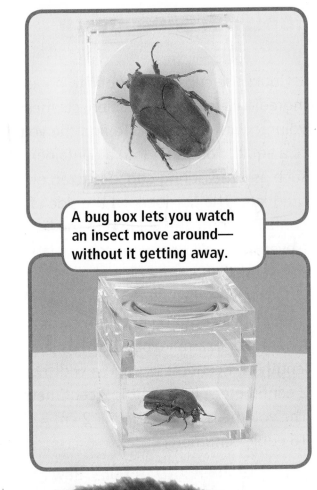

A bug box lets you watch an insect move around—without it getting away.

A hand lens allows you to see many details. When you use forceps to hold an object, you can observe it without your fingers getting in the way.

6

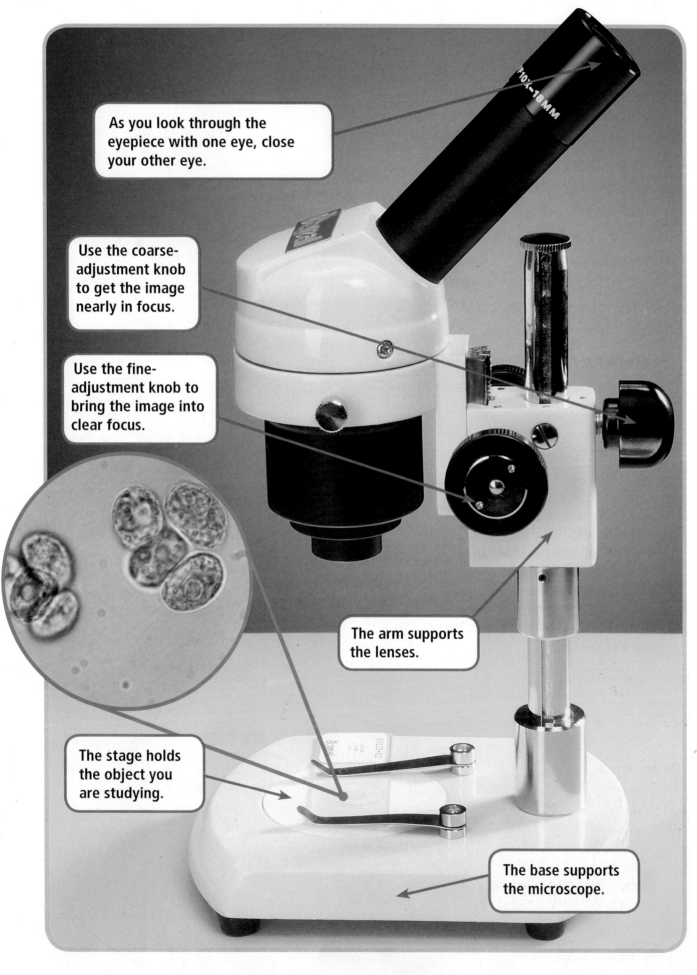

As you look through the eyepiece with one eye, close your other eye.

Use the coarse-adjustment knob to get the image nearly in focus.

Use the fine-adjustment knob to bring the image into clear focus.

The arm supports the lenses.

The stage holds the object you are studying.

The base supports the microscope.

Other Tools

Many other tools can help you measure. A thermometer can measure the temperature of the air or of a liquid. Be sure to touch the thermometer as little as possible. Otherwise, it will just measure the warmth of your fingers. Be careful! Glass thermometers break easily.

A **pan balance** measures mass. Mass is the amount of matter in an object. It is measured in grams (g). A **spring scale** measures forces, such as weight. The pull is measured in newtons (N).

MAIN IDEA AND DETAILS What do a pan balance and a spring scale each measure?

The number closest to the top of the liquid is the temperature.

This girl is using a spring scale to measure the rabbit's weight. ▶

▼ Before you use a pan balance, make sure the pointer is at the middle mark. Place the object in one pan, and add standard masses to the other pan. When the pointer is at the middle mark again, add the numbers on the standard masses. The total is the mass of the object.

pans

middle mark

standard masses

1. MAIN IDEA AND DETAILS Copy this graphic organizer and complete it.

MAIN IDEA: Scientists use many different tools to measure, observe, and handle.

 Two tools for measuring

 Two tools for observing

 One tool for handling

Ⓐ _____ Ⓑ _____ Ⓒ _____ Ⓓ _____ Ⓔ _____

2. SUMMARIZE Write two sentences that tell what this lesson is mostly about.

3. DRAW CONCLUSIONS How would scientific experiments change if scientists had no tools to use?

4. VOCABULARY Write a fill-in-the-blank sentence for each vocabulary term. Trade sentences with a partner.

FCAT Prep

5. Read/Inquire/Explain How can you decide which tool to use in a certain experiment?

6. Which tool would help you measure how different colors absorb the energy in sunlight?

A. beaker　　**C.** pan balance
B. meterstick　　**D.** thermometer

Links

Writing

Persuasive Writing

You are a scientist, but you can afford only two of the tools described in this lesson. Choose two tools, and write a persuasive **paragraph** about why they are the most important.

Math

Solve a Problem

You are using a measuring wheel to determine the width of a street. A rotation of the wheel is one meter (3.3 ft). The wheel rotates $9\frac{1}{2}$ times. About how wide is the street?

Art

Looking Closer

Draw an object as you would see it with your eyes. Then draw the same object as you think it would look under a hand lens. Now draw it as it looks under the highest-power microscope lens.

 For more links and activities, go to **www.hspscience.com**

2

What Are Inquiry Skills?

Fast Fact

Windows in the Roof The clear, curving roof of Telstra Stadium in Sydney, Australia, lets in light but keeps out rain. Engineers built and tested many models before the final stadium was built. In the Investigate, you'll make a model building.

Build a Straw Model

Materials • 16 plastic straws • 30 paper clips • 30 cm masking tape

Procedure

1 You will work with a group to construct a model of a building. First, discuss questions such as these: What should the building look like? What are some ways to use the paper clips and the tape with the straws? What will keep the building from falling down?

2 Have one group member record all the ideas. Be sure to communicate well and respect each other's suggestions.

3 Predict which techniques will work best, and try them out. Observe what works, draw conclusions, and record them.

4 Plan how to construct a model building, and then carry out the plan.

Draw Conclusions

1. Why was it important to share ideas before you began construction?

2. **Inquiry Skill** Scientists and engineers often use models to better understand how parts work together. Models help find problems before building. What did you learn about constructing a building by making the model?

Step 3

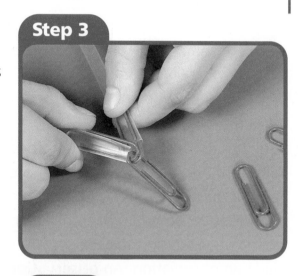

Step 4

Investigate Further

Choose one additional material or tool to use in constructing your model. Explain how it will improve your model.

Reading in Science

VOCABULARY
observation p. 12
inference p. 12
hypothesis p. 15
experiment p. 15

SCIENCE CONCEPTS
▶ how scientists think
▶ how asking questions helps scientists learn and understand

READING FOCUS SKILL

MAIN IDEA AND DETAILS

Look for inquiry skills scientists use.

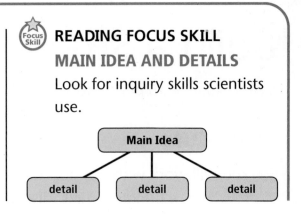

Scientists practice certain ways of thinking, or *inquiry skills.* You use these skills, too. Keep reading to learn more about inquiry skills.

Observe Did you notice the clouds when you woke up today? If so, you made an observation. An **observation** is information from your senses. You can observe how tall or smooth an object is.

Infer Did you ever try to explain why something is a certain color or why it smells like old socks? You were not observing. You were inferring. An **inference** is an untested conclusion based on your observations.

Scientists might observe that one star looks brighter than others. They could infer that the brighter star is bigger, hotter, or closer to Earth.

Predict You often use your knowledge to guess what will happen next. You are predicting. You figure out patterns of events. Then you say what will happen next. For example, scientists might observe a series of small earthquakes. Then they use that information to predict a nearby volcano eruption.

MAIN IDEA AND DETAILS Why do scientists observe, infer, and predict?

◀ You use inquiry skills to infer when a flower's buds will open. You might even predict what color the flowers will be.

▲ How are these plants different and the same? What words and numbers can be used to describe them?

Compare Scientists—and you—often compare things. You describe how the things are different and the same. For example, you learn about two rocks by comparing the minerals in them.

Classify/Order Is your music collection sorted in some way, such as by performer or type of music? Then you've classified it. You sorted it based on an observation. Scientists classify, or sort, things, too. For example, they might group rocks by color or texture.

You might also put objects or events in order. You could put planets in order by their size or their distance from the sun. You might put sounds in order by their pitch or their loudness. Putting things in order helps you see patterns.

Use Numbers Where would scientists be without numbers? They use exact numbers to show the mass of a seed. They use estimates to show the mass of a planet. Scientists—and you—use numbers to experiment and learn.

 MAIN IDEA AND DETAILS Name a way you use each skill on this page in your daily life.

Use Time and Space Relationships How do the orbits of planets relate to one another? What are the steps in the water cycle? How does a pulley work? To answer these questions, you need to understand time and space relationships. Scientists—and you—need to understand how objects and events affect each other. You also need to know the order in which events happen.

Measure You often need to measure the results of your experiments. How tall did each plant grow? How far did the block slide on sandpaper and on waxed paper? Measuring allows you to compare your results to those of others anywhere. Scientists use the International System (SI) of measurements. It is also called the *metric system.*

Formulate or Use Models Have you ever used a little ball and a big ball to show Earth orbiting the sun? Have you ever drawn the parts of a cell? You were making models. Models help you understand how something works. For example, a globe is a model of Earth.

Scientists often formulate, or make, models. Models help them understand things that are too big, small, fast, slow, or dangerous to observe in person.

 MAIN IDEA AND DETAILS How would you use these three skills to make a diorama of an ecosystem?

▼ These students are measuring how fast loaded and unloaded toys move. Which variables are they controlling? Which variable changes?

◀ **What is a possible hypothesis for an investigation using these materials?**

Plan and Conduct a Simple Investigation Your CD player will not work. You think of several possible causes, such as dead batteries. Then you plan and conduct a simple investigation. You find and fix the problem. Scientists also use this approach.

Hypothesize Suppose you have a more complex problem. Your class is making sandwiches to sell at a school fair. You must decide how to keep the sandwiches fresh.

A **hypothesis** is a statement of what you think will happen and why. You hypothesize that small, resealable bags work best because they keep air out. Next, you test your hypothesis.

You set up an **experiment** to test your hypothesis. You put different sandwiches in different wrappings. A day later, the meat and cheese sandwich in the resealable bag is freshest. However, maybe it was the cheese, and not the bag, that kept the sandwich fresh. You can't be sure!

Identify and Control Variables To make a fair test, you must identify the variables—the things that can change—in an experiment. Then you need to control—keep the same—all the variables except the one you change and the one you observe. So, only the kind of sandwich wrapping should change.

 MAIN IDEA AND DETAILS Why is it important to control variables?

Full Measure
Select an object in the classroom. Measure it as many ways as you can. Record the measurements. Give them to your teacher. You will be given another list. Try to find the object that the new list describes.

Draw Conclusions For the sandwich experiment, suppose the results support your hypothesis. You can draw a conclusion based on the data you collected. Small, resealable bags do keep sandwiches fresher than other wrappings. You are ready for the school fair!

Gather/Record/Interpret/ Display Data In this experiment, you gathered data by checking the freshness of each sandwich. You recorded the results for each wrapping so you would not mix them up. Then you interpreted the data by drawing a conclusion.

If this investigation were for a science class, you would display the results. You might organize the results into a graph, table, or map.

Communicate You would probably tell your friends which sandwich wrapping works best. If this experiment were for a science fair, you would use other tools to share information— writing, pictures, and graphs. You might even display some sandwiches. They would help communicate how well each kind of wrapping worked.

 MAIN IDEA AND DETAILS Why is communication an important skill?

▼ These students are using words, objects, and pictures to communicate. They are sharing how they conducted their experiment with toys and what conclusions they drew.

1. MAIN IDEA AND DETAILS Write details to complete this organizer.

> **MAIN IDEA: Scientists use many different inquiry skills.**

Ⓐ _____ **Ⓑ** _____ **Ⓒ** _____

2. SUMMARIZE Write a sentence that tells the most important information in this lesson.

3. DRAW CONCLUSIONS You cannot understand a friend's science project. What inquiry skill or skills does your friend need to strengthen?

4. VOCABULARY Create a word puzzle with the vocabulary words.

FCAT Prep

5. Read/Inquire/Explain Which skills could help you find out what kind of muscle tissue is on a slide?

6. Which inquiry skill helps you notice a change?
- **A.** communicate
- **C.** observe
- **B.** hypothesize
- **D.** predict

Links

Writing

Narrative Writing

Write a **story** about how you or an imaginary person your age uses several inquiry skills to solve a problem. At the end of the story, name the skills used.

Math

SI Units

Find out more about the International System (SI) of units. What SI units are most like these common units: inches, yards, miles, quarts?

Health

Get Moving

What do you believe is the main reason some people do not like to exercise? Now think of a way to find out whether your reason (hypothesis) is accurate. Write the steps you would take.

 For more links and activities, go to **www.hspscience.com**

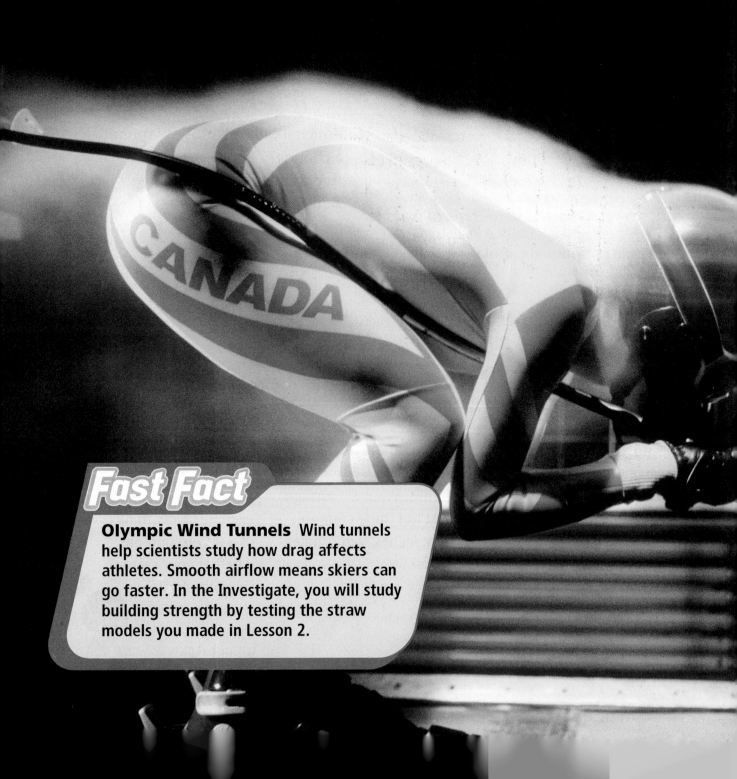

What Is the Scientific Method?

Fast Fact

Olympic Wind Tunnels Wind tunnels help scientists study how drag affects athletes. Smooth airflow means skiers can go faster. In the Investigate, you will study building strength by testing the straw models you made in Lesson 2.

Testing a Straw Model

Materials
- straw models from Lesson 2
- paper cups
- large paper clips
- pennies

Procedure

1. Bend a paper clip to make a handle for a paper cup, as shown.

2. With your group, predict how many pennies your straw model can support. Then hang the cup on your model and add one penny at a time. Was your prediction accurate?

3. Now work together to think of ways to strengthen your model. You might also look for other places on your model to hang the cup. Record your ideas.

4. Form a hypothesis about what will make the model stronger. Then experiment to see if the results support the hypothesis.

5. Discuss what made your straw model stronger, and draw conclusions.

6. Communicate your findings to the class.

Step 1

Step 2

Draw Conclusions

1. Were you able to increase the strength of your model? How?

2. **Inquiry Skill** Scientists experiment to test their hypotheses. What did you learn from your experiments in this activity?

Investigate Further

Will your model support more pennies if their weight is spread across the structure? Plan and conduct an experiment to find out.

VOCABULARY
scientific method p. 20

SCIENCE CONCEPTS
▶ how to explain the steps in the scientific method
▶ how the scientific method helps scientists gain knowledge

READING FOCUS SKILL

MAIN IDEA AND DETAILS
Look for the steps in the scientific method.

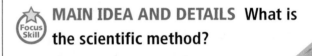

Using the Scientific Method

The **scientific method** is a way that scientists find out how things work and affect each other. The five steps of this method help test ideas. You learned the terms used in this method in Lesson 2. Now you will see how scientists—and you—can put these terms to work.

1 Observe and Ask Questions

After observing the straw models your class built, you might ask:

- Is a cube stronger than a triangle?
- Are straws more likely to bend if they are placed at an angle?
- Is a shorter straw stronger?
- Why do buildings use triangles?

MAIN IDEA AND DETAILS What is the scientific method?

▼ You can find triangle shapes in bridges and other structures. Why is that?

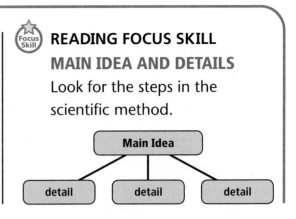

2 Form a Hypothesis

Maybe you wonder whether a pyramid or a cube is stronger. Now form a hypothesis. A hypothesis is a statement that tells what will happen and why. A hypothesis must be testable. Here is a possible hypothesis: *Pyramids hold more weight than cubes because triangles are stronger than squares.*

3 Plan an Experiment

How can you test your hypothesis? You think of a plan and then write it as steps. For example, you might hang a cup on each model, and then add one penny at a time to each cup.

Next, you need to think about all the variables. Make sure that you are changing only one each time you do the experiment.

In this experiment, both models are made of straws. Both are made the same way. The cups will be the same. Only one variable will be tested—the shape of the structures. The complete plan should list all the materials. After that, it should list what to do in order.

4 Conduct an Experiment

Now it's time to conduct, or carry out, your experiment. You follow the steps in the correct order. At each step, you record everything you observe, especially any results you didn't expect.

 MAIN IDEA AND DETAILS How do you plan an experiment?

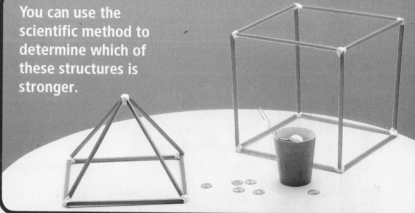

You can use the scientific method to determine which of these structures is stronger.

Insta-Lab

Observe and Ask Questions

Write down three questions about anything you can see while seated at your desk. Discuss the questions with two classmates. Choose one question none of you could answer. Plan a way to find the answer.

⑤ Draw Conclusions and Communicate Results

The final step is drawing conclusions. You look at the hypothesis again. Then you look at the observations you recorded. Do the results support your hypothesis? Was the pyramid able to support more pennies than the cube?

In this experiment, you could give the results in numbers. Other times, you might describe the results in other ways. For example, you might explain that a liquid turned blue or a plant wilted.

Scientists share the results of their investigations. That allows others to double-check the results. Then scientists can build new ideas on knowledge they are sure is reliable.

You can share your findings in a written or oral report. Charts, graphs, and diagrams help explain your results and conclusions. A written procedure allows others to repeat what you did.

★ **MAIN IDEA AND DETAILS** Why should a report on an investigation be clear and detailed?

▼ Your report should describe your hypothesis, the steps you carried out, the results, and your conclusions. Another person should be able to read your report, repeat your investigation, and get similar results.

1. MAIN IDEA AND DETAILS Draw and complete this graphic organizer.

> **MAIN IDEA: The scientific method consists of five steps.**

> Step 1: **A**_____ and ask questions.

> Step 4: Conduct an **C**_____ .

> Step 2: Form a **B**_____ .

> Step 5: **D**_____ and communicate results.

> Step 3: Plan an experiment.

2. SUMMARIZE Write a summary of this lesson, beginning with this sentence: *The scientific method helps us gain new knowledge.*

3. DRAW CONCLUSIONS Will the scientific method be different 100 years from now? Why or why not?

4. VOCABULARY Write a fill-in-the-blank sentence for the vocabulary term.

FCAT Prep

5. Read/Inquire/Explain Name a problem in a young person's life that could be solved using the scientific method.

6. When you use the scientific method, what are you testing?

A. conclusions   C. hypothesis

B. experiment   D. observations

Links

Writing

Expository Writing

Choose an investigation you conducted or observed. Write a **report** on it. Describe how each step of the scientific method was completed—or how it should have been.

Math

Solve a Problem

A penny weighs 2.8 grams (0.1 oz). Let's say a pyramid supports 10 pennies, and a cube supports 6. How much more weight will the pyramid support than the cube?

Social Studies

Super Scientists

Choose a scientist who interests you, and research his or her life, challenges, and successes. Then make a poster to share interesting facts about this scientist with others.

 For more links and activities, go to **www.hspscience.com**

Review and FCAT Preparation

Vocabulary Review

Use the terms below to complete the sentences. The page numbers tell you where to look in the chapter if you need help.

microscope p. 6
spring scale p. 8
inference p. 12
hypothesis p. 15
experiment p. 15
scientific method p. 20

1. Forces are measured by a _____.

2. A _____ is a testable explanation of an observation.

3. When you make an observation and then draw a conclusion, you make an _____.

4. To observe very small details, you might use a _____.

5. Scientists find out how things work and affect each other by using the _____.

6. A scientific test in which variables are carefully controlled is an _____.

Check Understanding

Write the letter of the best choice.

7. Which tool measures distance?
   A. forceps   **C.** meterstick
   B. graduate   **D.** microscope

8. Which of these is a hypothesis?
   F. I wonder how long a cactus can live without water here on a sunny windowsill.
   G. How long can a desert cactus live without water on a sunny windowsill?
   H. This experiment will test how long a desert cactus can live without water on a sunny windowsill.
   I. A cactus will live without water for a month on a sunny windowsill, since it can live in a desert.

9. **MAIN IDEA AND DETAILS** What is the main purpose of the scientific method?
   A. to ask questions
   B. to share information
   C. to test ideas
   D. to plan an experiment

10. In the scientific method, which of these do you do first?
    F. draw conclusions
    G. ask questions
    H. communicate
    I. hypothesize

11. Which of these is an observation?
    A. The plant needs more water.
    B. The plant wilted on the third day.
    C. The plant will need water daily.
    D. The plant will not live in a desert.

12. Which prediction for recycling in 2010 is based on the graph?

Waste Recycled

- **F.** The rate will increase a little.
- **G.** The rate will decrease a little.
- **H.** The rate will level off.
- **I.** The rate will decrease a lot.

13. Which tool measures volume?
- **A.** hand lens
- **C.** scale
- **B.** measuring cup
- **D.** ruler

14. Which inquiry skill is based on identifying common features?
- **F.** classify
- **H.** predict
- **G.** infer
- **I.** use numbers

15. Which of these is a possible inference based on seeing a bird eat seeds?
- **A.** The bird ate only the seeds.
- **B.** The bird has a thick beak.
- **C.** The bird doesn't eat meat.
- **D.** The males are quieter.

16. MAIN IDEA AND DETAILS Which of these is not an inquiry skill?
- **F.** infer
- **G.** communicate
- **H.** scale
- **I.** classify/order

Inquiry Skills

17. A model is not the real thing, so why do scientists **use a model**?

18. Which tool or tools would you use to **measure** and **compare** the mass of a cup of fresh water and a cup of salt water?

Read/Inquire/Explain

19. A scientist repeats another scientist's experiment but gets different results. What are possible causes?

20. You want to find out how water temperature affects the movement of goldfish.

Part A Write a hypothesis for your investigation.

Part B Identify the variables you will control in your experiment and the variable you will change.

The Nature of Matter

The chapters in this unit address these Grade Level Expectations from the Florida Sunshine State Standards.

The investigations and experiences in this unit also address many of the Grade Level Expectations in Strand H, The Nature of Science.

Science in Florida

Dry Tortugas

Dear Marianne,

Yesterday we left Key West and sailed 70 miles west to Dry Tortugas National Park. A park ranger told us how the islands got their name. Ponce de Leon discovered the islands in 1513, and he realized there was no supply of fresh water. There were many "tortugas" there, which is Spanish for sea turtles.

Talk to you soon,

Mark

The Sunshine State

USA

FCAT Writing

Writing Situation
Suppose you discover an island while sailing across the ocean. Write a story about the things you find on the island.

Experiment!

The Freezing Point of Water

When sidewalks and roads are covered with ice, people sprinkle salt on the ice to melt it. The salt combines with the ice, forming salt water. The ice melts because salt water freezes at a lower temperature than pure water. Do all liquids have the same freezing point? Plan and conduct an experiment to find out.

Chapter 1

Properties of Matter

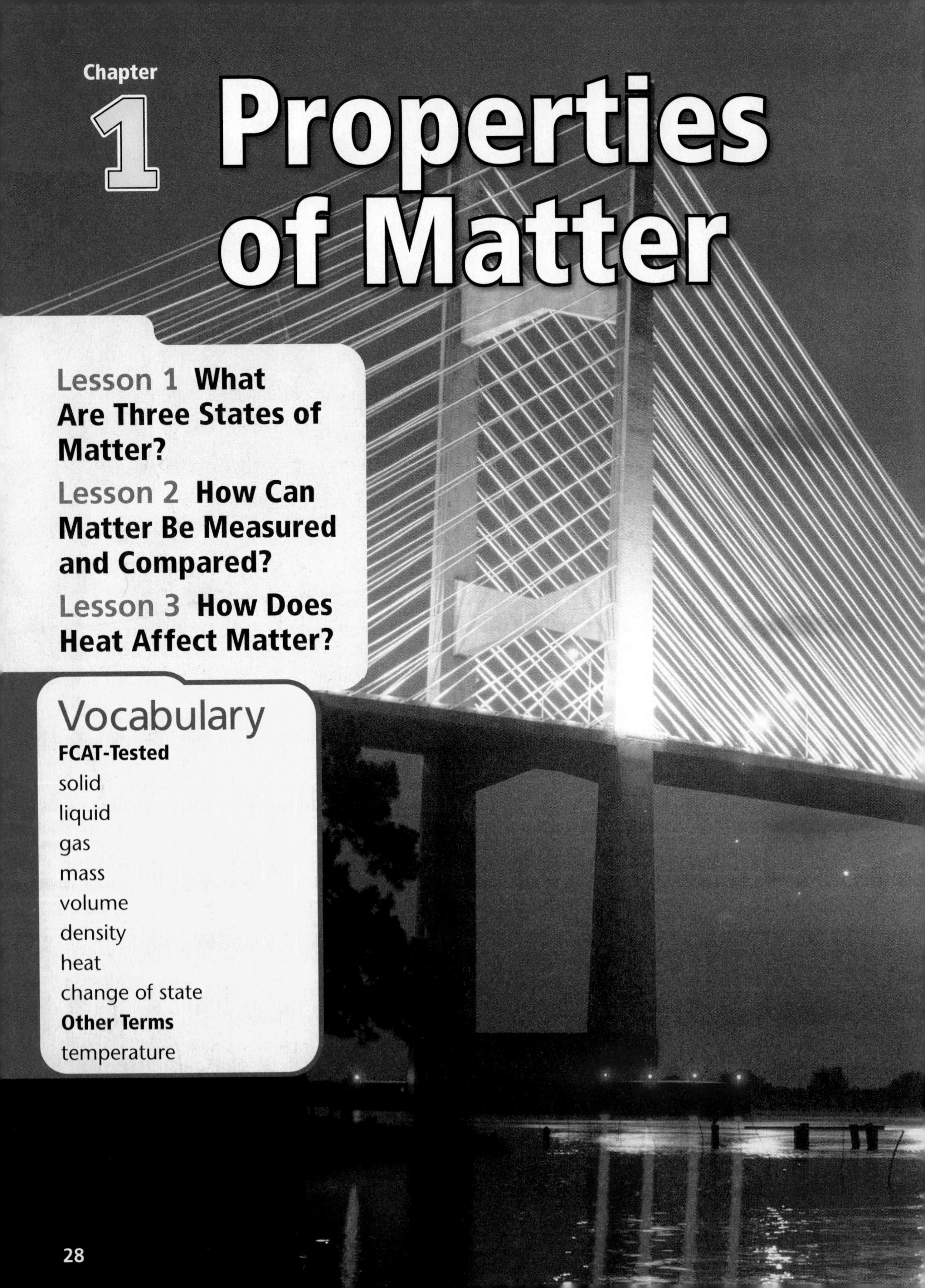

Vocabulary

FCAT-Tested

solid
liquid
gas
mass
volume
density
heat
change of state

Other Terms

temperature

What do YOU wonder?

The photo of Dames Point Bridge near Jacksonville, Florida, shows several kinds of matter. How many can you name? How are they alike? How are they different?

What Are Three States of Matter?

Fast Fact

Full of Hot Air In 1783, the first human flight took place in a hot-air balloon a little bit like this one. When a balloon is first filled with air, the balloon won't rise. But when the air inside the balloon is heated, the balloon lifts off! In this Investigate, you will discover more things about how air behaves.

What's the Matter?

Materials • plastic bag • plastic drinking straw • book

Procedure

1. Wrap the opening of a plastic bag tightly around one end of a straw. Hold the bag in place with your fingers. Don't squeeze the straw shut.

2. Blow into the straw. Observe what happens to the bag. Then record your observations.

3. Take the straw out of the bag. Lay the bag flat on the table, and place a book on top of the bag. Leave the opening of the bag free.

4. Repeat Steps 1 and 2.

Draw Conclusions

1. What happened to the bag? What happened to the book?

2. Draw Conclusions What conclusion can you draw about air?

Step 1

Step 3

Investigate Further

In a sink, place a full 2-L bottle on top of a plastic bag. Connect a tube to the faucet, and use it to fill the bag with water. What conclusion can you draw about water?

SC.A.1.2.1.4.1 physical properties of matter
SC.H.1.2.4.4.1 comparing experiments

Reading in Science

SC.A.1.2.1.4.1 physical properties of matter
LA.A.2.2.7 compare and contrast

VOCABULARY
solid p. 32
liquid p. 33
gas p. 34

SCIENCE CONCEPTS
▶ what a solid is
▶ what a liquid is
▶ what a gas is

 READING FOCUS SKILL
COMPARE AND CONTRAST
Look for similarities and differences among solids, liquids, and gases.

[alike]———[different]

Solids

Suppose you're putting books in a backpack. You can't put in as many books as you want. At some point, the books take up all the space in the backpack. That happens because books are matter. Matter is anything that takes up space and has mass.

What happens if you move this science textbook from your desk to your backpack? Does it take up more space in one place than it does in the other place? No, it doesn't.

What happens to the shape of the book when you move it? Does the shape change, or is it always the same? The book's shape stays the same because the book is a solid.

A **solid** is any matter that keeps its shape and always takes up the same amount of space.

 COMPARE AND CONTRAST How does a book's shape contrast with the shape of water?

Objects made of metal, stone, or rock are solids. They keep their shape and take up the same amount of space when moved from one place to another.

32

How many different shapes does the water have as it flows through this fountain?

Oil is a liquid. You can measure the space it takes up by pouring it into a marked container.

Liquids

You have a 1-liter (1-qt) bottle of juice. The bottle is full. You take off the top and pour all the juice into a bowl. How much juice is in the bowl? One liter. Pouring the juice into the bowl doesn't change the amount of space it takes up.

What happened to the shape of the juice? When it was in the bottle, the juice had the shape of the bottle—tall and thin. Now that it's in the bowl, the juice is wide and flat, like the bowl.

Juice is a liquid. A **liquid** is any matter that always takes up the same amount of space but doesn't have any definite shape. If a liquid is in a container, it takes the shape of the container. If it isn't in a container, it spreads out into a thin layer.

If you've ever spilled water on a table, you know that.

 COMPARE AND CONTRAST How is a liquid like a solid? How are they different?

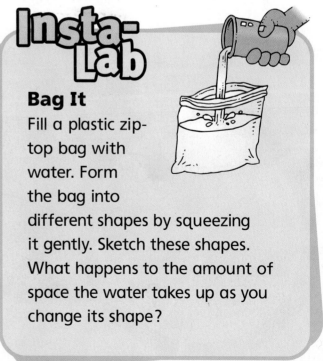

Insta-Lab

Bag It
Fill a plastic zip-top bag with water. Form the bag into different shapes by squeezing it gently. Sketch these shapes. What happens to the amount of space the water takes up as you change its shape?

33

Gases

Did you ever blow up a balloon? A balloon may be round, or it may be long and thin. You can squeeze it into other shapes. The air inside the balloon has the shape of its container. What happens if the balloon pops? The matter inside the balloon goes all over the place!

The air you use to blow up a balloon is a gas. A **gas** is matter that doesn't have a definite shape and doesn't take up a definite amount of space. A gas always takes up whatever space there is.

Think of gas in a container as being like students in school. The bell rings at the end of the school day. Students rush out of the building and spread out all over the neighborhood. In the same way, a gas spreads into whatever space it has. For example, Earth's atmosphere is gas that isn't in a container. It spreads all over the planet. Earth's gravity holds most of the atmosphere in place.

 COMPARE AND CONTRAST How is a gas similar to and different from a solid?

▼ The pump squeezes outside air into a smaller space to fill the tire.

▲ The air in the diver's tank is squeezed into a much smaller space than it takes up in the atmosphere. This lets the tank hold much more air so that the diver can stay under water longer.

1. COMPARE AND CONTRAST Draw and complete the graphic organizer.

	Different	Alike
Solids	Shape **A** _____ .	All three states have **D** _____ and take up **E** _____ .
Liquids	Shape **B** _____ to match container.	
Gases	**C** _____ to fill available space.	

2. SUMMARIZE Write three sentences that tell about this lesson.

3. DRAW CONCLUSIONS Your teacher puts a jar on the desk. The matter inside the jar is blue. Something blue starts drifting out of the jar. What type of matter is in the jar?

4. VOCABULARY Use each vocabulary word in a sentence that begins
One example of a _____ is _____ .

FCAT Prep

5. Read/Inquire/Explain Why does a bicycle tire get harder to pump up as it gets fuller?

6. Which of the following is a liquid?
   A. ice on a pond
   B. a bar of soap
   C. an ocean breeze
   D. sea water

Links

Writing

Expository Writing
Imagine that your class is making a video about matter. Write the **narration** for that video. If you want, you may also describe the images that appear with your narration.

Math

Select the Operation
There are four bottles of water on a counter. Each bottle is a different size and shape. Write one or more ways you could find the total amount of water in the bottles.

Music

Impressions of Matter
Find three pieces of music that make you think of a solid, a liquid, and a gas. They may be pop songs or parts of classical works. Play a sample of each piece for your class.

 For more links and activities, go to www.hspscience.com

How Can Matter Be Measured and Compared?

Fast Fact

Size Matters Canals like this join two bodies of water that are at different levels. A ship enters the canal at one level. Water is let in or out to raise or lower the ship. It takes about 200 million liters (52 million gal) of water to move a boat through the Panama Canal. The Investigate will help you understand more about the volume of matter.

How Much and How Heavy?

Materials • 3 plastic cups • raisins • cereal • pan balance

Procedure

1. Fill a plastic cup all the way to the top with raisins.

2. Fill another cup all the way to the top with cereal.

3. Observe the amount of space taken up by the raisins and by the cereal. Record your observations.

4. Adjust the balance so the two pans are level. Put one cup on each pan. Observe and record your observations.

Step 1

Draw Conclusions

1. Compare the amount of space taken up by the cereal and by the raisins.

2. **Draw Conclusions** Why didn't the cups balance? Explain your answer.

Step 4

Investigate Further

Fill the third cup with a mixture of raisins and cereal. Predict what will happen if you put it on the balance with each of the other two cups. Check your prediction.

VOCABULARY
mass p. 38
volume p. 39
density p. 40

SCIENCE CONCEPTS
▶ what several properties of matter are

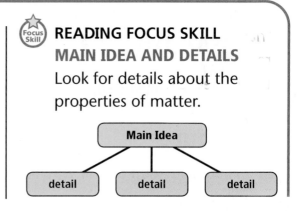

READING FOCUS SKILL
MAIN IDEA AND DETAILS
Look for details about the properties of matter.

Basic Properties

How would you describe this book? You might say that it's big or that it's heavy. You might describe its cover or tell how many pages it has.

A single piece of information about an object or a substance is a *property*. One property of this book is that it's big. Another property is that it's heavy.

Properties can help you tell one thing from another. Can you name a property of glass? That's right! You can see through it. Does that property apply to the paper in this book? No, it doesn't. You can use that property to tell one difference between glass and paper.

Some properties apply to all matter. They are basic properties of matter. For example, all matter has a property called mass. **Mass** is the amount of matter in an object. This book is big and solid. It has a lot of matter.

◀ This student is using a balance to measure the mass of the toy dinosaur. When the pointer lines up, the mass shown on the balance equals the mass of the toy.

A single page doesn't have as much matter. The mass of a book is greater than the mass of one page. Scientists measure the amount of mass by using these metric units: grams (g) and kilograms (kg). A textbook has a mass of about 1 kilogram. A page has a mass of about 1 gram.

A second basic property of all matter is volume. **Volume** is how much space an object takes up. The volume of this book is greater than the volume of a pencil. You can't always judge an object's volume from its mass. A brick has greater mass than a pillow, but a pillow has greater volume than a brick.

The volume of liquids is often measured in pints, quarts, and gallons. Scientists measure the volume of liquids and gases in liters (L) and milliliters (mL). A milliliter is $\frac{1}{1000}$ liter. A 10-centimeter (4-in.) cube of liquid is 1 liter.

Scientists measure the volume of solids in cubic centimeters (cm^3). A cube that measures 1 centimeter on each side takes up 1 cubic centimeter of space. One cubic centimeter has the same volume as 1 milliliter.

 MAIN IDEA AND DETAILS What are two basic properties of matter?

▲ You can find the volume of this cube by multiplying its length by its width by its height (*length* × *width* × *height*) in centimeters. The volume would be in cubic centimeters.

The red cube and green liquid both take up space. If you drop the cube into 250 milliliters of liquid, the level rises to 300 milliliters. What is the volume of the cube? ▶

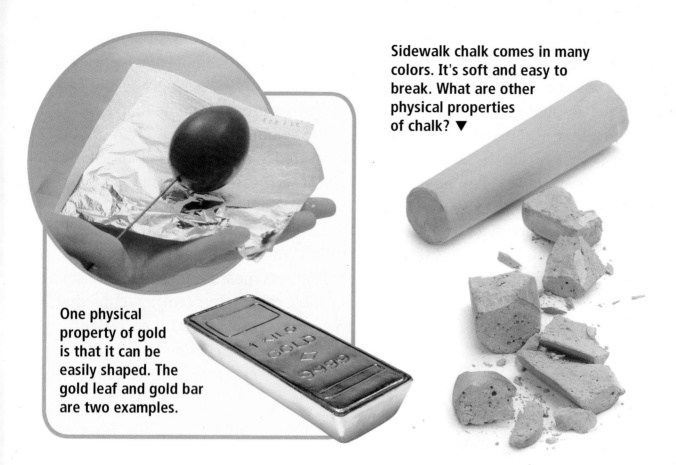

Sidewalk chalk comes in many colors. It's soft and easy to break. What are other physical properties of chalk? ▼

One physical property of gold is that it can be easily shaped. The gold leaf and gold bar are two examples.

Physical Properties

Mass and volume are two basic properties of all matter. Many other properties help you tell one type of matter from another. Most of the properties that you notice are physical properties.

A physical property is information you can observe without changing what the matter is made of. For example, you can measure the volume of a piece of wood. This doesn't change the wood in any way. You can also observe that wood breaks when bent. In this case, the original piece of wood changes, but the pieces are still wood. So breaking is a physical property. To find out whether wood burns, you have to burn it! Then it's no longer wood. So the ability to be burned is not a physical property.

Physical properties can describe an object, such as a book. They can also describe the matter from which the book is made—paper. Mass, volume, and color are physical properties. So are shape, texture, smell, and taste. Copper can be stretched into wires or hammered into sheets. Those are also physical properties.

Think about a glass marble and a wooden bead that are the same size. The marble has more mass in the same amount of space. The matter in glass is more concentrated than the matter in wood. The relationship between the mass and volume of a substance is given by its density.

Density is the mass of one unit of volume of a substance. Because all matter has mass and volume, all matter has density. Density is another basic property of matter.

Scientists often measure density in grams per cubic centimeter. For example, a block of plastic has a mass of 3 grams and a volume of 1 cubic centimeter. The density of the plastic is 3 grams per cubic centimeter, or 3 g/cm³. The density of lead is about 11 g/cm³. This means that 1 cubic centimeter of lead has a mass of about 11 grams. You find density by dividing mass by volume. If a piece of glass has a mass of 12 grams and a volume of 3 cubic centimeters, its density is $12 \div 3 = 4$ g/cm³.

 MAIN IDEA AND DETAILS **What is a physical property?**

Insta-Lab

Stretchable or Stiff?

Work with a piece of chalk, a paper clip, and a rubber band. Observe and record the physical properties for each item. How could you use physical properties to help you tell the items apart if you were blindfolded?

Science Up Close

Why Objects Float

What would happen if you shook this container of liquids and solids and then left the container standing on a table? After a time, the liquids and solids would be back in the same "order" as before you shook the container. A substance will float on any liquid or gas that has a density greater than its own. In the container, the substance with the greatest density is at the bottom. The substance with the least density is at the top.

wood floating on corn oil

plastic floating on water

ball of tar floating on glycerin

rubber eraser floating on corn syrup

copper wire floating on mercury

Electrical Properties

Electrical properties are another type of physical property. An electrical property describes how a substance interacts with electricity.

The first electrical property most people think of is how well a substance allows electricity to pass through it. You may know that most electrical equipment uses copper wire. The wiring in your home is probably copper. The cords on lamps, radios, and television sets are copper wire. Why?

Copper can easily be shaped into thin wires. That's one of its physical properties. One of copper's electrical properties is that copper allows electricity to pass through it easily. In other words, it *conducts* electricity well.

Why does most of the copper wire in your home have a rubber or plastic covering? Among the reasons are the physical properties of rubber and plastic. They can easily be formed into different shapes. An electrical property of rubber and plastic is even more important. Rubber and plastic don't allow electricity to pass through them. In other words, rubber and plastic don't conduct electricity. Because of this electrical property, it's usually safe to touch an unbroken lamp cord when the lamp is on. The rubber prevents the electricity from reaching you. The plug is covered with rubber or plastic for the same reason.

 MAIN IDEA AND DETAILS **What is one important electrical property?**

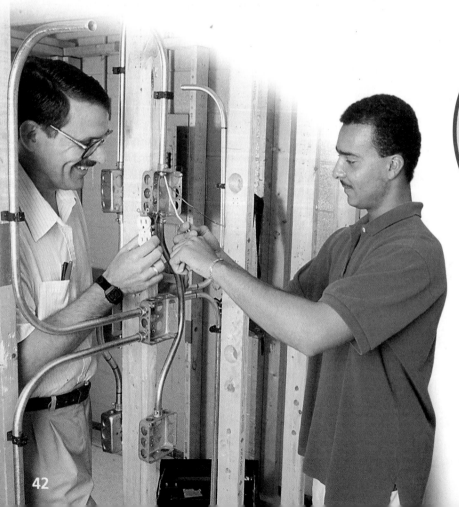

Why does this screwdriver have a plastic-covered handle?

◄ Rubber-handled tools are important to the safety of people who work with electricity. How else might this worker be protected from electricity?

1. MAIN IDEA AND DETAILS Copy and complete the graphic organizer.

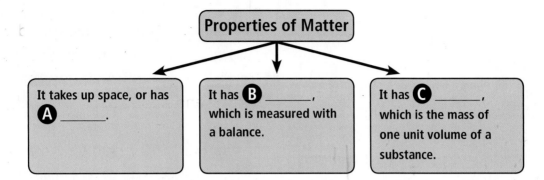

Properties of Matter

It takes up space, or has **A** _____.

It has **B** _____, which is measured with a balance.

It has **C** _____, which is the mass of one unit volume of a substance.

2. SUMMARIZE Use your completed graphic organizer to write a lesson summary.

3. DRAW CONCLUSIONS Some video cables are made of gold. What does that tell you about one of gold's electrical properties?

4. VOCABULARY Write a dictionary definition of each vocabulary word.

FCAT Prep

5. Read/Inquire/Explain Most kinds of wood float on water, but some don't. What can you infer about wood that doesn't float?

6. Which is **not** a physical property of glass?
  A. transparent   **C.** brittle
  B. used in windows   **D.** fragile

Links

Writing

Narrative Writing
Think of something you have used today, and write a **description** of its physical properties. Describe how its properties affected the way you used the object.

Math

Round Decimals
The density of ice is 0.917 g/cm³. What is the density of ice, rounded to the nearest hundredth?

Health

Human Properties
Human beings have mass and volume. Therefore, they have density. Some people can easily float on water. Others have to fill their lungs with air in order to float. What can you infer about the density of humans?

 For more links and activities, go to **www.hspscience.com**

How Does Heat Affect Matter?

Fast Fact

What's in a Flame? A burning candle contains three states of matter. The flame's heat melts the solid wax. The liquid wax moves up the wick. The flame changes the liquid to a gas. Then the gas burns and releases energy. In the Investigate, you will see how heat and cold affect other kinds of matter.

Hot and Cold

Materials
- desk lamp
- string
- large bowl
- safety goggles
- ruler
- water
- 3 balloons
- clock with second hand
- ice

Procedure

1. Turn on a lamp. Wait at least 3 minutes for the bulb to get hot.

2. **CAUTION: Put on safety goggles.** Blow up three balloons, and tie them closed.

3. Measure the length of a balloon. Record your measurement.

4. Hold the balloon about 3 cm above the light bulb. **CAUTION: Do not touch the bulb with anything.** Hold the balloon in place for 2 minutes.

5. Repeat Step 3.

6. Add water and ice to a bowl until it is half full. Gently push the balloon under the water. Hold it there for 2 minutes.

7. Repeat Step 3.

8. Repeat Steps 3–7 with the other balloons.

Draw Conclusions

1. Compare the measurements of the three balloons.

2. **Inquiry Skills** Scientists use numbers to help them see patterns. How did you use numbers to infer what happened to the air inside the balloon?

Step 3

Step 4

Investigate Further

Fill a balloon with water at room temperature. **Predict** what will happen if you put the balloon in a bowl of hot water for 15 minutes. Test your prediction.

SC.A.1.2.2.4.1 heating, cooling/phase changes
SC.H.1.2.2.4.2 metric tools

45

Reading in Science

VOCABULARY
heat p. 47
temperature p. 47
change of state p. 48

SCIENCE CONCEPTS
▶ what heat is
▶ how heat affects matter

READING FOCUS SKILL
CAUSE AND EFFECT Look for the effects of heat on matter.

cause ⟶ effect

Thermal Energy

To a scientist, *energy* means "the ability to make something move or change." What does that mean? Here's an example.

You put a piece of butter into a hot pan. The butter is cold, pale yellow, and firm. A few minutes later, the butter has changed. It's a clear, bubbling liquid. What caused the butter to change?

To understand what happened to the butter, you need to know more about matter. Tiny particles make up

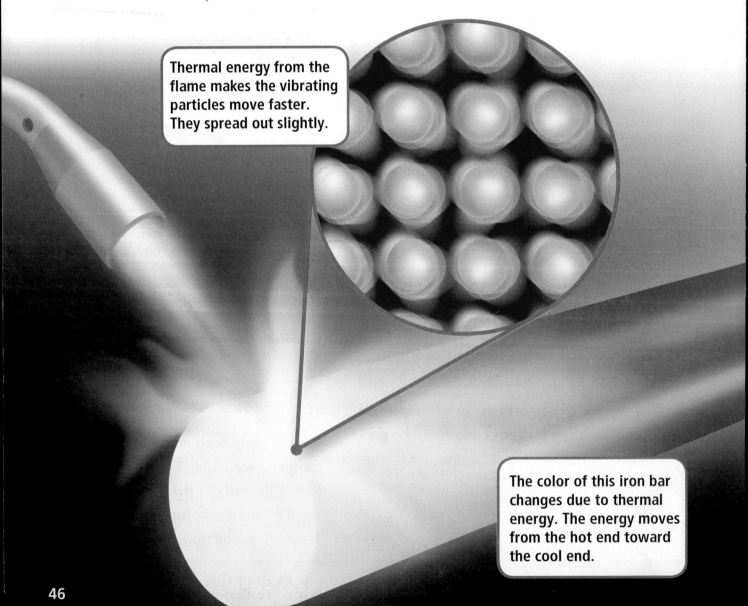

Thermal energy from the flame makes the vibrating particles move faster. They spread out slightly.

The color of this iron bar changes due to thermal energy. The energy moves from the hot end toward the cool end.

all matter. These particles are too small to be seen, and they're always moving. *Thermal energy* is the energy of moving particles of matter. In solid objects, such as the pan, the particles keep the same neighbors. They just move back and forth quickly.

When the burner is turned on, thermal energy flows from the burner into the pan. The thermal energy causes the particles in the pan to move faster. Energy then passes from the particles of the pan to the butter. The energy makes the butter change into a substance with different properties.

Heat is the flow of thermal energy from warmer to cooler objects. Thermal energy always moves naturally from warmer to cooler.

One end of the iron rod in the picture is gaining energy from the flame. The iron particles move faster. Objects with faster moving particles feel hotter compared with objects around them. You can measure how "hot" an object is with a thermometer.

Temperature is a measure of the average motion of the particles. The faster the particles move, the more heat they transfer to the thermometer. This energy causes the liquid particles in the thermometer tube to move faster. The liquid takes up more space and moves higher in the tube.

 CAUSE AND EFFECT What causes the particles that make up a substance to move?

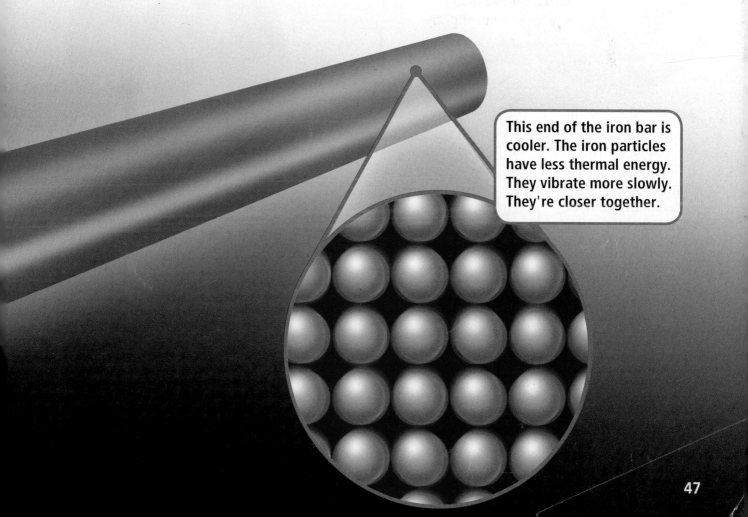

This end of the iron bar is cooler. The iron particles have less thermal energy. They vibrate more slowly. They're closer together.

Warming and Cooling Matter

What if the iron bar on the last page is replaced with an ice bar? What happens as the ice is heated?

At first, the particles vibrate faster and faster. At some point, they have so much energy that they move around and slide past one another. Because of that, the ice no longer has a definite shape. It becomes a liquid. The ice has melted into water.

What happens if you catch that water in a pan and keep heating it? The water particles gain more energy. They move faster. After a while, the particles have so much energy that they separate altogether. They spread out as far as they can. They take up whatever space they're in. The water no longer has a definite volume. It's now a gas, because the water has boiled.

These kinds of changes—for example, from solid to liquid—are known as a **change of state**. A change of state takes place at a different temperature for each substance.

▲ Water particles in this beaker gain thermal energy from the burner. As they move faster, the temperature rises.

▲ At 100°C (212°F), water particles have so much energy that they form large bubbles and escape from the liquid. The water quickly becomes a gas—water vapor.

48

▲ At 0°C (32°F), water particles have so little energy that they just vibrate in place. The water is a solid—ice.

▲ Ice particles on the surface gain energy from the air. When they have enough energy, they change to a liquid—water.

An iron bar can also melt and change to a gas. It takes much more thermal energy to get the particles moving fast enough. Iron melts at 1535°C (2795°F) and boils at 2750°C (4982°F).

Other substances go through phase changes at different temperatures. For example, mercury in a thermometer melts at –39°C (–38°F) and boils at 357°C (675°F). Mercury stays liquid whether the thermometer is in ice or in boiling water.

Dry ice is solid carbon dioxide. It's much colder than water ice. Carbon dioxide melts at –56°C (–69°F), and when it reaches –79°C (–110°F), it changes directly from a solid to a gas. It's a gas at room temperature.

 CAUSE AND EFFECT What causes changes of states?

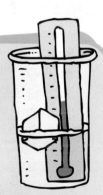

Insta-Lab

Where's the Ice?
Add cold tap water to a plastic foam cup until the cup is half full. Measure and record the temperature of the water. Place some ice chips in the cup. Observe and record the temperature of the water until the ice melts. What happens to the temperature?

Thermal Properties

A *thermal property* describes how a substance reacts to thermal energy. Thermal properties are part of a substance's physical properties. One thermal property describes how well a substance conducts heat. How easily can thermal energy pass through it?

If you put a silver spoon in a bowl of hot soup, the handle of the spoon gets hot. A thermal property of silver is that it conducts heat well. What happens if you put the hot soup in a plastic foam cup? The cup stays fairly cool. A thermal property of plastic foam is that it doesn't conduct heat well.

When a substance gets hotter, its particles move faster. The particles spread apart. The substance *expands,* or gets bigger. When the substance cools down, the particles slow down. The substance *contracts,* or gets smaller. The amount that a substance expands and contracts is another thermal property.

 CAUSE AND EFFECT What causes a substance to expand when heated?

Math in Science
Interpret Data

Expanding Metals

Most things expand when they're heated. *How much* they expand is a thermal property.

Four metal bars each measured the same length at 20°C (68°F). After the temperature went up to 620°C (1150°F), they were measured again. The bar graph shows their new lengths. Which bar expanded the most?

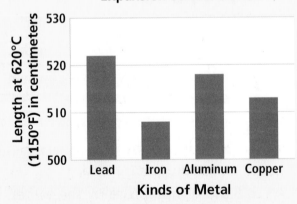

This bridge has gaps in it. The gaps give the material a place to expand on a hot day. The gaps help keep the bridge from breaking.

Focus Skill

1. CAUSE AND EFFECT Copy and complete the graphic organizer.

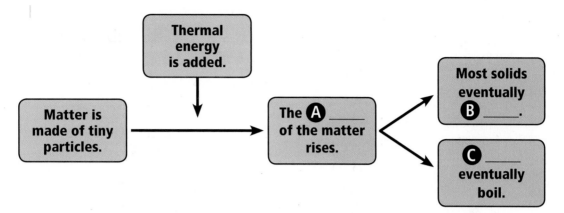

Thermal energy is added.

Matter is made of tiny particles.

The Ⓐ _____ of the matter rises.

Most solids eventually Ⓑ _____.

Ⓒ _____ eventually boil.

2. SUMMARIZE Write a paragraph that describes what this lesson is mostly about.

3. DRAW CONCLUSIONS Why does placing a metal jar lid below hot running water make it easier to open the jar?

4. VOCABULARY Write a question and answer for each vocabulary term.

FCAT Prep

5. Read/Inquire/Explain What happens in a freezer that makes water change to ice?

6. What happens if a substance loses enough thermal energy?

A. It boils.   **C.** It freezes.

B. It expands.   **D.** It melts.

Links

Writing

Narrative Writing

Suppose that, for the next 10 minutes, you shrink to become a particle in an ice cube. Write a **story** about what you see and do when a source of thermal energy comes close.

Math   9÷3

Subtract Decimals

A bar of metal at 20°C is 500 centimeters long. At 635°C, it's 518.6 centimeters long. How much did it expand?

Language Arts

Word Parts

Use a dictionary to find three words with the prefix *thermo-*. Don't use words from this lesson. List the words, and tell how their meanings are related.

 For more links and activities, go to www.hspscience.com

PB and J

A Sticky Problem

A peanut butter and jelly sandwich is usually easy to make. You take two slices of bread and slather peanut butter and jelly on them. But, for the U.S. Army, making the sandwich is not that easy.

Some of the Army's top scientists have been trying to make peanut butter and jelly sandwiches for four years! The Army's sandwiches have to taste good and last for three years without refrigeration.

Two New Sandwiches

This sandwich research is done by scientists at the Natick Soldier Center in Massachusetts. The center has already made the Army pepperoni and barbecued chicken sandwiches that can last unrefrigerated for three years in 80-degree heat.

But keeping such sandwiches from growing mold over a couple of years is no easy task. To keep the sandwiches fresh, one important step by Army scientists is to control the "water activity" or the amount of water in the sandwich. By keeping as much moisture as possible out of the sandwich, they reduce the risk that mold will grow.

In addition, scientists made sure that the sandwich contents, such as pepperoni or barbecue sauce, were slightly acidic. That way bacteria are prevented from growing.

One Sandwich, Three Years?

As a result of all this research, one Army scientist said that the sandwiches "will last a minimum of three years at 80 degrees and six months at 100 degrees. They will travel to the swampiest swamp, the highest mountain, the most arid desert."

Peanut butter and jelly sandwiches, however, pose a special problem. Mold keeps growing on them as a result of too much moisture. But mold or no mold, some soldiers say the long-lasting sandwiches leave a bad taste in their mouths. "I don't think I've ever wanted a sandwich that's that old," said Master Sergeant Kelly Tyler.

THINK ABOUT IT

1. Why is it important to the Army to be able to keep food fresh for three years?
2. If you could, what kind of sandwich would you create to last for three years?

Find out more! Log on to
www.hspscience.com

Building the Bridge

In the late 1800s, most people did not consider building the Brooklyn Bridge to be a job for a woman. Emily Roebling was married to the bridge's master builder, Washington Roebling. In 1872, her husband became seriously ill. She knew a lot about building, so she became his assistant.

Builders and engineers asked Emily Roebling's advice. She understood what materials could be used and how they should be put together. Emily Roebling played an important role in building the bridge.

Career   Welder

When you need to join two pieces of metal together, you have to call a welder. To join metal together, a welder must use a lot of heat. Heat is applied to metal pieces, which then melt along their edges to form a permanent bond. Welding is used to build ships, make cars and airplanes, and many other things.

You Can Do It!

Quick and Easy Project

Make It Float!

Procedure

1. Fill a bowl with water.
2. Place a test tube in the water. Allow water to flow into the test tube. Observe what happens.
3. Fill the test tube with water, and stopper it.
4. Place the test tube in the bowl of water. Observe and record the behavior of the tube.
5. Repeat Step 4, using different amounts of water in the stoppered test tube.

Materials

- large bowl
- water
- test tube
- stopper

Draw Conclusions

What conclusion can you reach from Step 2? What conclusion can you reach from Step 3? What did you have to do to make the test tube float? Why did it float?

Design Your Own Investigation

Changing Density

Do you think adding salt to water changes the density of the water? Plan and conduct an experiment to find out. (Hint: use a floating object to observe differences in the liquids.)

Review and FCAT Preparation

Vocabulary Review

Use the terms below to complete the sentences. The page numbers tell where to look in the chapter if you need help.

solid p. 32   **volume** p. 39
liquid p. 33   **density** p. 40
gas p. 34   **heat** p. 47
mass p. 38   **change of state**
    p. 48

1. The space an object takes up is its
   _____.

2. A substance with a definite volume but no definite shape is a _____.

3. The amount of matter an object is made up of is its _____.

4. Boiling and melting are examples of a _____.

5. A substance with no definite volume and no definite shape is a _____.

6. If you divide an object's mass by its volume, you find its _____.

7. The flow of thermal energy from warmer to cooler substances is
   _____.

8. A substance with a definite volume and a definite shape is a _____.

Check Understanding

Write the letter of the best choice.

9. **COMPARE AND CONTRAST** Which of the following would probably have the greatest mass?
   A. a bicycle   **C.** a car
   B. a brick   **D.** a flower

10. **CAUSE AND EFFECT** What is true of the bottom substance in the picture?

    F. It has the same density as the top substance.
    G. It is the least dense substance.
    H. It is the most dense substance.
    I. It has a density of 1 g/cm^3.

11. As the temperature of an object rises, what happens to the tiny particles that make up the object?
    A. They move faster.
    B. They move more slowly.
    C. They move closer together.
    D. They stop moving.

12. Which of the following is most likely to happen to an object that is being cooled?
    F. It boils.   **H.** It expands.
    G. It contracts.   **I.** It melts.

13. What type of property is the amount that a substance expands when heated?

    A. a basic property

    B. a thermal property

    C. a chemical property

    D. an electrical property

14. Which parts of the cord in the diagram are probably good conductors of heat?

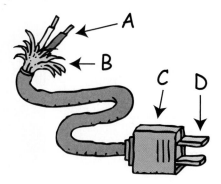

    F. A and C   **H.** A and D

    G. B and C   **I.** B and D

15. Which of the following have no definite shape?

    A. a liquid and a solid

    B. a solid and a gas

    C. a solid, liquid, and gas

    D. a liquid and a gas

16. What is the density of an object with a mass of 15 grams and a volume of 5 cubic centimeters.

    F. 3 g/cm^3

    G. 5 g/cm^3

    H. 10 g/cm^3

    I. 20 g/cm^3

Inquiry Skills

17. Draw a conclusion about what is happening to the particles in the diagram. Explain your answer.

18. In August, when the temperature is 35°C (95°F), you find a steel beam on a construction site. It is 10 meters (33 ft) long. **Predict** what you will find if you measure it in January, when the temperature is 5°C (41°F).

Read/Inquire/Explain

19. Why are concrete sidewalks poured in short sections with cracks between them instead of in one long strip?

20. Pots used on stoves typically have handles covered in hard plastic or wood.

    Part A Why do pots have handles like this?

    Part B What property of plastic and wood makes them useful as handles?

Energy

The chapters in this unit address these Grade Level Expectations from the Florida Sunshine State Standards.

PHYSICAL SCIENCE

Chapter 2 Sound

SC.B.1.2.2.4.2   knows the relationship between attributes of all waves (for example wavelength, frequency) and attributes of sound waves (for example pitch, intensity).

Chapter 3 Light and Heat

SC.B.1.2.1.4.1   knows that most living things use energy from the sun to live and grow.

SC.B.1.2.3.4.1   knows that most objects that emit light also emit heat.

SC.B.1.2.4.4.1   knows ways that energy can be transformed (for example, electricity to light, light to heat, mechanical to heat).

SC.B.1.2.5.4.1   extends and refines use of a variety of tools to measure the gain or loss of energy.

Chapter 4 Making and Using Electricity

SC.B.1.2.1.4.2   knows how to trace the flow of energy in a system.

SC.B.1.2.2.4.1   knows that there are a variety of sources for electricity.

SC.B.1.2.4.4.1   knows ways that energy can be transformed.

SC.B.1.2.4.4.2   knows that moving electric charges produce magnetic forces and moving magnets produce electric currents.

SC.B.2.2.1.4.1   understands the reasons for energy conservation.

The investigations and experiences in this unit also address many of the Grade Level Expectations in Strand H, The Nature of Science.

Science in Florida

Ponce Inlet

Dear Mrs. Williams,

I am on vacation with my family in Ponce Inlet. We saw the lighthouse and I remembered everything you taught the class about light last year. My mom and dad were impressed! I told them how light bends when it travels from one material to another. Thanks for teaching me so much.

See you after the break,

Renata

The Sunshine State

USA

FCAT Writing

Writing Situation
Think about a time when the power went off. Write a story about what happened when there was no electricity.

Experiment!

Color and Light Energy Absorption

Matter and energy are constantly interacting with each other. Light and heat are two forms of energy that interact differently with different types of matter. Does the color of an object affect the amount of energy it absorbs? Plan and conduct an experiment to find out.

Chapter

2 Sound

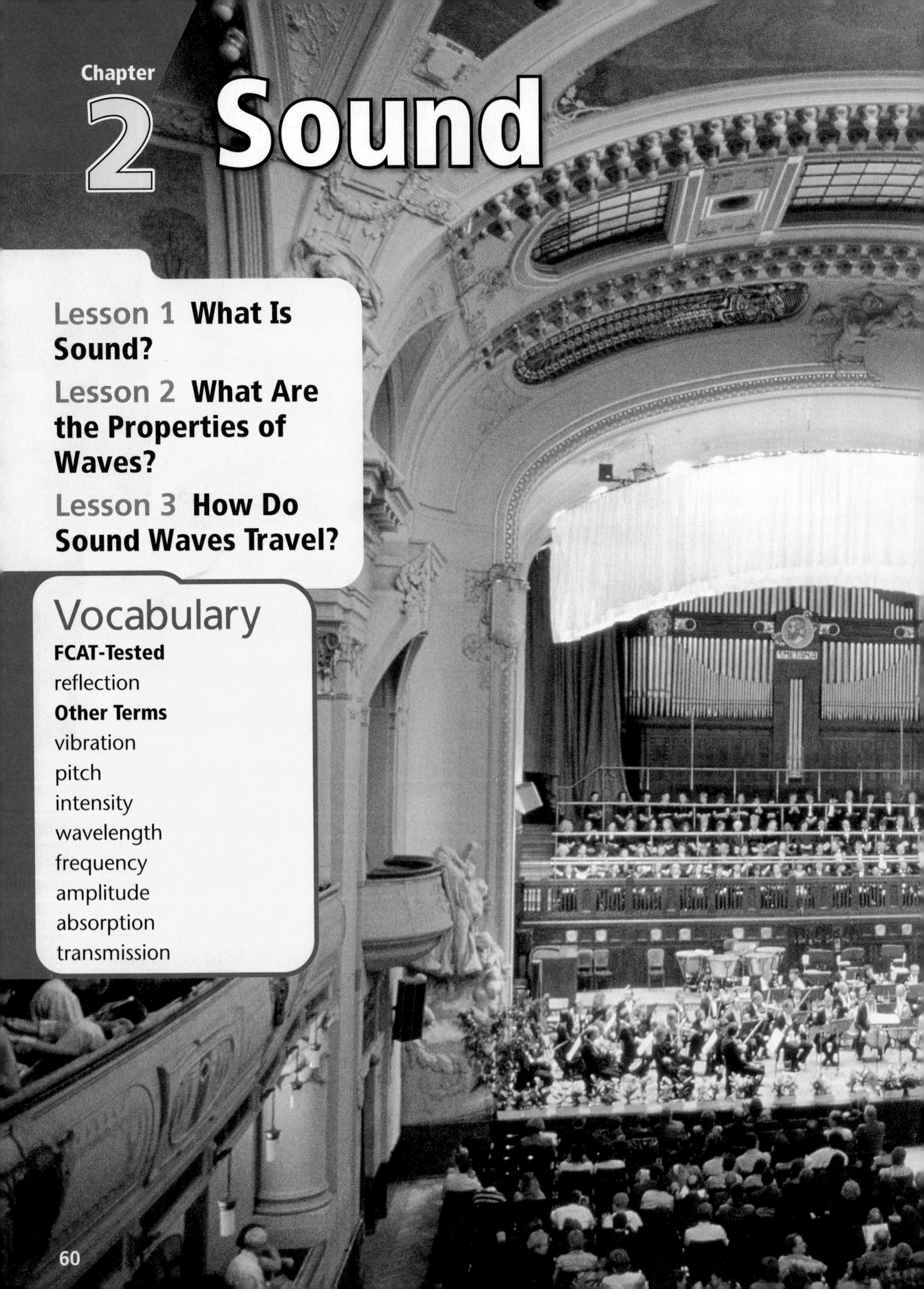

Vocabulary

FCAT-Tested

reflection

Other Terms

vibration

pitch

intensity

wavelength

frequency

amplitude

absorption

transmission

What do YOU wonder?

When people design a concert hall, their goal is to provide high-quality sound to every person in the hall. How do you think the sound differs between the first and last rows in this hall?

61

What Is Sound?

Fast Fact

Listen to the Drums! Every year, the people of Ako, Japan, hold a festival that honors warriors of long ago. Drums are a major part of that festival. The largest of the drums can be about 1 to 2 meters (3 to 6 ft) across. Hitting a drum is one way to make a sound. In the Investigate, you'll explore other ways to make sounds.

Feel the Vibes

Materials   • **plastic ruler**

Procedure

1. Place the ruler on a desk or table. Let 20 cm of the ruler stick out over the edge.

2. With one hand, firmly press down on the end that is on the tabletop. With the other hand, flick the other end of the ruler.

3. Observe the ruler with your eyes. Record your observations.

4. Repeat Step 2. Observe the ruler with your ears. Record your observations.

5. Change the strength with which you flick the end of the ruler. Observe the results and record your observations.

6. Move the ruler to change the length that hangs over the edge of the tabletop. Repeat Steps 2–5. Observe the results and record your observations.

Step 1

Step 6

Draw Conclusions

1. What did you observe in Step 3? In Step 4? How do you think these observations are related?

2. **Inquiry Skill** Hypothesize how changing the ruler affects the sound it makes. Tell how you would test your hypothesis.

Investigate Further

Place one ear on the tabletop, and cover the other ear with your hand. Have a partner repeat Steps 1 and 2. What do you observe?

SC.B.1.2.2.4.2 wave attributes
SC.H.1.2.2.4.2 metric tools

63

VOCABULARY
vibration p. 64
pitch p. 66
intensity p. 67

SCIENCE CONCEPTS
▶ how sound is produced
▶ how sounds can vary

READING FOCUS SKILL
MAIN IDEA AND DETAILS
Find details about the nature of sound.

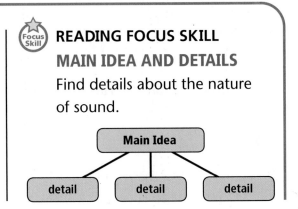

Sources of Sound

Try this. Place your hand on your throat, and hum softly. What do you feel? You may feel slight movements. Your vocal cords are moving quickly back and forth. A quick back-and-forth movement is a **vibration**.

Have you ever plucked a guitar string? As you watched the string move, it was probably a blur. It looked that way because it was vibrating quickly. The string was moving back and forth so fast that you couldn't see it clearly.

In the Investigate, you made the ruler vibrate. You also changed how much or how little the ruler vibrated. What do a moving ruler, a plucked guitar string, and your humming throat all have in common? They all make sounds, and they all vibrate.

When something vibrates, the air around it vibrates, too. Then

◀ **What part of this speaker actually makes the sound?**

You hear a phone ring because a small speaker inside it vibrates. The vibrations spread through the air in all directions.

the vibrations move through the air. When they reach your ear, you hear them as sounds.

Sound travels through the air, but it can also travel through other materials. You can hear sounds through a liquid when you swim underwater. In the Investigate Further activity, you heard sounds traveling through a solid tabletop. You can hear all those sounds because vibrations can travel through liquids and solids, as well as through gases like air.

The vibrations that cause sounds are called *sound waves.* When sound waves reach your ear, they make parts inside your ear vibrate. Then a signal travels to your brain, and you hear the sound.

Sounds can be loud or soft, high or low, but they are all produced by sound waves. You'll learn that the properties of the waves are what make sounds different from each other.

 MAIN IDEA AND DETAILS How is sound produced?

Pitch

Little dogs and big dogs both bark, but their barks are different. One sound is high, and the other is low. **Pitch** is how high or low a sound is. The two barks have different pitches.

What makes the barks different? Think about the size of the dogs. A smaller dog has smaller vocal cords, parts in the throat that vibrate. Smaller objects usually vibrate faster than larger ones. They make sound waves that are close together. Big objects vibrate more slowly. They produce sound waves that are more spread out. When the sound waves reach your ears, the close-together waves sound higher than the spread-out waves.

You can find many examples of sounds that differ in pitch. Adults' voices are deeper than children's voices. Thin guitar strings make higher sounds than thick ones do. What other examples can you think of?

 MAIN IDEA AND DETAILS What waves make high-pitched sounds?

This bird's tiny vocal cords make a high sound. ▶

◀ Long, thick bass strings make a low sound.

Lower Pitch

Higher Pitch

What can you infer about the strings on the left side of the piano?

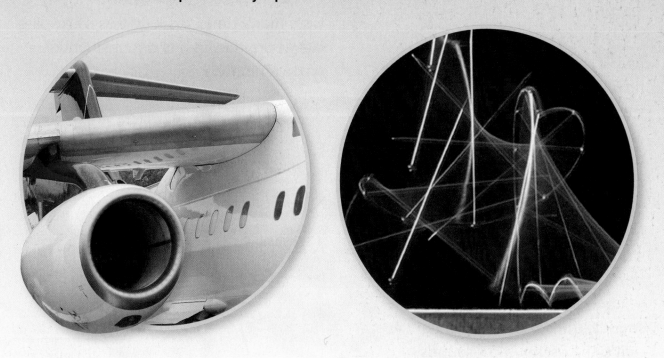

Intensity

Imagine that you drop a small paperback book on the floor. Then you drop a huge encyclopedia. How would the sounds differ? The encyclopedia would make a much louder sound than the paperback. These sounds would differ in **intensity**—the measure of how loud or soft a sound is.

But what makes such sounds different? You can probably guess that the difference is in the sound waves. Sound waves have a certain amount of energy. A heavier book would have more energy when it hits the floor, so it would produce sound waves with more energy.

When a door closes slowly, it produces sound waves. But when the door slams shut, it produces higher-energy sound waves. The sound waves you produce when you whisper don't have as much energy as the sound waves you produce when you shout. You hear sound waves with more energy as louder sounds.

 MAIN IDEA AND DETAILS What kind of waves make soft sounds?

Hands-On Vibrations!

Place two fingers gently on your Adam's apple. Now hum. Hum high notes and low notes. Hum loudly and softly. Say something and then shout it. What changes do you notice in your throat each time?

67

Measuring Sound Intensity

You know a loud sound when you hear it, but how could you measure how loud it is? Scientists measure sound intensity by using a unit called a *bel*. The bel was named after Alexander Graham Bell. He invented the telephone, but he also studied sound and hearing.

For most common sounds, the bel is too big a unit to be useful. Most sounds are measured in decibels. A decibel (dB) is one-tenth of a bel.

You'd probably think that a 20-dB sound is twice as loud as a 10-dB sound. But it isn't. A 20-dB sound is ten times as loud as a 10-dB sound. Any difference of 10 dB means that one sound is ten times as loud as another.

MAIN IDEA AND DETAILS What unit is used to measure the intensity of most sounds?

How many times the loudness of rustling leaves are the sounds of a residential area at night?

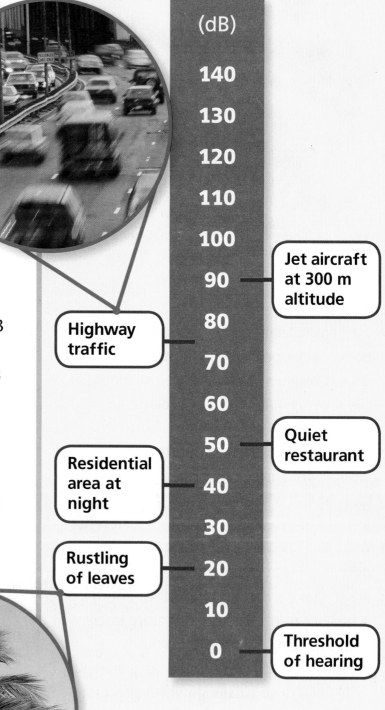

(dB)

- 140
- 130
- 120
- 110
- 100
- 90 — Jet aircraft at 300 m altitude
- 80 — Highway traffic
- 70
- 60
- 50 — Quiet restaurant
- 40 — Residential area at night
- 30
- 20 — Rustling of leaves
- 10
- 0 — Threshold of hearing

68

1. MAIN IDEA AND DETAILS Draw and complete this graphic organizer.

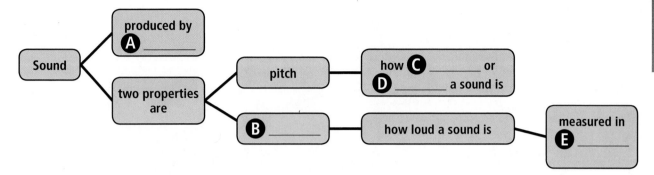

2. SUMMARIZE Use your completed graphic organizer to write a lesson summary.

3. DRAW CONCLUSIONS If you strike a piano key hard and hold it, the note takes some time to fade out. Why?

4. VOCABULARY Use each of the lesson vocabulary words in a separate sentence.

FCAT Prep

5. Read/Inquire/Explain If you tap the longest bar on a xylophone, it makes a sound. As you go up the scale to the shorter bars, the pitch of the sound rises. Why?

6. What converts waves into sound?

A. air   C. your brain

B. your ear   D. vibration

Links

Writing

Expository Writing

Explaining something to someone else can often help you understand it better yourself. Write a **friendly letter** to a relative or friend. In the letter, explain the sound you heard at a concert.

Math

Compare Whole Numbers

Two bells are vibrating. The first bell vibrates 16,597 times each second. The second bell vibrates 16,832 times each second. Which bell has a higher pitch? Why?

Language Arts

Sound Poetry

Poetry uses the sounds of words. Write a poem about sounds and how they travel. Try to include sounds differing in pitch and intensity for an audience to chant with you.

 For more links and activities, go to **www.hspscience.com**

What Are the Properties of Waves?

Fast Fact

Take Note Guitar strings produce different notes because they vibrate at different speeds. When a guitar is in tune, the string that makes the lowest sound vibrates 164.8 times a second. The string that makes the highest sound vibrates 659.2 times a second. Most people can "vibrate" (tap) a finger only about 10 times a second. In the Investigate, you'll observe the vibration of rubber "strings."

Feel the Vibes II

Materials
- safety goggles
- pencil
- foam cup
- thin rubber band
- 2 paper clips
- ruler
- tape
- thick rubber band

Procedure

❶ **CAUTION: Put on the safety goggles.** Use the pencil to poke a hole in the bottom of the cup.

❷ Thread the thin rubber band onto the paper clip. Put them in the cup, and then pull the rubber band through the hole.

❸ Place the cup on a table upside down. Tape the ruler to the cup as shown in the picture, with the 1-cm mark at the top. Pull the end of the rubber band over the end of the ruler, and tape it to the back.

❹ Pull the rubber band to one side, and then let it go. Observe the sound. Record your observations.

❺ Repeat Step 4, but this time, pull the rubber band farther.

❻ Use one finger to press the rubber band against the 2-cm mark and then the 4-cm mark. Repeat Step 4 each time.

❼ Repeat Steps 2–6, using the thick rubber band.

Step 2

Step 3

Draw Conclusions

1. Compare the sounds you made.

2. **Inquiry Skill** How did using the numbers on the ruler help you to give a reason for the sounds that you made?

Investigate Further

Hypothesize **how you could use your setup to play a musical scale. Test your hypothesis.**

SC.B.1.2.2.4.2 wave attributes
SC.H.1.2.2.4.2 metric tools

71

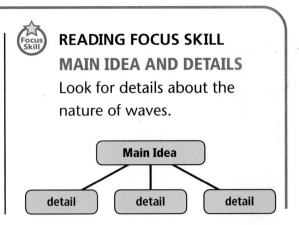

VOCABULARY
wavelength p. 73
frequency p. 73
amplitude p. 73

SCIENCE CONCEPTS

▶ what the properties of waves are

▶ how frequency relates to pitch

▶ how amplitude relates to volume

READING FOCUS SKILL

MAIN IDEA AND DETAILS
Look for details about the nature of waves.

Main Idea
detail | detail | detail

Sound Waves

Have you ever watched the water along the shore of an ocean or a lake? Then you've seen waves. Waves also travel in air, carrying sound. But water waves and sound waves are different.

Water waves move up and down. You can see this if you look at a raft when a passing boat makes waves. When the waves hit the raft, it bobs up and down.

Waves that move up and down like this are called *transverse waves*. In the ocean, the waves travel forward, but the water moves up and down. The two directions cross each other. The word *transverse* means "across."

Sound waves are different. Have you ever played with a spring toy? If you hold one end of the spring and move it forward and back, you create waves. What you see is a bunching up of some coils that moves down to the end of the spring and back. That's a wave, although it doesn't move up and down. Waves that move this way, along the travel direction of the waves, are

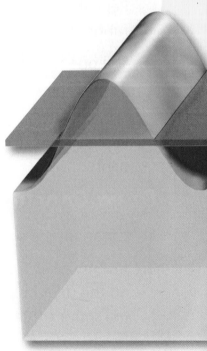

◀ **How is the movement of water waves like the movement of sound waves?**

longitudinal waves. Longitudinal means "along." Spring-toy waves move along the spring.

If you wanted to describe waves, how would you begin? You could start with length. You'd choose a point on one wave, such as the top of a water wave. Then you'd measure to the same point on the next wave. The distance between the two points is the **wavelength**.

Another property you can use to describe waves is **frequency**—the number of waves that pass in a second.

If you were to count water waves as they crash on a beach, you'd be measuring the waves' frequency.

You could also describe how much energy waves have. This property is called **amplitude**. For transverse waves, such as water waves, the amplitude is how tall the waves are. For longitudinal waves, such as sound waves, the amplitude is how tightly bunched the particles or sections are.

MAIN IDEA AND DETAILS Name three properties of waves.

▼ For longitudinal waves, one wavelength is the distance from one bunched-up section to the next.

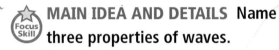

▼ For transverse waves, you measure amplitude from the rest position to the top of the wave. The red surface shows the rest position.

amplitude

wavelength

Frequency and Pitch

Imagine that you could see sound waves moving past you. If you were amazingly fast, you could check their frequency by seeing how many waves go by each second. If the waves were close together, more would pass by during each second. That would mean that the frequency of the waves is high.

Remember, an object that vibrates quickly produces sound-wave peaks that are close together. The waves have a shorter wavelength than the waves produced by objects that vibrate slowly.

When the wave peaks are close together, the sound has a high pitch. As you can see, frequency and pitch are related. When the sound waves reach your ears, the waves with close-together peaks have a high-pitched sound. The higher the frequency of the waves, the higher the pitch of the sound.

 MAIN IDEA AND DETAILS How are frequency and pitch related?

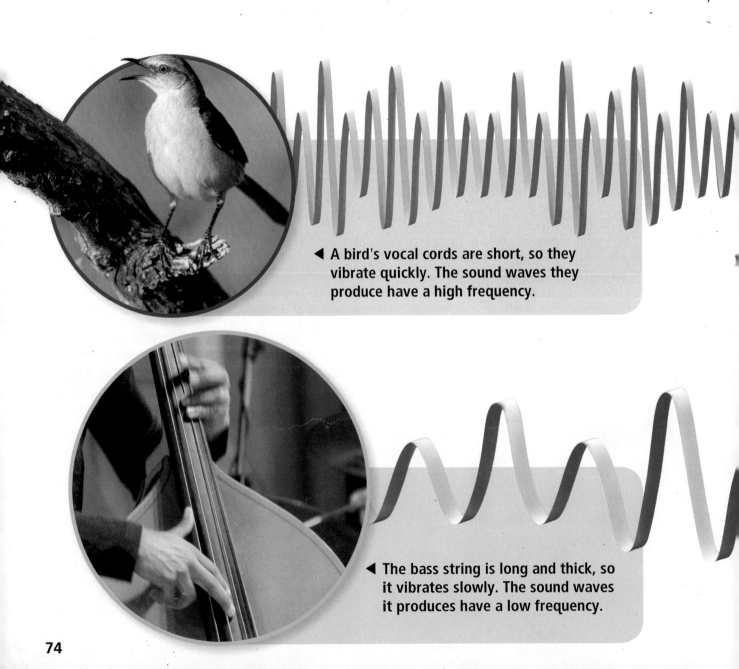

◀ A bird's vocal cords are short, so they vibrate quickly. The sound waves they produce have a high frequency.

◀ The bass string is long and thick, so it vibrates slowly. The sound waves it produces have a low frequency.

Amplitude and Loudness

You know that sound waves with more energy make a louder sound. And you've learned that amplitude is a measure of how much energy a wave has. Put those two statements together, and what do you get? Sound waves with larger amplitudes are louder.

Imagine that you're tossing stones into a pond. First, you throw in a pebble. It hits the water with little energy and makes a small "bloop" sound. It also makes small ripples in the water. Both the sound waves and the water waves have small amplitudes.

Then, you throw in a big rock. It hits the water with a lot of energy. It makes a loud splashing sound and big ripples in the water. Both types of waves produced by the big rock have large amplitudes.

MAIN IDEA AND DETAILS How does the amplitude of sound waves relate to their intensity?

A pin has very little energy when it hits a table. It produces sound waves with very small amplitudes. ▶

◀ A jet engine has a lot of energy. It produces sound waves with very large amplitudes.

Insta-Lab

Making Waves

Tie one end of a rope to a tree, a doorknob, or anything that's roughly 1 meter off the ground. Move the rope to make transverse waves. Change the amplitude and frequency of the waves.

Measuring Sound Waves

You now know several properties of sound waves—wavelength, frequency, and amplitude. But how do you measure those properties? After all, you can't just hold a ruler up to a sound wave. It's very hard to count things you can't see! Fortunately, technology has a solution.

To measure sound waves, you can use an oscilloscope (uh•SIL•uh•skohp). This instrument has a screen on the front that displays a picture of sound waves.

This may seem far-fetched, but it really isn't. After all, you're used to machines that take in sound waves and change them into magnetic code on a tape or into laser marks on a disc.

An oscilloscope isn't all that different. Like a tape recorder or a CD recorder, it has a microphone. The microphone picks up sound waves in the air, and the oscilloscope changes them into pictures on the screen, like those shown below.

MAIN IDEA AND DETAILS What machine can be used to measure the properties of sound waves?

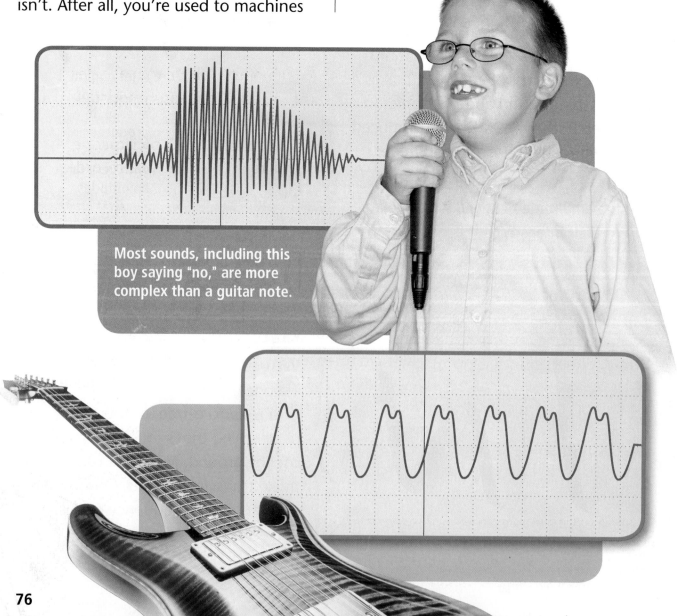

Most sounds, including this boy saying "no," are more complex than a guitar note.

1. MAIN IDEA AND DETAILS Draw and complete this graphic organizer.

MAIN IDEA	There are two types of waves	The properties of sound waves affect the sound you hear.	
DETAILS	**A** _____ waves move across the direction of travel.	**B** _____ is the number of waves that pass by in a second.	Higher frequency waves make a **D** _____ pitched sound.
	Longitudinal waves move back and forth along direction of travel.	Amplitude measures the **C** _____ of a wave.	**E** _____ amplitude waves make a softer sound.

2. SUMMARIZE Write two sentences that tell what this lesson is about.

3. DRAW CONCLUSIONS You hit a key on the left side of a piano. Then you hit a key on right side harder. How are the sound waves different?

4. VOCABULARY Draw and label a picture to show the wavelength and amplitude of a transverse wave.

FCAT Prep

5. Read/Inquire/Explain How are the amplitudes of sound waves and of water waves related?

6. Which of the following machines can be used to measure sound waves?

A. CD burner   **C.** oscilloscope

B. microphone   **D.** tape recorder

Writing

Expository Writing
Imagine that you're playing the piano. Your brother says he doesn't understand why some strings produce higher notes than other strings. Write a brief **explanation** telling why.

Math

Name Decimals
You strike a B key on a piano. The sound wave that is produced has a wavelength of 0.69 m. Write the word form of this decimal.

Music

Notes and Frequencies
There is a direct relationship between frequency and the notes of a scale. Research this topic. Then write the names for the notes of a scale. Beside each name, write its frequency.

 For more links and activities, go to **www.hspscience.com**

How Do Sound Waves Travel?

Fast Fact

Sing Me a Song Humpback whales communicate underwater by using sound. Scientists call the sounds whale songs. Those sounds are among the loudest made by any animal on Earth. In the Investigate, you'll study how sound travels through different materials.

Do You Hear What I Hear?

Materials
- 2 x 4 pine board
- cardboard tube
- paper cup
- water

Procedure

1. Have a partner rub a fingernail on a desktop. Listen, and record your observations. Press one ear against the desktop, and listen to the rubbing again. Record your observations.

2. Have your partner hold the board. Press your ear against one end of the board. Then have your partner, at the other end, lightly rub a fingernail against the wood. Listen, and record your observations.

3. Hold one end of the cardboard tube up to your ear. Have your partner lightly rub a fingernail on the other end of the tube. Listen, and record your observations.

4. Press the side of the paper cup against your ear. Have your partner lightly rub a fingernail on the other side of the cup. Listen, and record your observations.

5. Fill the cup with water, and repeat Step 4.

Step 2

Step 4

Draw Conclusions

1. What differences did you observe in the sounds?

2. **Inquiry Skill** Identify the variable that you changed in this Investigate. What variable did you observe?

Investigate Further

Can you observe how sound travels through a liquid other than water? Plan and conduct a simple investigation to find out.

SC.C.1.2.2.4.1 waves in different media
SC.H.1.2.2.4.1 experimental design

79

VOCABULARY
reflection p. 82
absorption p. 83
transmission p. 84

SCIENCE CONCEPTS
▶ how the human ear works
▶ how sound waves react when they strike a surface

READING FOCUS SKILL
COMPARE AND CONTRAST
Look for differences in the way sound waves interact with objects.

| alike | different |

Hearing Sounds

When a rocket is launched into space, it makes a huge roar. The engines vibrate, sending out sound waves in all directions. But how do you actually hear the sound?

First, the sound waves have to travel through matter to your ear. Usually, they travel through air.

In space, there is no air. Once the rocket engine is out in space, it's completely silent. If you flew past it, you wouldn't hear any sound at all. Out there, sound waves have nothing to travel through.

But here on Earth, air carries the sound from the rocket to your ears. When the vibrations reach one of your ears, they make your eardrum vibrate. Those vibrations travel through bones and tissues until they reach your inner ear. There, special cells change the vibrations into electrical signals. These signals travel along a nerve to your brain. A special part of your brain recognizes the electrical signals. You hear the loud noise from the rocket.

COMPARE AND CONTRAST How is hearing on Earth different from hearing in space?

▼ How does the sound of the alarm travel to the girl's right ear? How does it travel to her left ear?

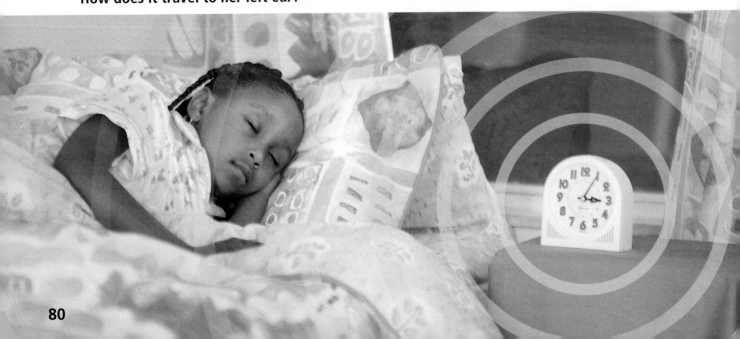

How Hearing Works

The way sound travels from the air to become signals in your brain is complex. Follow the numbers, and then read the other information.

Vibrations from the eardrum travel along three tiny bones, called the hammer, anvil, and stirrup.

Nerve signals from the cochlea travel along this nerve to your brain.

❶ Outer ear
Your outer ear catches sound waves and funnels them inward to your eardrum.

❷ Eardrum
The sound waves make your eardrum vibrate.

❸ Cochlea
Bones pass vibrations to a snail-shaped organ called the cochlea (КАНК•lee•uh). Hairlike cells inside change vibrations into nerve signals.

Reflection

What happens when a sound wave strikes a surface other than your ear? That depends on the surface.

It's helpful to compare sound waves and light waves. When light waves strike a mirror, they are reflected back in the same pattern in which they struck it. That's why you see a reflection. When sound waves strike a smooth, flat surface, they are also reflected back in the same pattern. The result is that you hear the sound again. That's what an echo is.

But when light waves strike a rough wall, they are scattered all over. You can't see a reflection in the wall. When sound waves strike a rough surface, they are scattered all over, too.

Whether they echo or not, the sound waves are bouncing off the surface, a process called **reflection**.

COMPARE AND CONTRAST What is different about the two ways sound waves can reflect off a surface?

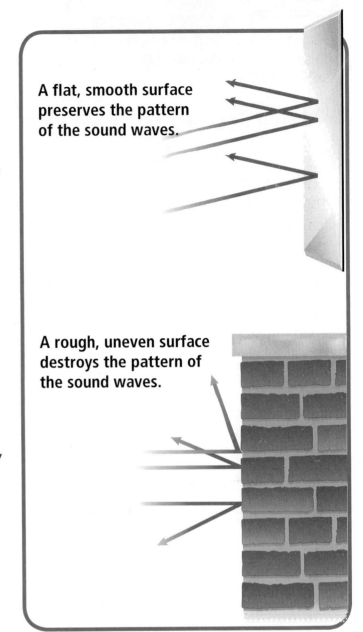

A flat, smooth surface preserves the pattern of the sound waves.

A rough, uneven surface destroys the pattern of the sound waves.

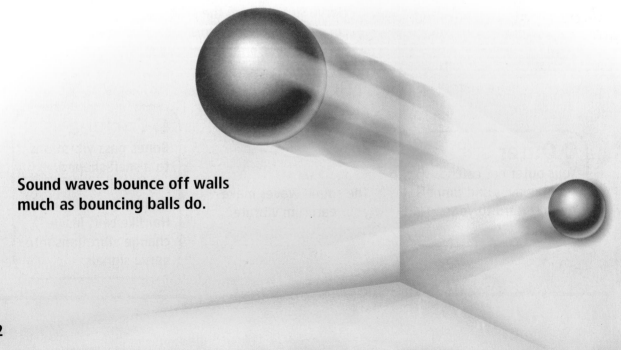

Sound waves bounce off walls much as bouncing balls do.

This anechoic (an•eh•кон•ik), or "without echoes," chamber is carefully designed to absorb any sounds that are made inside it.

Absorption

Imagine making a loud sound in a bare room. You hear the sound reflecting off the hard floors and walls. What a noisy place!

But what if you make the same sound in a room with carpets and curtains? This time, you don't hear any echoes. This room seems much more quiet, because the carpets and the curtains take in the sound. They stop the sound waves from reflecting or traveling any farther. This process is called **absorption**.

What happens to a sound wave that is absorbed? It just dies out. There is no more vibration and no more sound.

This can be very useful. Imagine that you're trying to read and your neighbor is running noisy power tools. If materials in the walls of your home absorb the loud sounds, the sounds can't travel to your ears. Then you can have some peace and quiet!

⭐ **COMPARE AND CONTRAST** How is absorption different from reflection?

How would you describe what is happening to the sound waves in this diagram?

Insta-Lab

Quiet, Please
Find something that makes a steady, even sound, such as a clock that ticks loudly. Place your hands over your ears. Can you still hear the sound? Place other materials over your ears to see how well they conduct or absorb sound waves.

Transmission

You know that the parts of your ear don't reflect sound. And they don't absorb sound, either. If they did, how would you hear the sounds around you?

You can hear sounds when sound waves keep vibrating through some kinds of material. They travel through air or other matter, all the way to your inner ear. The sound waves keep moving along—a process called **transmission**. Your eardrum transmits, or moves along, the sound waves to the hammer, then to the anvil and the stirrup, and finally to the cochlea.

Have you ever heard someone talking in the next room, even though the door was closed? The sound waves were transmitted through the air in that room, through the wall, through the air in your room, and then into your ear. Materials that can vibrate are materials that can transmit sounds.

⭐ (Focus Skill) **COMPARE AND CONTRAST** How is transmission similar to absorption? How is it different from absorption?

How does this diagram relate to the example of someone talking in the next room?

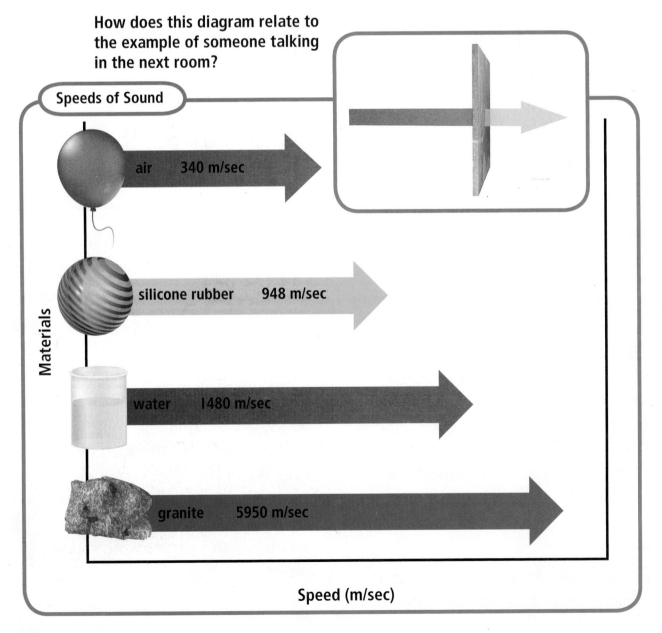

Speeds of Sound

Materials

air   340 m/sec

silicone rubber   948 m/sec

water   1480 m/sec

granite   5950 m/sec

Speed (m/sec)

1. COMPARE AND CONTRAST Draw and complete this graphic organizer.

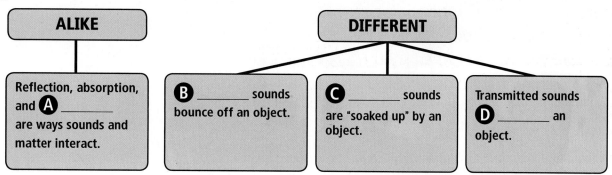

ALIKE

Reflection, absorption, and **A** _____ are ways sounds and matter interact.

DIFFERENT

B _____ sounds bounce off an object.

C _____ sounds are "soaked up" by an object.

Transmitted sounds **D** _____ an object.

2. SUMMARIZE Summarize this lesson by writing one sentence that summarizes each section.

3. DRAW CONCLUSIONS As people get older, some of the hairlike cells in their cochleas die off. How might that affect their hearing?

4. VOCABULARY Write a dictionary definition of each vocabulary word.

FCAT Prep

5. Read/Inquire/Explain Why do people often hear echoes in the mountains?

6. Which would do the **best** job of absorbing sounds?

   A. air   **C.** rocks

   B. blankets   **D.** water

Links

Writing

Expository Writing

Some people find it easier to understand words than pictures. Look back at the diagram in Science Up Close. Then write an **explanation** that conveys the same information.

Math

Round Whole Numbers

A human cochlea has about 35,000 hairlike cells in it. To what place has that number been rounded?

Health

Protect Your Hearing

Infections and accidents that damage the ear usually affect hearing. Do some research on hearing. Then write a brief report describing what people can do to protect their hearing.

For more links and activities, go to www.hspscience.com

President's
SUNKEN SHIP
Discovered

John F. Kennedy

In May 2002, underwater explorer Robert Ballard discovered a famous sunken ship. The ship is named *PT-109*. Its captain, John F. Kennedy, survived the sinking and later became a U.S. President.

Ballard is best known for finding the *Titanic*. Even though Ballard has made many amazing underwater discoveries, the search for *PT-109* was one of the most difficult tasks he has ever faced.

"It was like conducting a search in the Sahara Desert during a blinding sandstorm," Ballard said. "To succeed, we needed all our skills and technology, plus a healthy dose of luck."

Searching the Deep

Ballard discovered *PT-109* in the South Pacific Ocean off the Solomon Islands. The ship had sunk there after being rammed by a Japanese warship in 1943.

The Solomon Islands are about 1900 kilometers (1200 miles) northeast of

Approximate search area

Amagiri and *PT–109* collide

Kolombangara Island

PT–109 wreck drifts south

Route swum by survivors

Kennedy Island (Plum Pudding Is.)

PT–109 wreck found

Japanese destroyer *Amagiri* route

Olasana Island

Naru Island

Australia. To find the sunken ship, Ballard used SONAR, or sound navigation and ranging. SONAR uses sound waves to locate objects under water.

Sound waves pass through water but bounce off solid objects, such as the seafloor. After sound waves bounce off an object, a receiver can show an image of the object.

By using sound, Ballard was able to map the ocean floor.

He found an unusual feature on the seafloor—a small mound in an otherwise flat area.

Ballard and his crew then used a robot submarine to explore the unusual area. The robot took photos of the mound. The photos showed a torpedo gun in the sand. Ballard and his crew had discovered *PT-109!*

THINK ABOUT IT

1. Why do you think it was important to discover the wreck of *PT-109?*
2. What do the letters SONAR mean?

Spin In

Find out more! Log on to
www.hspscience.com

THE MOSQUITO KID

larvae

Michael Nyberg lives in an area where mosquitoes are a big problem. After visiting a sound lab in Michigan, Michael decided that he could fight mosquitoes with sound.

Michael placed mosquito larvae in the fish tank and hooked up a loudspeaker. The teen scientist used the speaker to send sound waves through the water in the tank.

"The sound vibrations caused air sacs, which are like lungs, inside the larvae to explode," Michael said. "When the air sacs exploded, the larvae died." Now some pest companies are hoping to use Michael's idea to fight mosquitoes.

You Can Do It!

Quick and Easy Project

Materials

- 2 paper cups
- pencil
- string, 4 m long
- 2 paper clips

Quick and Easy Project

Sound over a Distance

Procedure

1. Use the pencil to poke a hole in the bottom of each paper cup.

2. Pass one end of the string through the hole in a cup, from outside to inside. Tie the end onto a clip. Repeat with the other end.

3. Go outside with a partner. Move apart until the string is almost stretched tight.

4. Hold your cup over one ear while your partner speaks into the other cup in a normal voice.

5. Tighten the string, and then repeat.

Draw Conclusions

What factors affected whether you could hear your partner at a distance? How could you change materials to make another test?

Design Your Own Investigation

Long-Distance Listening

How far can sound travel to reach your ears? Choose an object, such as an alarm clock, that makes a sound with a constant intensity. Design an investigation to find out how far away from the object you can hear its sound. Make a prediction of that distance. Then gather the materials, and carry out your investigation. Compare your results with those of other students. What hypotheses might you test?

Review and FCAT Preparation

Vocabulary Review

Use the terms below to complete the sentences. One term will be used twice. The page numbers tell you where to look in the chapter if you need help.

vibration p. 64   **amplitude** p. 73
pitch p. 66   **reflection** p. 82
intensity p. 67   **absorption** p. 83
wavelength p. 73 **transmission** p. 84
frequency p. 73

1. A word that means "bouncing off" is _____.

2. Quick back-and-forth motion is called _____.

3. The distance from the rest position to the top of a wave is called the wave's _____.

4. How high or low a note sounds is called its _____.

5. The process of a sound wave's traveling through matter is called _____.

6. The measure of the loudness of a sound is called _____.

7. The number of waves that pass a certain point in one second is called the _____.

8. The process of taking in and stopping a sound is called _____.

9. The distance from the top of one wave to the top of the next wave is called the _____.

10. An echo in the mountains can be an example of a sound's _____ off of cliffs.

Check Understanding

Write the letter of the best choice. Use the diagram to answer Questions 11–13.

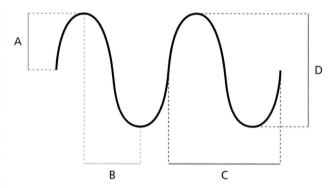

11. What kind of wave is shown?
    A. a longitudinal wave
    B. a transverse wave
    C. a sound wave
    D. a water wave

12. Which shows the amplitude of the wave?
    F. A
    G. B
    H. C
    I. D

13. Which shows the wavelength of the wave?

A. A   **C.** C

B. B   **D.** D

14. COMPARE AND CONTRAST One bell produces sound waves with a greater amplitude than those of another bell. How do the sounds of the two bells differ?

  F. The first bell sounds higher.

  G. The first bell sounds lower.

  H. The first bell is louder.

  I. The first bell is softer.

15. What unit is most often used to measure the intensity of a sound?

  A. bel

  B. centimeter

  C. decibel

  D. meter

16. MAIN IDEA AND DETAILS Where are sound waves changed into electrical signals that travel to your brain?

  F. the eardrum

  G. the hammer

  H. the stirrup

  I. the cochlea

Inquiry Skills

17. Ronald is taking out the trash. He drops a trash can lid, and it makes a huge crash. A second later, he hears an echo of that crash. What can you **infer** about Ronald's surroundings? Explain.

18. Janel is looking at a musical instrument she's never seen before. It has five strings. The thickest string is on the left, and the strings get thinner to the right. **Predict** which string will produce the lowest note. Explain your **prediction**.

Read/Inquire/Explain

19. Imagine that you want to give a friend a chirping toy bird as a gift. Describe how you will wrap the toy so that the sound can't be heard until the gift is opened. Tell what happens to the sound when you wrap the toy that way.

20. Dr. Jeffers places an oscilloscope and a microphone inside a vacuum chamber. He then removes all the air from the chamber.

Part A Outside the chamber is a CD player. Dr. Jeffers plays a recording of a single, pure note— a G. What should appear on the screen of the oscilloscope? Explain.

Part B Inside the vacuum chamber is another CD player. Using a remote control, Dr. Jeffers plays a recording of another note—an A. Now what should appear on the screen of the oscilloscope? Explain.

Chapter 3

Light and Heat

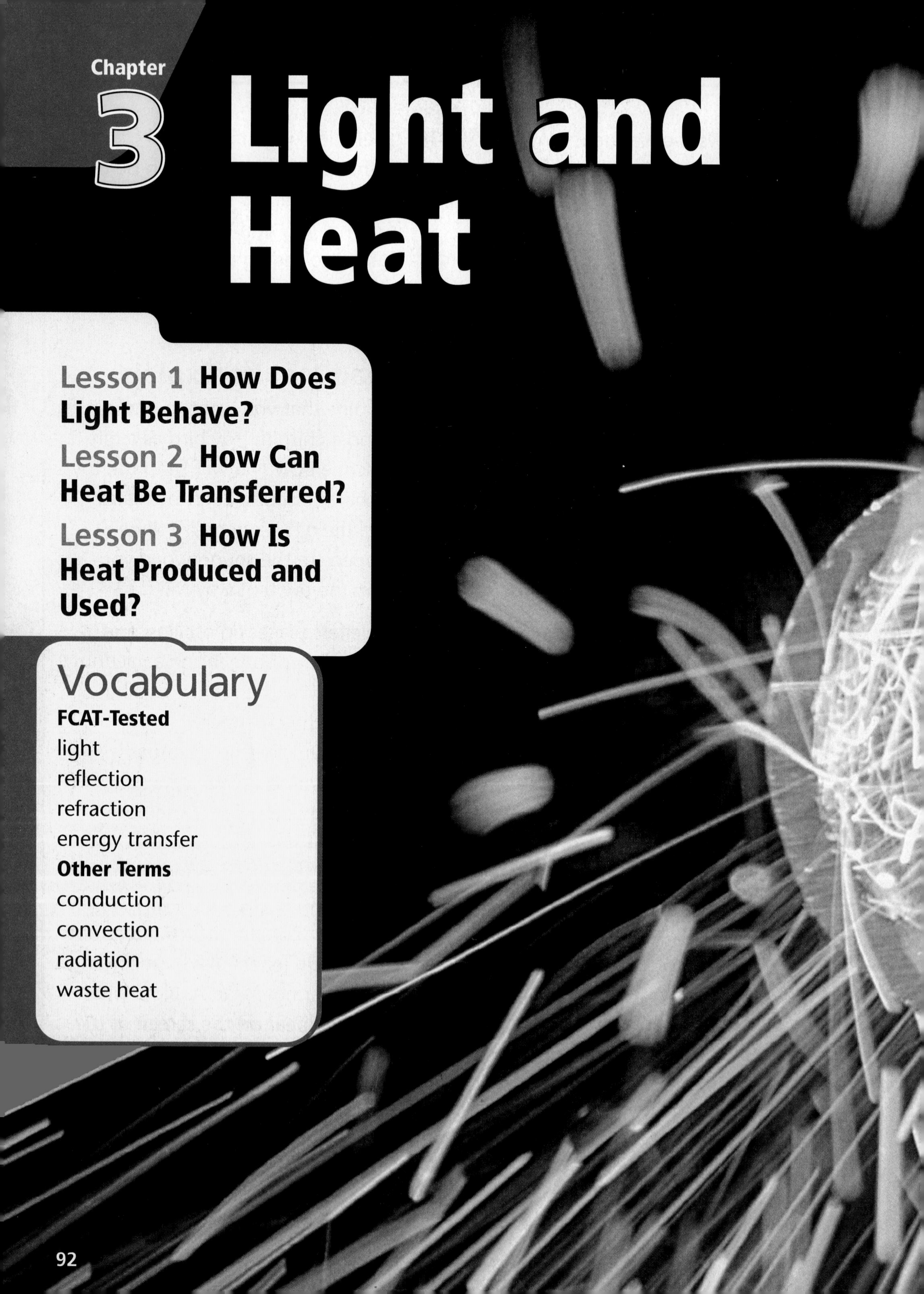

Vocabulary

FCAT-Tested

light

reflection

refraction

energy transfer

Other Terms

conduction

convection

radiation

waste heat

What do YOU wonder?

Laser light can be used to cut wood and metals. Some lasers get so hot that they can burn right through steel. How do you think light makes things hotter?

How Does Light Behave?

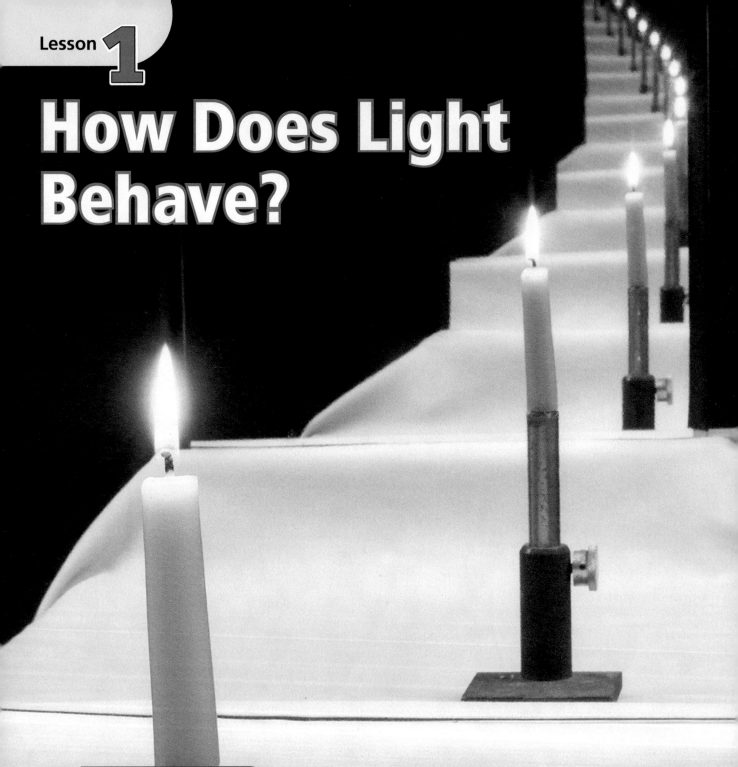

Fast Fact

Chain of Candles How many candles do you see? Light bounces from mirror to mirror and back again. Every bounce makes you see another candle. In the Investigate activity, you will find out about the path of a beam of light.

How Light Travels

Materials
- ruler
- small lamp without a lampshade
- clay
- 3 index cards
- pencil

Procedure

1. Using the ruler, draw lines on each card from corner to corner to make a large X.

2. Use a pencil to make a hole at the center of each X. Stack the cards, and use the pencil to make sure all the holes are at the same height.

3. Make a clay stand for each card. Stand the cards on the desk, one in front of the other and a few centimeters apart.

4. Place the lamp on the desk, and turn it on. Look through the holes in the cards. Move the cards until you can see the light bulb through all the holes at once. Draw a diagram to show your setup.

5. Move the cards to new places. Each time you move them, draw a diagram to show your setup. Try to observe the light through the holes each time.

Step 1

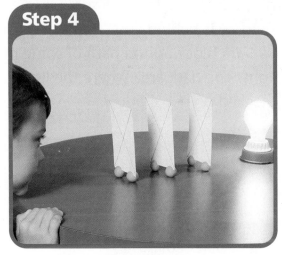

Step 4

Draw Conclusions

1. In what position were the cards when you were able to see the light bulb?

2. **Inquiry Skill** How did drawing diagrams help you communicate your results?

Investigate Further

Would your results be the same if the cards were not on a level surface? Plan and conduct a simple investigation to find out.

VOCABULARY
light p. 96
reflection p. 97
refraction p. 99

SCIENCE CONCEPTS
▶ how matter affects the path of light
▶ how the eye receives light

 **READING FOCUS SKILL**
CAUSE AND EFFECT Look for ways in which matter affects light.

cause	→	effect

Properties of Light

Remember how warm you feel when you stand in the sun? **Light** is a form of energy that can travel through space. Light from the sun gives plants the energy they need to make food. Animals get their energy from plants and from animals that have eaten plants.

Think about your shadow on a sunny day. When you face the sun, your shadow is behind you. That's because you are blocking the path of some of the light. The dark area where the light is blocked is your shadow.

Light travels in straight lines until it hits something. When the light hit you, its path was blocked. Light doesn't go around corners. That's why the area behind you was dark.

Think back to the Investigate. The only time you could see the light bulb was when the holes in the cards were in a straight line. If you moved one card out of line, it blocked the light. When you tried to look through the holes, you saw the card, not the light.

 CAUSE AND EFFECT What causes a shadow?

This stop sign makes a shadow because it blocks light from the sun. As the sun's position in the sky changes, the size and position of the shadow change.

▲ When the surface of water is smooth, it acts just like the regular mirror does, as you can see in this reflecting pool.

Reflection

When you comb your hair, do you look in a mirror to make sure you look okay? What you see in the mirror is called an image. You can see your image because light bounces off the mirror and back to you.

When light hits an object, the light bounces off the surface of the object. The bouncing of light off an object is called **reflection**.

Most objects have rough surfaces. You can't see an image in something with a rough surface, such as cloth, because the roughness makes light reflect in many different directions. A mirror or a calm lake has a smooth, flat surface. Almost all the light reflects in the same direction. This is the kind of reflection that allows you to you see yourself.

Your image in a mirror looks just like you—except for one thing. It's backward! Images in a mirror are reversed from left to right.

 CAUSE AND EFFECT What causes a mirror to reflect an image?

Absorption

Not all of the light that hits an object is reflected. You know that light passes through glass. That's why you can see through glass. *Transparent* materials let most of the light that hits them pass through. Glass, water, and many kinds of plastic are transparent.

Translucent (tranz•LOO•suhnt) materials let some of the light that hits them pass through, but they also absorb or scatter some of the light. This is why you can't see through them clearly. Wax paper, frosted glass, and some kinds of plastic are translucent.

Can you see through a metal door or a brick wall? Of course not! The reason is that these materials absorb or reflect all of the light. No light passes through them. *Opaque* (oh•PAYK) materials do not allow light to pass through. Metal, brick, and wood are opaque.

 CAUSE AND EFFECT Why can't you see through opaque materials?

The dark red vase on the left is opaque. The middle vase is transparent. The vase on the right is translucent. ▼

▲ This beautiful stained-glass window is made up of translucent and opaque materials.

▲ When a beam of light enters water it slows down. If it hits at an angle, the light bends. Light travels faster in air than in water.

▲ A beam of light doesn't bend if it enters the water straight on.

Refraction

Have you ever used a net to catch a fish in a tank? You probably had a hard time telling where the fish was. That's because your eyes were fooled by the direction the light came from.

Light reflecting off the fish passed through the water, into the air, and to your eye. When the light moved from the water to the air, its speed changed. The change in speed made the beam of light bend. The bending of light is called **refraction** (rih•FRAK•shuhn).

⭐ **CAUSE AND EFFECT** What causes refraction?

Is It Broken?
Put a pencil into a glass. Observe the pencil. Now pour water into the glass. Observe the pencil again. Explain your observations.

Seeing Light

Light is all around you. This sun gives off light. So do streetlights and desk lamps. Light also bounces off objects. When light bouncing from an object reaches your eyes, you see the object.

How do you see light? It enters the front of the eye and passes through an opening called the pupil. Around this opening is the iris, the colored part of the eye. The iris controls how much light can pass into the eye. When light is bright, the iris makes the pupil small. When light is dim, the iris makes the pupil large so that more light can enter.

The transparent lens of your eye bends the rays of light to make them focus, or meet, on the retina, at the back of your eye. A nerve carries information about the light to your brain. Your brain tells you what you're seeing.

 CAUSE AND EFFECT **What causes an image to form inside the eye?**

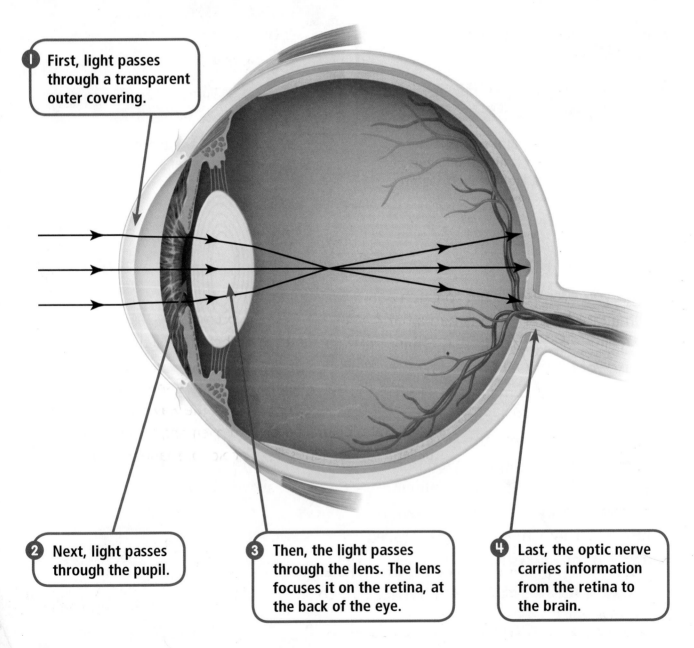

1 **First, light passes through a transparent outer covering.**

2 **Next, light passes through the pupil.**

3 **Then, the light passes through the lens. The lens focuses it on the retina, at the back of the eye.**

4 **Last, the optic nerve carries information from the retina to the brain.**

1. CAUSE AND EFFECT Copy and complete the graphic organizer.

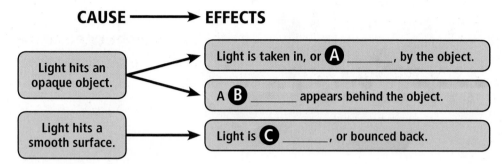

CAUSE ⟶ EFFECTS

Light hits an opaque object.	→	Light is taken in, or **A** _____, by the object.
		A **B** _____ appears behind the object.
Light hits a smooth surface.	→	Light is **C** _____, or bounced back.

2. SUMMARIZE Write two sentences that tell what this lesson is mainly about.

3. DRAW CONCLUSIONS Why can't you see around corners?

4. VOCABULARY Write a paragraph that shows how the vocabulary terms in this lesson are related.

FCAT Prep

5. Read/Inquire/Explain You put your arm into a tank of water. Why does your arm look broken?

6. Which part of the eye controls the amount of light that enters?
   A. pupil   **C.** lens
   B. iris   **D.** retina

Writing

Expository Writing
Think about a time when you have seen a lake, pond, or even a puddle reflect a scene. Write a **paragraph** that describes the scene and its reflection.

Math

Compare Lengths
A sign is 200 cm tall. Its shadow is 100 cm long at 10 A.M. What ratio compares the sign's height to the shadow's length? Will the ratio be greater or smaller just after sunrise?

Art

Sun Sculpture
Use what you know about how light moves to make a sculpture. The sculpture should change in some way due to sun movement, for example, color or shadow shape.

 For more links and activities, go to www.hspscience.com

2

How Can Heat Be Transferred?

Fast Fact

Seeing Temperature A thermogram (THER•muh•gram) is a picture that shows how hot things are. Blue and black show the coldest objects. Yellow and red show the hottest objects. You can tell that the car has just been driven because the tires and engine are hot. In the Investigate, you will build a device that uses a much older method to measure temperature.

Build a Thermometer

Materials
- apron
- food coloring
- clear plastic 1-L bottle with narrow mouth
- funnel
- tape
- clear plastic drinking straw
- water
- modeling clay

Procedure

1. Put on an apron. Add water to the bottle until it is about one-third full.

2. Add two or three drops of food coloring. Swirl the bottle to mix the color evenly.

3. Put the straw in the bottle. Hold the straw so that the end is half-way down in the water. Tape the straw in place at the neck of the bottle.

4. Use clay to seal the top of the bottle so that no air can get in or out. *Do not squeeze the bottle.*

5. Make a drawing of your thermometer. Show the water level in the straw.

6. Put the thermometer in a warm place for five minutes. Observe the water level in the straw. Make a drawing to record this observation.

Draw Conclusions

1. Did the water level in the straw change when the thermometer was in a warm place? If so, how did it change?

2. **Inquiry Skill** Suppose you put your thermometer in a cold place, such as a refrigerator. Predict what would happen.

Step 3

Step 4

Investigate Further

Predict **which places in your classroom will be the warmest and coolest. Then** plan and conduct a simple investigation **to check.**

SC.B.1.2.5.4.1 measuring gain/loss of energy
SC.H.1.2.5.4.1 using models

Reading in Science

SC.B.1.2.3.4.1 light and heat
SC.B.1.2.1.4.1 living thing/energy from the sun
LA.A.2.2.1 main idea and details

VOCABULARY

conduction p. 106
convection p. 107
radiation p. 108

SCIENCE CONCEPTS

▶ how temperature and heat are different

▶ ways in which heat moves

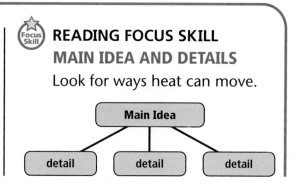

READING FOCUS SKILL

MAIN IDEA AND DETAILS

Look for ways heat can move.

```
            Main Idea
         /     |     \
   detail    detail    detail
```

Temperature and Heat

You step outside on a bright summer day and feel the hot air right away. You look up at the thermometer. It shows that the temperature is 33°C (92°F). No wonder you feel hot! A thermometer measures the temperature of matter—in this case, the air outdoors. Temperature is the measure of how hot or cold something is.

The particles in matter are always moving. The more energy they have, the more they move. The particles in a solid can't move very far. They vibrate in place. In a liquid or a gas, the particles can move faster and farther. Temperature is actually the measure of the average energy of this movement.

On a hot day, particles in the air have more energy than they do on a cooler

◀ A thermometer measures temperature. It tells how hot or cold matter is.

day. The air particles move faster. This gives them a higher temperature.

Which has a higher temperature— steaming tea in a teapot or water in a swimming pool? If you said the tea, you'd be right. It's much hotter than the water in the pool.

Which has more energy—the tea or the water in the pool? Even though it's cooler, the water in the pool has more thermal energy. Thermal energy is the total amount of energy in an object. There is a much larger amount of matter in the pool, so the total of its energy is larger. The tea in the teapot is a small amount of matter. It has less total energy.

It's a hot day, so you jump into the swimming pool. Ahh, you feel cooler already! And you *are* cooler. Energy is moving from your body into the water. As you learned in Chapter 1, the term for this transferred energy is *heat*. Heat always moves from matter that is warmer to matter that is cooler. In the pool, as the heat from your body moves into the cool water, you cool off.

Focus Skill **MAIN IDEA AND DETAILS** How does heat move?

▼ The small mass of liquid in this teapot has a high temperature.

▼ The liquid in this wading pool is cool. However, its total thermal energy is greater than that of the liquid in the teapot because the pool water has much more mass.

105

Conduction

Have you ever left a metal spoon in a bowl of hot soup? When you touched the spoon handle, it felt hot. The handle of the spoon wasn't in the soup, so how did it get hot? Heat moved from the soup into the spoon. Then it moved along the spoon until the whole spoon was hot.

Heat travels by **conduction** through materials that are touching. The heat from the soup moved by conduction to the handle of the spoon and then from the spoon to your fingers.

Some materials conduct heat better than others. Most metals conduct heat well. Other materials do not conduct well at all. A foam cup, for example, is a poor conductor of heat. Glass, air, water, and wood also do not conduct heat well.

 MAIN IDEA AND DETAIL What kinds of matter conduct heat well?

The blacksmith's forge warms the pieces of metal. Heat spreads through the metal by conduction. ▼

Math in Science
Interpret Data

Heat Conductors

The table lists some metals in order of how well they conduct heat. The best conductor is listed first. Some steel cooking pots have a thin layer of copper on the bottom. Why do you think they are made that way?

Conductivity	
good ⬆	Silver
	Copper
	Steel
poor ⬇	Lead

Convection

The particles in liquids and gases move constantly. The movement of heat in liquids and gases from a warmer area to a cooler area is called **convection**.

Warm liquid or gas is forced up by cooler liquid or gas. When water boils in a pot, the water near the heat source gets hot first and is forced up by the cooler water. Then the cool water gets hot and is forced up. This happens over and over in a circular current, or flow. This is an example of convection.

 MAIN IDEA AND DETAILS What kinds of matter carry heat by convection?

Hot Air

Cut a spiral shape from a sheet of construction paper. Make a hole in its center. Tie thread through the hole. Hold the spiral above a warm desk lamp. What happens? Why? Next, hold the spiral beside the lamp. What happens? Why?

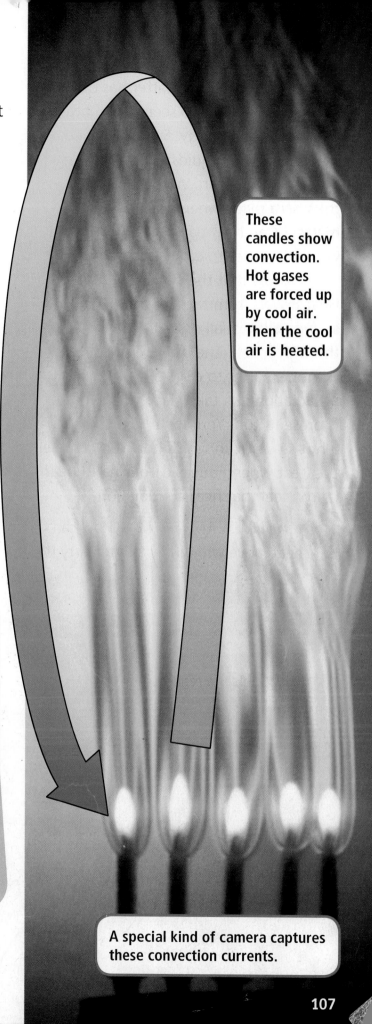

These candles show convection. Hot gases are forced up by cool air. Then the cool air is heated.

A special kind of camera captures these convection currents.

Radiation

You have seen that matter has heat energy. You have also seen that matter can carry heat energy. Solids carry heat by conduction. Liquids and gases carry heat by convection. What happens, then, in a place where there is no matter? Can heat pass through space without matter to carry it? Yes, it can.

You know that the sun warms Earth. Heat travels from the sun to Earth's surface. Almost all of that distance is through space. The movement of heat without matter to carry it is **radiation**.

Radiation can take place when matter is present, too. You don't have to touch a hot stove to know it's hot. You can feel the heat when you hold your hand near it. You feel that heat by radiation.

MAIN IDEA AND DETAILS **How can heat move without matter to carry it?**

▼ Heat from the wires in a toaster moves to a slice of bread by radiation. The glowing wires of the toaster also give off light.

▼ This is a regular photograph of an elephant.

▼ This photograph shows how heat radiates from the body of an elephant.

108

Focus Skill

1. MAIN IDEA AND DETAILS Copy and complete the graphic organizer.

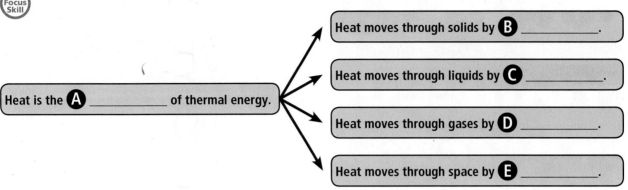

Heat is the **A** _____ of thermal energy.

Heat moves through solids by **B** _____.

Heat moves through liquids by **C** _____.

Heat moves through gases by **D** _____.

Heat moves through space by **E** _____.

2. SUMMARIZE Write a summary of this lesson, beginning with the sentence *Heat is a form of energy that can move in three ways.*

3. DRAW CONCLUSIONS How is radiation different from conduction and convection?

4. VOCABULARY Draw a picture to illustrate the lesson vocabulary.

FCAT Prep

5. Read/Inquire/Explain Two glasses hold water at 22°C. One holds 250 mL. The other holds 350 mL. Which glass holds more thermal energy? Explain.

6. Which material conducts heat well?
 A. brick   **C.** plastic
 B. glass   **D.** silver

Links

Writing

Narrative Writing

Write a **personal story** about a very hot day and what you did to cool off. Explain why what you did cooled you off.

Math

Measure Temperature

Fill an ice cube tray with water. Place a thermometer in one section. Put the tray in a freezer. Just as the water freezes, measure the temperature. What is it?

Social Studies

Time Line

Find out who invented the first thermometer and who developed the two temperature scales. Make a time line that shows what you learned.

 For more links and activities, go to www.hspscience.com

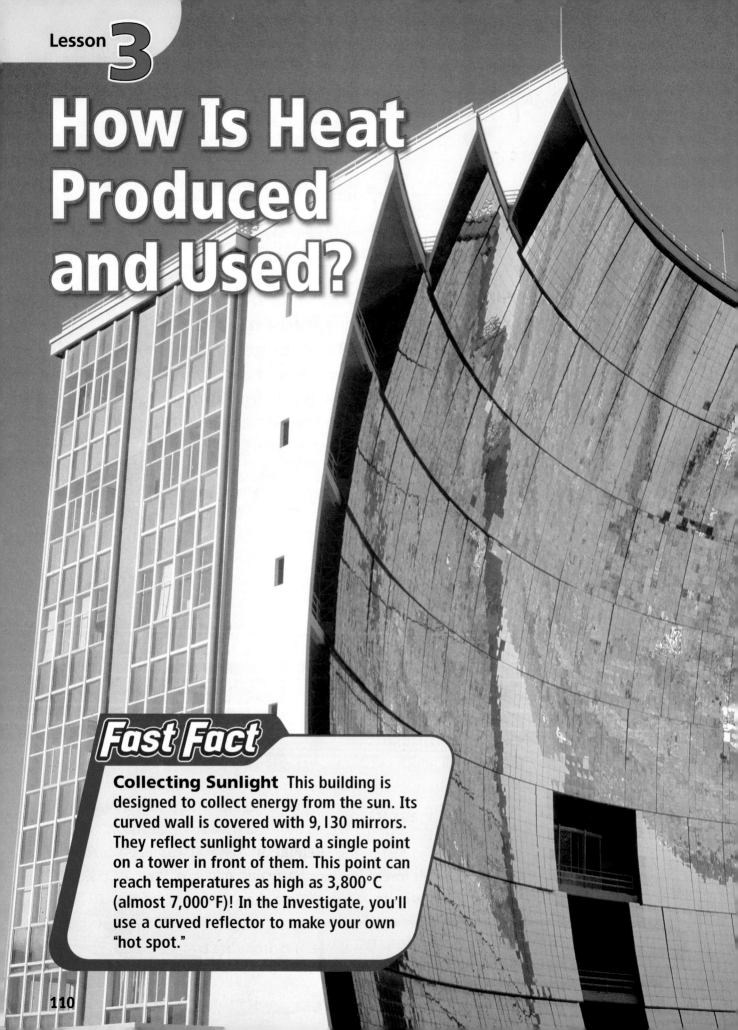

How Is Heat Produced and Used?

Fast Fact

Collecting Sunlight This building is designed to collect energy from the sun. Its curved wall is covered with 9,130 mirrors. They reflect sunlight toward a single point on a tower in front of them. This point can reach temperatures as high as 3,800°C (almost 7,000°F)! In the Investigate, you'll use a curved reflector to make your own "hot spot."

Build a Solar Hot Spot

Materials
- poster board
- scissors
- clock or watch
- 2 sheets of graph paper
- thermometer
- shoe-box lid
- aluminum foil
- string
- glue
- hole punch
- ruler

Procedure

1. **CAUTION: Be careful when using scissors.** Cut a piece of poster board 10 cm by 30 cm. Glue foil to one side. Let it dry for at least 10 minutes.

2. Place a thermometer in the shoe-box lid.

3. Place the lid in sunlight. Record the temperature each minute for 10 minutes.

4. Punch a hole 2 cm from the middle of each 10-cm side of the poster board. Use string to pull these sides toward each other until they are about 20 cm apart. Then tie the string to hold the shape.

5. Put the curved reflector in the shoe-box lid, with the thermometer in its center. Repeat Step 3.

6. Make line graphs of the data from Steps 3 and 5. Show time on the horizontal axis and temperature on the vertical axis.

Step 3

Step 5

Draw Conclusions

1. Describe the temperature changes shown on each graph.

2. **Inquiry Skill** Interpret the data. What do you infer caused the differences in the temperatures on the two graphs?

Investigate Further

Repeat the experiment, using black construction paper instead of foil. Make a chart to compare your results. Explain the difference in your results from the two surfaces.

SC.B.1.2.5.4.1 measuring gain/loss of energy
SC.H.2.2.1.4.1 making predictions
111

Reading in Science

SC.B.1.2.1.4.1 living things/energy from Sun;
SC.B.1.2.4.4.1 transformation of energy; SC.B.1.2.1.4.2 flow of energy; LA.A.2.2.1 main idea and details

VOCABULARY
energy transfer p. 113
waste heat p. 116

SCIENCE CONCEPTS
▶ how heat energy is transferred to other forms of energy
▶ how people use heat

(Focus Skill) **READING FOCUS SKILL**
MAIN IDEA AND DETAILS
Look for examples of how heat is produced and used.

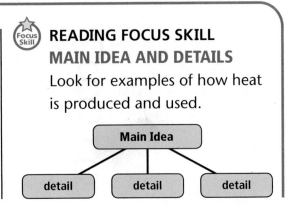

Heat Sources

Did you know that you can absorb heat just by going outside? During the day, even if it's cloudy, energy from the sun reaches Earth. It warms you, and it warms Earth. The sun is the main source of light and heat for Earth.

Heat from the sun can be used in other ways. In the Investigate, you made a curved reflector. You used it to collect the sun's energy. Large groups of mirrors can do the same thing. This is how some solar power plants work. The mirrors reflect light onto a tower. The tower contains materials that collect the heat. The heat is used to make electricity.

Have you ever noticed something that looks like a window propped up on the roof of a house? That's a solar panel. Solar panels collect and store heat from the sun. This heat is used to warm water for use in the home.

Solar Two, in California, is a power plant. The mirrors reflect the sun's energy onto the tower, which collects the heat.

▲ When a fuel such as wood is burned, it gives off light and heat.

◀ A thermostat (THER•muh•stat) allows a person to control how much heat the furnace sends into the rooms.

Some homes collect heat from the sun naturally because they have large windows that face the sun. In many areas, however, the sun doesn't provide enough heat to keep a whole house warm. In those areas, houses have to be warmed by changing other forms of energy to heat. The change of energy from one form to another is called **energy transfer**.

Fuels are sources of energy to make heat. Wood and any other materials that burn are fuels. Many homes have furnaces that burn oil or natural gas. A furnace warms water or air. As the warmed material is pumped through the house, it gives off its heat to the rooms.

Other homes don't have fuel-burning furnaces. Instead, they have electric heaters in each room, usually along the bottom of a wall. When electricity flows through wires, the wires get hot. The wires in the heaters in each room warm the home.

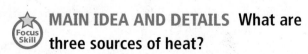 **MAIN IDEA AND DETAILS** What are three sources of heat?

Using Heat

People use heat in many ways. You already know that it's used to warm homes. Heat is also used to warm water for bathing and washing dishes. Heat is used to dry clothes, either in a dryer or outside on a line in the sun. If the clothes are wrinkled, heat from an iron makes the cloth smooth again.

Heat is also used to make changes in matter. People do this every day at home when they cook. Some stoves burn natural gas. Other stoves use electricity. Food is put into a pan, and the pan is put on top of the stove or in the oven. Heat from the stove moves into the pan. Then the heat moves into the food, making it hot and causing changes in its matter.

Heat also changes matter in factories. For example, metals such as iron and brass are heated until they melt. Then the liquid metals are poured into molds. When the metals cool, they harden and have the shapes of the molds. Plastics are molded in a similar way.

◀ A wok is like a large frying pan. The whole wok is heated by the flame. Food cooks quickly because it touches the hot pan.

In a popcorn popper, hot air heats the kernels until they pop. ▶

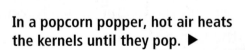

Motion from Heat

A heat engine burns fuel to produce heat. Then the engine transfers the heat into the energy of motion. Steam engines are heat engines.

In a steam engine, fuel is burned to heat water. The water boils, making steam.

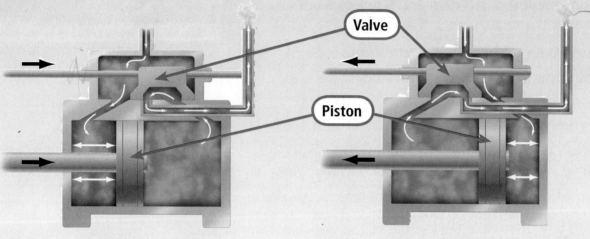

Valve

Piston

First, a valve lets hot steam into the left side. The steam pushes the piston to the right. The valve lets out cooler steam from the right side.

Then, the valve opens to let steam into the right side. The steam pushes the piston back. This left-right cycle repeats.

Heat can be used to produce motion. In some power plants, heat is used to boil water. This heat may come from burning fuel or from the sun. The boiling water becomes steam. The expanding steam pushes the blades of fanlike machines called turbines (TER•binz). The energy of the turbines' motion is changed to electricity. When that electricity gets to your home, you can turn it back into heat by turning on the stove.

 MAIN IDEA AND DETAILS What are four ways heat is used in the home?

Insta-Lab

Zap It!

Do this experiment on a sunny day. **CAUTION: Put on safety goggles.** Take a kernel of popcorn and a raisin outside. Set both on concrete or brick in the sun. Hold a hand lens so that it focuses a small dot of light on the kernel. Wait one minute. Repeat with the raisin. What happens? Why?

Waste Heat

As you have learned, making heat often involves burning a fuel. People burn fuels to heat homes and to make car engines work. Most electricity is made in power plants that burn fuel. When fuel is burned, not all of the heat it produces can be put to use. The heat that can't be used to do work is **waste heat**.

The engine of a car uses heat to produce motion. If you stand near the front of a car that has just been driven, you can feel heat being given off into the air around the car. It doesn't do any work. It's waste heat.

Sometimes waste heat can be harmful. The electricity that flows through a computer makes heat. The computer has no use for this heat. If the heat builds up, it can damage the computer. That's why computers have fans to remove the waste heat.

 MAIN IDEA AND DETAILS What is waste heat?

The computer fan moves hot air. The heat sink conducts heat away from chips. ▼

A car radiator collects waste heat to protect the car's engine from overheating.

A light bulb turns energy to light and heat. The heat is waste heat.

fan

heat sink

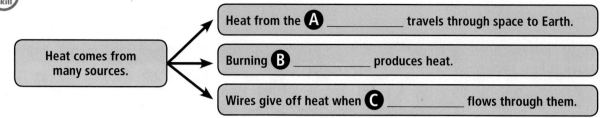

Focus Skill

1. MAIN IDEA AND DETAILS Copy and complete the graphic organizer.

Heat comes from many sources.

Heat from the **A** _____ travels through space to Earth.

Burning **B** _____ produces heat.

Wires give off heat when **C** _____ flows through them.

2. SUMMARIZE Write a sentence that tells the most important information in this lesson.

3. DRAW CONCLUSIONS Why does a car engine need a radiator?

4. VOCABULARY Give two examples of energy transfer.

FCAT Prep

5. Read/Inquire/Explain If you sit in the sun, you will feel warmer in dark-colored clothing than in light-colored clothing. Explain how energy transfer causes this effect.

6. Which property must be different between two objects for heat to be transferred from one to the other?

A. mass   C. temperature

B. shape   D. volume

Links

Writing

Persuasive Writing
Imagine that you sell furnaces to homeowners. Write a **business letter** explaining why your furnaces are the best ones to buy.

Math (9÷3)

Make a Bar Graph
About nine-tenths of the energy that some light bulbs use produces heat rather than light. Make a bar graph showing how much of a light bulb's energy makes light and how much makes heat.

Physical Education

Overheated!
Your body also produces waste heat. If it builds up, overheating can lead to heatstroke. Research heatstroke. Make a poster about its signs and the treatment for it.

 For more links and activities, go to
www.hspscience.com

Heat from Earth

How does your family heat the house when it's cold outside? They might use oil. They might burn gas. Some people heat their homes using thermal heat.

In Iceland, pools of naturally heated water called hot springs warm homes and greenhouses. Hot springs are places where heat from deep inside Earth comes to the surface to warm pools of water. This heating process is caused by *geothermal energy*.

Hot springs can be found around the world. In Iceland, homes and greenhouses are warmed by heat from hot springs. People in Japan or Iceland aren't the only ones to use Earth's heat to warm or cool their houses, however.

Several feet below the ground, the soil temperature stays at an almost constant temperature. Depending on the location, the temperature of the soil below the surface ranges from 7 to 24 degrees Celsius (45 to 75 degrees Fahrenheit). During winter, the ground temperature is usually warmer than the air temperature above ground. In the summer, the ground temperature is usually cooler than the air temperature above ground. Those temperature differences can be used to make indoor temperatures warm or cool.

To make use of the temperature differences, a house must be equipped with a heat pump. A heat pump is connected to pipes buried in the ground. A special liquid moves through the pipes and into the *heat pump.* In the winter, the pump brings heat from the ground into the house. In the summer, the heat from the house is carried by the liquid to the underground pipes. Ducts carry the heated or cooled air throughout the house.

Hot springs and geothermal power plants rely on heat from deep inside Earth.

THINK ABOUT IT

1. How else could geothermal energy be used?
2. Do you know of any other places where hot springs are found?

Find out more! Log on to
www.hspscience.com

SCIENCE Spin from WEEKLY READER®

People

SC.H.3.2.1.4.1
technologies,
costs/benefits
SC.H.3.2.4.4.1
solving problems/
new ideas

A Bright Idea

Riding a bike at night can be dangerous. Car drivers often cannot see cyclists. Everyone sees Chris Niezrecki as he pedals around town after the sun has gone down. That's because his bike glows in the dark.

Niezrecki invented a glow-in-the-dark bike by using the same technology, *electroluminescence,* that makes the face of a watch glow in the dark.

Drivers can see the glowing bike up to 180 meters (600 feet) away. That's far enough so that drivers can steer to avoid the bike. The glow-in-the-dark bike should help keep cyclists safe.

You Can Do It!

Quick and Easy Project

Conductors

Procedure

1. Carefully tape the bulb of a thermometer to the top of the handle of each spoon.
2. Put warm water into the jar. The water should not be deep enough to touch the thermometers when the spoons are placed in the water.
3. Carefully put the spoons into the jar.
4. Measure and record the temperature of each spoon every minute for 5 minutes.

Materials

- 3 thermometers
- tape
- warm water
- large jar
- plastic, wood, and metal spoons of about the same size

Draw Conclusions

Which spoon conducted heat the fastest? How do you know?

Design Your Own Investigation

Seeing Around Corners

You have seen that light travels in straight lines. That's why you can't see around corners. How could you use a mirror to see around corners? Experiment to find the best position in which to place the mirror so that you have a good view around a corner.

Review and FCAT Preparation

Vocabulary Review

Match the terms to the definitions below. The page numbers tell you where to look in the chapter if you need help.

light p. 96   **radiation** p. 108
reflection p. 97   **energy**
refraction p. 99   **transfer** p. 113
conduction p. 106   **waste heat** p. 116
convection p. 107

1. Heat that can't be used to do work is _____.

2. The bending of light is called _____.

3. The change of energy from one form to another is called _____.

4. Heat flows through a liquid or a gas by _____.

5. _____ is a form of energy that travels in straight lines.

6. The bouncing of light off an object is called _____.

7. Heat travels through solids that are touching by _____.

8. _____ moves heat through space, where there is no matter.

Check Understanding

Write the letter of the best choice.

9. In which container does the water have the most thermal energy?

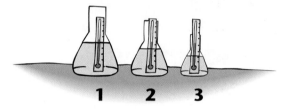

1   2   3

  A. Beaker 1
  B. Beaker 2
  C. Beaker 3
  D. They're equal.

10. **MAIN IDEA AND DETAILS** Which of the following removes waste heat?
  F. car radiator
  G. furnace
  H. heat engine
  I. turbine

11. **CAUSE AND EFFECT** Which causes an image to form inside the eye?
  A. The cornea is transparent.
  B. The lens bends light rays.
  C. The pupil changes size.
  D. The optic nerve leads to the brain.

12. Which of these is translucent?

  F.   **G.**   **H.**   **I.**

13. Jack was standing on a bridge, looking into a pond. He could see himself in the pond. What made it possible for Jack to see himself?

A. absorption
B. energy transfer
C. radiation
D. reflection

14. Which energy transfers are taking place?

F. light to heat and electricity
G. electricity to heat and light
H. heat to light and electricity
I. waste heat to light and electricity

15. Kira walked by the stove and said, "Wow! That's hot!" What allowed her to feel how hot the stove was without touching it?

A. conduction
B. fuel
C. radiation
D. refraction

16. Which does a thermometer measure?

F. number of particles of matter
G. total energy of movement of particles of matter
H. fuel energy of particles of matter
I. average energy of movement of particles of matter

Inquiry Skills

17. **Predict** what will happen to the handle of a metal spoon when you put the spoon into a cup of hot cocoa. Explain your answer.

18. **Interpret Data** Suppose you measure temperature in two cups. Each holds 250 mL of water. Both begin at 80°C. Over time, Cup A cools more quickly than Cup B. What **conclusion** can you draw about what each cup is made of?

Read/Inquire/Explain

19. Lenses in eyeglasses change the direction of light rays to help the lens of the eye form an image inside the eye. What process takes place in the eyeglass lenses? Explain your answer.

20. You are helping with the dishes after supper, and you notice that the pots have wooden handles.
Part A What is the reason for wooden handles on a pot?
Part B What other materials might be used to make pot handles?

Vocabulary

FCAT-Tested	conductor	hydroelectric power
potential energy	insulator	
kinetic energy	magnet	geothermal energy
Other Terms	magnetic pole	
static electricity	magnetic field	solar energy
current electricity	electromagnet	chemical energy
series circuit	generator	mechanical energy
parallel circuit	electric motor	

What do YOU wonder?

These huge machines are turbines and generators. Where might you find them? What do you think they do?

What Is Electricity?

Fast Fact

Ceramic Insulators Insulators are made of a ceramic material through which electricity can't flow. Sparks heat the air around the insulators to 3,000°C (5,400°F) or more! In the Investigate, you'll see what kinds of paths let electricity flow.

Light a Bulb

Materials
- D-cell battery
- flashlight bulb
- masking tape
- insulated electric wire, about 30 cm with ends stripped

Procedure

CAUTION: Don't touch the sharp ends of the wire!

1 Using these materials, how can you make the bulb light? Predict the kind of setup that will make the bulb light.

2 Draw a picture of your prediction.

3 Test your prediction. Put the materials together the way your drawing shows.

4 Record your results. Beside your drawing, write *yes* if the bulb lit. Write *no* if it didn't.

5 Make more predictions and drawings. Test them all. Record the results of each try.

Draw Conclusions

1. How must the materials be put together to make the bulb light?

2. **Inquiry Skill** Look at your drawings and notes. How did you record data? Scientists publish their results so that others can check them. Could someone use your records to double-check your tests? Explain.

Step 2

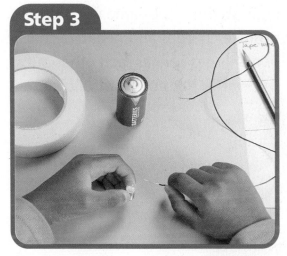

Step 3

Investigate Further

Predict the kind of setup that will light two bulbs at the same time. Test your prediction.

VOCABULARY

static electricity p. 128
current electricity p. 130
series circuit p. 132
parallel circuit p. 132
conductor p. 134
insulator p. 134

SCIENCE CONCEPTS

▶ what electricity is
▶ how electricity moves

READING FOCUS SKILL

SEQUENCE Look for the steps by which electricity is generated and the ways it moves.

Static Electricity

Have you ever pulled your sweater out of the clothes dryer and found your socks stuck to it? If so, you have seen static electricity in action. **Static electricity** is an electrical charge that builds up on an object. Static electricity results from changes in matter.

Most of the time, matter is electrically neutral. It has the same number of positive charges and negative charges. The charges cancel each other out, so the matter has no electrical charge.

In the dryer, your socks rub against other clothes. Some clothes gain negative charges. These clothes end up with a negative electrical charge. Other clothes lose negative charges and end up with a positive electrical charge.

Objects with opposite charges attract, or pull, each other. That's why your socks stick to your sweater. Objects with the same charge repel, or push away, each other.

Static electricity stays in an object until something happens to remove it.

◀ **What electric charges make this girl's hair stand on end?**

Objects with the same charges move away from each other. What happens if their charges are different? ▼

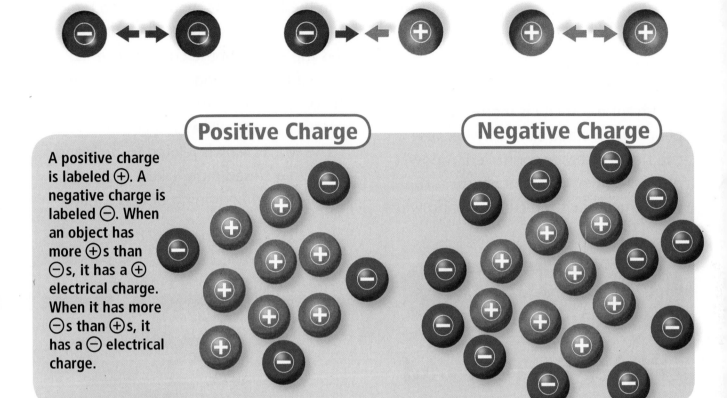

Positive Charge

Negative Charge

A positive charge is labeled ⊕. A negative charge is labeled ⊖. When an object has more ⊕s than ⊖s, it has a ⊕ electrical charge. When it has more ⊖s than ⊕s, it has a ⊖ electrical charge.

Pulling your socks off your sweater forces charges to move. You hear a crackle of sparks as extra negative charges move between the sweater and the socks. Then the socks aren't charged anymore.

Lightning is caused by static electricity. During a storm, ice crystals in clouds rub together and gain negative charges. The ground loses negative charges, so it has a positive charge. Soon the difference in charges becomes large. Negative charges move from the clouds to the ground as a giant spark. Flash! You see lightning.

 SEQUENCE Explain the sequence of events that leads to a flash of lightning.

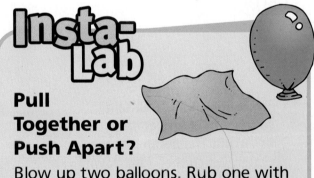

Insta-Lab

Pull Together or Push Apart?

Blow up two balloons. Rub one with wool. Hold it up to a wall. What happens? Tie a string to each balloon. Rub the balloons together. Hold them by their strings. Put them close together. What happens? Why?

Current Electricity

Static electricity is one form of electricity. Another form is **current electricity**, or a steady stream of charges. In current electricity, an electric current moves through a material such as a copper wire.

Current electricity is more useful to people than static electricity because it can be more easily controlled. A power plant produces a flow of charges. The plant then sends the current along wires to homes and businesses, where people use it to provide light and heat and to run machines.

In the Investigate, you lit a bulb by using an electric current. The battery was the source of the current. The current moved along a path that linked the battery and bulb. The path that an electric current follows is a circuit.

The word *circuit* is related to *circle* and refers to a closed path. Like a circle, a circuit has no beginning or end. Charges

Science Up Close

Water Current and Electric Current

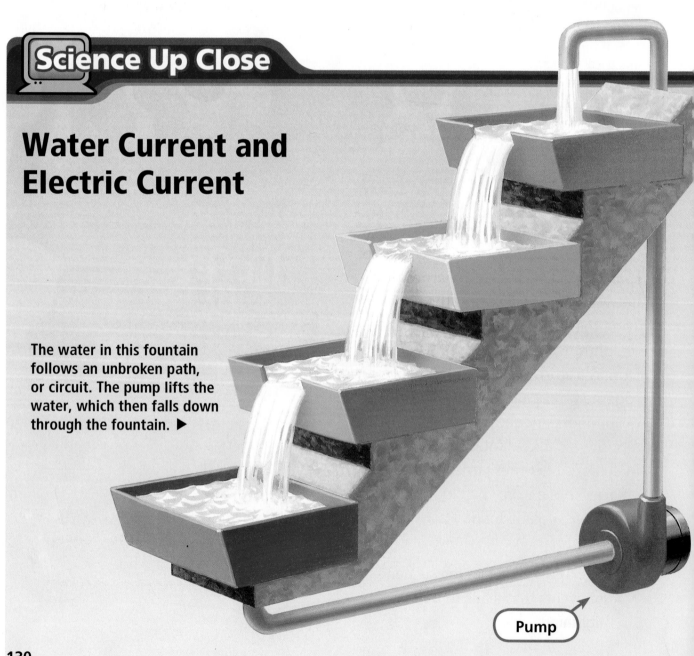

The water in this fountain follows an unbroken path, or circuit. The pump lifts the water, which then falls down through the fountain. ▶

Pump

flow around a circuit without starting or stopping. For any electrical machine to work, the circuit must be complete, or closed.

In the Investigate, the bulb lit only when the path of wire connecting it to the battery was closed. You needed a circuit with no gaps in it. Unhooking a wire at any point broke the circuit, leaving it incomplete, or open. Then the bulb stayed dark because no electric current flowed through it.

Light bulbs aren't the only things that work when they are part of a closed circuit. Turning the key in a car's ignition closes a circuit. The closed circuit starts the car's engine. Pushing the power button on a computer closes a circuit and starts the computer. Closing an electrical circuit can make a doorbell ring or the beaters of an electric mixer spin.

 SEQUENCE **What happens when a driver presses on the steering wheel to honk the horn of a car?**

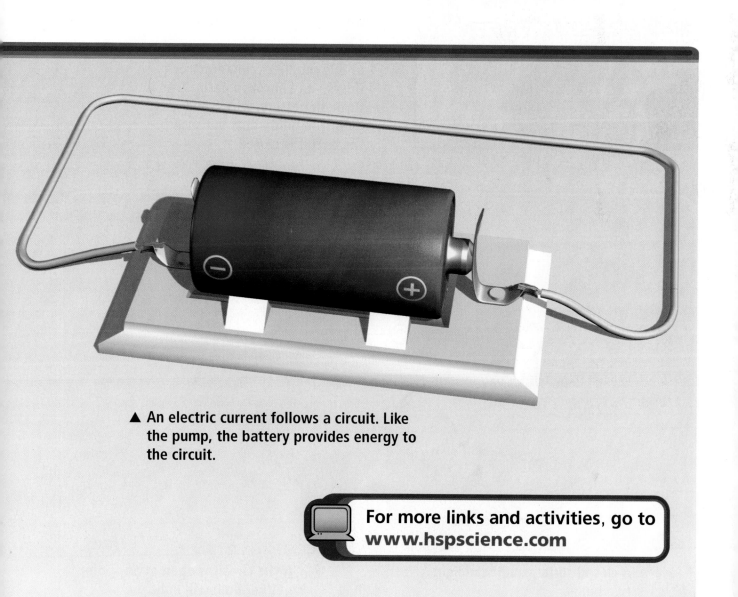

▲ **An electric current follows a circuit. Like the pump, the battery provides energy to the circuit.**

For more links and activities, go to www.hspscience.com

Electrical Circuits

Electrical circuits are not all laid out in the same way. A circuit that has only one path for the current to follow is a **series circuit**.

A simple example has two bulbs, one battery, and wires. The current flows in a path from the battery, through the first bulb, through the second bulb, and back to the battery. While both bulbs are in place and undamaged, they glow. But the flow of charges stops if either bulb burns out or is unscrewed. If one part of a series circuit fails, the whole circuit fails.

A **parallel circuit** has more than one path for the electric current to follow. If something stops charges from moving along one path, they can take another.

In the pictures of a parallel circuit, you can see two circular paths. The current can travel through both bulbs and light them both. If one bulb is missing or damaged, however, the current can still travel through the other bulb. Breaking

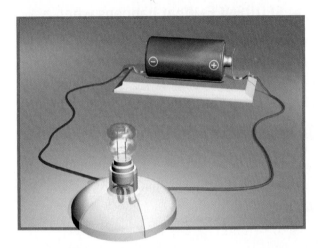

◄ **In this simple circuit, electrons flow in an unbroken path through battery, wires, and bulb. The bulb lights because the circuit is closed.**

Series Circuit

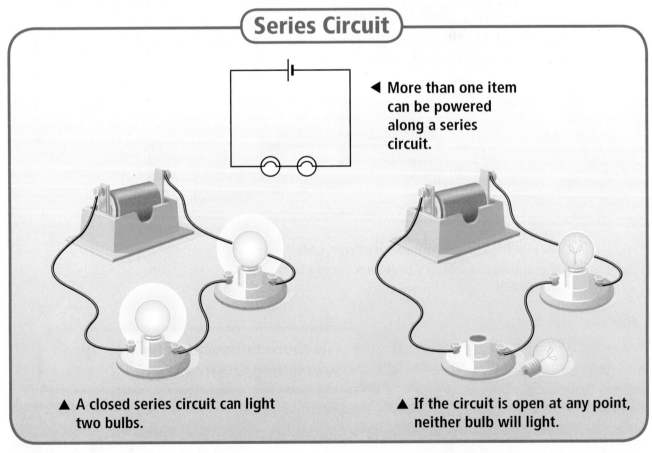

◄ **More than one item can be powered along a series circuit.**

▲ **A closed series circuit can light two bulbs.**

▲ **If the circuit is open at any point, neither bulb will light.**

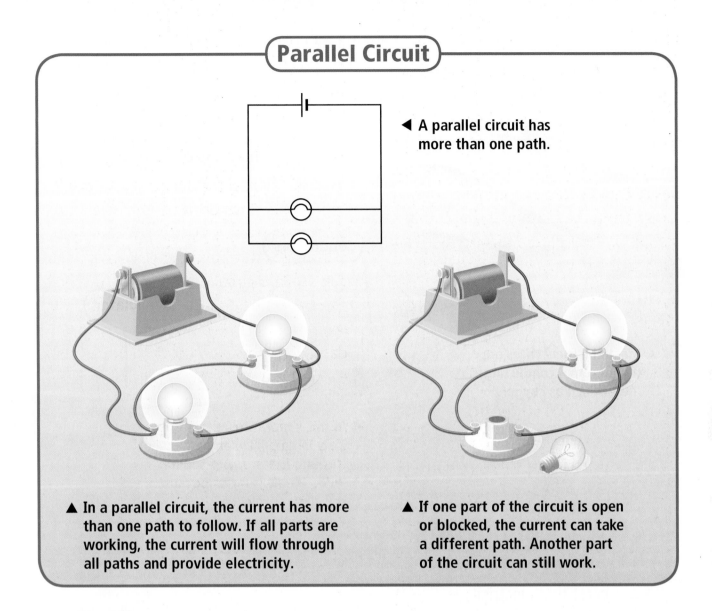

Parallel Circuit

◀ A parallel circuit has more than one path.

▲ In a parallel circuit, the current has more than one path to follow. If all parts are working, the current will flow through all paths and provide electricity.

▲ If one part of the circuit is open or blocked, the current can take a different path. Another part of the circuit can still work.

one path doesn't stop the current. When one part of a parallel circuit fails, other parts of the circuit continue to work. The electric current still has a path along which it can travel.

Think of electrical circuits as streets in a city. A series circuit is like a single street that goes around in a circle. If the street is blocked at any point, all traffic stops. A parallel circuit is more like several streets that cross one another. If traffic backs up on one street, cars and buses can turn and take a different route.

Series and parallel circuits make many devices work. In a flashlight, a series circuit lets current flow between the batteries and the bulb. Homes and schools have many lights. These lights are wired in parallel circuits. Any of these lights can work alone, or many can work at the same time. If one light burns out or is turned off, the others can still work because the electric current travels through parallel circuits.

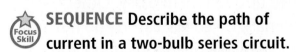

SEQUENCE Describe the path of current in a two-bulb series circuit.

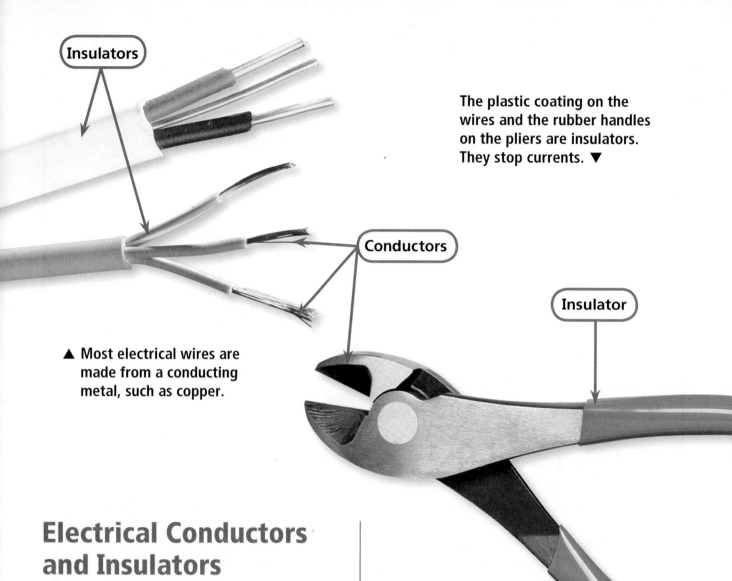

Insulators

Conductors

Insulator

The plastic coating on the wires and the rubber handles on the pliers are insulators. They stop currents. ▼

▲ Most electrical wires are made from a conducting metal, such as copper.

Electrical Conductors and Insulators

It's no secret that electricity is dangerous. It can cause painful shocks, burns, injuries, or even death. Parents often put plastic covers over wall outlets. The covers stop small children from poking their fingers into the outlets. Yet it's safe to touch the electrical cord of a lamp or an appliance. Have you ever wondered why?

The answer is connected with the properties of materials. Some materials, called **conductors**, let electric charges move through them easily. Other materials, called **insulators**, do not.

Most metals are good conductors of electricity. That's why the working parts of an electrical outlet are metal. Most electrical wires are metal, too—usually copper. You should never touch any bare metal electrical wires at home. The electrical cords of appliances have a coating of plastic or rubber around the metal wire to protect you when you handle them. Plastic and rubber are good insulators.

Many everyday things do their jobs safely and well because of the way insulators and conductors work together. If you look at the bottom of a light bulb,

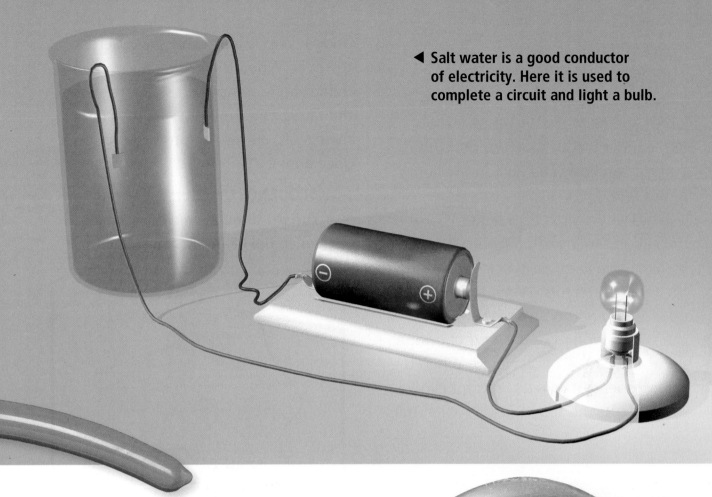

◄ Salt water is a good conductor of electricity. Here it is used to complete a circuit and light a bulb.

Light comes from a bulb because an electric current makes a thin wire inside it glow. ▶

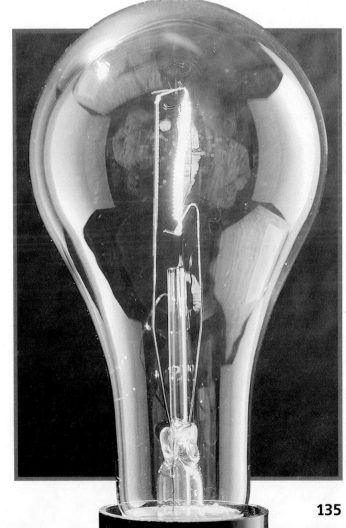

you will see the small metal tip that conducts the current from the socket into the bulb. Just above the tip, you will see a black band. This band is an insulator. It does not allow the current to flow from the metal tip to the metal screw threads above it.

SEQUENCE What happens when a current reaches a conductor? What happens when it reaches an insulator?

135

Switches

A switch is a device that opens or closes a circuit. When you switch on a lamp, you close the circuit. You allow two conductors to touch so that the current can flow. The bulb in the lamp glows.

When you switch off a lamp, you open the circuit. An insulator—which may be as simple as an air space—separates the two conductors. When the circuit is open, the bulb doesn't glow.

A switch works like the kind of bridge that can be raised or lowered. When the switch opens the circuit, current can't travel across the space, just as when the bridge is up, traffic can't travel across the river. When the bridge is lowered, traffic can continue across the river. In the same way, when the switch closes the circuit, current can travel through it once again.

 SEQUENCE Describe the flow of current through an electric heater when the heater is switched on.

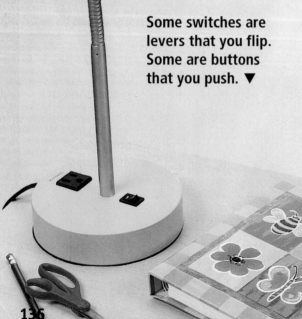

Some switches are levers that you flip. Some are buttons that you push. ▼

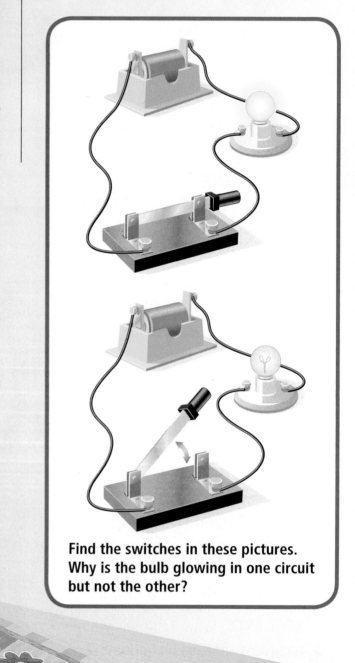

Find the switches in these pictures. Why is the bulb glowing in one circuit but not the other?

Focus Skill

1. SEQUENCE Copy and complete the graphic organizer. Write these terms in the boxes to describe a working series circuit.

wire switch more wire bulb battery or wall outlet

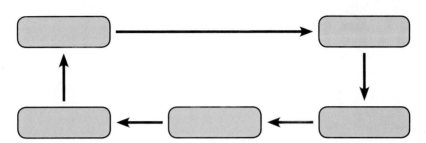

2. SUMMARIZE Use the graphic organizer to tell what a circuit is and how it works.

3. DRAW CONCLUSIONS Suppose you want to decorate a room for a party. You plan to buy strings of lights. Which type of circuit would it be better to get? Why?

4. VOCABULARY How are insulators and conductors different? Why are both important?

FCAT Prep

5. Read/Inquire/Explain How are static electricity and current electricity alike? How are they different?

6. What does a switch bring together?
   A. circuits   **C.** currents
   B. conductors   **D.** charges

Writing

Expository Writing
Write a **report** about a charge that travels through a circuit. Tell how it moves from a power plant, where electricity is generated, to the lights in your home and back to the power plant.

Math

Compare Whole Numbers
Electrical power is measured in units called watts. Which light bulb do you think would burn brighter—a 100-watt bulb or a 60-watt bulb? Explain.

Music

Compose a Tune
Connect some bells and buzzers in series and parallel circuits with switches. Use the switches to make the bells and buzzers play a rhythm or a tune.

 For more links and activities, go to www.hspscience.com

137

How Are Electricity and Magnetism Related?

Fast Fact

Mighty Magnets! The world's strongest magnets are made from iron, boron, and neodymium, a metal. A tiny 50-mm (2-in.) magnet made of these materials can lift up to 30 kg (66 lb)! This sculpture uses pairs of these strong magnets. In the Investigate, you'll learn how to make a different kind of magnet.

Can Electricity Make a Magnet?

Materials
- bar magnet
- small compass
- sheet of cardboard
- tape
- D-cell battery
- 30-cm length of insulated wire with stripped ends

Procedure

1. Move a bar magnet around a compass. Observe what the compass needle does. Put the magnet away.

2. Tape the battery to the cardboard. Tape one end of the wire to the flat end of the battery. Leave the other end loose.

3. Tape the wire to the cardboard in a loop, as shown in the picture.

4. Place the compass on top of the loop. Observe the direction in which the compass needle points.

5. Touch the loose end of the wire to the pointed end of the battery. Observe what the compass needle does. Record your observations.

Draw Conclusions

1. How does a magnet affect a compass needle?

2. How does an electric current affect a compass needle?

3. **Inquiry Skill** Compare electricity and magnetism. How are they alike?

Step 3

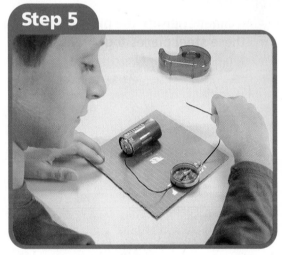
Step 5

Investigate Further

Repeat steps 4 and 5, with the compass *under* the loop. Compare your observations.

SC.B.1.2.4.4.2 charges, magnetism, currents
SC.H.1.2.4.4.1 comparing experiments

139

VOCABULARY

magnet p. 140
magnetic pole p. 142
magnetic field p. 143
electromagnet p. 144
generator p. 146
electric motor p. 147

SCIENCE CONCEPTS

▶ how electric currents are like magnets
▶ how generators and motors work

 READING FOCUS SKILL
COMPARE AND CONTRAST
Look for ways in which magnets and electric currents are alike and different.

[alike]——[different]

Magnets

Have you ever played with a magnet? If you haven't, you may want to now! As you move a magnet around and bring it close to objects, you can discover what a magnet does.

A **magnet** is an object that attracts iron and a few (not all) other metals. Magnets attract steel because it contains iron. When you bring an iron object or a steel object close to a magnet, the object moves toward the magnet. Try this for yourself. Place a steel paper clip near a magnet. What happens? Try the same thing with a plastic paper clip. How do your results compare?

All magnets attract iron, but they may not look alike. Some magnets are shaped like bars. Others are U-shaped. Some magnets that stick to refrigerator doors are thin, flat shapes.

A magnet inside the plastic base holds these steel pieces together. ▼

▲ The horseshoe magnet attracts these metal objects. What metal do the objects contain?

Some magnets are shaped like bars.

Why do these plastic letters stick to this refrigerator door? ▶

Distance affects the strength of a magnet's attraction. A small steel object that is close to a magnet moves toward it. However, if the same object is farther away, it will not move toward the magnet.

Other forces can overcome the force of a magnet. Refrigerator magnets stick well to the door, but you can easily pull them off.

Barriers can interfere with a magnet's pull, too. A refrigerator magnet may hold one or two sheets of paper to the door, but if you put too many sheets under it, the magnet will fall.

Magnets can make some other objects magnetic. For example, if you rub a needle over a magnet several times in the same direction, the needle will become magnetic enough to pick up other needles.

COMPARE AND CONTRAST **How are all magnets alike? How are they different?**

Magnetic Poles and Magnetic Fields

A magnet has two places at which its force is the strongest. Each of these is called a **magnetic pole**, or *pole* for short. If you tie a string around the middle of a bar magnet and let it swing, one end will point north. That end is the magnet's north-seeking pole. It is often marked with an *N*. The end that points south is often marked *S*.

Forces between magnetic poles act like forces between electrical charges. Opposite poles attract, and like poles repel. If you hold two S poles or two N poles near each other, they push apart. If you hold an N pole and an S pole near each other, they attract.

Magnets of every shape have N and S poles. Try holding two round refrigerator magnets close together. If you turn them in one direction, they attract each other. If you turn them in the other direction, they repel each other.

Magnets keep their poles even if you change their shape. If you cut a bar magnet into pieces, each piece would be a magnet with both an N pole and an S pole.

Magnetic Poles

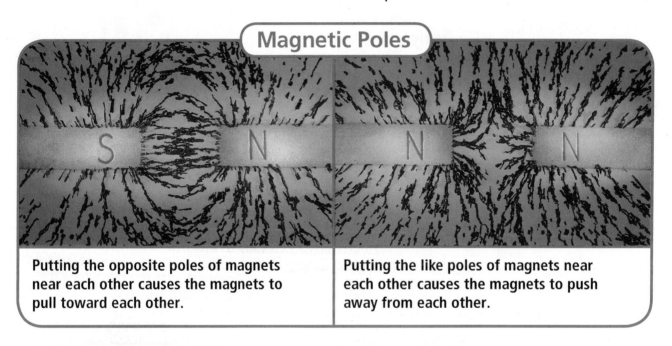

Putting the opposite poles of magnets near each other causes the magnets to pull toward each other.

Putting the like poles of magnets near each other causes the magnets to push away from each other.

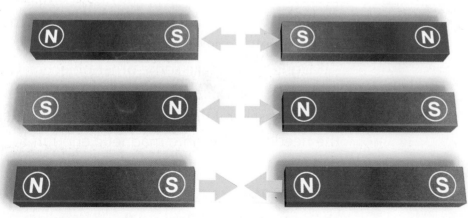

◀ All magnets have N and S poles. Poles that are the same repel, or push apart. Poles that are opposite attract, or pull together.

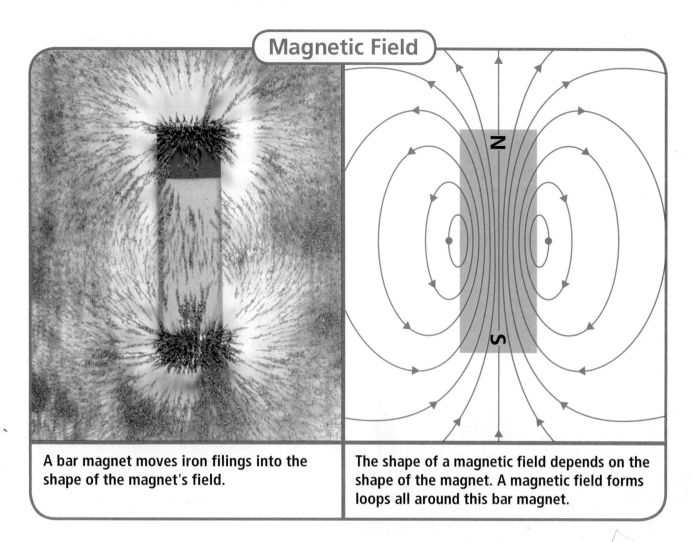

A bar magnet moves iron filings into the shape of the magnet's field.

The shape of a magnetic field depends on the shape of the magnet. A magnetic field forms loops all around this bar magnet.

You can use a compass to see a magnet's force. If you put a compass close to a bar magnet, the needle will point toward the magnet's N pole and away from the magnet's S pole.

A **magnetic field** is the space around a magnet in which the force of the magnet acts. If you put iron filings around the magnet, you will be able to see the shape of the magnet's field. The filings will form circles that start and end at the poles, where the magnet's pull is the strongest.

COMPARE AND CONTRAST How are a magnet's magnetic force and magnetic field different?

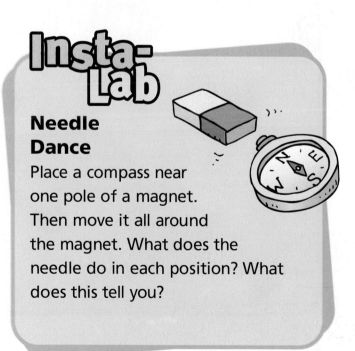

Insta-Lab

Needle Dance

Place a compass near one pole of a magnet. Then move it all around the magnet. What does the needle do in each position? What does this tell you?

Electromagnets

In the Investigate, you saw that a current of electricity causes a magnetic force. You showed that electricity and magnetism are related.

Actually, an electric current produces a magnetic field around a wire. You can't see the field, but it circles the wire. The field around a single wire is weak. The field around many wires close together is strong. When coils wrap around an iron core, such as a nail, the core becomes an **electromagnet**.

An electromagnet is a temporary magnet. It has a magnetic force only when an electric current moves through the wire. The electromagnet does not work if the current is switched off.

With many coils of wire and a strong current, electromagnets can be made very strong. In junkyards, such electromagnets lift many tons of scrap iron and steel.

 COMPARE AND CONTRAST How are a magnet and an electromagnet alike? How are they different?

A steel nail is not normally a magnet, but it becomes one when an electric current runs around it. How can you tell that this nail is now a magnet? What would happen if you took one of the wire ends off the battery?

In one experiment, a student built and tested an electromagnet. This graph shows the results. What hypothesis was the student testing? How did the student measure the magnet's strength? What conclusion can you draw from this graph?

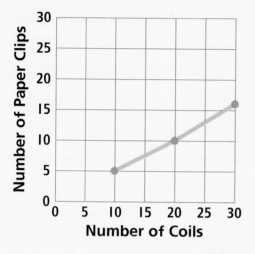

▲ This powerful electromagnet is being used to move scrap iron in a junkyard.

▼ This is an MRI (magnetic resonance imaging) machine in a hospital. It uses a magnetic field to take pictures of the brain, the muscles, and other soft tissues inside the body.

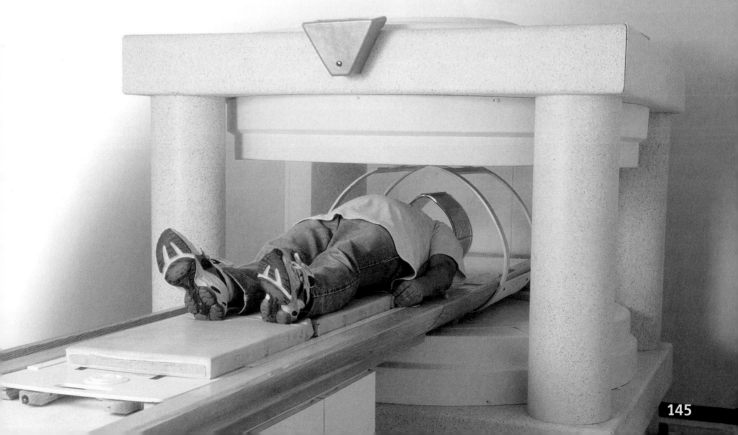

Generators and Motors

Electricity can produce a magnetic field. Luckily for us, the reverse is also true—a magnetic field can produce electricity. If you move a coil of wire near a magnet, current electricity flows in the wire. That is how a **generator**, a device that produces an electric current, works.

Any source of energy that can turn a coil of wire in a magnetic field can produce electricity. Hand-cranked generators use human power to turn the coil. During a power failure, you might use a gasoline-powered generator to produce electricity for lights.

Power plants in large cities use many huge generators to produce enough electricity to meet people's needs. Most power plants burn coal, oil, or natural gas. The fuel heats water until it turns to steam. The steam's pressure turns a turbine. A turbine is a machine that produces electricity. The turbine spins a coil inside the field of a magnet to produce electricity. Then the electricity is sent out along power lines to homes and businesses.

Generators use motion to produce electricity. Can electricity produce motion? If you have ever seen someone

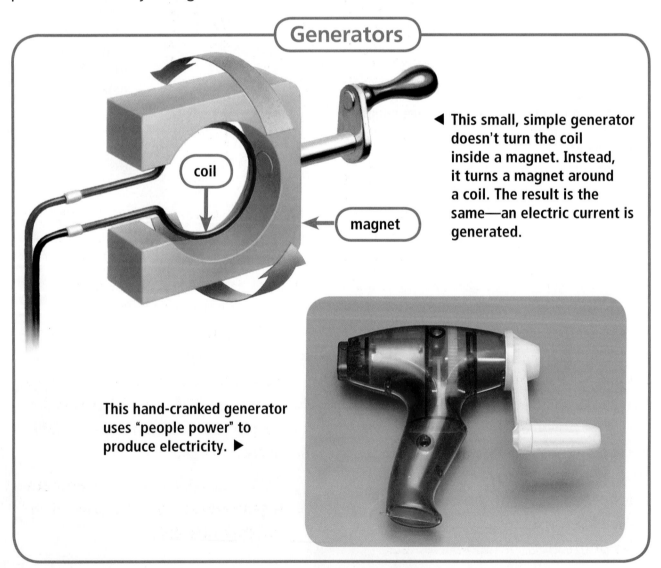

Generators

coil

magnet

◀ This small, simple generator doesn't turn the coil inside a magnet. Instead, it turns a magnet around a coil. The result is the same—an electric current is generated.

This hand-cranked generator uses "people power" to produce electricity. ▶

Motors

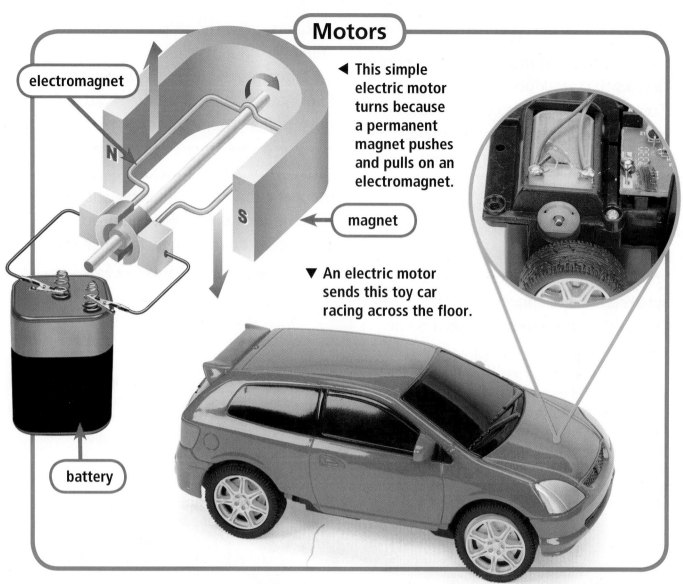

electromagnet

N

S

◄ This simple electric motor turns because a permanent magnet pushes and pulls on an electromagnet.

magnet

▼ An electric motor sends this toy car racing across the floor.

battery

use a mixer or an electric drill, you know that the answer is yes. Such tools have an electric motor in them. An **electric motor** is a device that changes electrical energy into mechanical energy.

In some motors, an electromagnet lies between the poles of a permanent magnet. Like all magnets, the electromagnet has an N pole and an S pole. The poles are pushed away from the like poles of the permanent magnet. They are pulled toward the opposite poles of the permanent magnet.

The motor's shaft turns until the poles of the electromagnet are near

the opposite poles of the permanent magnet. Then the current of the electromagnet reverses. Its N pole becomes its S pole, and its S pole becomes its N pole. The shaft turns again. The current keeps reversing, and the shaft keeps spinning.

Electric motors do many useful things. They start cars. They run CD players. The next time you turn on a fan, thank the inventors of motors!

 COMPARE AND CONTRAST How are a generator and a motor alike? How are they different?

Other Uses of Magnets

Generators and motors aren't the only devices that work because of magnets. Compasses point north because they respond to Earth's natural magnetic field. This helps people find their way on land and at sea.

Magnets are used in computers, compact disc players, and magnetic recording devices, such as VCRs. They are also inside headphones, stereo speakers, and telephone receivers. Doorbells and phones ring because of magnets. Even the strip on the back of a credit card is a magnet.

Magnets are used for recording information. On a computer hard drive or floppy disk, for example, electromagnets move across the disk's surface. They make one disk area more magnetic than another. Later, the disk spins under a part called the head. The head reads the magnetic information.

 COMPARE AND CONTRAST How are a videotape and a computer hard drive alike?

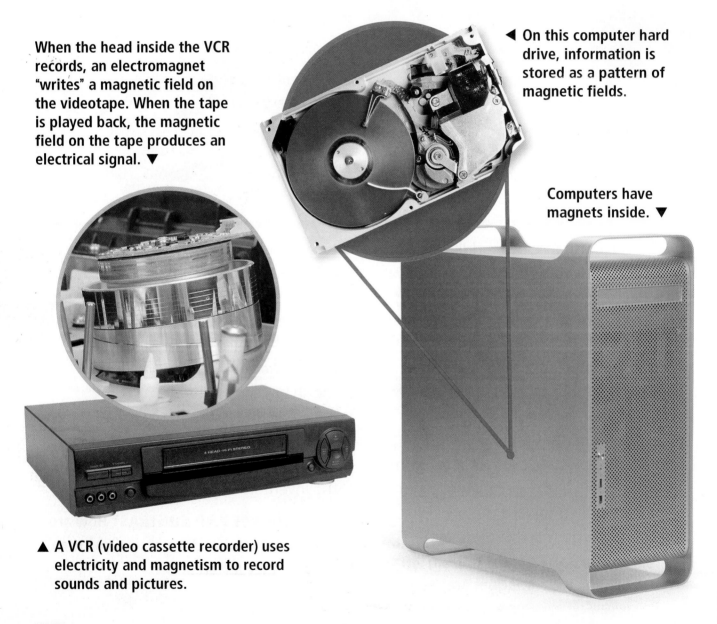

When the head inside the VCR records, an electromagnet "writes" a magnetic field on the videotape. When the tape is played back, the magnetic field on the tape produces an electrical signal. ▼

◀ On this computer hard drive, information is stored as a pattern of magnetic fields.

Computers have magnets inside. ▼

▲ A VCR (video cassette recorder) uses electricity and magnetism to record sounds and pictures.

1. COMPARE AND CONTRAST Draw and complete this graphic organizer to explain how electricity and magnetism are related.

Alike	Different
Opposite types **A** _____ .	Magnetic **B** _____ interact.
Like types repel.	Electrical charges interact.
	Moving magnets make **C** _____ .
	Moving charges make an electromagnet.

2. SUMMARIZE Use the completed graphic organizer to write a lesson summary.

3. DRAW CONCLUSIONS Tell why the relationship between electricity and magnetism is important to people.

4. VOCABULARY Use the terms *electricity* and *magnet* in a sentence to explain how a generator works.

FCAT Prep

5. Read/Inquire/Explain Why is an electromagnet not a permanent magnet?

6. If you turn the N poles of two magnets toward each other, what will they do?

A. attract   **C.** repel

B. produce electricity   **D.** spin

Links

Writing

Expository Writing
Write a **paragraph** for a friend. Tell your friend how an electric motor works.

Math

Make a Bar Graph
Test the strength of one magnet by measuring how many paper clips it can pick up. Then test two, three, and four magnets stuck together. Does it matter how the magnets are put together? Make a bar graph of your results.

Social Studies

History of Names
Electricity is measured in amperes, coulombs, ohms, watts, and volts. Find out more about the famous scientists whose names are used for these units of measurement. Share what you learn with the class.

For more links and activities, go to
www.hspscience.com

3

What Are Some Sources of Electricity?

Fast Fact

Where Does It Come From? Wind farms provide the energy to produce only a small fraction of the electricity used in the United States. In the Investigate, you'll see two kinds of energy.

The Ups and Downs of Energy

Materials
- piece of lightweight poster board, about 30 cm x 70 cm
- ballpoint pen
- masking tape
- books
- marble
- ruler

Procedure

1 Build a "roller coaster" for the marble. Using the ruler, draw a line along both long edges of the piece of poster board, about 1 cm in from each edge. Press hard with a ballpoint pen. Fold up along the marked lines to make walls to keep the marble from rolling off the edges.

2 Place the poster board between two stacks of books so that it forms a valley. Tape the two ends of it to the books.

3 Hold a marble at the top on one side. Let it go, and observe what happens. Does it go past the bottom and all the way up the other side? Hypothesize about what affects the marble's path.

4 Change your setup as necessary so that the marble goes all the way up the hill the way a roller coaster car does.

Step 1

Step 2

Draw Conclusions

1. What was the source of energy for the marble?

2. **Inquiry Skill** To make a roller coaster that worked, you had to change a variable. Which variable did you change? Explain.

Investigate Further

Plan and conduct an investigation. **Determine whether the weight of a marble affects how it behaves on the ramp.**

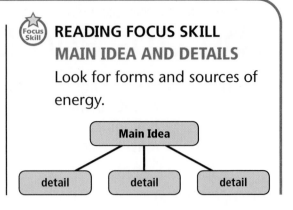

SC.B.1.2.2.4.1 sources of electricity
SC.E.1.2.3.4.1 solar energy
LA.A.2.2.1 main idea

VOCABULARY

potential energy p. 153
kinetic energy p. 153
hydroelectric power
    p. 154
geothermal energy p. 155
solar energy p. 156

SCIENCE CONCEPTS

▶ how energy
  changes form
▶ how people
  produce electricity
  from other forms of
  energy

Focus Skill **READING FOCUS SKILL**

MAIN IDEA AND DETAILS

Look for forms and sources of energy.

```
            ┌──────────┐
            │ Main Idea │
            └──────────┘
          ╱       │       ╲
  ┌────────┐ ┌────────┐ ┌────────┐
  │ detail │ │ detail │ │ detail │
  └────────┘ └────────┘ └────────┘
```

Potential and Kinetic Energy

You can't always see energy, but you know it's there. A pot of water boils on the stove. An egg fries in a pan. Cooking takes a lot of energy. So does moving around. Jet airplanes speeding between cities use energy. So do birds soaring through the sky.

Anytime something gets warmer, gets cooler, or moves, energy is being changed from one form to another. Often you can see or feel the effects of released energy. For example, your body gets energy from food. This energy keeps you alive and provides power for all you do. The energy stored in the food is released in your body. The gasoline used in a car also has stored energy. Burning the fuel releases the energy.

Objects can also have energy because of their position or because of what is done to them. A roller coaster car at the top of a hill has energy. A rubber band has energy when it is stretched. These

◀ The bicycle's position at the top of the hill gives it potential energy. It can coast down the hill.

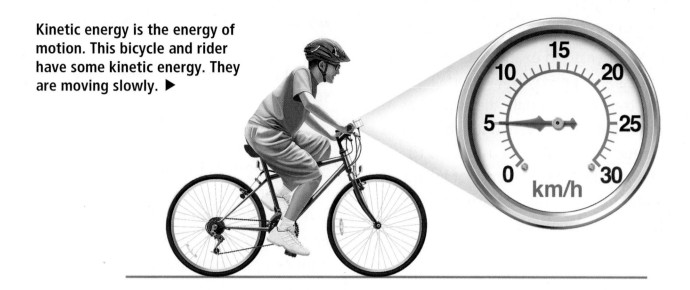

Kinetic energy is the energy of motion. This bicycle and rider have some kinetic energy. They are moving slowly. ▶

This bicycle and rider have greater kinetic energy. They are moving faster. ▶

are both examples of **potential energy**, or energy due to an object's position or condition. You can't always see evidence of it, but you can guess that it exists when an object is in a high place or in a stretched condition. When an object moves, it has **kinetic energy**, or the energy of motion. You can see evidence of kinetic energy.

How are potential and kinetic energy related? Suppose you push a bicycle up a hill. At the top, the bicycle has potential energy because of its position. It can coast down the hill. If it does, its potential energy will change to kinetic energy as it rolls downhill.

You can measure kinetic energy. The faster an object moves, the more kinetic energy it has. For example, if you pedal a bicycle slowly, your kinetic energy is less than if you race it at top speed.

MAIN IDEA AND DETAILS What are two main differences between potential and kinetic energy?

(Focus Skill)

153

Hydroelectric Power

Another good example of potential and kinetic energy is a waterfall. At the top of a waterfall, the water has potential energy. When it falls, it gains kinetic energy. People use dams to change the kinetic energy of falling water into electrical energy called **hydroelectric power**.

Many hydroelectric power plants are on rivers. A dam blocks the flow of the river. A reservoir (REZ•er•vwar), or human-made lake, forms behind the dam. To produce electricity, water is released. The falling water flows through and turns a large, fanlike turbine. The turning turbine causes a generator to spin.

Another kind of dam stores energy by pumping water from a lower reservoir to a higher one. When electricity is needed, the water is released.

A huge dam can produce enough electricity to supply a big city. A small dam can produce enough for a farm or ranch.

 MAIN IDEA AND DETAILS What is hydroelectric power?

▼ Dams change the kinetic energy of falling water into electricity.

▲ As water flows down from the reservoir, it turns the turbine. The turbine turns the generator, which produces an electric current.

Inside a geothermal plant, heat from below ground is used to make steam that turns turbines.

▲ The Geysers Power Plant in Calistoga, California, is the world's largest producer of geothermal power.

Geothermal Power

It might surprise you to learn that people can use the heat inside Earth. You know that Earth is hot deep underground. Heat from inside Earth is called **geothermal energy**.

In some places, reservoirs of hot water lie 3 kilometers (2 mi) or more below Earth's surface. A deep well can reach the hot water. Then people can pump up the water and use it to heat buildings.

Not all geothermal heat pumps must go so deep. In winter, the upper 3 meters (10 ft) of the ground is warmer than the air. In summer, it is cooler than the air. Pipes can move heat between the ground and a building to warm or cool the building.

Geothermal energy can be used to produce electricity. Most power plants burn coal, oil, or natural gas to produce heat to turn water to steam. The steam turns turbines, and the turbines spin generators. Geothermal power plants don't need to burn fuel for heat. The heat is ready to use right from the ground.

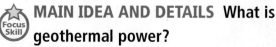 **MAIN IDEA AND DETAILS** What is geothermal power?

Solar Power

You feel heat and see light—two forms of energy—when you go outside on a sunny day. People can use **solar energy**, or the energy of sunlight, to meet some of their energy needs.

Solar energy can heat buildings without any special equipment. The south side of a building gets more sunlight than the other sides. Big windows on the south side can let in sunlight to heat the building.

Solar energy can also heat water. A flat solar panel, or collector, on a roof stores water in clear tubes. The sun shines on this water and heats it. Then the hot water is pumped inside the building for people to use.

Solar energy can also be used to produce electricity. Solar cells use sunlight to produce electricity. This solar power is used to run many devices, including watches, calculators, and outdoor garden lights.

⭐ (Focus Skill) **MAIN IDEA AND DETAILS** What is solar power?

◀ Solar cells change the sun's energy to electrical energy to power this highway emergency phone.

44 S.O.S.

Insta-Lab

Solar Heating

Take two empty soft drink cans. Put a thermometer into each can, and seal the opening around it with clay. Tape white paper around one can and black paper around the other. Leave the cans on their sides in the sun. What happens? Why?

1. MAIN IDEA AND DETAILS Draw and complete this graphic organizer. List details about kinds and sources of energy.

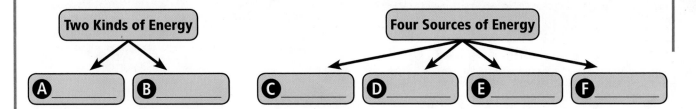

Two Kinds of Energy

A _____ B _____

Four Sources of Energy

C _____ D _____ E _____ F _____

2. SUMMARIZE Use the completed graphic organizer to write a lesson summary.

3. DRAW CONCLUSIONS What energy source do you think people will use most in the future? Explain.

4. VOCABULARY Write a sentence to explain the difference between potential energy and kinetic energy.

FCAT Prep

5. Read/Inquire/Explain Tell how a dam is used to make electricity.

6. Which energy source can provide both direct heat and electricity?
A. a turbine   **C.** sun
B. falling water   **D.** wind

Links

Writing

Expository Writing
Write a **paragraph** about ways to classify energy. Give examples of different forms of energy. Tell why they are important and how people use them.

Math

Using Angles
Earth's surface absorbs the most solar energy when the sun's rays shine straight down. It absorbs less when the rays strike the surface at a slant. Draw pictures of two solar water heaters on roofs. Show one that would work well and one that wouldn't.

Health

Sun Safety
The sun is a good source of energy, but it also causes risks to human health. Research the dangers of too much exposure to sunlight. Make a list of "Sun Safety Rules" to post in the classroom.

 For more links and activities, go to www.hspscience.com

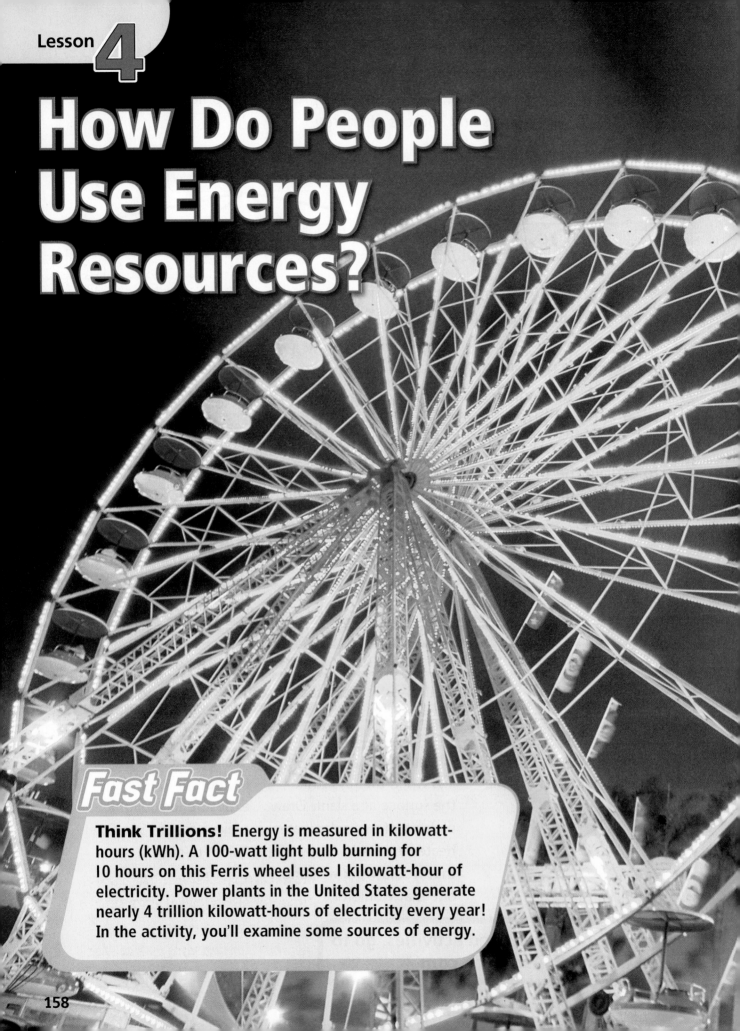

How Do People Use Energy Resources?

Fast Fact

Think Trillions! Energy is measured in kilowatt-hours (kWh). A 100-watt light bulb burning for 10 hours on this Ferris wheel uses 1 kilowatt-hour of electricity. Power plants in the United States generate nearly 4 trillion kilowatt-hours of electricity every year! In the activity, you'll examine some sources of energy.

Energy Sources and Uses

Materials
- 10 index cards (5 yellow and 5 blue)
- pens, pencils, drawing materials

Procedure

1. On each blue card, write *Uses of Energy.* On each yellow card, write *Sources of Energy.*

2. With your classmates, brainstorm ways you use energy every day. Choose five of these ways, and draw a picture of each way on a separate blue card. Label each picture with a word or two.

3. Determine the source of energy for each use you named. Draw and label the sources on the yellow cards.

4. Match your energy source cards with your energy use cards.

5. Exchange sets of cards with classmates, and work to match up their sources and uses.

Draw Conclusions

1. In what ways do you and your classmates use energy? What are the sources of the energy you use?

2. **Inquiry Skill** Sort your cards to classify the uses and sources of energy you listed. Give reasons for the way you sorted the cards.

Step 1

Step 2

Investigate Further

Make cards that show how energy moves and changes from a source through one use of it. Communicate this sequence to your classmates.

SC.B.1.2.4.4.1 transformation of energy
SC.H.1.2.3.4.1 working collaboratively

159

Reading in Science

SC.B.1.2.4.4.1 transformation of energy
SC.B.2.2.2.4.1 energy conservation
LA.A.2.2.1 main idea

VOCABULARY
chemical energy p. 162
mechanical energy p. 163

SCIENCE CONCEPTS
▶ ways people use energy
▶ ways people can save energy

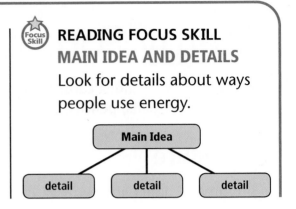

READING FOCUS SKILL
MAIN IDEA AND DETAILS
Look for details about ways people use energy.

Main Idea
detail detail detail

Uses of Electricity

Can you imagine a world without electricity? Strange as it may seem, people have been using electricity for only a short time. Thomas Edison made his first successful electric light bulb in 1879. The first electric power plant opened that same year. That may seem like a long time ago to you, but it's a short time in human history.

The refrigerator was invented in 1913. Microwave ovens were invented in the 1950s, but few people had them before 1970. The first wind farm for making electricity started working in 1980.

Today, we often take electricity for granted. We use it in our homes and in businesses. About one-third of the electricity used in the United States is used in homes. It warms and cools

◀ We use electricity to light our homes, schools, and businesses. Can you imagine living without electric lights?

The heater uses electricity to heat a room. In what other ways do we use electricity for heat? ▼

In computer speakers, electricity is changed to sound energy.

rooms. It heats water for showers. It cooks food, and it keeps food cold to preserve it.

Businesses such as stores and offices use another one-third of our energy. Like homes, these businesses use electricity for heating, cooling, and light. They also use it to run machines, such as computers and photocopiers. Businesses use electricity to keep offices clean and to provide services to their customers.

Another one-third of our electricity is used in manufacturing businesses.

Workers in factories use electricity to make or prepare many of the products we buy. For example, in food processing factories, electricity runs the canning and freezing equipment.

Electricity is used to mine metals and to drill for and refine oil. It is used to make cars, trains, and airplanes. It's hard to imagine what life was like before people learned to use electricity!

 MAIN IDEA AND DETAILS **How is electricity used in homes and businesses?**

Uses of Chemical Energy

Electricity is an important form of energy. However, it is not the only one we use. We use the energy stored in gasoline to move the cars and airplanes that take people from one place to another. Gasoline also fuels trucks, ships, and trains that carry goods.

Chemical energy is energy stored in the arrangement of particles of matter. Gasoline, which is made from oil, has chemical energy. So do coal and natural gas. Coal, oil, and natural gas all formed inside Earth from the remains of ancient plants and animals. The remains decayed under great pressure millions of years ago.

Because they come from ancient living things, these fuels are called fossil fuels. Fossil fuels remained underground for centuries. Then, people started mining coal and drilling for oil. Today, we burn huge amounts of fossil fuels.

Chemical energy can be changed into other forms of energy. Many power plants burn fossil fuels to change their stored chemical energy into heat. The heat is used to produce steam to turn

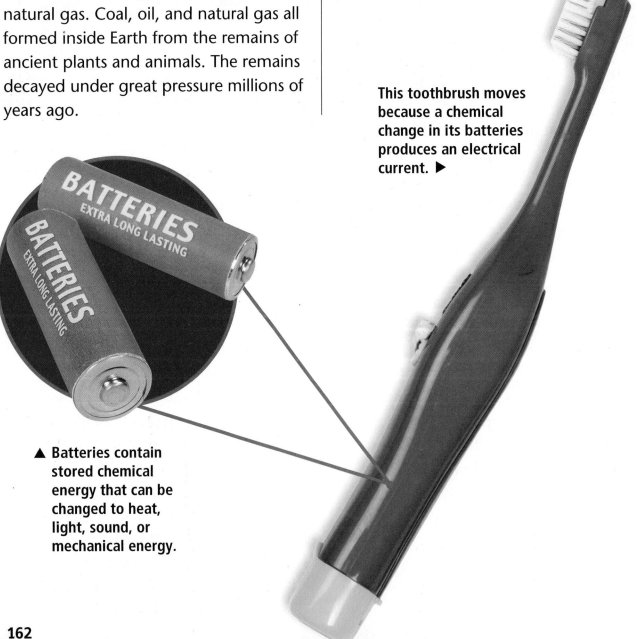

This toothbrush moves because a chemical change in its batteries produces an electrical current. ▶

▲ **Batteries contain stored chemical energy that can be changed to heat, light, sound, or mechanical energy.**

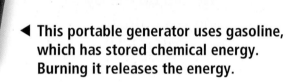

When it is finished, this combustion turbine will work like a jet engine. It will burn natural gas to generate electricity. ▶

◀ This portable generator uses gasoline, which has stored chemical energy. Burning it releases the energy.

the turbines that generate electricity. Car engines burn gasoline to change its chemical energy into mechanical energy. **Mechanical energy** makes machine parts move.

Chemical energy is what makes batteries work. A chemical change inside the battery releases charges from atoms. The current causes CD players to make sound or battery-operated toys to move.

⭐ **MAIN IDEA AND DETAILS** Explain
(Focus Skill) **two ways people use chemical energy.**

Insta-Lab

Chemical Energy
Wrap a dry pad of steel wool around the base of a thermometer. Put them together into a clear jar, and close it. Wait 5 minutes. Read the temperature. Remove the pad and thermometer from the jar. Soak the pad in vinegar for 1 minute. Squeeze out the extra vinegar, and wrap the pad around the base of the thermometer again. Put them back in the jar and close it. Wait 5 minutes. Read the temperature again. What happens? How can you explain it?

Energy Conservation

Most of the energy you use comes from burning fossil fuels. Today, people are using Earth's stores of energy faster than ever. Fossil fuels were formed millions of years ago. When they have been used up, it will take millions of years for more to form.

When fossil fuels are gone, we will need other energy sources to take their place. It will take time to develop new energy sources, so we must make the fossil fuels last as long as possible. We can do this by conserving, or using less of them.

How can you help with this? You can turn off the TV when you aren't watching it. You can take shorter showers or use cooler water. Talk about ways you can save energy at school. See what you and your classmates can do to conserve energy.

Focus Skill MAIN IDEA AND DETAILS Tell why people should conserve energy.

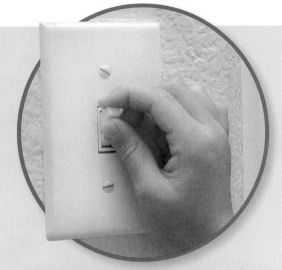

▲ Turning off lights that you are not using is a good way to conserve energy.

▲ Insulation in attics and walls helps save energy. Insulated buildings lose less heat in winter and stay cooler in summer than uninsulated ones.

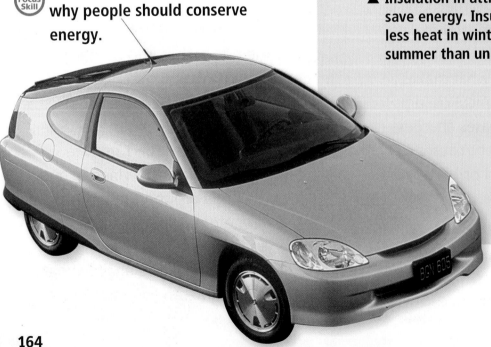

◄ This car may look ordinary, but it isn't. It's a "hybrid" car. A hybrid car's engine uses both gasoline and electricity.

1. MAIN IDEA AND DETAILS Draw and complete this graphic organizer. Give details about forms and uses of energy.

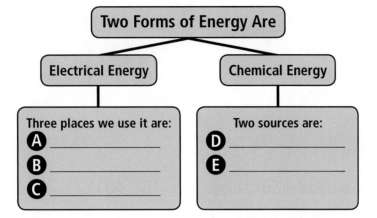

Two Forms of Energy Are

Electrical Energy — Chemical Energy

Three places we use it are:
- **A** _____
- **B** _____
- **C** _____

Two sources are:
- **D** _____
- **E** _____

2. SUMMARIZE Use the completed graphic organizer to write a lesson summary.

3. DRAW CONCLUSIONS Which kind of energy is most important? Why?

4. VOCABULARY Use the terms *chemical energy* and *mechanical energy* to explain how a battery-operated toy works.

FCAT Prep

5. Read/Inquire/Explain List some things you can do to conserve energy.

6. In which form is energy stored inside a battery?
- **A.** chemical
- **B.** electrical
- **C.** kinetic
- **D.** mechanical

Links

Writing

Persuasive Writing
Write a **letter** someone might send to the editor of your local newspaper. Explain why you think people in your community should work harder to conserve energy.

Math

Solve a Problem
Energy use is measured in kilowatt-hours (kWh). *Kilo-* means "one thousand," so 1 kWh equals 1,000 watts used for 1 hour. How long would five 100-watt bulbs need to burn to use 1 kWh?

Literature

Write a Poem
Use a thesaurus to find words related to energy. Use them to write a rhyming poem about ways people can save energy. Trade poems with a partner, and read them aloud. Display your poems on a bulletin board.

 For more links and activities, go to **www.hspscience.com**

These BOOTS Were Made for WALKING

In the future, recharging the battery in your MP3 player may be as simple as taking a walk. Why? A California company has developed a material that can be placed in a pair of boots. It changes the mechanical energy of walking into electrical energy that can charge batteries and other devices.

Charge It!

The material is an electroactive polymer that's called "artificial muscle." When a person walks, the electroactive polymer in the boots' soles compresses and releases.

The polymer is a very thin film of rubbery material. It bends when an electric current flows through it. This is why the polymer is called *artificial muscle*. The polymer also works in reverse. When it is bent or squeezed, it makes a weak electric current. A wire connected to the boot can then store the energy in a battery or use it to power a device, such as a cell phone.

Used in the Field

A team of scientists worked for 15 years to develop the artificial muscle. Some of the first people to make use of the material might be U.S. soldiers in the field. By going on a march, soldiers could power up hand-held gear such as computers.

Scientists working on the project believe that the artificial muscle material could also be used by recreational hikers and walkers to power such things as a radio or a CD player.

THINK ABOUT IT

1. What other inventions can you think of that might help U.S. soldiers in the field?
2. How might artificial muscles in your shoes help you?

Find out more! Log on to
www.hspscience.com

SCIENCE Spin from WEEKLY READER®

People

SC.B.1.2.2.4.1
sources of
electricity
SC.H.3.2.4.4.1
solving problems/
new ideas

LIGHTING THE WAY

Without the help of Lewis Latimer (1848–1929), you would have to read at night by candlelight. Latimer helped to design the electric light bulb.

In the early 1880s, Thomas Edison invented an electric lamp. Electricity passed through a thin thread of carbon to make light. The thread was inside a glass bulb. The thin thread burned out after only a few days.

Latimer worked to design a light bulb that would last longer. In 1882, he succeeded. He later was awarded patents for the new design.

Career   Power Plant Technician

Electricity plays a huge role in our daily lives. The people who make electricity possible are the power plant operators. These technicians control and monitor the machines that generate the electricity to power homes, schools, and businesses. The plant operators also control the complex network of circuits that carries the electricity.

You Can Do It!

Quick and Easy Project

Insulators and Conductors

Procedure

1. Build a series circuit, but leave two wire ends open. Touch them together to make sure the circuit works.

2. Touch the ends to a test material to see if it will complete the circuit. Does the bulb light? Record your results.

3. Repeat Step 2 for each test material.

Materials

- three 30-cm pieces of wire, with insulation trimmed from the ends
- D-cell battery
- flashlight bulb
- test materials of your choice

Draw Conclusions

Which materials are conductors? Which are insulators? How do you know?

Design Your Own Investigation

Generate Electricity

Does moving a bar magnet inside a coil of wire generate an electric current? You can use a compass to find out. Use wire, a bar magnet, and a compass to build and test a simple generator. Record and explain your findings. How can you make sure that it's an electric current, and not the magnet, that's affecting your compass? How can you make your generator stronger? Test your ideas.

4 Review and FCAT Preparation

Vocabulary Review

Use the terms below to complete the sentences. The page numbers tell you where to look in the chapter if you need help.

static electricity
p. 128

magnet
p. 140

current electricity
p. 130

electromagnet
p. 144

series circuit
p. 132

generator
p. 146

parallel circuit
p. 132

potential energy
p. 153

conductor
p. 134

kinetic energy
p. 153

1. An object that attracts iron is a _____.

2. The charge that builds up on an object is _____.

3. A circuit that has only one path for electricity to follow is a _____.

4. The energy of motion is _____.

5. A device that produces an electric current is a _____.

6. A material that electricity can flow through easily is a _____.

7. An _____ is a temporary magnet.

8. Electricity that flows along a wire is _____.

9. The energy an object has because of its position is _____.

10. A circuit that has two or more paths that electricity can follow is a _____.

Check Understanding

Write the letter of the best choice.

11. **COMPARE AND CONTRAST** What is one way in which all magnets are alike?
   A. They stick to aluminum cans.
   B. They attract iron.
   C. They need a current to work.
   D. They have one or two poles.

12. **MAIN IDEA AND DETAILS** What kind of energy does water at the top of a dam have?

   F. chemical
   G. kinetic
   H. mechanical
   I. potential

13. How do charges move in a circuit?
   A. along two or more paths
   B. along a loop with no beginning and no end
   C. through an insulator
   D. up and down

14. What energy source is used to produce most of the electricity we use today?

  F. fossil fuels
  G. geothermal energy
  H. falling water
  I. wind

15. Which pair is made up of two things that work in opposite ways?

  A. bar magnet and horseshoe magnet
  B. chemical energy and mechanical energy
  C. generator and motor
  D. solar energy and geothermal energy

16. What does an electromagnet have that a bar magnet does not have?

  F. attraction for iron
  G. magnetic field
  H. two poles
  I. wire coil

Inquiry Skills

17. The needle of a compass moves when you put a bar of metal close to it. What can you **infer** from this observation?

18. A student team builds two electromagnets. The students use 20 coils of wire in one. They use 40 coils in the other. Everything else is the same. **Compare** the strengths of the two electromagnets.

Read/Inquire/Explain

19. Suggest a practical use for an electromagnet. Explain why it would be a good use for it.

20. Suppose you woke up one morning and one use of electricity had disappeared.

Part A How would your life change?

Part B How would your community change?

Force and Motion

 The chapters in this unit address these Grade Level Expectations from the Florida Sunshine State Standards.

Chapter 5

Forces and Motion

SC.C.1.2.1.4.1   knows that velocity describes a change in distance over time.

SC.C.2.2.2.4.1   uses tools to measure changes in position, direction, and speed of an object after a push or pull has been applied.

Chapter 6

Simple Machines

SC.C.2.2.1.4.1   understands how simple machines are used to make tasks possible.

The investigations and experiences in this unit also address many of the Grade Level Expectations in Strand H, The Nature of Science.

PHYSICAL SCIENCE

Science in Florida

Everglades City

Dear Dominique,
I had so much fun today with my aunt and uncle in the Everglades. They have an airboat, and we took a ride through a swamp near their house. The fan on the airboat is taller than my uncle! As the fan blew the air, we zoomed across the water. I was holding on tight as my uncle steered us through the swamp.

See you soon,
Marty

The Sunshine State

USA

FCAT Writing

Writing Situation
Think about times when you were moving very fast. Explain how you were able to move quickly.

Experiment!

Airboats are powered by strong fans that blow air and push the boats forward. Sailboats have large sails that catch the wind, which causes the boats to move. What kind of sail is able to catch the most wind and make a boat move the fastest? Plan and conduct an experiment to find out.

Chapter

5 Forces and Motion

Vocabulary

FCAT-Tested
force
inertia
gravity
gravitation
weight
friction

Other Terms
position
motion
speed
velocity
acceleration

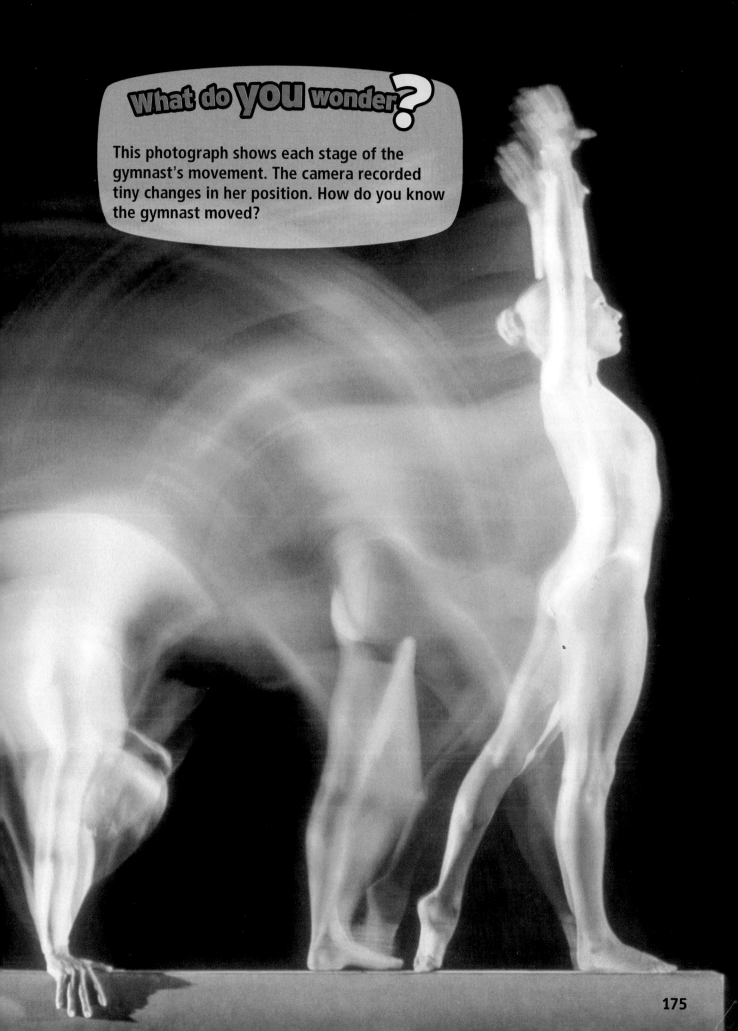

How Is Motion Described and Measured?

Fast Fact

Higher Speed Means Higher Risk On a highway, cars often go as fast as 120 kilometers per hour (75 mi/hr). High-speed accidents are much more deadly than low-speed ones. A driver is 15 times as likely to die in a crash that takes place at 80 kilometers per hour (50 mi/hr) than in one that takes place at 40 kilometers per hour (25 mi/hr). In the Investigate, you'll describe moving at a very low speed.

Walk This Way

Materials • paper • pencil

Procedure

1. Choose a location in your school. The location could be an exit door or bench, for example. A person going there from your classroom should have to make some turns.

2. Start walking to the selected location. As you walk, record the way you move. Include the distance you walk, where you turn, any landmarks you see, and how fast you move.

3. Return to the classroom. On a piece of paper, write directions to the location. Use your notes to add details. Don't name the location. Your partner should follow the directions and try to match your speed.

4. Get feedback from your partner about how well your directions worked. Use the feedback to improve your directions. Then follow the improved directions.

5. Switch roles with your partner, who should repeat Steps 1–4.

Step 2

Step 3

Draw Conclusions

1. How did your partner know how far and how fast to walk and where to turn?

2. **Inquiry Skill** Tell why the revised directions and a good experiment plan are examples of clear communication.

Investigate Further

Draw a map to your location. Trade maps with a new partner. Compare using a map to using written directions.

SC.C.2.2.2.4.1 position, direction, speed
SC.H.1.2.3.4.1 working collaboratively
SC.H.1.2.1.4.1 scientists publish, enabling repetition   **177**

SC.C.2.2.2.4.1 position, direction, speed
LA.A.2.2.7 compare and contrast

VOCABULARY
position p. 178
motion p. 178
speed p. 180

SCIENCE CONCEPTS
▶ how to define motion
▶ how to measure speed

READING FOCUS SKILL
COMPARE AND CONTRAST
Look for similarities and differences between motion and speed.

| alike | different |

Changing Position

Where are you located right now? Are you *at* your desk? *Under* a light? To the *right* of a door, or *2 meters (6 ft) away from* the board? Words such as these describe your position. **Position** is the location of an object.

Every object has a position. The position of your nose is the center of your face. How would you describe the position of the doorway in your classroom? These positions don't change.

But sometimes an object's position does change. When it does, the object is in motion. **Motion** is a change of position of an object.

There are many kinds of motion. You can walk forward or backward. An elevator goes up and down. A pendulum swings from side to side. Things may move quickly or slowly. They may follow a straight, curved, or circular path. But whenever something moves, its position changes.

◀ **The soccer players are in constant motion. Their positions are always changing.**

The still pictures don't show the actual motion of the boats, but you can tell that the boats moved. How do you know? Without even thinking about it, you interpret an object's change of position as motion. ▶

In the boat race pictures, have the boats in the second picture moved from where they were in the first picture?

You can tell that the boats have moved, because their positions have changed. In the first picture, the boats were close to the docks. They were to the right of the man with the flag. In the second picture, the boats have moved past the man with the flag. The docks can't be seen anymore.

You sensed the boats' motion by looking at the shore and assuming it was still. In other words, you used the shore as your *frame of reference.* Relative to the shore, the boats have moved.

You can change your frame of reference. You might say you're not moving when you're sitting at your school desk. But change your frame of reference to the solar system. Now you realize that you're spinning and moving around the sun with Earth. You're moving at about 1000 kilometers per hour (600 mi/hr)!

 COMPARE AND CONTRAST How are the boat and the shore different frames of reference for the rowers?

Measuring Motion

How fast can you run? If you run faster than your friend, your speed is greater. **Speed** tells you how the position of an object changes during a certain amount of time.

You can use words like *fast* and *slow* to describe speed. Fast-moving objects change their position quickly. Slow-moving objects change their position slowly. But you can be more exact if you use numbers and units, such as 10 meters per second or 5 miles per hour.

To find an object's speed, you need to measure two things. You need to measure distance. This distance is the change in the object's position. You also need to measure the time it takes the object to move through the distance.

Once you have both the distance and time measurements, you can find the object's speed with this formula:

speed = distance ÷ time

In other words, find speed by dividing the movement distance by the time it takes to move that distance.

For example, suppose you're going by car to a campground for a vacation. You travel 225 kilometers in 3 hours. You can find your speed this way:

225 km ÷ 3 hr = 75 km/hr

When you know the speed of an object, you know how much distance

◄ In a close race, times can be nearly the same. Judges use precise stopwatches to measure time in tenths or hundredths of a second to determine who is fastest.

To know speed, you must know two other things—distance and time. In a race, the distance is the same for all the runners, but their times vary.

For drivers, speed is often measured in miles per hour. ▼

▲ The police officer uses a radar gun to measure the speeds of cars moving toward him.

it can move in a certain amount of time. Suppose an insect moves 100 centimeters per second (40 in./sec). This means that in 1 second, it can travel 100 centimeters (40 in.). Does that seem fast? It is fast, for an insect. An insect that moves this fast probably has wings!

Speed tells you only how quickly or slowly an object moves. It doesn't tell you the direction of the motion.

COMPARE AND CONTRAST Which travels faster—a bicycle that travels 24 kilometers in 1 hour or a bicycle that travels 48 kilometers in 2 hours?

Insta-Lab

Fast Walk, Slow Walk

Compare walking speeds. Mark off a distance of at least 10 m. Walk that distance twice while measuring the time. Cover the distance first in 10 seconds and then in 15 seconds. How do you determine how quickly you need to walk?

Comparing Speeds

Suppose you're watching a horse race between Lightning and Thunder. Lightning's speed so far is 55 kilometers per hour (34 mi/hr). Thunder's speed so far is 60 kilometers per hour (37 mi/hr). The race is half over. Can you say which horse is moving faster right now? You might guess Thunder. But you need more information to be sure.

You just learned that speed is the total distance divided by time. This formula gives *average* speed. For example, you saw how to find the average speed during a three-hour car trip. You can also measure speed over a shorter time. The speedometer of a car shows the car's speed moment by moment.

Now let's go back to the horse race. Thunder has a greater average speed so far. However, Lightning could be moving faster at this moment. To be sure, you have to watch the race closely and compare the horses' positions. If Lightning is catching up to Thunder, you know Lightning is running faster now.

 COMPARE AND CONTRAST How is speed at one moment different from average speed?

Math in Science
Interpret Data

Top Speeds of Vehicles
The graph shows the fastest speed for each type of vehicle. Which vehicle is fastest? Slowest?

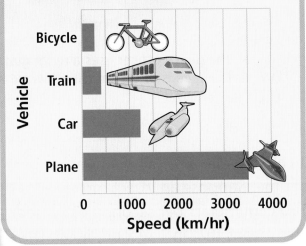

Can you tell from the pictures whether the horse in front was running faster? Explain. ▶

1. COMPARE AND CONTRAST Draw and complete this graphic organizer to compare a moving car with a person walking on a sidewalk.

ALIKE	DIFFERENT
Both are examples of **A** _____.	The car has a greater **B** _____ than the walker.
Both changes in position are compared to a **C** _____.	The driver is **D** _____ compared to the car seat but is **E** _____ compared to the sidewalk.

2. SUMMARIZE Use lesson vocabulary terms to write a lesson summary.

3. DRAW CONCLUSIONS A top spins in place without changing its location. Is it moving? Why or why not?

4. VOCABULARY Write one question for each of the terms *position, motion, speed.* Trade questions with a partner, and answer your partner's questions.

FCAT Prep

5. Read/Inquire/Explain What does it mean to say that the average speed of a car is 35 miles per hour?

6. What is the speed of a dog that runs 9 meters in 3 seconds?

A. 3 meters per second

B. 9 meters per second

C. 12 meters per second

D. 27 meters per second

Links

Writing

Descriptive Writing
Write a paragraph about how you experience motion. **Describe** examples of each of these kinds of motion: forward, backward, back-and-forth, side-to-side, and rotating.

Math

Speed Fact Family
Write the related fact-family members for this formula.

speed = distance ÷ time

Physical Education

Sprint the Distance
Go outside with a partner. Bring a meterstick, masking tape, and a stopwatch. Mark off a distance of at least 10 meters (33 ft). Walk or run as your partner times you. Use the formula to find your speed.

For more links and activities, go to **www.hspscience.com**

What Is Acceleration?

Fast Fact

Tennis Serves Stopping and returning a tennis serve can be a real challenge. The world's fastest serve was a sizzling 239.8 kilometers per hour (149 mi/hr)! In the Investigate, you'll see how a force changes the motion of an object such as a table tennis ball.

Which Way the Ball Blows

Materials
- ruler
- masking tape, 10-cm strip
- table tennis ball
- straw

Procedure

1. Put the strip of tape on a table or your desktop. Place the table tennis ball at one end of the tape.

2. Blow through the straw onto the ball. Blow gently and steadily. Make the ball roll along the tape. Observe whether the ball rolls in the direction in which you blow.

3. Return the table tennis ball to the end of the tape. Blow on the ball at a right angle to the tape. Observe whether the ball rolls in the direction in which you blow.

4. Roll the ball gently. Blow on the ball in a direction different from where the ball is rolling. Observe what happens.

Draw Conclusions

1. In what direction did you blow to make the ball roll along the tape? To make it roll at right angles to the tape?

2. Inquiry Skill What tools could you use to measure the motion of the ball?

Step 2

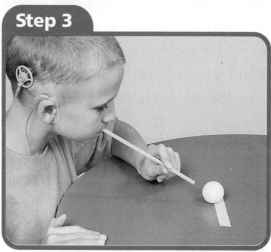

Step 3

Investigate Further

Blow on the ball in one direction. Have a partner blow at right angles to the direction in which you blow. Observe the path of the ball.

SC.C.1.2.1.4.1 velocity
SC.H.1.2.2.4.2 metric tools

185

VOCABULARY

velocity p. 186
acceleration p. 187
force p. 188
inertia p. 190

SCIENCE CONCEPTS

▶ how velocity relates to acceleration

▶ how forces cause acceleration

 READING FOCUS SKILL

CAUSE AND EFFECT Look for ways in which forces cause acceleration.

cause ⟶ effect

Velocity

If you were asked to describe the motion of a bird, a bike, or a train, you'd probably tell how fast it was going. You'd probably also mention its direction. When you tell both the speed and the direction of an object, you give its **velocity**.

To describe the direction part of velocity, you can use compass directions or words such as *right, left, up,* and *down.* For example, suppose you're riding a bicycle at 30 kilometers per hour (19 mi/hr) toward the west. Your

speed is 30 kilometers per hour. But your velocity is 30 kilometers per hour, west.

Two objects with the same speed have different velocities if they are moving in different directions. While your velocity is 30 kilometers per hour, west, your friend's velocity might be 30 kilometers per hour, north.

▼ Velocity includes both speed and direction. A rocket's velocity is at least 11 kilometers per second (7 mi/sec), up. These riders' velocity is 24 kilometers per hour (15 mi/hr), east.

▼ Acceleration may be a change in speed, direction, or both. This boat is changing direction. This skier is changing both speed and direction.

Changing Velocity

Like your bicycle, objects don't always move steadily in one direction. They stop and start, slow down and speed up, and turn. These changes are examples of acceleration. **Acceleration** is any change in the speed or direction of an object's motion. So acceleration is any change of velocity.

Think about what happens to your bicycle when you ride it. It accelerates when it speeds up and rolls away from a stop sign. It also accelerates when it slows to a stop at a stop sign. Slowing down is acceleration, just as speeding up is. If the bicycle moves in a circle at

a constant speed of 10 kilometers per hour (6 mi/hr), is it accelerating? Yes, it is. It is always turning in the circle—changing direction—so it is always accelerating.

You can measure acceleration. The larger the change in speed, the larger the acceleration. Getting a car up to top speed is a larger acceleration than doing so for your bicycle. Stopping a large jet plane that is moving at top speed is a larger acceleration than doing so for a car.

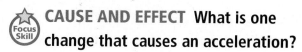 **CAUSE AND EFFECT** What is one change that causes an acceleration?

More Force, More Acceleration

When forces push or pull in the same direction, they simply add up. Suppose you double the force on an object by pushing it twice as hard. Then you double its acceleration as well.

▲ The athletes push the sled, and it accelerates.

◀ More athletes push this sled with more force. Its acceleration is greater than that of the sled shown above.

Force and Acceleration

Push a door, and it moves. Pull the door, and it moves the other way. Pushes and pulls of all kinds are **forces**. Forces are measured in newtons (N).

Forces change motion. If a soccer ball is still, it stays still until a force moves it. If you kick the soccer ball, it keeps moving in the same direction until a force changes its motion. Any change of speed or direction requires a force. In other words, *forces cause acceleration.*

The direction in which an object moves depends on the direction of the force that is used on the object. You used a force on the table tennis ball in the Investigate. The ball rolled in the direction in which you blew.

What if there's more than one force? In that case, the forces work together. You saw this in the Investigate Further. The ball rolled in a direction between the direction of your force and the direction of your partner's force. Two forces of the same size but opposite in direction will cancel each other out. Forces that cancel each other out are called balanced forces.

▲ This sled is pulled by six dogs. The sled with more dogs is pulled harder. It accelerates more than the other sled.

◄ One dog pulls this sled.

For more links and activities, go to www.hspscience.com

How does the size of a force affect acceleration? If you tap a basketball with your finger, it may roll a little. You've used a small force. But if you kick the ball hard, it takes off. You've used a large force. A larger force results in a larger acceleration. For example, a windmill's blades are turned by the wind. A gentle breeze turns them slowly. A strong wind spins them so fast that they're a blur!

 CAUSE AND EFFECT What causes the speed or direction of objects to change?

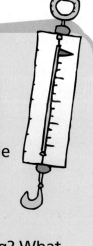

Insta-Lab

Spring-Scale Follow the Leader
You will need a spring scale and a box. Hook the scale to the box. Drag the box. What happens when the scale shows a large reading? What happens when it reads zero?

Mass and Acceleration

Which would you rather move by pushing—a bicycle or a car? Pushing the bicycle would take much less force. You'd need to push the car much harder to get it moving.

The acceleration of an object depends on its mass. It takes more force to accelerate a large mass than to accelerate a small mass. This is because all matter has inertia. **Inertia** is the property of matter that keeps it moving in a straight line and keeps unmoving matter at rest. A truck has more inertia than a motorcycle. It needs a bigger engine, because more force is needed to get it moving quickly.

The more mass an object has, the more inertia it has. And the more inertia an object has, the harder it is to change its motion.

⭐ **Focus Skill** **CAUSE AND EFFECT Why is it harder to get a loaded wheelbarrow moving than an empty one?**

◄ **Which ball accelerates more when you throw it—the basketball or the tennis ball? Why?**

1. CAUSE AND EFFECT Draw and complete this graphic organizer.

A **A** _____ is a push or pull → that can cause → **B** _____ , a change in **C** _____ .

2. SUMMARIZE Write a summary of this lesson. Begin with this sentence: *I use forces every day.*

3. DRAW CONCLUSIONS Describe the acceleration of a downhill skier.

4. VOCABULARY Describe an everyday situation in which you might notice forces. Use the terms *velocity, acceleration, force,* and *inertia.*

FCAT Prep

5. Read/Inquire/Explain A polar bear walks toward the North Pole. It walks 15 kilometers in 1 hour. What is the bear's velocity?

6. The acceleration of an object depends on the size of the force used on it and what other property?

A. color   C. temperature

B. mass   D. volume

Links

Writing

Narrative Writing
Write an action-packed adventure **story** that describes motion and uses the vocabulary from this lesson.

Math

Compare Accelerations
A car goes from 0 to 100 kilometers per hour in 10 seconds. Another car slows from 100 to 0 kilometers per hour in 10 seconds. Compare these accelerations.

Social Studies

History of Science
Use library resources to learn more about Isaac Newton. Explain what Newton's second law of motion is and how it relates to the ideas in this lesson.

For more links and activities, go to www.hspscience.com

3

Why Is the Force of Gravity Important?

Fast Fact

What Goes Up . . . The same force that pulls sky divers to Earth keeps planets in their orbits around the sun. In the Investigate, you'll learn how an object can travel a circular path like the orbits of the planets.

Making Circular Motion

Materials • safety goggles • string, 1-m length • cardboard tube
• rubber stopper • tape

Procedure

1 CAUTION: **Put on safety goggles.** Tie the stopper to the end of the string.

2 Put tape over the string on the stopper to hold the string in place. Be sure the stopper is securely fastened. Thread the string through the tube.

3 Go outdoors. Stand where you have a clear space 3 meters around you in all directions.

4 Holding the string, move the tube to whirl the stopper in a circular path over your head. Be sure to hold the string securely. You may want to wrap it once around your hand. Don't hit anything with the stopper! The circular path of the stopper should be level with the ground.

5 Observe the direction in which you are pulling the string as the stopper moves around the circle.

Step 2

Step 4

Draw Conclusions

1. In what direction did you pull the string to keep the stopper moving in a circle?

2. Inquiry Skill What materials would you need for an experiment to test the hypothesis that spinning the stopper faster requires a stronger pull?

Investigate Further

Try whirling the stopper in an up-and-down circle in front of you. Observe the direction in which you pull. Compare it with the direction in Step 5.

SC.E.1.2.5.4.1 gravity and planets
SC.H.1.2.2.4.1 experimental design **193**

Reading in Science

SC.E.1.2.5.4.1 gravity and planets
LA.A.2.2.1 main idea

VOCABULARY
gravity p. 195
gravitation p. 195
weight p. 196
friction p. 197

SCIENCE CONCEPTS
▶ what weight measures
▶ how weight differs from mass

 READING FOCUS SKILL
MAIN IDEA AND DETAILS
Look for details about gravity, gravitation, and weight.

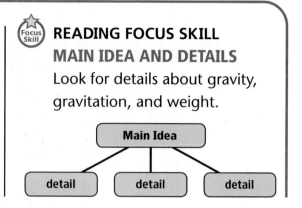

Natural Forces

Every day, you use the force of your muscles to sit, stand, and walk. What other forces do you use every day? You've seen how magnets interact. You've also explored electric charges. You use electric devices and machines with magnets all the time.

The force between electric charges is one of the most important in nature. It holds together tiny particles of matter.

These particles are so small that you don't see how electricity affects their motion.

You do see the result of electric force when it pulls and pushes charged objects. For example, you've probably seen a balloon stick to a wall after you rubbed it against fabric or your hair.

MAIN IDEA AND DETAILS Give an example of how you used the force of your muscles today.

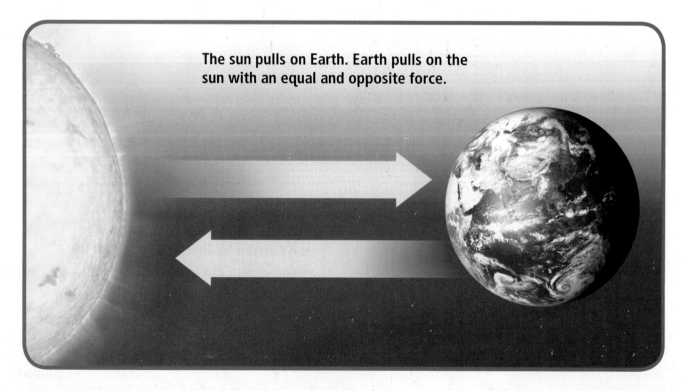

The sun pulls on Earth. Earth pulls on the sun with an equal and opposite force.

Gravity

Besides the force of your own muscles, gravity is probably the force you notice most. **Gravity** is the force that pulls things toward Earth. If you toss a ball upward, gravity pulls it back down to the ground.

Gravity is an effect of gravitation. **Gravitation** is a force that acts between all masses and causes them to attract one another. It acts everywhere, all the time. Gravitation helps hold the moon in its orbit around Earth. It pulls the moon and Earth toward each other. This pull prevents the moon from flying off in a straight line because of its inertia. It is similar to the pull that held the stopper in its path in the Investigate.

Gravitation also holds Earth in its orbit around the sun. The other planets, too, are held in their orbits by gravitation.

The larger and closer two masses are, the more gravitation affects them. Sometimes the force is very weak, but it's always there. Earth's gravitation affects you more than any other object's, because Earth is so large and so close to you.

MAIN IDEA AND DETAILS What keeps the moon in a circular path?

▼ Gravity is the force that pulls you toward Earth. Roller coasters use this force to provide thrills.

Weight

How can you measure the force of gravity on an object? Simple—just weigh the object on a scale.

An object's **weight** is the gravitational force acting on it. Because it is a force, weight is measured in newtons (N). One newton is about the weight of an apple, or just under a quarter of a pound.

Don't confuse weight with mass— they aren't the same thing. Mass is the amount of matter in an object. It's measured on a balance, not on a scale. The unit of mass is the gram.

Your weight is the gravitational force acting on you. So your weight would change if you were away from Earth's gravity. The moon's gravitational force is less than Earth's. On the moon, you would weigh only one-sixth of what you weigh on Earth. Your mass, however, is the same wherever you are.

MAIN IDEAS AND DETAILS Is a person on a diet trying to lose weight or mass? Explain your reasoning.

The child weighs 250 newtons (56 lb). She's being weighed on a doctor's scale. The bear cub is much lighter. A different kind of scale is being used to measure the force of gravity acting on the cub.

▲ A bike's brakes use friction to slow down the bike, to stop it, or to keep it from moving in the first place.

Friction

Have you ever heard tires squeal when a car stopped suddenly? That sound is caused by another familiar force—friction. **Friction** is a force that resists the motion of objects, relative to each other, when the objects are touching. Friction changes kinetic energy to heat. Over time, friction slows down motion and stops it. Friction is measured in newtons, just like other forces.

The force of friction is always present when one surface touches another. Often, friction is useful. For example, your bike slows down when you apply the brakes. The brakes are rubber pads that create friction when they press against a wheel. The friction slows the wheel and finally stops it.

Sports shoes have rubber soles that increase friction. This helps keep you from slipping while you run and play.

 MAIN IDEA AND DETAILS **If your friend pushes you to the right, in what direction does friction act?**

Insta-Lab

Get the Feel of Friction

Rub your hands together. Put a drop of cooking oil on your hands, and rub them together again. Now put on some rubber gloves, and rub your hands together. How is the friction different each time?

197

Controlling Friction

Friction acts between any two surfaces. For example, it slows or stops motion of the parts within machines. Friction causes machines to lose energy as waste heat. Did you notice your hands warm up when you rubbed them together in the Insta-Lab?

Friction is useful when you want to brake your bicycle. However, surfaces wear out quickly when a lot of friction is present. So friction can also be a problem. People reduce friction by making surfaces smooth. Also, surfaces may be covered with oil or another slippery material to reduce friction.

Several moving parts of a bicycle are oiled to reduce friction. The chain, gears, and pedals are oiled. The oil allows the moving parts to slide smoothly over one another.

⭐ **Focus Skill** **MAIN IDEA AND DETAILS** What are two ways that friction can be controlled?

Water on a water slide reduces friction, making the ride faster and more exciting. ▶

The bike rider oils his chain and gears to reduce friction and make his ride easier. ▼

The surfer waxes his board to increase the friction between the board and his feet. ▼

1. MAIN IDEA AND DETAILS Draw and complete this graphic organizer.

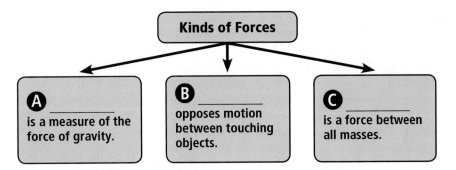

Kinds of Forces

A _____ is a measure of the force of gravity.

B _____ opposes motion between touching objects.

C _____ is a force between all masses.

2. SUMMARIZE Use your completed graphic organizer to write a lesson summary.

3. DRAW CONCLUSIONS Explain how friction keeps nails from falling out of walls.

4. VOCABULARY Use the vocabulary terms from this lesson to make a word puzzle.

FCAT Prep

5. Read/Inquire/Explain What happens to motion when friction is reduced?

6. What is weight a measurement of?
  A. electrical force   **C.** gravity
  B. friction   **D.** acceleration

Links

Writing

Expository Writing
Write about a product that reduces or increases friction. **Explain** how the product works and why people need it.

Math

Solve a Problem
You push an eraser forward with a force of 2 newtons. The eraser doesn't move. What is the force of the friction acting on the eraser?

Music

Make a Glass Sing
The friction between a wet finger and the rim of a thin-walled glass can make a pleasing sound. See if you can make music this way. Be careful! Hold the glass with one hand while you run a finger around its rim.

For more links and activities, go to **www.hspscience.com**

SCIENCE SOARS AT THE OLYMPICS

Chris Soule races down a hill on his sled to train for the Winter Olympics.

To train for the Winter Olympics, athlete Chris Soule stands at the top of a long hill holding a small sled. He springs forward, jumps on the sled, and races down the hill as fast as he can. Soule competes in a kind of Olympic sled race called *skeleton*. To compete in skeleton takes speed, strength, and science. That's right—science.

Shaving Time

A top skeleton racer must be fast. The athlete who finishes with the fastest time wins the race and the gold medal. "Some of the sports events are won by one-hundredth or even one-thousandth of a second," Peter Davis told *Weekly Reader.* Davis is the head of coaching and sport sciences for the United States Olympic Committee.

Racing with Science

To shave hundredths of a second off their times, many athletes have turned to science.

At the U.S. Olympic Training Facility in Lake Placid, New York, scientists called biomechanists (by•oh•MEH•kuhn•ists) use computer software to help skeleton racers improve their push starts.

To do this, scientists videotape the athletes during their push starts. The tapes are fed into a computer. The scientists can then study every movement and every angle of the athletes' bodies. They decide, for example, whether the athlete is leaning too far forward at the start or whether his or her feet are in the best position.

Virtual Training

Another training tool that's being used more and more is virtual reality. "We can set up an athletic event on a computer," Davis said. "An athlete uses video goggles to see the event and react to what is happening." By using virtual reality, athletes who compete in winter sports can train throughout the year.

THINK ABOUT IT

1. Why are even small improvements important for some sports?
2. How is videotape used to help racers?

MORE SPORTS SCIENCE

- Uniforms are being made with new kinds of slick fabrics that help speed skaters perform better and stay cooler.
- Blood tests can show how much lactic acid is in an athlete's blood. Too much lactic acid makes the muscles work harder than they should.
- Skiers practice in wind tunnels that show them how to go faster.

Find out more! Log on to
www.hspscience.com

SC.H.3.2.4.4.1 solving problems/new ideas
SC.H.1.2.4.4.1 comparing experiments

SCIENCE Spin™ from WEEKLY READER®

People

SC.H.1.2.5.4.1
using models
SC.H.3.2.4.4.1
solving problems/
new ideas

Testing the Wind

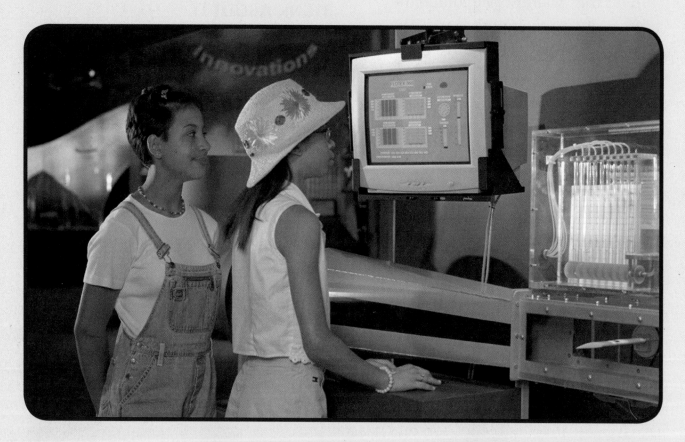

If you have ever wondered how engineers test a new airplane before flying it, check out a wind tunnel. That's what Melinda Lee did recently when she visited a science center.

A wind tunnel is exactly what it sounds like. A powerful fan at one end blows air through a tunnel and out an exhaust. Melinda was able to test the effects of wind speed on an airfoil, or wing-shaped piece of metal.

Melinda used the computer to change the position of the airfoil and the wind speed. The display showed the lifting forces on the airfoil.

Materials
- wagon
- round ball, such as a soccer ball

Motion and Frames of Reference

Procedure

1. Work in a group of three students. Have Student A sit in the wagon and hold the ball. Have Student B pull the wagon at a constant velocity.
2. While the wagon is moving, have Student A toss the ball upward about 2 m and catch it. Observe this yourself from about 6 m away.
3. Have Students A and B repeat the motions so that all of you can verify your observations. Ask Student A if the ball appears to be going straight up and down.

Draw Conclusions
Discuss each person's observations. How are the observations affected by each person's frame of reference?

Change of Reference

Switch roles with your group members. Be sure each of you has a chance to observe from both places when the ball is tossed. Now change one variable. See if you get different results. You might try changing the way the ball is tossed, the location of the observer, or the velocity of the wagon. Be careful not to go too fast!

Review and FCAT Preparation

Vocabulary Review

Use the terms below to complete the sentences. The page numbers tell you where to look in the chapter if you need help.

position p. 178	**force** p. 188
motion p. 178	**inertia** p. 190
speed p. 180	**gravitation** p. 195
velocity p. 186	**weight** p. 196
acceleration p. 187	**friction** p. 197

1. The force that slows or stops the motion of objects, relative to each other, when the objects are touching is _____.

2. A push or pull measured in newtons is a _____.

3. The measurement of the gravity acting on an object is the object's _____.

4. A change in velocity is _____.

5. A change in position is _____.

6. The property that describes an object's resistance to changing its motion is _____.

7. The force of attraction that exists between any two masses anywhere in the universe is _____.

8. Speed and direction taken together are _____.

9. The distance an object travels divided by the time it takes to travel is its _____.

10. An object's location is its _____.

Check Understanding

Write the letter of the best choice.

11. **MAIN IDEA AND DETAILS** What force holds the moon in its orbit around Earth?
    - **A.** friction
    - **B.** gravitation
    - **C.** position
    - **D.** weight

12. If an object has a large mass on Earth, what else does it have a lot of?
    - **F.** inertia and volume
    - **G.** weight and inertia
    - **H.** weight and speed
    - **I.** weight and volume

Use the picture to answer Questions 13 and 14.

13. A dial in the picture tells you how many kilometers per hour the car is going. What does this measure?
    - **A.** acceleration
    - **B.** speed
    - **C.** velocity
    - **D.** weight

14. What information about the car can you find by using the dial and compass together?

   F. its acceleration

   G. its motion

   H. its speed

   I. its velocity

15. What force is shown by Arrow 2?

   A. electric force   **C.** gravity

   B. friction   **D.** magnetic force

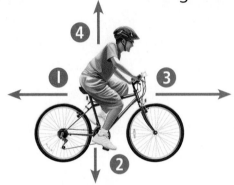

16. CAUSE AND EFFECT If you increase the force on an object, what do you probably also increase?

   F. acceleration   **H.** inertia

   G. gravity   **I.** mass

Inquiry Skills

17. How do you **observe** friction when you erase a pencil mark?

18. A girl pulls a wagon by applying a force to it. What other force can you **infer** acts on the wagon in the opposite direction?

Read/Inquire/Explain

19. Can an object that moves at a constant speed be accelerating? Explain your answer.

20. A truck, a car, and a bicycle are driving away from a stoplight. The truck uses a big engine for this acceleration. A car uses a smaller engine, and the bicycle rider uses the force of his own muscles.

Part A Why does each vehicle require a different amount of force to accelerate?

Part B Suppose each vehicle is pushed forward with a force of the same size. Which vehicle will be moving fastest after one minute? Why?

6 Simple Machines

Lesson 1 How Do Simple Machines Help People Do Work?

Lesson 2 How Do a Pulley and a Wheel-and-Axle Help People Do Work?

Lesson 3 How Do Other Simple Machines Help People Do Work?

Vocabulary

FCAT-Tested
lever
fulcrum
pulley
wheel-and-axle
inclined plane

Other Terms
work
simple machine
screw
wedge

What do YOU wonder?

Simple machines can be found just about anywhere there are people. What simple machines do you think this person is using? How would you define *simple machine*?

How Do Simple Machines Help People Do Work?

Boinnng! The two people on the left end dropped 2 meters ($6\frac{1}{2}$ ft) onto the seesaw. That sent the person on the right end flying almost 3 meters (10 ft) into the air! In the Investigate, you'll make a model that shows the forces on a seesaw.

Up and Down

Materials
- safety goggles
- tape
- 2 rubber bands
- 2 wooden rulers

Procedure

1 CAUTION: **Put on safety goggles.** Work in groups of three. Tape a rubber band 2 cm from each end of one ruler.

2 One person should hook a finger through each rubber band and lift the ruler. This person should pull enough to keep the ruler level while a second person presses down on the 15-cm mark.

3 The third person should measure the length of each rubber band. Record your observations and measurements.

4 Repeat Steps 2 and 3, with the second person pressing on the 17-cm mark.

5 Repeat Steps 2 and 3, with the second person pressing on the 19-cm and 21-cm marks.

Draw Conclusions

1. What happened as the second person pressed farther from the ruler's center?

2. Inquiry Skill Sometimes scientists can learn about what they can't see by watching how it affects other things. For example, the ruler affected the rubber bands. How did you use space relationships to observe what was happening to the ruler and rubber bands?

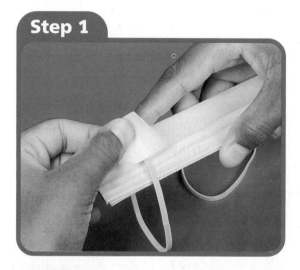
Step 1

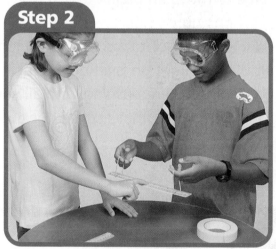
Step 2

Investigate Further

What do you predict would happen if you pressed down on the 10-cm mark? Test your prediction.

SC.C.2.2.1.4.1 simple machines
SC.H.1.2.3.4.1 working collaboratively
SC.H.1.2.5.4.1 using models

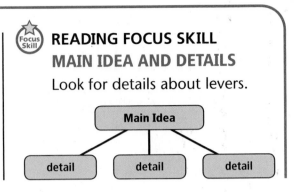

VOCABULARY

work p. 210
simple machine p. 211
lever p. 212
fulcrum p. 212

SCIENCE CONCEPTS

▶ what a scientist means by *work*

▶ what a simple machine is

▶ how a lever changes the way work is done

READING FOCUS SKILL

MAIN IDEA AND DETAILS

Look for details about levers.

Main Idea → detail | detail | detail

Work and Simple Machines

You do schoolwork in class and at home. You may help with work at home by baby-sitting or mowing lawns. For most people, these are examples of work. But to a scientist, *work* has a different meaning. **Work** is the use of force to move an object over a distance.

When you do homework, you have to concentrate. But to a scientist, the only work you might do is lifting a pencil.

Imagine you're pushing with all your might on a door that's stuck. If it doesn't move, you're not doing work.

For work to be done, an object also has to move in the direction of the force applied to it. If you lift a box, you apply a force upward and the box moves up. That's work.

But what if you then carry the box across the room? Your arms are lifting up, but the box is moving sideways. So, your arms aren't doing any work on the box, no matter how tired they might get.

The girl uses an upward force on the dog, and the dog moves up. The girl is having fun but is doing work, too.

A lawn mower makes the work of mowing lawns easier. It's a complex machine with many parts.

This wheelbarrow is a simple machine—a lever. The boy lifts the handles, and the pile of leaves goes up. He does the same amount of work as carrying the leaves by hand. It takes less force, but he lifts further. ▶

Here's another scientific definition: A *machine* is anything that changes the way work is done. You just read that work is the use of force applied over a distance. A machine might change the direction of a force or the amount of force that is needed.

You probably use a lot of machines every day. Most machines have many moving parts. But some machines are very simple. In fact, they're called simple machines.

A **simple machine** is a machine with few or no moving parts to which you apply just one force. Some simple machines have very few moving parts.

Others have no moving parts.

Imagine that you want to pry up a board nailed to the floor. You slide one end of a pry bar under the board and press down on the other end. After a good push, the board comes up.

The pry bar is a simple machine. You applied a force when you pushed down. The bar changed the direction of the force, and the board moved up. The bar also changed the amount of force that was needed. After all, you couldn't pry up the board with just your hands!

 MAIN IDEA AND DETAILS How might a machine change the way work is done?

Levers

A **lever** is a bar that pivots on a fixed point. The fixed point is called the **fulcrum**. For example, a seesaw is a lever. The board of the seesaw is the bar, and the place in the middle, where the board pivots, is the fulcrum.

The pry bar you just read about is one kind of lever. The fulcrum was the point where the pry bar touched the floor. A force was applied at one end of the bar. The thing that moved—the board—was at the other end.

With the seesaw and the pry bar, the fulcrum is between the force and the thing that moves. But there are other kinds of levers. In a picture on the previous page, a boy lifts one end of a wheelbarrow. He applies force at that end, and the wheelbarrow pivots at the other end. The thing that is moved—the pile of leaves—is between the force and the fulcrum.

A broom is a third kind of lever. You hold the handle at one end—the fulcrum. The thing that is moved—the dirt—is at the other end. You apply force between the thing that is moved and the fulcrum.

★ **MAIN IDEA AND DETAILS** Give three examples of a lever.
(Focus Skill)

A hockey stick is one kind of lever. The girl holds one end of the stick. That's the fulcrum, where the stick pivots. The other end moves the puck. The girl applies force between the two ends. ▶

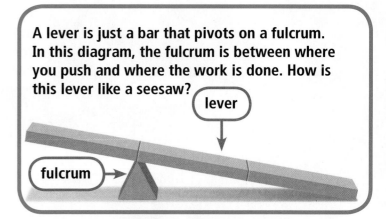

A lever is just a bar that pivots on a fulcrum. In this diagram, the fulcrum is between where you push and where the work is done. How is this lever like a seesaw?

lever

fulcrum

fulcrum

lever

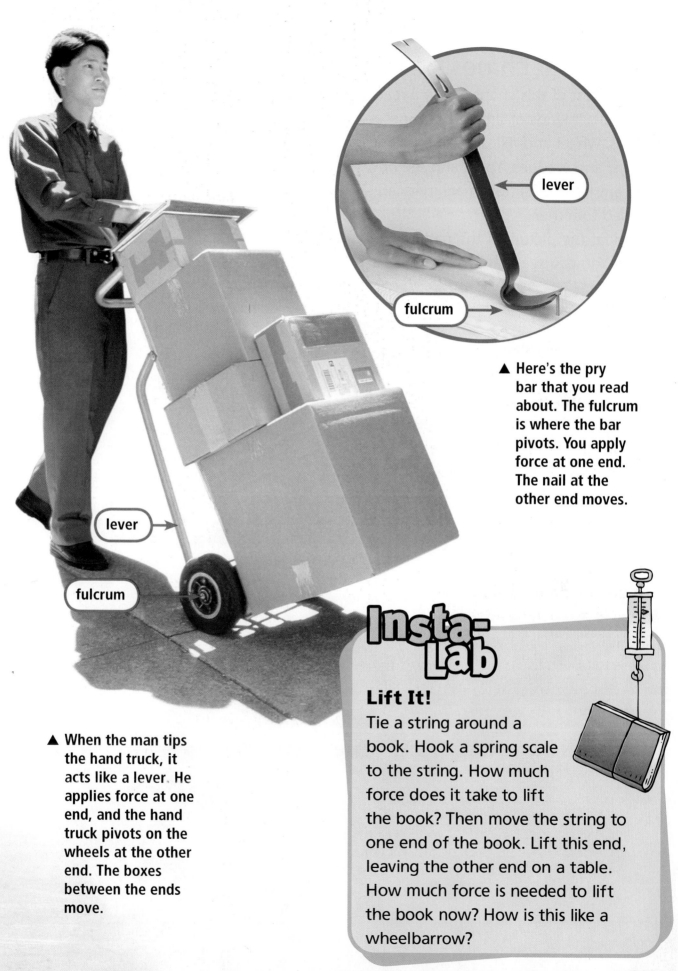

lever

fulcrum

▲ Here's the pry bar that you read about. The fulcrum is where the bar pivots. You apply force at one end. The nail at the other end moves.

lever

fulcrum

▲ When the man tips the hand truck, it acts like a lever. He applies force at one end, and the hand truck pivots on the wheels at the other end. The boxes between the ends move.

Insta-Lab

Lift It!
Tie a string around a book. Hook a spring scale to the string. How much force does it take to lift the book? Then move the string to one end of the book. Lift this end, leaving the other end on a table. How much force is needed to lift the book now? How is this like a wheelbarrow?

Levers with Other Simple Machines

In the rest of this chapter, you'll read about other kinds of simple machines—pulleys, wheel-and-axles, inclined planes, screws, and wedges. You'll also see how different kinds of simple machines can be used together.

Look at the picture of the paper cutter. You can see that it's a lever with the fulcrum at one end. But the blade of the paper cutter is another simple machine—a wedge. The two simple machines work together to cut paper.

A hedge clipper is made up of two levers. Each has its fulcrum between the two ends. And just as in the paper cutter, the blades are wedges.

 MAIN IDEA AND DETAILS Give an example of a lever working with another simple machine.

This paper cutter consists of a lever and a wedge working together. ▶

▼ This hedge clipper is made up of two levers and two wedges.

Focus Skill

1. MAIN IDEA AND DETAILS Draw and complete this graphic organizer.

	Work	Simple Machine	Lever
Description	Ⓐ	Ⓑ	Ⓒ
Example	Ⓓ	Ⓔ	Ⓕ

2. SUMMARIZE Use the graphic organizer to help you write a summary of this lesson.

3. DRAW CONCLUSIONS There are three kinds of levers. How do you think they are classified?

4. VOCABULARY Write a definition for each of the vocabulary terms in this lesson.

FCAT Prep

5. Read/Inquire/Explain Annie is using a screwdriver to pry open a can of paint. To get the lid to pop up, she has to press down on the screwdriver's handle. Why?

6. Which of the following is a lever?
   A. a bottle opener   **C.** a match
   B. a drinking straw   **D.** a pencil

Links

Writing

Expository Writing
Many everyday objects, such as pry bars and seesaws, are levers. Choose one such object, and write a **how-to** paragraph that tells how to set it up and how to use it.

Math

Solve Problems
Mrs. Ikeda has three pry bars. The shortest is 50 centimeters long. The second is twice as long. The longest is three times as long. What is the length of each bar?

Language Arts

Find a Word Origin
The word *lever* comes to English from words in older languages. Use a dictionary to find one of those words. Then write a sentence or two telling how the word relates to levers.

 For more links and activities, go to www.hspscience.com

How Do a Pulley and a Wheel-and-Axle Help People Do Work?

Fast Fact

Quite a Haul Every April, more than 500 people of all ages gather in Phoenix, Arizona, for the Phoenix Boulder Blast. It's the largest event in the sport of rock climbing in the United States. Many of the climbers practice indoors with equipment like this pulley. In the Investigate, you'll make and use a model to help you see how pulleys work.

Hoist Away

Materials
- string
- book
- wire coat hanger
- ruler
- scissors
- spring scale

Procedure

1. Work with a partner. Tie a loop of string tightly around the book.

2. Bend the hanger into a diamond shape. Hang it from a doorknob or coat hook.

3. Cut a 1-m length of string. Tie one end to the loop of string around the book. Pass the other end through the hanger, and attach it to the spring scale.

4. One partner should lift the book by pulling down on the spring scale. Note the reading on the spring scale. The other partner should measure the distance the spring scale moved and the distance the book moved. Record your observations and measurements.

5. Hook the hanger to the loop of string on the book. Untie the long string. Pass it through the hanger, and tie it to the doorknob or coat hook. Repeat Step 4, but pull up on the spring scale.

Step 4

Step 5

Draw Conclusions

1. How did the force needed to lift the book change?

2. **Inquiry Skill** What variable changed the second time?

Investigate Further

Experiment. How could you use two hangers with the spring scale and string to lift the book? Try it!

Reading in Science

VOCABULARY
pulley, p. 218
wheel-and-axle, p. 220

SCIENCE CONCEPTS
▶ how a pulley changes the way work is done
▶ how a wheel-and-axle changes the way work is done

READING FOCUS SKILL
MAIN IDEA AND DETAILS
Look for details about pulleys and wheel-and-axles.

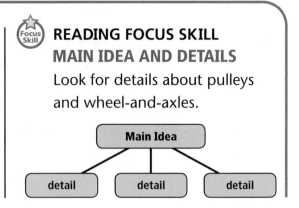

Pulleys

Changing the direction of the force can make a job much easier. For example, imagine you want to raise a flag up a pole. You could climb to the top of the pole and pull the rope up. But who would do that?

Instead, you can use a pulley that's at the top of the flagpole. A rope attaches to the flag, goes up around the wheel, and runs back down to the ground. You pull down on one end of the rope, and the other end goes up, taking the flag with it. That's easier, isn't it?

A **pulley** is a wheel with a line around it. The line might be a rope, a cord, or a chain. The wheel has a lip around its edge to keep the line from slipping off.

Most sailboats have pulleys attached to the sails. Pulleys enable the sails to move in different directions—up, down, and even sideways. ▼

Pulling one end of the rope in one direction moves the other end in a different direction.

pulley

pulley

As you know, all simple machines change the way work is done. A pulley changes the direction of the force. If you pull down on one end of the line, the other end goes up.

A single, fixed pulley doesn't change the amount of force needed. For example, suppose you wanted to lift a 200-newton (44-lb) box. You'd still need to lift 200 newtons, even with a pulley. Pulleys come in all sizes. A child might use a tiny pulley to open a window blind. A mechanic might use a large group of pulleys with a chain to lift an engine out of a car.

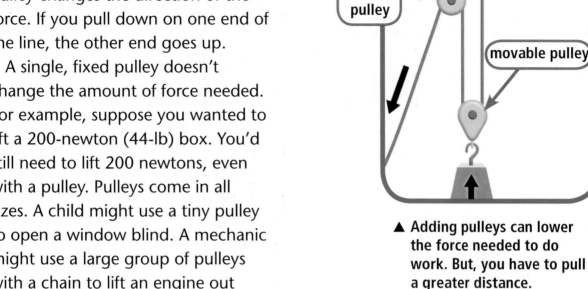

▲ Adding pulleys can lower the force needed to do work. But, you have to pull a greater distance.

MAIN IDEA AND DETAILS How does a pulley change the way work is done?

This man is using a large group of pulleys to increase his lifting force.

Wheel-and-Axles

A wheel-and-axle is exactly what its name says—a wheel and an axle. An axle is a rod that goes into or through a wheel. You can see wheels as well as axles on wheelbarrows and on skateboards, but those wheels and those axles are not simple machines.

To be a simple machine, a **wheel-and-axle** must have a wheel and an axle that turn *together*. If you turn the axle, the wheel turns with it. If you turn the wheel, the axle turns, too.

A wheel-and-axle changes the way work is done. If you turn the wheel, the axle turns with more force. You have to move the wheel over a greater distance, but you use less force. If you move the axle, the wheel moves a greater distance. You have to use more force, but you don't have to move the axle as far.

 MAIN IDEA AND DETAILS What must a wheel and an axle do to be a simple machine?

▼ A wheel-and-axle can work in two ways. You can turn the wheel to make the axle move. Or you can turn the axle to make the wheel move.

wheel

axle

The Faucet: A Wheel-and-Axle in Use

Did you ever wonder how a faucet works? The water flows through a small opening inside the faucet. When a washer blocks that opening, no water can get out. If you raise the washer a little, a little water does flow. When the opening is completely unblocked, lots of water flows.

water

Insta-Lab

A Model Wheel-and-Axle

Hold a 2-L bottle by the cap. Have a partner turn the bottle by the base so it tightens the cap. Can you stop the bottle from turning? Now roll the bottle along your desk by turning the cap. How far do your fingers move? How far does the bottle roll?

The moving part of the faucet is a wheel-and-axle. The handle is like one spoke of a wheel. The washer is on the end of an axle. The axle moves up and down because of a screw. Without the handle, you'd have to turn the axle by hand to adjust the water. That would be hard to do. But when you turn the handle, you turn the axle, too. You can use much less force, which makes it easier to open and close the faucet.

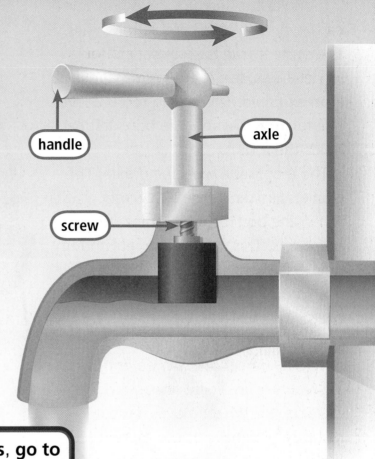

handle

axle

screw

For more links and activities, go to
www.hspscience.com

This salad spinner handle is a wheel-and-axle. The outside part is the wheel. The axle is inside. It is what moves the basket. ▶

wheel

axle

Machines Working Together

In the last lesson, you read how levers can work with other simple machines. The same is true for pulleys and for wheel-and-axles. A fishing rod and reel is an example. The fishing rod is a lever. The fulcrum is where the boy's left hand holds the rod.

The reel uses a wheel-and-axle. The crank is like the spoke of a wheel. When the boy turns the crank, the axle turns. This makes the reel wind up fishing line.

Focus Skill **MAIN IDEA AND DETAILS Is a rod and reel one simple machine? Explain.**

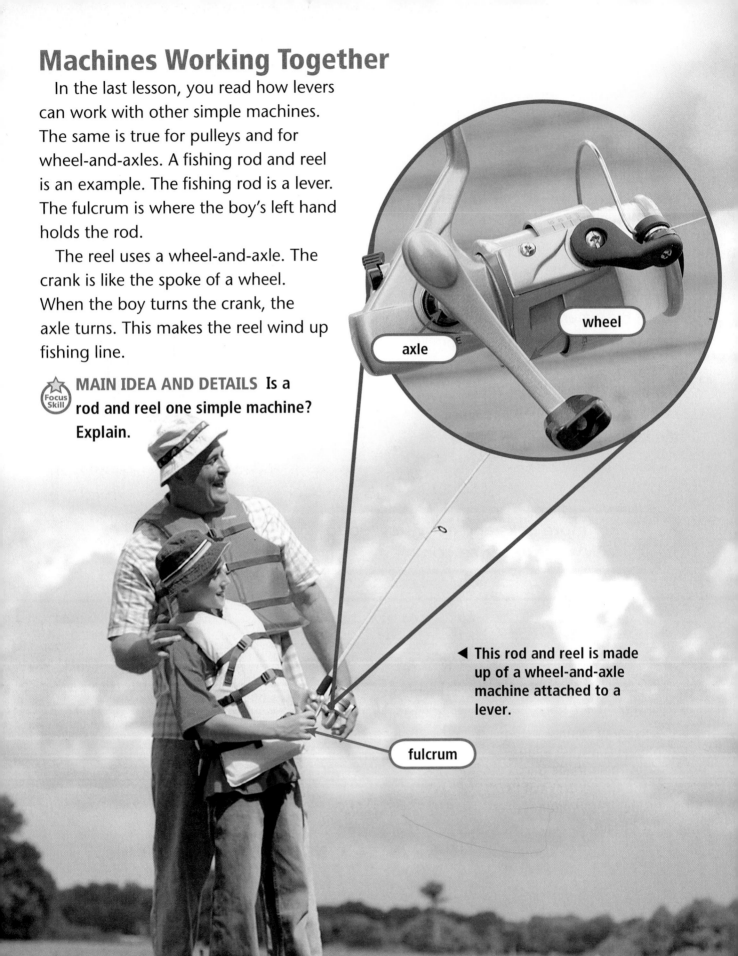

axle

wheel

◀ This rod and reel is made up of a wheel-and-axle machine attached to a lever.

fulcrum

222

Focus Skill

1. MAIN IDEA AND DETAILS Draw and complete this graphic organizer.

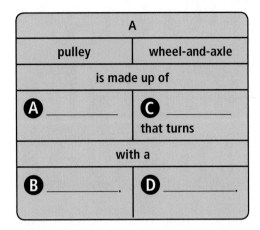

A	
pulley	wheel-and-axle
is made up of	
Ⓐ _____	Ⓒ _____ that turns
with a	
Ⓑ _____ .	Ⓓ _____ .

2. SUMMARIZE Write a short paragraph telling what this lesson is mainly about.

3. DRAW CONCLUSIONS How does the pulley in a window blind change the way work is done?

4. VOCABULARY Use each of the vocabulary terms in a sentence.

FCAT Prep

5. Read/Inquire/Explain How is a screwdriver an example of a wheel-and-axle?

6. Which kind of simple machine is the beater part of an electric mixer?

A. pulley   **C.** pulley and lever

B. wheel-and-axle   **D.** two pulleys

Links

Writing

Narrative Writing

Imagine that you are the person who invented the pulley. Write a paragraph **describing** how you invented it.

Math

Define Geometric Relationships

A wheel is a short, wide cylinder, and an axle is a long, thin cylinder. What do the two cylinders of a wheel-and-axle have in common?

Social Studies

Ancient Simple Machines

Research how pulleys may have been used to help build the Egyptian pyramids. Write a paragraph or draw a picture to report what you find out.

 For more links and activities, go to **www.hspscience.com**

How Do Other Simple Machines Help People Do Work?

Fast Fact

Screws Machines like those shown here can move large amounts of water uphill. These are screws that each move about 38,000 liters (10,000 gal) of water each minute. In the Investigate, you'll use another kind of simple machine—a ramp—that makes lifting things easier.

Moving Up

Materials
- cardboard
- tape measure
- toy car
- scissors
- string
- spring scale

Procedure

1. Use some of the cardboard to make a ramp from the floor to a chair seat. Make a second ramp, twice as long as the first. Using the tape measure, find and record the distance from the floor to the seat, both straight up and along each ramp.

2. Tie a loop of string to the toy car. Attach the spring scale to the string.

3. Hold on to the spring scale, and lift the car from the floor directly to the chair seat. Record the force shown.

4. Hold on to the spring scale, and pull the car up the short ramp from the floor to the chair seat. Record the force shown. Do the same for the long ramp.

Draw Conclusions

1. How did using the ramps affect the amount of force needed to move the car to the chair seat?

2. **Inquiry Skill** Scientists interpret data to draw conclusions. After examining your data, what conclusions can you draw?

Step 1

Step 4

Investigate Further

Predict what variables affect the force needed to lift the car. With a partner, plan and conduct a simple investigation to test your ideas.

SC.C.2.2.1.4.1 simple machines
SC.H.1.2.3.4.1 working collaboratively
225

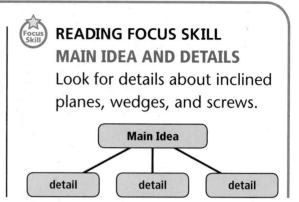
VOCABULARY
inclined plane, p. 226
screw, p. 228
wedge, p. 230

SCIENCE CONCEPTS
► how an inclined plane, a wedge, and a screw change the way work is done

⭐ **READING FOCUS SKILL**
MAIN IDEA AND DETAILS
Look for details about inclined planes, wedges, and screws.

```
            ┌──────────┐
            │ Main Idea │
            └──────────┘
           /      |      \
    ┌────────┐ ┌────────┐ ┌────────┐
    │ detail │ │ detail │ │ detail │
    └────────┘ └────────┘ └────────┘
```

Inclined Planes

An inclined plane may be the simplest simple machine of all. An **inclined plane** is simply a slanted surface. How can a surface be a machine? It changes the way work is done. An inclined plane changes the amount of force needed, and it changes the direction of the force.

Look at the sloping shore in the picture on this page. This sloping shore is an inclined plane.

Suppose that raising the boat out of the water involves lifting it up 2 meters (7 ft). You'd need a crane to lift the boat 2 meters straight up. It's much easier to use a truck to pull the boat up the slope.

There's something else, too. A truck's engine might not be able to lift the boat straight up. But with the slope, it doesn't have to. To lift the boat 2 meters (7 ft), the truck might actually move forward 15 meters (49 ft). But the truck will use a lot less force to move the boat.

There are two ways that the sloping shore changes how the work is done in lifting the boat.

1 The truck moves forward to move the boat up.

2 The truck moves 15 meters (49 ft) to lift the boat 2 meters (7 ft), and it uses less force.

An inclined plane enables you to lift an object by using less force. But you must move that object a greater distance.

The pictures on this page show other examples of inclined planes. It may seem odd to think of something in nature as being a simple machine, but a hill is an inclined plane. Remember, an inclined plane is simply a slanted surface.

Imagine that the bikers in the two pictures are riding to the top of the same hill. The biker in the red shirt is on a steep path. He has to pedal hard to reach the top. Even so, taking the path is easier than lifting the bike straight up would be.

The biker in the striped shirt is on a path that is less steep. He doesn't have to pedal as hard to reach the top. But because the path is less steep, it's longer. He has to pedal a greater distance to reach the top of the hill.

 MAIN IDEA AND DETAILS How does an inclined plane change the way work is done?

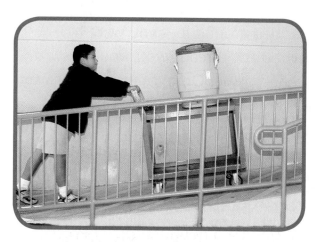

▲ How would the work of pushing the cart be different if the ramp were steeper?

▲ The road is less steep than the rocky hill. It's easier to pedal along the road. But you have to travel farther to reach the hilltop.

Screws

You've read that using an inclined plane enables you to use less force to move something, even though you must apply the force over a greater distance. A screw is another type of simple machine. It does exactly the same thing.

A **screw** is a post with threads wrapped around it. If you were to unwrap the threads, you would have an inclined plane. Or, to put it another way, the threads are an inclined plane that curls around a post.

Look at the neck of the bottle. Imagine an ant climbing from the bottom of the neck to the opening. It can climb straight up. Or it can walk along the threads. It will use less force if it follows the threads, but it will walk farther.

 MAIN IDEA AND DETAILS What is a screw?

There are two screws here. The threads on the neck of the bottle slide along the threads on the inside of the cap. ▼

An Inclined Plane and a Screw

Moving something up an inclined plane requires less force over a greater distance than moving it straight up.

A screw is just an inclined plane wrapped around a post. When something moves along the threads of a screw, it is actually moving along an inclined plane.

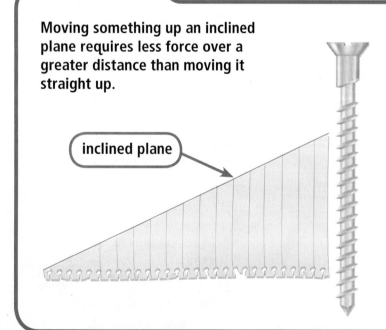

inclined plane

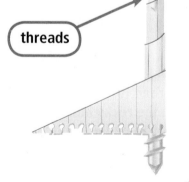

threads

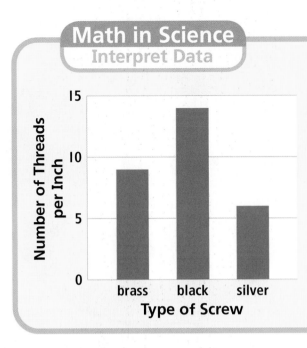

The graph describes the three kinds of screws in Beth's workshop. You know that the threads of a screw form an inclined plane. Which kind of screw has the steepest threads? Explain.

◄ A drill bit is a kind of screw. The sharp tip cuts into the wood. The groove is a screw. It lifts the wood out.

A nut and a bolt both have screw threads, like a cap and a bottle. The threads inside the nut slide along the threads on the bolt. ▶

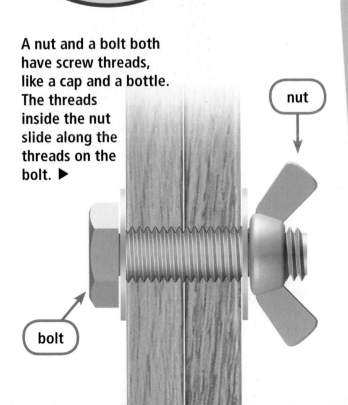

nut

bolt

Insta-Lab

WEDGE

Spreading Spines

Work with a partner. One person should press two books tightly together. The other person should insert the narrow edge of a wedge-shaped building block or doorstop between the books. That person should then press gently toward the books. What happens to the books? Change roles and do this again.

229

Wedges

Another simple machine related to the inclined plane is the wedge. A **wedge** is two inclined planes placed back to back.

An inclined plane and a wedge both change the direction of a force. If you want to raise a heavy object, you can slide it along the slanted part of an inclined plane.

Imagine using a wedge to split wood. You stick the narrow edge into the wood. Then you use a big hammer to apply a downward force. The wedge makes that force greater. The pieces of wood are pushed apart by the slanted parts of the wedge.

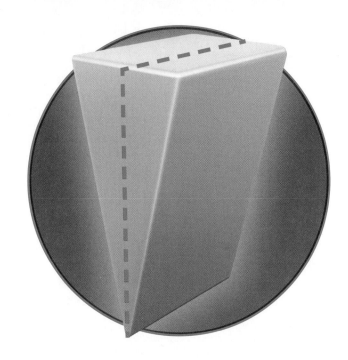

▲ A wedge is really just two inclined planes back to back.

MAIN IDEA AND DETAILS How is a wedge like an inclined plane?

Like many blades, the blade of this tile cutter is a wedge.

▲ This cleaver is a wedge. The cook moves the cleaver down, and the slices of onion move sideways, away from each other.

1. MAIN IDEA AND DETAILS Draw and complete this graphic organizer. Define each machine and give two examples.

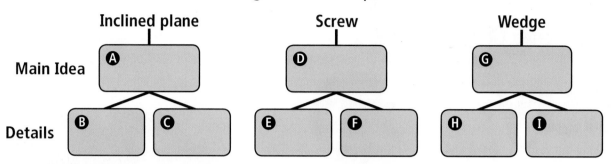

Inclined plane   Screw   Wedge

Main Idea   **A**   **D**   **G**

Details   **B**   **C**   **E**   **F**   **H**   **I**

2. SUMMARIZE Write a summary of this lesson by using each lesson vocabulary term in a sentence.

3. DRAW CONCLUSIONS How does the screw on a bottle cap change the direction of a force?

4. VOCABULARY Make a flash card for each lesson vocabulary term. Include a definition and a labeled diagram on each flash card.

FCAT Prep

5. Read/Inquire/Explain One screw has many threads close together. Another screw has few threads, and they're spread out. Which screw is like a steep inclined plane? Explain.

6. Which kind of simple machine is an ax?

   A. inclined plane   **C.** wedge

   B. screw   **D.** ramp

Links

Writing

Expository Writing

An inclined plane is like a screw and like a wedge, but it is also different from them. Write a **paragraph** comparing and contrasting an inclined plane and a screw. Then write a **paragraph** comparing and contrasting an inclined plane and a wedge.

Math

Classify Geometric Figures

Draw separate diagrams for an inclined plane, a screw, and a wedge. Label geometric figures on each diagram.

Health

Surgical Simple Machines

Research screws that are used in surgery. Write a paragraph telling what you find out.

For more links and activities, go to www.hspscience.com

Gadget Guy

Inventor Dean Kamen is on a roll. Kamen invented a super-scooter called the Segway Human Transporter.

Now Kamen has another invention. It's a wheelchair that allows disabled or injured people to get around more easily. Called the iBOT, it is unlike most wheelchairs in that it has two pairs of back wheels that can turn on top of each other. The design allows the iBOT to safely climb steps.

The Segway relies on sensors to control speed. If a rider leans forward, the Segway goes forward. If a rider leans back, it stops. The Segway uses *gyroscopes* to balance. A gyroscope is a wheel that spins inside a frame, causing the frame to balance in position.

Spin axis

The seat of the iBOT can even be raised, so that the person using the wheelchair can see eye to eye with others. "The iBOT allows people who cannot walk to basically do all the ordinary things you take for granted—things they can't do even with a [regular] wheelchair," said Kamen.

Sensor Science

Kamen's most famous invention is probably the Segway Human Transporter. After keeping it secret for years, Kamen unveiled the battery-powered Segway to intense public attention. It is now used by some police departments and mail carriers.

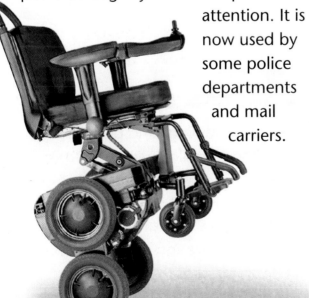

Kids First

Kamen has been inventing since he was a child. Today, he shares his excitement about science and inventions with kids around the country. "The most important thing we can invent is inventors," said Kamen.

Kamen's favorite invention is the FIRST program. Kamen created the program in 1990 to show kids that science and engineering can be fun. Every year, FIRST runs a *robotics* competition. Robotics is the use of computers to guide robots that perform tasks. Teams of middle-school students build robots from plastic blocks and race them against other teams.

THINK ABOUT IT

1. What are some other ways people who use wheelchairs might be helped to move about more easily?

2. If you could build a robot, what tasks would you want it to perform? Why?

Find out more! Log on to
www.hspscience.com

SC.H.3.2.4.4.1 solving problems/
new ideas

233

SCIENCE Spin™ from WEEKLY READER®

People

SC.H.1.2.5.4.1 using models
SC.H.3.2.4.4.1 solving problems/new ideas

Flying High

Recently, Judy Leden strapped a pair of wings on her back. The 30-foot-wide wings carried Leden about 35 feet into the air. Her flight lasted for 17 seconds.

Between 1490 and 1505, artist Leonardo Da Vinci made several drawings of a glider. The wings that Leden used were based on Da Vinci's glider. No one knew whether the glider would actually fly. Leden flew Da Vinci's glider a total of 20 times.

Career   Drafter

Drafters make drawings and plans. These plans are used to build everything from toys to buildings to spacecraft. A drafter's tools include pencils, paper, calculators, and computers.

Quick and Easy Project

Book Balance

Materials
- meterstick
- book
- tape

Procedure

1. Tape the book to one end of the meterstick. Keep it balanced so it doesn't fall off.
2. Brace the other end of the meterstick so that it does not slip.
3. Slide one finger of your other hand under the meterstick. Lift the book.
4. Repeat Step 3 with your finger in different places on the meterstick.

Draw Conclusions

How does the position of your finger affect your lifting the book?

Design Your Own Investigation

Many Pulleys

How exactly do pulley systems work? Must a pulley stay in one place, or can it move along with the object that's being lifted? How many pulleys can you use at the same time? Design an investigation that will help you find out more about pulley systems. Then gather the materials you need, and carry out your investigation.

Vocabulary Review

Use the terms below to complete the sentences. The page numbers tell you where to look in the chapter if you need help.

work p. 210   **simple machine** p. 211
lever p. 212   **fulcrum** p. 212
pulley p. 218   **inclined plane** p. 226
screw p. 228   **wedge** p. 230

1. A paper cutter is made up of a wedge and another _____.

2. A hill is an example of an _____.

3. A bar that pivots on a fulcrum is a _____.

4. Two inclined planes that are back to back form a _____.

5. A wheel with a rope or chain around it is a _____.

6. A post with threads wrapped around it is a _____.

7. The point where a lever pivots is the _____.

8. Using force to move an object over a distance is _____.

Check Understanding

Write the letter of the best choice.

9. Which of the following is an example of work, to a scientist?
   A. solving a mental math problem
   B. carrying a book across the room
   C. pushing against the floor
   D. lifting a chair off the floor

10. Where can the fulcrum of a lever **not** be?
    F. the end of the bar
    G. the middle of the bar
    H. between the middle and the end
    I. not touching the bar

11. How is the screwdriver being used in this picture?

    A. as a lever
    B. as a screw
    C. as a pulley
    D. as a wheel-and-axle

12. **MAIN IDEA AND DETAILS** An inclined plane is a part of which other simple machine?

   F. lever   **H.** screw

   G. pulley   **I.** wheel-and-axle

13. Which of the following does **not** change the direction of a force?

   A. inclined plane

   B. pulley

   C. wedge

   D. wheel-and-axle

14. **MAIN IDEA AND DETAILS** Which detail about an ax lets you know that it is a wedge?

   F. It has just one inclined plane.

   G. It changes the way work is done.

   H. It has two inclined planes.

   I. It changes the direction of the force applied.

15. Which simple machine could you use to hold two objects together?

   A. lever

   B. pulley

   C. screw

   D. wheel-and-axle

16. Which kind of simple machine is the wheelchair resting on?

   F. inclined plane

   G. lever

   H. pulley

   I. screw

Inquiry Skills

17. Think about a spiral staircase. Which simple machine can you **compare** it to? Explain.

18. This table shows the force needed to lift a heavy box 1 meter by using four different methods. What conclusions can you draw about the distance the box traveled by **interpreting the data**?

Method Used	Force Needed
Lever	200 newtons
Inclined plane	300 newtons
Pulley	500 newtons
Lifting straight up	500 newtons

Read/Inquire/Explain

19. Tamyra and Marv are loading boxes onto identical trucks. Tamyra slides the boxes up a ramp that is 1 meter long. Marv uses a ramp that is 2 meters long. Who uses more force? Explain.

20. You have to put a 20-kilogram box on a shelf. You can lift it 1 meter, or you can push it up a ramp. The ramp is 2 meters long. If you use the ramp, you'll feel as if you're moving 10 kilograms.

   Part A Which method for putting the box on the shelf would you choose? Why?

   Part B Which method might make you feel more tired? Explain.

Processes That Shape the Earth

EARTH SCIENCE

 The chapters in this unit address these Grade Level Expectations from the Florida Sunshine State Standards.

Chapter 7
The Rock Cycle

SC.D.1.2.1.4.1   understands the stages of the rock cycle.
SC.D.1.2.1.4.2   knows the properties of different types of soil.
SC.D.1.2.4.4.1   understands how processes of weathering and erosion constantly change the surface of the Earth.

Chapter 8
The Water Cycle

SC.D.1.2.3.4.1   understands how the water cycle is influenced by temperatures and land features.

Chapter 9
Conserving Resources

SC.D.2.2.1.4.1   knows ways in which people can conserve natural resources.
SC.D.2.2.1.4.2   knows ways misuse of natural resources affects the quality of life for all species.

The investigations and experiences in this unit also address many of the Grade Level Expectations in Strand H, The Nature of Science.

Science in Florida

Deltona

The Sunshine State

USA

Dear Carli,

I can't believe what I saw today. We were in the car and noticed a lot of black smoke out the window. On the radio, we heard that there was a large wildfire that started when lightning struck a tree. As we were driving, we saw some charred trees where the fire had already passed through. All of the leaves in the forest were gone and black tree trunks were all that was left. I took some pictures to show you.

Can't wait to get home,

Gabrielle

FCAT Writing

Writing Situation
Think about the good and bad ways that fire affects our lives. Explain how fire can be both beneficial and harmful.

Experiment!

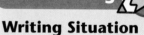

A forest fire is only one thing that changes Earth. The weather changes from day to day and from season to season. Rain can help fight a forest fire. A drought can make forest fires more likely. Can you use the clouds to predict the weather? Is there a pattern of changes that goes with certain clouds? Plan and conduct an experiment to find out.

239

Chapter 7

The Rock Cycle

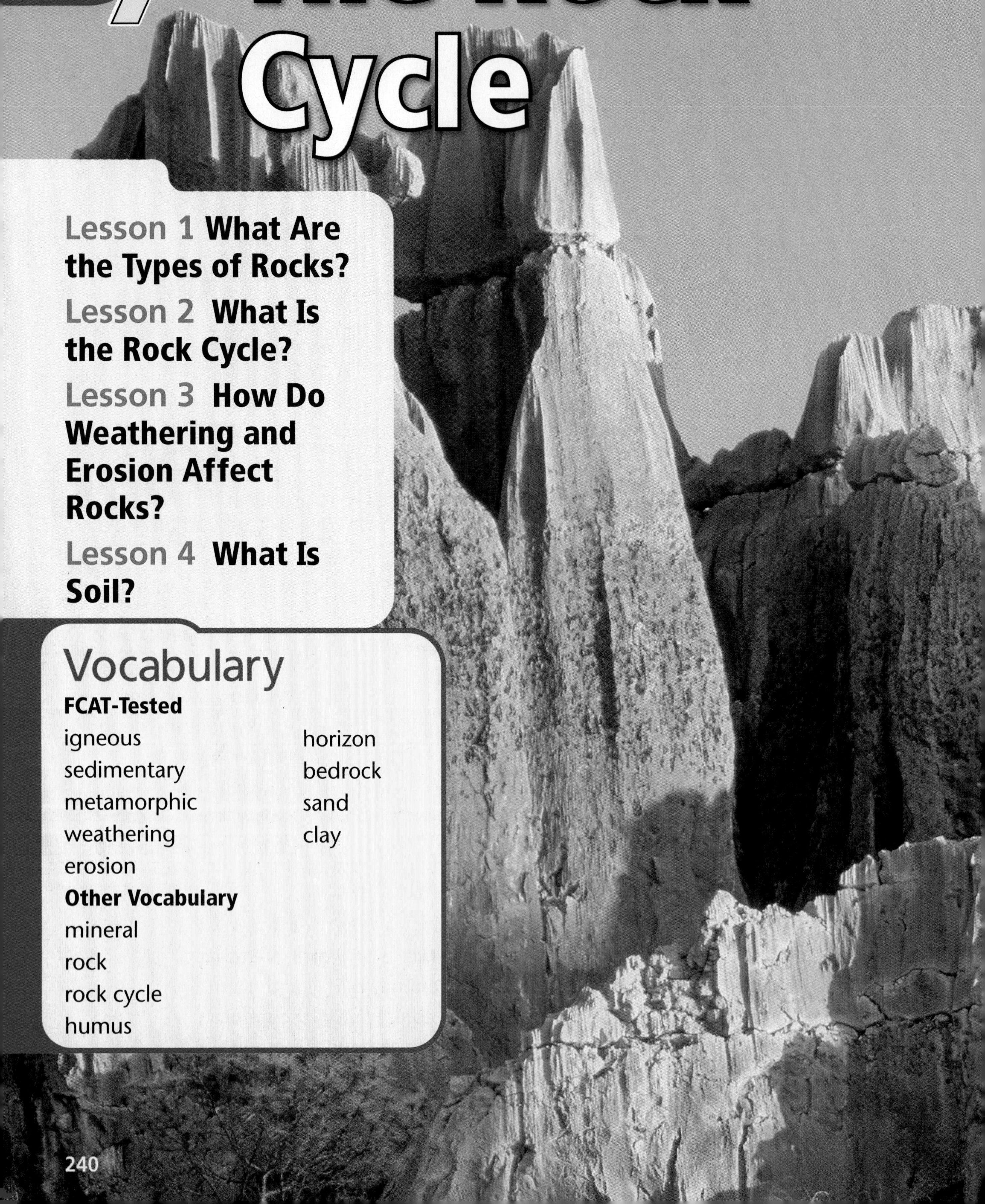

Vocabulary

FCAT-Tested

igneous
sedimentary
metamorphic
weathering
erosion
horizon
bedrock
sand
clay

Other Vocabulary

mineral
rock
rock cycle
humus

What do YOU wonder?

Rocky Forest These formations are part of the Stone Forest near Kunming, China. How do you think such landscapes might form?

What Are the Types of Rocks?

Fast Fact

Tiny Particles Sandstone is made of tiny grains of sand. You would need to line up more than 315 grains to reach 2 centimeters (0.8 in.). The picture shows layers of sandstone rock. In the Investigate, you'll look at one way rocks can form.

Making Sedimentary Rock

Materials
- 2 small plastic cups
- sand
- measuring cup
- white glue
- water
- plastic stirrer for mixing
- pushpin
- ring stand
- hand lens
- aluminum pan
- scissors

Procedure

1. Use the pushpin to make a small hole in the bottom of one cup. The hole should be big enough to let water out but not sand.

2. Place 60 mL water and 60 mL white glue in the other cup. Mix and set aside.

3. Fill the first cup with sand.

4. Using a ring stand, suspend the cup holding sand over the pan.

5. Pour the glue mixture into the sand. Let the liquid drain into the pan. Let the glue dry. This could take two or three days.

6. When the liquid stops draining, remove the cup with the sand in it. Cut away the plastic cup with the scissors.

Draw Conclusions

1. Observe and describe the structure that has formed in the cup. Use a hand lens.

2. Inquiry Skills Scientists often use models to study real-world processes. Compare the way you made your rock with the way you think an actual rock would form. Check your answer when you finish the lesson.

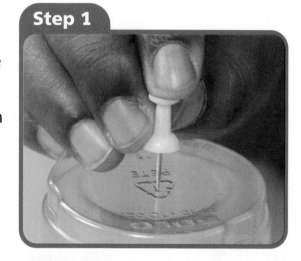

Step 1

Step 4

Investigate Further

Make a sandstone rock with several layers. Plan the investigation so you can easily observe each layer in the rock.

VOCABULARY

mineral p. 244
rock p. 244
igneous p. 246
sedimentary p. 247
metamorphic p. 248

SCIENCE CONCEPTS

▶ what minerals are
▶ what the three types of rocks are

READING FOCUS SKILL

MAIN IDEA AND DETAILS

Look for details about the three types of rock.

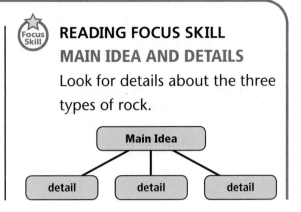

Minerals

Do you remember the last time you picked up a pebble? Maybe it had sparkling specks or wavy lines. Maybe it was as clear as glass.

Minerals formed the colors and patterns in the pebble. A **mineral** (MIN•er•uhl) is a solid, nonliving substance that occurs naturally in rocks or in the ground. Every mineral has unique properties. Earth's surface is **rock**, a solid substance made of minerals. Rock can be made of many minerals or of one mineral with different-sized grains. Look at the granite. Each of its colors is a different mineral.

There are more than 4000 minerals. Many of them look alike. Scientists use the minerals' physical properties to tell them apart. For example, scientists can compare the hardness of two minerals by how easily they can be scratched. Gypsum and calcite can look alike, but gypsum is easier to scratch than calcite.

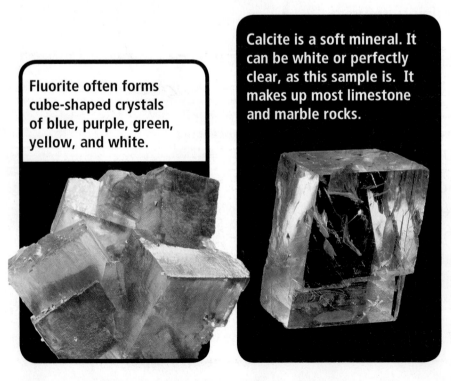

Fluorite often forms cube-shaped crystals of blue, purple, green, yellow, and white.

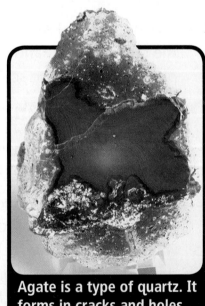

Calcite is a soft mineral. It can be white or perfectly clear, as this sample is. It makes up most limestone and marble rocks.

Agate is a type of quartz. It forms in cracks and holes in other rocks. The colored bands take the shape of the hole in which it formed.

▼ Silvery galena is a common mineral from which we get lead.

These two minerals are types of mica. The darker one is biotite. The yellowish one is muscovite.

▼ Copper is produced from the mineral chalcopyrite (kal•koh•PY•ryt).

▲ Hornblende is one of a group of hard green, black, and brown minerals.

The way a mineral reflects light is its *luster.* Two minerals may be the same color, but one may have a shiny luster and the other a dull luster.

When you rub a mineral across a surface, the mineral leaves a *streak* of powder. This colored streak can help scientists identify two minerals that look alike.

Minerals have other properties, too. Is the mineral magnetic? What shape are its crystals?

Two minerals might look alike and share some properties, but they don't share all properties. Gold and pyrite are both shiny and gold in color. Pyrite is sometimes called "fool's gold," because people have mistaken it for gold. Gold is much softer than pyrite. Gold leaves a golden streak. Pyrite's streak is greenish black.

MAIN IDEA AND DETAILS What properties can scientists use to identify minerals?

Igneous Rocks

Scientists classify rocks into three groups, based on how they form. One group is **igneous** (IG•nee•uhs) rocks. Igneous rocks form when melted rock cools and hardens.

The idea of melted rock might seem strange. Deep inside Earth, it is so hot that some rock is liquid, like syrup. This melted rock is *magma.* Inside Earth's crust, magma cools slowly. Volcanic eruptions release magma. Magma on Earth's surface is *lava.* Lava cools quickly.

 MAIN IDEA AND DETAILS How does igneous rock form?

Sometimes two igneous rocks form from the same magma, so they have the same chemical makeup. How they look depends on how deep in Earth they form. On Earth's surface lava cools quickly and grains don't have time to grow big. Inside Earth's surface magma cools slowly, giving grains time to grow big.

▼ **Basalt**

▼ **Rhyolite**

Gabbro ▶

◀ **Diorite**

Granite ▶

▼ Conglomerate forms from very large sediments. Notice the grains have rounded edges.

Shale is Earth's most common sedimentary rock. It forms from very fine sediments of silt and clay.

▼ Sandstone rock forms from sand-sized sediment.

▲ Scientists group sedimentary rocks by how they form and the size of the sediment grains that form them. This picture shows grains of sand, silt, and clay.

Sedimentary Rocks

Another type of rock is very common on Earth's surface. **Sedimentary** (sed•uh•MEN•ter•ee) rock forms from sediment. *Sediment* is pieces of rock that have been broken down and moved. Water, wind, and ice break down rock and then carry the sediment. When the wind or water slows down, the sediment falls to the surface. It piles up in layers. The layers get pressed together. Water, carrying minerals, moves through the sediment. Over time, the minerals cause the sediment to stick together. This is what you modeled in the Investigate.

MAIN IDEA AND DETAILS How does sedimentary rock form?

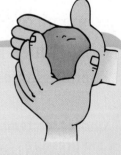

Insta-Lab

Making Layered Rock

Use small round pieces of clay to make a model of a sedimentary rock. How are these layers like the layers of real sedimentary rocks? How are they different?

Metamorphic Rocks

Another group of rock is metamorphic (met•uh•MAWR•fik) rock. **Metamorphic** rock is rock that has changed from another type of rock. High temperature and pressure form this type of rock.

Mountain building often causes metamorphic rock to form. Mountains form when plates that make up Earth's surface push together. Rock near the surface can get pushed down. Pressure on the rock squeezes it. Mineral grains in the rock get pressed more tightly together. If pressure is great enough, minerals in the rock change.

As natural forces push the rock deeper into Earth's crust, the temperature around it rises. High temperatures can change the minerals in rock. But the rock must not melt if it is to become metamorphic rock. If the rock melts, it becomes magma and eventually igneous rock.

Metamorphic rock can form from any type of rock. This includes other metamorphic rock.

 MAIN IDEA AND DETAILS What two processes form metamorphic rock?

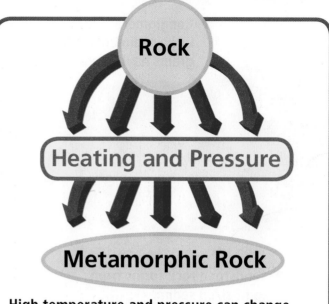

High temperature and pressure can change one type of rock into metamorphic rock.

Metamorphic slate forms from shale or mudstone.

Gneiss (NYS) is a metamorphic rock that forms from schist or granite.

Under high temperature and pressure, sedimentary limestone becomes metamorphic marble.

The grains in the rock show the effect of pressure on this metaconglomerate rock.

1. MAIN IDEA AND DETAILS Fill in the graphic organizer below.

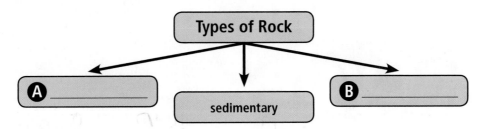

Types of Rock

 A _____

sedimentary

 B _____

2. SUMMARIZE Write two sentences that summarize this lesson.

3. DRAW CONCLUSIONS Igneous rocks are the most common type of rocks in Earth's crust. Why do you think this is so?

4. VOCABULARY In your own words, write definitions of the three types of rock.

FCAT Prep

5. Read/Inquire/Explain You find a mineral that is shiny and a golden color. How can you tell if it is gold?

6. Under which of these conditions would igneous rock form?
  A. water breaks down rock
  B. pressure builds
  C. magma cools
  D. sediment collects

Links

Writing

Expository Writing
Choose a type of mineral or rock. Write a **description** of how it forms, where it is found, and what it is used for.

Math

Make a Circle Graph
About 75 percent of rock on Earth's surface is sedimentary. Together, what percent are the other two types? Draw a circle graph to show the relationship.

Art

Rock Art
Draw a picture of the type of rock or mineral you wrote about in your description. Include details that would help someone else identify it.

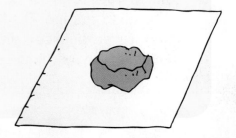

 For more links and activities, go to www.hspscience.com

What Is the Rock Cycle?

Hot Rock Basalt rock doesn't melt easily. It can stay solid at 1000°C (1832°F). This basalt lava flowed from a Hawaiian volcano. The Hawaiians call this pāhoehoe (pah•HOH•ee•hoh•ee) lava. In the Investigate, you'll model how rocks change over time.

Model a Rock Cycle

Materials
- small plastic pencil sharpener
- crayons of three colors
- metal cookie sheet
- wax paper
- iron
- aluminum pie pan
- toaster oven

Procedure

1. Use the sharpener to make three piles of crayon shavings, each a different color.

2. Place the crayon shavings in three layers, on a cookie sheet. Press down the layers with your hand.

3. Place wax paper over the shavings. Your teacher will press down on the shavings lightly with a warm iron. The teacher will leave the iron for a few seconds, until the shavings soften. They should not melt completely. Let the shavings cool for a few minutes.

4. Place the block of shavings into the pie pan. **CAUTION: Your teacher will put the pan in the toaster oven. Let the shavings melt. Your teacher will remove the shavings and let them cool.**

Step 2

Step 3

Draw Conclusions

1. What type of rock does Step 2 represent? What type of rock does Step 3 represent? How about Step 4?

2. **Inquiry Skill** How would you plan and conduct a simple investigation that uses the "rock" from Step 4 to model how sedimentary rock forms?

Investigate Further

Design a similar investigation that models the same cycle but with the events in a different sequence.

Reading in Science

 SC.D.1.2.1.4.1 the rock cycle,
LA.A.2.2.1 sequence

VOCABULARY
rock cycle p. 252

SCIENCE CONCEPTS
▶ what the rock cycle is
▶ what processes take place during the rock cycle

READING FOCUS SKILL
SEQUENCE Look for the steps of the rock cycle.

The Rock Cycle

Earth's surface is always changing. Forces inside Earth push mountains upward. Rain and wind wear down the rocks in those mountains. Rivers, winds, and oceans carry sediment. They deposit it in different places. New layers of rock form. Volcanoes erupt lava onto Earth's surface. Lava cools and hardens into rock. This rock wears away, too.

Often you can't see these changes. Many of them take thousands of years. They can even take millions of years. All of these changes are part of the rock cycle. The **rock cycle** is the sequence of processes that change rocks over long periods. In the rock cycle, the materials in rocks change again and again.

The rock cycle can follow many paths. There is a close-up look at one of them later in the lesson.

 SEQUENCE Is there a first and last step in the rock cycle?

The Rock Cycle

During the rock cycle, each type of rock can be changed into any of the others. Notice that there is more than one path to each type of rock.

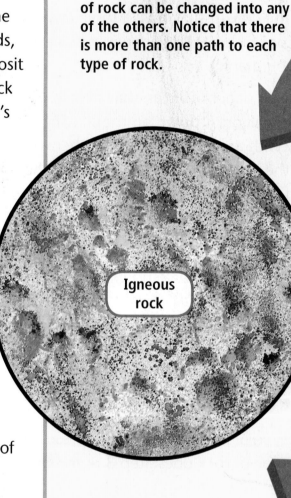

Igneous rock

■ = Melting and cooling
■ = Being broken down and carried by water, wind, and ice
■ = Pressure and heat

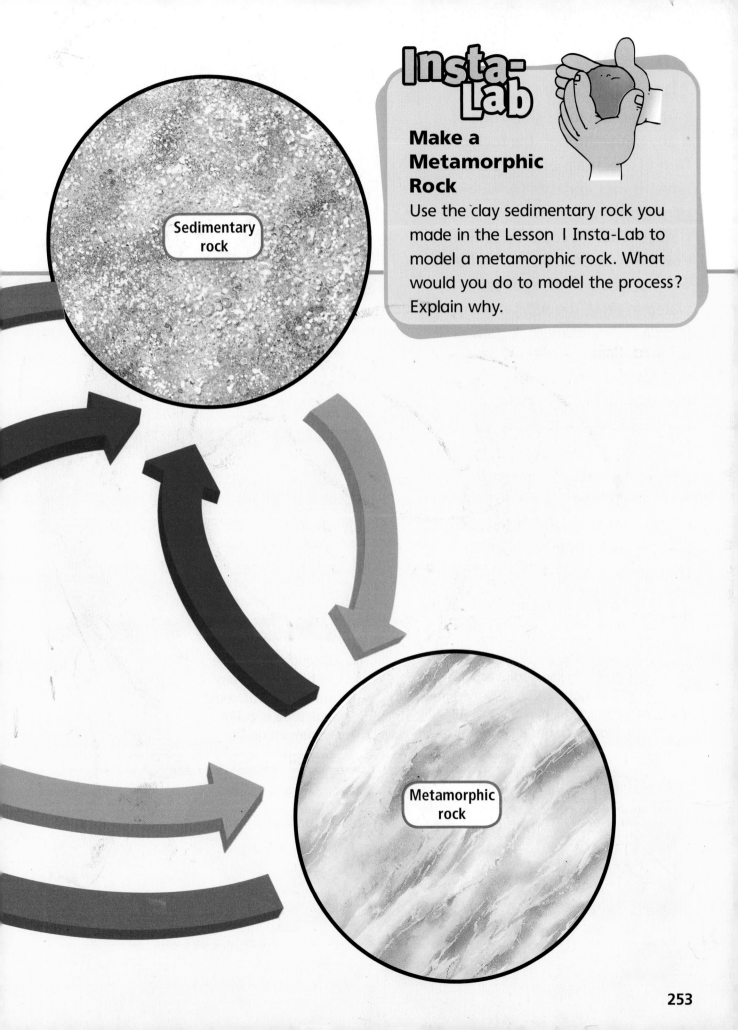

Sedimentary rock

Metamorphic rock

Insta-Lab

Make a Metamorphic Rock

Use the clay sedimentary rock you made in the Lesson 1 Insta-Lab to model a metamorphic rock. What would you do to model the process? Explain why.

One Path Through the Rock Cycle

These three rocks show one of many paths through the rock cycle. During mountain building, the igneous rock andesite (AN•duh•zyt) might be pushed upward to Earth's surface. There it could be broken down into smaller pieces, and this sediment could be deposited in water. In time, the sediment might form a sedimentary rock such as sandstone. This sandstone may get pushed deep into Earth's crust. With high temperature and pressure, the sandstone may become quartzite (KWAWRT•syt). Suppose even higher temperature acts on quartzite. The rock would melt, and eventually it would cool. It could harden as an igneous rock. Then the rock cycle continues.

 SEQUENCE What new type of rock can form after quartzite melts?

▲ Andesite is a common rock that forms from volcanic lava.

▲ Although sandstone can be made of any small sediment, most sandstone is made of rounded quartz sediment.

▼ The grains in sandstone are pressed together tightly. The new metamorphic rock, quartzite, is much harder than sandstone and has different properties.

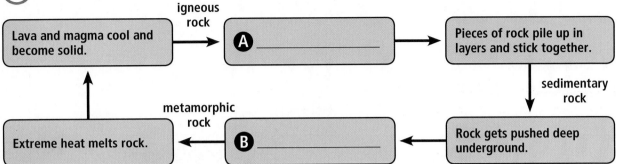

1. SEQUENCE Copy and add processes to complete the graphic organizer.

Lava and magma cool and become solid.

igneous rock →

A _____

→ Pieces of rock pile up in layers and stick together.

↓ *sedimentary rock*

Rock gets pushed deep underground.

← **B** _____

metamorphic rock

← Extreme heat melts rock.

↑

2. SUMMARIZE Write a paragraph that summarizes this lesson. Begin with the sentence *The rock cycle works slowly and never stops.*

3. DRAW CONCLUSIONS How might igneous rock become metamorphic?

4. VOCABULARY Define the term *rock cycle* in your own words without using the word *cycle*.

FCAT Prep

5. Read/Inquire/Explain Identify a part of the rock cycle that you might see.

6. Which of these isn't produced by the rock cycle?

A. lava   **C.** sediment

B. minerals   **D.** fungi

Links

Writing

Expository Writing

Choose one path through the rock cycle. Write a step-by-step **explanation** of the way one rock changes into another. Don't choose the path explained on the opposite page.

Math

Solve Problems

A layer of sedimentary rock is 5 meters thick. The layer was deposited at a rate of 1 centimeter per year. How many years did it take to form?

Language Arts

Word Origins

Research the origins of the words *igneous, sedimentary,* and *metamorphic.* Write a short explanation about each one.

For more links and activities, go to www.hspscience.com

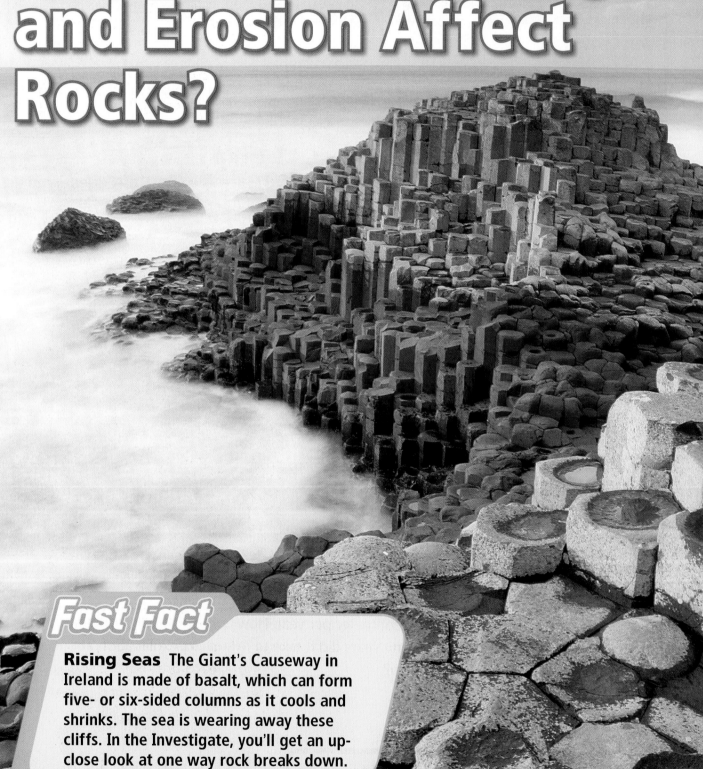

How Do Weathering and Erosion Affect Rocks?

Fast Fact

Rising Seas The Giant's Causeway in Ireland is made of basalt, which can form five- or six-sided columns as it cools and shrinks. The sea is wearing away these cliffs. In the Investigate, you'll get an up-close look at one way rock breaks down.

Shake Things Up

Materials
- **6 medium-sized rocks**
- **2 pieces of chalk**
- **empty clear plastic juice container with lid (2 qts)**

Procedure

1. Make a model of the way rocks break down in nature. Add two pieces of chalk to the container.

2. Place six rocks in the container.

3. Put the lid on the container.

4. Shake the container so that the rocks and chalk rub against each other. Do this for several minutes. You can take turns with your lab partner.

Draw Conclusions

1. Compare the way the rocks and chalk looked at the start and at the end of the investigation.

2. **Inquiry Skill** Scientists often infer the reasons for an investigation's results. Why do you think some of the materials in the cup broke down faster than other materials? How do you think this relates to rocks in nature?

Step 2

Step 4

Investigate Further

First, weigh the chalk that is left after the investigation. Then, add water to the container and repeat the test. Compare the mass of the chalk before and after the water. What conclusion can you draw?

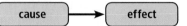

VOCABULARY
weathering p. 258
erosion p. 262

SCIENCE CONCEPTS
▶ how weathering affects rock
▶ how erosion affects rock

READING FOCUS SKILL

CAUSE AND EFFECT
Look for the causes of weathering.

cause → effect

Weathering

Have you ever seen a weed growing through a crack in a sidewalk? Maybe you've seen a statue with its features worn away. These are examples of weathering. **Weathering** is the breaking down of rock on Earth's surface into smaller pieces. Weathering helps shape landforms. It also helps make soil.

There are two types of weathering. One type of weathering physically breaks rock into smaller pieces.

The other type of weathering is different. It changes the chemical makeup of rock. This softens and weakens the rock, helping water wear it away. Water causes most weathering. It can break down some rock by itself. For example, water can wear away rock salt, calcite, and limestone.

Sinkholes are the result of weathering. They form when water slowly dissolves underground rock.

▼ Water can help wear away bits of surface rock.

A chemical change has turned the surface of this rock brown. Iron oxide, or rust, breaks down the outer layer of some kinds of rock.

Some rocks break down when oxygen combines with minerals in them. This often happens in rocks that have iron. When iron mixes with oxygen, iron oxide, or rust, forms. Rust makes it easier for other processes to weather the rock.

 **CAUSE AND EFFECT** What is the effect of weathering?

Science Up Close

Formation of a Sinkhole

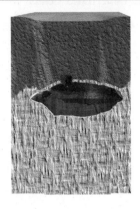

1 Rain soaks into the ground. The rainwater eats away limestone rock under the surface. Water carries away the dissolved rock. A small opening forms.

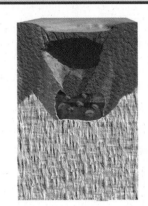

2 The opening in the rock becomes larger as time passes.

3 Rock and soil that covered the underground opening cave in. A sinkhole forms on the surface. Do you think this process happens quickly or slowly? Explain.

This 15-story-deep sinkhole formed in Florida in 1994. It formed in an area where large amounts of minerals were taken out of the ground.

For more links and activities, go to **www.hspscience.com**

Weathering by Other Processes

The other type of weathering doesn't change the rock chemically. It breaks rock down through physical processes. Water, ice, living things, and wind are causes of this type of weathering.

You see the results of this weathering around you each day. It can cause cracks in sidewalks and potholes in streets. Rain enters cracks in rock and cement. If the water freezes into ice, it expands. The ice cracks and breaks rock around it. Stones in streams are also a sign of weathering. These stones were broken from larger pieces of rock. As they tumble against each other, they break down even more.

Large ocean waves weather coastlines. Waves smash into the bottom of a cliff. The rock that the waves hit cracks and breaks. In time, rock at the top of the cliff falls into the sea.

Even temperature changes can weather rock. Rock expands when it heats up. It contracts when it cools. Repeated heating and cooling can

Pounding waves force air into cracks. This helps split the rock. Water also carries sediment. This scrapes rock like sandpaper.

▼ Waves hit cliffs like this with great force. Thousands of tons of water smash into coastal rocks during storms.

▲ Running water carries sediment. The sediment scrapes against itself and against rocks in the streambed as the water moves.

Scraping and bumping against each other in a moving stream gives these rocks rounded edges.

weaken some rock. The rock can then crack or break.

Living things can cause weathering. You have probably seen plants grow through cracks in rocks. The roots wedge into the rocks, splitting the rock around them as they grow. Animals can cause weathering, too. When animals dig in soil, they move rocks closer to Earth's surface. Then rainwater can reach them more easily.

Wind also causes weathering. Wind picks up bits of rock and soil and throws them against other rocks. This chips away the rocks' surface bit by bit.

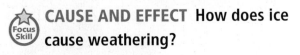

Insta-Lab

Observe Weathering

Use a large rock or brick to press down on a handful of rock salt. What happens to the rock salt? What kind of weathering does this model?

CAUSE AND EFFECT How does ice cause weathering?

(Focus Skill)

Erosion

What happens after weathering breaks down rock into sediment? Erosion takes over. **Erosion** is the process of moving sediment.

Water can cause erosion. Rivers carry sediment downstream. They drop it on their banks or at their mouths. Ocean waves pick up sediment and leave it on the shore as sand.

Wind erosion is most common in deserts. With few plants to hold sediment in place, wind picks it up easily. Wind stacks sand into huge mounds called sand dunes.

Glaciers are important causes of erosion. As these giant sheets of ice move, they scrape the ground. They pick up rocks and soil. During the last Ice Age, huge glaciers covered large parts of what is now the northern United States. They eroded and helped shape the plains and other landforms we see today. As glaciers moved over land, they also formed lakes. When the glaciers melted, they left behind huge ridges of sediment and large amounts of water.

 CAUSE AND EFFECT What are the main causes of erosion?

Math in Science
Interpret Data

What is the largest type of sediment? What is the smallest? Which would erosion affect more, boulders and cobbles or silt and clay? Why is that?

SEDIMENT COMES IN ALL SIZES		
256 mm and up	BOULDERS	
64-256 mm	COBBLES	GRAVEL
2-64 mm	PEBBLES	
0.0625-2 mm	SAND	
0.002-0.0625 mm	SILT	
0.002 mm and under	CLAY	

This photo shows one river flowing into another. Soil washes into rivers from areas along its banks. One of these rivers is carrying much more sediment than the other. The sediment has turned parts of the water brown.

Water that washes over areas of bare soil can create gullies. Planting vegetation can help prevent this type of soil erosion.

Focus Skill

1. CAUSE AND EFFECT Copy and complete the graphic organizer below.

CAUSE　　　　　　　　　　　　**EFFECT**

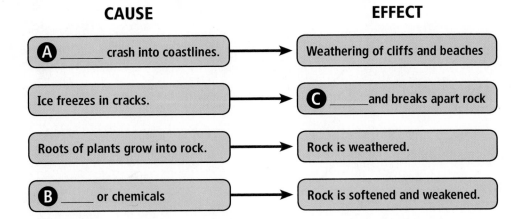

A _____ crash into coastlines. → Weathering of cliffs and beaches

Ice freezes in cracks. → **C** _____ and breaks apart rock

Roots of plants grow into rock. → Rock is weathered.

B _____ or chemicals → Rock is softened and weakened.

2. SUMMARIZE Summarize the lesson section on physical weathering.

3. DRAW CONCLUSIONS The Colorado River flows through the bottom of the Grand Canyon. Does the river cause weathering or erosion? Explain.

4. VOCABULARY Make a crossword puzzle using the vocabulary for the first three lessons in this chapter.

FCAT Prep

5. Read/Inquire/Explain You see a marble sign. Its letters are too worn to read. What caused this?

6. Which of these doesn't cause weathering?
  A. wind　　　**C.** water
  B. magma　　**D.** plants

Links

Writing

Narrative Writing

Write the **story** of a grain of sediment that has been weathered from a mountain, carried to the sea by a river, and left on a beach. Write from the sediment's point of view.

Math

Solve Problems

A farmer plants $\frac{1}{5}$ of his land with trees to stop erosion. If he plants trees on 525 hectares, how much land does he have? Show your work.

Social Studies

Famous Features

Research a famous natural feature, such as a canyon, mountain, or rock formation. Explain how it formed. Draw a map that shows where the feature is located. Share with the class what you find.

 For more links and activities, go to **www.hspscience.com**

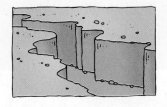

263

What Is Soil?

Fast Fact

Forming Soil This tree is starting soil formation by weathering rock. Over a long time, the rock will be broken down into soil. It can take up to 1000 years for 2 centimeters ($\frac{3}{4}$ in.) of topsoil to form!

Testing Soil

Materials
- measuring scoop
- sand
- 2 large jars with wide mouths
- potting soil
- 250 mL measuring cup
- water

Procedure

1. Place several scoops of sand in a jar. Place an equal amount of potting soil in another jar.

2. Put 200 mL of water in the measuring cup.

3. Slowly pour the water into the sand. Stop when water starts to puddle on top.

4. Record how much water you used.

5. Repeat Steps 2, 3, and 4 for the potting soil.

Draw Conclusions

1. Compare the amounts of water the two types of soil absorbed. Infer where the water you poured into the soil and the sand went.

2. **Inquiry Skill** When scientists do an experiment, they often do it in more than one way and compare results. What do your results tell you about how the size of particles and the spaces between them compare in sand and potting soil?

Step 2

Step 3

Investigate Further

Repeat the investigation, using a different type of soil. Predict how the new results will compare with the results of the Investigate. Is your prediction correct?

SC.H.1.2.2.4.2 metric tools, **SC.H.1.2.4.4.1** comparing experiments, **SC.H.1.2.5.4.1** using models, **SC.H.2.2.1.4.2** making predictions

265

VOCABULARY
humus p. 266
horizon p. 267
bedrock p. 267
sand p. 268
clay p. 268

SCIENCE CONCEPTS
▶ what soil is
▶ how soil forms and how soils differ

READING FOCUS SKILL
COMPARE AND CONTRAST
Look for ways that soils are alike and different.

| alike | — | different |

Soil Formation

If you walk in the woods, you are walking on soil. If you grow flowers on a windowsill, you use soil. Soil is one of the most important things on Earth. Plants can't grow without soil. Without plants, animals could not exist.

So what is soil? The largest part of soil is weathered rock. Sediment makes up almost 50 percent of soil.

Soil has living and nonliving parts. It contains **humus** (HYOO•muhs), or the remains of decayed plants and animals. Soil is crawling with living organisms. There are worms and insects as well as bacteria, fungi, and roots that you can't see with just your eyes.

Water and air make up about half the volume of a soil sample. Water and air are in the spaces between soil particles.

▼ These three pictures show steps of soil formation.

Bedrock is broken down into smaller pieces.

Subsoil is partly weathered rock.

Topsoil is a mix of humus, minerals, and small sediment.

Most soil has **horizons**, or layers. Some soils have several horizons that are easy to see. Other soils have few horizons.

Because horizons form differently, each has particles of different sizes. Horizons also may have different minerals. Horizons all share some properties. The upper layer is topsoil. It includes humus. The lower horizons have partly weathered rock. The lower horizons also contain minerals that rain has carried from upper layers. The bottom horizon is **bedrock**, or the solid rock that forms Earth's surface.

Soil is always forming, but it takes a long time. Some soils take thousands of years to form. That is one reason why soil is such an important resource.

 COMPARE AND CONTRAST How are the top and bottom horizons of soil different?

This well-developed soil has several horizons.

Decayed plant and animal matter (humus) is on the soil surface.

Topsoil is dark and is a mixture of minerals and humus.

Subsoil contains partly weathered rock.

Layer of bedrock is the bottom level.

Types of Soil

You might think that one type of soil is very much like another, but there are many types of soil. Soils are classified by their physical properties. The size of soil particles is one property. Each type of soil is a mix of particles of different sizes. The largest particles are **sand**. A sand particle might be 1 to 2 millimeters (0.04 to 0.08 in.) across. The smallest soil particles are **clay**. Clay particles might be $\frac{1}{1000}$ the size of sand particles. The size of silt is between sand and clay.

Different amounts of sand, silt, and clay in soil give it texture. Texture is how the soil feels in your hands. Soil with more sand feels rough, while soil with more clay feels smooth. Soils differ in other ways, also. They have different compositions. Soil under a desert has less humus than grassland soil. Some soils hold water well, while others don't. Soil horizons can be just a few centimeters thick, or they can reach several meters underground.

Soil type depends on the area where it forms. Bedrock breaks down to form

Sandy soils have large particles. Water passes through quickly. They can be good for growing crops.

Fertile soils often have a thick layer of topsoil. Large amounts of humus make the soil dark.

Clay soils have tiny particles. They hold nutrients and water so well it's hard for plants to grow.

Soil Horizons in Three Different Places

Soils of grasslands often have a thick top horizon that is full of humus. They are loose, soft, and fertile.

Desert soils don't have much humus. They are pale gray to red in color and high in salts. Horizons are not well developed.

This typical Florida soil is sandy, with a thin layer of humus. It forms from limestone bedrock.

the soil above it. Granite bedrock forms coarse soil. Soil formed by basalt bedrock is fine-grained.

A soil's color is also dependent on where the soil forms. A dark soil may have formed in a place with a lot of humus, such as a forest. A light-colored soil may have little organic matter, such as in a desert.

 COMPARE AND CONTRAST How might desert soil and forest soil be alike? Different?

Insta-Lab

How Much Water?

With a dropper, drop water onto a tablespoon of soil and onto a small sponge. Compare how much water soaks in and how much runs off in each case. What property of soil are you modeling?

269

Soil and Plants

Most plants need soil. Their roots draw nutrients, water, and oxygen from soil.

Some soils are fertile. They are good for growing plants. Other soils lack nutrients. To make the soil better for growing plants, many farmers and gardeners add nutrients to soil. The nutrients they add are fertilizer (FERT•uhl•eye•zer).

There are natural fertilizers and artificial fertilizers. Artificial fertilizers are human-made mixtures of chemicals. They add to the soil nutrients that plants need. Natural fertilizers include compost and animal waste. People make compost by putting food and plant scraps in a pile. The scraps decay to make fertilizer.

Some soils hold more moisture than other soils. Humus helps soil hold water. Soils with small particles hold water better than soils with large particles. When soil is too dry for plants, people add water. They pump water from wells and other sources and sprinkle it on soil.

 COMPARE AND CONTRAST **Compare and contrast the two types of fertilizers.**

Soils can lose nutrients because of erosion or heavy use. Fertilizers put back important nutrients, such as phosphorus, nitrogen, and potassium.

Many farmers use fertilizers on their soil.

FEEDS 5,000 SQ. FT.
NET WT. 13 LBS.

FALL FERTILIZER 10-18-10

Many farmers and gardeners use compost to give soil nutrients. Compost is a natural fertilizer that adds humus to soil.

1. COMPARE AND CONTRAST Fill in the graphic organizer below.

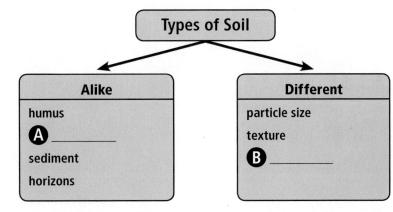

Types of Soil

Alike
humus
A _____
sediment
horizons

Different
particle size
texture
B _____

2. SUMMARIZE Write one sentence to summarize each section in the lesson.

3. DRAW CONCLUSIONS Erosion can wash away soil. Why is it important to control this type of erosion?

4. VOCABULARY Make a page for a picture dictionary, using the five lesson vocabulary words.

FCAT Prep

5. Read/Inquire/Explain Why is it useful to all people to understand soil and how it forms?

6. Which of these makes up the largest part of soil?

A. water   **C.** air
B. humus   **D.** sediment

Links

Writing

Persuasive Writing
Write a short **e-mail** to the editor of a newspaper. Persuade gardeners to use compost instead of other fertilizers in their gardens. Explain why you think compost is a better choice.

Math

Solving a Problem
Soil in a certain area erodes at a rate of 3.2 centimeters per month. How much soil erodes over a period of 5 years?

Social Studies

Report
Write a **report** about the problems of drought and soil erosion that led to the "Dust Bowl." If possible, interview someone who was affected by the "Dust Bowl." Include a map.

 For more links and activities, go to **www.hspscience.com**

Crumbling HISTORY | WILL THE GREAT SPHINX CRUMBLE LIKE A COOKIE?

The Great Sphinx in Egypt has stood the test of time. For at least 4,500 years, the sphinx has towered over a desert in Egypt. Now, however, rising groundwater may cause the ancient statue to crumble.

The Mysterious Sphinx

A sphinx is a figure with the head of a person and the body of a lion. No one knows for sure why the Great Sphinx was built. Some say it honors an ancient king named Khafre. Others say the sphinx was made to represent an ancient Egyptian god.

The sphinx was built at about the same time that the Great Pyramid was built. Even though scientists know little about the sphinx, they do know something about the Great Pyramid and the other nearby pyramids.

The ancient Egyptians built the pyramids as tombs for their kings. When an Egyptian king died, his body was mummified. The body was then placed in the tomb. Many of the king's belongings were also placed in the tomb.

Wind has blown desert sand into the Great Sphinx, wearing away the monument.

Damaging History

The sphinx and pyramids have suffered damage over time. For example, wind has blown the desert sand into the monuments, causing them to wear away. Some of the blocks that make up the monuments have come loose and fallen.

Now the ancient monuments are facing the most serious threat ever—water. A dam built near the monuments traps water. That water is used to irrigate farm crops grown nearby. Irrigation has caused the level of groundwater to increase. The water is filled with salts. The salts and water react with the stone that makes up the monuments. The chemical reaction causes the stones to crumble and turn into dust.

Two scientists are now trying to protect the ancient monuments. They want to find ways to keep groundwater from flowing under the monuments. If the water isn't stopped, the Great Sphinx and pyramids may one day crumble into dust blown by the desert wind.

THINK ABOUT IT

1. Why did the ancient Egyptians build the pyramids?

2. Can you think of any monuments in the United States that need protecting?

THE GREAT SPHINX

20 meters (66 ft) high
73 meters (240 ft) long
4-meter-wide (13-ft-wide) face
2-meter-high (7-ft-high) eyes

Spin-In

Find out more! Log on to
www.hspscience.com

SC.H.2.2.1.4.2
patterns in nature
SC.H.3.2.2.4.1
evaluating
information

The Color of Dirt

What's the color of dirt? Brown right? Not always!

In the early 1900s a scientist named Dorothy Nickerson helped scientists who test soil. Nickerson helped to make standards that scientists can use when they study dirt and rocks.

As part of her work, Nickerson worked with Albert H. Munsell. Munsell had invented a color chart system. Nickerson worked with Munsell so that the chart could be used for describing soil color.

Why is studying dirt important? Experts use the Munsell color chart and color names when surveying soil. The surveys show scientists what kind of soil exists in our country. Then scientists can decide the best way to use the soil.

Career Landscaper

Where to plant that Japanese maple? What kind of grass would grow best in this yard? These are questions a landscaper can answer. Landscapers study how plants live in different soils and in different climates. They know which soil is good for which plants and how to help soil that is not good for planting.

You Can Do It!

Quick and Easy Project

Deep Freeze

Materials
- drinking straw
- glass of water
- clay
- freezer

Procedure
1. Put a straw into a glass of water.
2. Suck on one end of the straw to fill it completely with water.
3. Keep your tongue over the top end of the straw to stop water from running out. Then pull the straw from the water. Plug the bottom end with a small piece of clay.
4. After removing your tongue, plug the other end of the straw with clay.
5. Put the straw into a freezer. Leave it for about 3 hours.
6. Take out the straw. Observe the ends.

Draw Conclusions
Describe what happened to the straw. Draw conclusions about why this happened. What Earth process does this model?

Design Your Own Investigation

Signs of the Rock Cycle

Look for evidence of a stage of the rock cycle in the area where you live. Explain the change that is going on. Take photos or draw sketches of what you see. How would you design a way to observe changes over time? Which stages of the rock cycle are you most likely to see? Which are you not likely to see? Share what you find with other students.

Vocabulary Review

Use the terms below to complete the sentences. The page numbers tell where to look in the chapter if you need help.

mineral p. 244
igneous p. 246
sedimentary p. 247
metamorphic p. 248
rock cycle p. 252

weathering p. 258
erosion p. 262
humus p. 266
horizon p. 267
bedrock p. 267

1. Rock that formed from other weathered rock is _____.

2. The process of moving sediment from one place to another is _____.

3. Rock that forms when melted rock cools and hardens is _____.

4. A group of processes that change rocks over a long time is the _____.

5. A soil layer is a _____.

6. A solid substance that occurs naturally in rocks or in the ground is a _____.

7. The breaking down of rock on Earth's surface into smaller pieces is _____.

8. The solid rock that forms Earth's surface is _____.

9. Rock that has changed from another type of rock is _____.

10. The remains of dead plants and animals is _____.

Check Understanding

Write the letter of the best choice.

11. Of which substance are rocks made?
    A. clay
    B. horizons
    C. humus
    D. minerals

12. Identify the rock below.

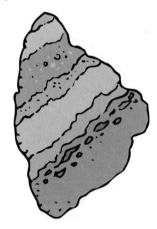

    F. igneous granite
    G. metamorphic quartzite
    H. sedimentary conglomerate
    I. sedimentary sandstone

13. **MAIN IDEA AND DETAILS** Which of these is **not** a part of the rock cycle?
    A. Metamorphic rock melts.
    B. Lava hardens into rock.
    C. Nitrogen enters soil.
    D. Plants weather rock.

14. COMPARE AND CONTRAST Which describes how some igneous rock forms?

   F. Water freezes in cracks in rock.

   G. Magma cools underground.

   H. Pressure changes minerals in rock.

   I. Water erodes sediment.

15. What is the name of the lowest soil horizon?

   A. bedrock

   B. magma

   C. subsoil

   D. topsoil

16. What makes up humus?

   F. decayed plants and animals

   G. fertilizer

   H. minerals

   I. sediment

Inquiry Skills

17. Why is the ability to **use models** important when studying processes that are part of the rock cycle?

18. What are you looking for when you **compare** rocks?

Read/Inquire/Explain

19. Why is most metamorphic rock harder than the sedimentary rock from which it formed?

20. Jameer is on vacation with his family in Hawai'i. He sees rock formations all around the Kīlauea volcano. Some of these look like the diagram below. Help Jameer identify the part of the rock cycle shown in the diagram.

   Part A What happened just before this step?

   Part B List two possible steps in the cycle after this one.

The Water Cycle

Vocabulary

FCAT-Tested	tornado
water cycle	hurricane
evaporation	sea breeze
condensation	land breeze
Other Terms	rain shadow
precipitation	air mass
rain	cold front
sleet	warm front
snow	barometer
hail	anemometer

What do **YOU** wonder?

Each spring as the weather warms, snow and ice in the Yukon begin to melt. The snow and ice turn into millions of gallons of moving water. Where do you think this water goes?

1

What Is the Water Cycle?

Fast Fact

Got Water? Almost all of Earth's water is in the oceans. In fact, more than 97 percent of Earth's water is ocean water! In the Investigate, you will find out what ocean water is like.

From Salt Water to Fresh Water

Materials
- 500 mL of warm water
- cotton swabs
- plastic wrap
- salt
- large bowl
- large rubber band
- masking tape
- spoon
- small glass jar
- small ball

Procedure

1. Stir two spoonfuls of salt into the warm water. Dip a cotton swab into the mixture. Touch the swab to your tongue. Record what you observe. **CAUTION: Do not share swabs. Throw the swab away.**

2. Put the jar in the center of the bowl. Pour the salt water into the bowl. Be careful not to get any salt water in the jar.

3. Put plastic wrap over the bowl. The wrap should not touch the jar. Use the rubber band to hold the wrap in place.

4. Put the ball on the wrap over the jar. Make sure the wrap doesn't touch the jar.

5. Mark the level of the salt water with a piece of tape on the outside of the bowl. Put the bowl in a sunny spot for one day.

6. Remove the wrap and the ball. Use clean swabs to taste the water in the jar and in the bowl. Record what you observe.

Step 2

Step 4

Draw Conclusions

1. What did you observe during the investigation?

2. **Inquiry Skill** Scientists infer based on what they observe. What can you infer is a source of fresh water for Earth?

Investigate Further

What would happen if you left the bowl and jar in the sun for several days? Write a hypothesis. Try it!

SC.D.1.2.3.4.1 water cycle
SC.H.1.2.5.4.1 using models
SC.H.2.2.1.4.2 patterns in nature
281

Reading in Science

LA.A.2.2.1 sequence
SC.D.1.2.3.4.1 water cycle
SC.H.2.2.1.4.2 patterns in nature

VOCABULARY

water cycle p. 282
precipitation p. 282
evaporation p. 284
condensation p. 285

SCIENCE CONCEPTS

▶ what processes make up the water cycle

▶ how a raindrop is formed

READING FOCUS SKILL

SEQUENCE Look for the order in which events of the water cycle occur.

The Water Cycle

As you are on the way home from school, it suddenly starts raining. Where does rain come from? When rain reaches the ground, where does it go?

Water is constantly moving through the environment. Water moves from the surface of Earth to the air and then back to Earth's surface again in a never-ending process called the **water cycle**.

Energy from the sun drives the water cycle. When the sun's energy warms water on Earth's surface, the water changes from a liquid to a gas.

The gas form of water, called water vapor, goes into the air. If the water vapor cools, it becomes liquid water again and falls back to Earth. Water that falls back to Earth is called **precipitation** (pree•sip•uh•TAY•shuhn). Precipitation can be rain, snow, sleet, or hail. Rain is liquid water. Snow, sleet, and hail are frozen water. Energy from the sun changes precipitation to water vapor once again. This continues the water cycle.

 SEQUENCE What steps must take place in order for ocean water to become rain?

A cloud forms when water vapor cools. The water vapor becomes liquid again in a process known as condensation. The liquid water in clouds is in the form of tiny droplets that can stay up in the air.

When the sun warms the surface of water, the water changes to water vapor, a gas. The gas then becomes part of the air.

In the clouds, water droplets can bump into each other and join to make larger droplets. Soon the droplets become heavy and fall to Earth as precipitation.

Some precipitation soaks into the ground. Precipitation can also run over the ground and flow into streams, rivers, lakes, and eventually the ocean.

Parts of the Water Cycle

It's a hot day. To cool off, you take a swim. When you get out of the water, you dry yourself with a towel. You leave the towel in the sunlight while you play with your friends. When you come back, the towel is dry. Where did the water in the towel go?

The water evaporated. **Evaporation** (ee•vap•uh•RAY•shuhn) is the process by which a liquid changes into a gas. A large amount of water evaporates from Earth's oceans, lakes, and rivers every day. But water also evaporates from the soil, from puddles, and even from your skin as you sweat.

Water vapor mixes with other gases in the air. When the wind blows, air moves. The water vapor moves with the air. Sometimes the water vapor can move very long distances. The water vapor can also move high up into the air.

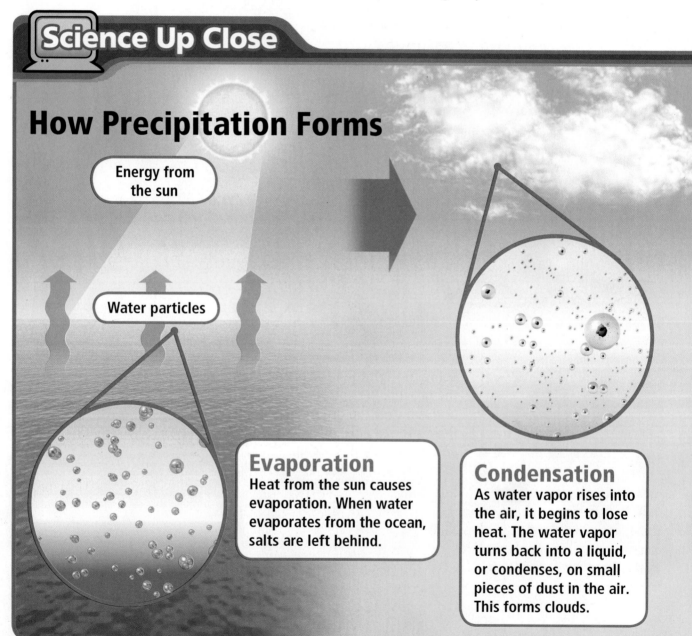

Science Up Close

How Precipitation Forms

Energy from the sun

Water particles

Evaporation
Heat from the sun causes evaporation. When water evaporates from the ocean, salts are left behind.

Condensation
As water vapor rises into the air, it begins to lose heat. The water vapor turns back into a liquid, or condenses, on small pieces of dust in the air. This forms clouds.

When the water vapor moves up in the air, it becomes cooler. If the water vapor cools enough, condensation (kahn•duhn•SAY•shuhn) happens. **Condensation** is the process by which a gas changes into a liquid. Have you ever seen water dripping from an air conditioner? The dripping water is from water vapor that condensed as it cooled.

Air has many small bits of dust in it. When water vapor cools, it condenses on the dust particles. The condensed water and dust particles form clouds. Inside clouds, tiny droplets of water can join to make larger droplets. These droplets can join to make even larger, heavier droplets. When the droplets become too heavy to stay in the air, they fall to Earth as precipitation. The type of precipitation that falls depends on the temperature of the air around it.

 SEQUENCE Heat causes a piece of ice to melt. What will happen next?

 For more links and activities, go to **www.hspscience.com**

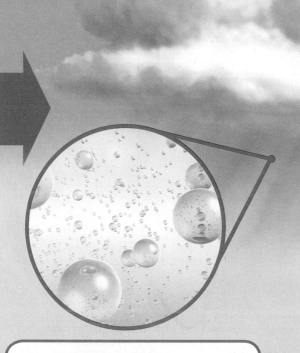

Precipitation
Inside clouds, small water droplets join to form larger droplets. In time, these larger droplets become raindrops that fall to Earth. The water in raindrops is fresh water.

Forms of Water
Fill a glass with ice. Fill another glass with room temperature water. Observe the glasses for at least five minutes. Describe any changes you see. What property of the glasses was different? What process occurred on the outside of one glass? Why did this process occur? Can you control the process? Try it.

Groundwater and Runoff

When rain falls on land, some of it soaks into the soil. Plants use much of this water. Also, some of the water in the soil evaporates back into the air. But not all of the water in soil evaporates or is used by plants.

Some of the water that goes into soil moves deeper into the ground. The water in the ground moves down until it gets to solid rock. Because the water cannot move through the rock, it begins to collect there. After a while, a lot of collected water forms a body of groundwater.

Many people rely on groundwater for their drinking water. They dig wells to reach the groundwater. Then they pump the water up to the surface.

Rain that is not soaked up by the soil becomes runoff. The runoff flows into creeks and streams, which flow into rivers. Large rivers, such as the Mississippi River and the Columbia River, flow into larger bodies of water.

 SEQUENCE **In what sequence of events does groundwater form?**

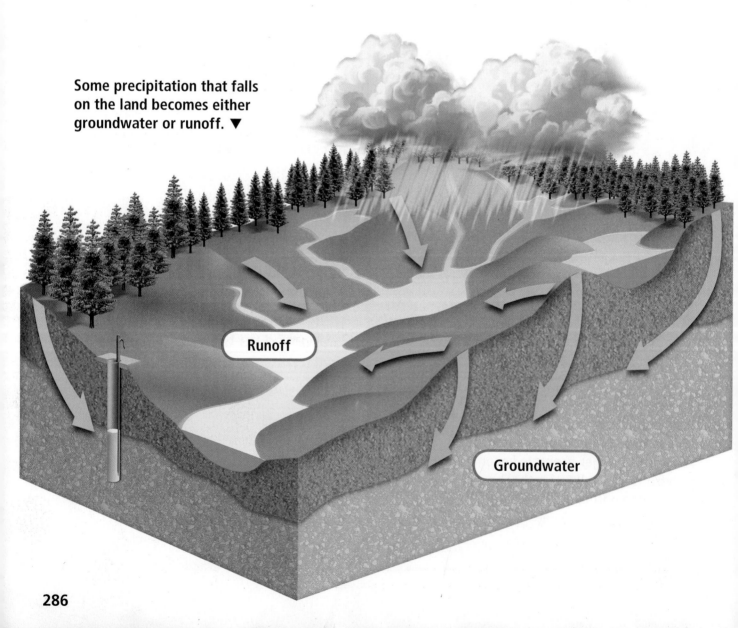

Some precipitation that falls on the land becomes either groundwater or runoff. ▼

Runoff

Groundwater

Focus Skill

1. SEQUENCE Draw and complete each graphic organizer.

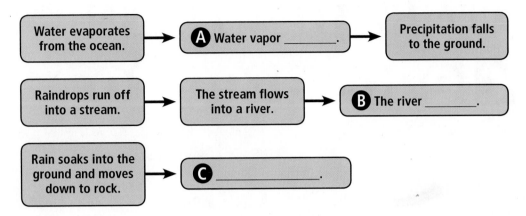

| Water evaporates from the ocean. | → | **A** Water vapor _____. | → | Precipitation falls to the ground. |

| Raindrops run off into a stream. | → | The stream flows into a river. | → | **B** The river _____. |

| Rain soaks into the ground and moves down to rock. | → | **C** _____. |

2. SUMMARIZE Draw a diagram that summarizes this lesson.

3. DRAW CONCLUSIONS Will pond water evaporate faster on a warm, sunny day or on a warm, cloudy day? Explain.

4. VOCABULARY Write one sentence that uses all the vocabulary terms for the lesson.

FCAT Prep

5. Read/Inquire/Explain Most rainwater comes from the ocean, but rainwater is not salty. Why not?

6. Which of the following happens when water vapor cools?
 A. condensation   **C.** heating
 B. evaporation   **D.** vaporization

Links

Writing

Persuasive Writing
Less than 3 percent of Earth's water is fresh. Write a **speech** that explains to people why it's important to protect Earth's freshwater resources. Present your speech to the class.

Math

Make a Circle Graph
Earth is known as "the water planet." Find out how much of Earth's surface is covered by water. Make a circle graph that shows this information.

Social Studies

Where Is Water?
Find a world map. Make a list of all the major bodies of water you see. Research one of the bodies of water, and report on it. Include information such as how the body of water formed.

 For more links and activities, go to **www.hspscience.com**

2

How Is the Water Cycle Related to Weather?

Fast Fact

When It Rains, It Pours Floods cause billions of dollars of damage to property every year. It takes only 60 cm (2 ft) of moving floodwater to sweep away a car. Higher waters sweep away trees, bridges, and even buildings! In the Investigate activity, you will model a flood.

Modeling a Flood

Materials
- aluminum baking pan
- plastic bag
- plastic gloves
- soil
- water
- toothpick
- beaker

Procedure

1 Half-fill the aluminum baking pan with soil. Make a path in the soil to form a "river channel" that runs through the center of the pan. Build up some small hills around the river channel. Press the soil in place.

2 Use the toothpick to poke several holes in the bottom of the plastic bag.

3 Measure 150 mL of water in the beaker. One partner should hold the plastic bag over the pan while the other partner slowly pours the water into the bag. Let the water drip over the pan to model a rainy day. Record what you observe.

4 Repeat Step 3 several times until the pan becomes three-fourths full of water.

Draw Conclusions

1. What happened to the soil in the pan after the first "rainy day"? What happened after the last "rainy day"?

2. **Inquiry Skill** Scientists often gather, record, and interpret data to understand how things work. Interpret what you observed and recorded using your model. What do you think causes floods?

Step 1

Step 3

Investigate Further

Would the results be the same if there were several days between each rainfall? Plan and conduct a simple investigation to find out.

SC.D.1.2.3.4.1 water cycle; **SC.H.1.2.3.4.1** working collaboratively; **SC.H.1.2.5.4.1** using models; **SC.H.2.2.1.4.2** patterns in nature

289

Reading in Science

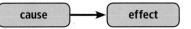
LA.E.2.2.1 cause and effect
SC.D.1.2.3.4.1 water cycle
SC.H.2.2.1.4.2 patterns in nature

VOCABULARY
rain p. 290
sleet p. 290
snow p. 291
hail p. 291
tornado p. 292
hurricane p. 292

SCIENCE CONCEPTS
▶ what some kinds of precipitation are
▶ what causes different kinds of weather

READING FOCUS SKILL
CAUSE AND EFFECT Look for the causes of certain types of weather.

```
cause ──────▶ effect
```

Kinds of Precipitation

You may think of precipitation as bad weather. After all, rain keeps you from playing outdoors. It can also cause floods. Hail can damage cars and homes. Sleet can make roads dangerous. Snow can pile up on driveways and on sidewalks. However, all of these kinds of precipitation are simply part of the water cycle.

What causes different kinds of precipitation? Most water on Earth, such as ocean water, is liquid. You learned in Lesson 1 that if water is heated enough, it becomes water vapor, a gas. If water is cooled enough, it freezes.

Rain, the most common kind of precipitation, is liquid water. Rain falls if the temperature is higher than 0°C (32°F). **Sleet** is frozen rain. Sleet is

Kinds of Precipitation

Types	Causes
Rain	Water vapor condenses in air.
Snow	Water vapor turns into ice crystals instead of a liquid.
Sleet	Falling rain passes through a layer of freezing-cold air and turns into ice.
Hail	Rain freezes and then falls to a warmer pocket of air. The frozen rain is coated with liquid water and then carried back up to a cold pocket of air, where the liquid coating also freezes.

RAIN
Rain is liquid precipitation. Tiny raindrops are called drizzle. Heavy rain can cause floods.

caused when rain falls through a layer of freezing-cold air. This turns the rain into ice pellets. **Snow** is made of ice crystals. Snow is caused when the air temperature is so cold that water vapor turns directly into ice. **Hail** is round pieces of ice. Hail is caused when rain freezes and then falls to a warmer part of the air. Raindrops coat the frozen rain before it is carried back up to a colder part of the air by wind. The new liquid coating then freezes also. This happens over and over until the hail is too heavy and it falls to the ground.

 CAUSE AND EFFECT What causes rain to become sleet?

SNOW
Snow is made of ice crystals. The crystals, which come in many different shapes, form high in the air.

▲ **SLEET**
Sleet is made of frozen raindrops. Sleet forms when rain falls through a pocket of cold air.

▲ **HAIL**
Hail can be as small as a pea or as large as a grapefruit. The size of a piece of hail depends on how many times it is carried up and down in a storm cloud.

Severe Storms

Heat from the sun powers the water cycle. This same energy causes severe storms.

One type of severe storm is a thunderstorm. Thunderstorms are storms with lightning, strong winds, and heavy rain. Sometimes tornadoes form during thunderstorms. A **tornado** is a fast-spinning spiral of wind that stretches from the clouds of a thunderstorm to the ground. Tornadoes can have wind speeds greater than 400 kilometers (250 mi) per hour! Every year, there are about 800–1000 tornadoes in the United States.

Another kind of severe storm is a hurricane. **Hurricanes** are large tropical storms with wind speeds of 119 kilometers (74 mi) per hour or

▲ The United States has more tornadoes per year than any other country in the world.

Blizzards are severe snowstorms that can last for hours. Blizzards have strong winds, blowing snow, and very low air temperatures. ▼

Hurricanes are categorized by their wind speed. Does a hurricane's wind speed relate to the amount of damage it causes?

Hurricane Strength

Category/Wind Speed	Hurricanes	Cost of damage in dollars
5 (>155 mph)	Hurricane Andrew, 1992	$34.1 billion
4 (131–155 mph)	Hurricane Charley, 2004	$14 billion
3 (111–130 mph)	Hurricane Betsy, 1965	$9 billion
2 (96–110 mph)	Hurricane Floyd, 1999	$4.9 billion
1 (74–95 mph)	Hurricane Agnes, 1972	$9.1 billion

Three pictures of Hurricane Andrew

more. Hurricanes form over warm water in the tropical oceans. These storms can last for weeks out at sea. But when a hurricane reaches land, it no longer gets energy from warm water. It soon becomes weaker.

The winds of a hurricane spin around the calm center of the storm, called the "eye." Rain, waves, and "storm surge," a huge bulge of water pushed onto the land by the storm, can cause flooding.

 CAUSE AND EFFECT What causes flooding during a hurricane?

Tornado in a Bottle

Fill a clear, plastic bottle three-fourths full of water. Tape a washer over the mouth of the bottle. Tape a second clear, plastic bottle upside down on top of the first bottle. Turn the bottles over and swirl the top bottle around quickly. What do you observe?

Weather Safety

Severe storms are dangerous. Injuries can be caused by downed power lines and trees. Floods can occur. It's important to keep yourself safe during severe weather. One way to stay safe is to follow safety rules in your community. Local radio or TV stations will tell you if there is a severe storm in your area.

There are other ways to warn people about severe weather. For example, some areas have weather sirens that are turned on when a severe storm is detected. Some sirens can even detect nearby tornadoes on their own and warn people in the area.

When there is a severe storm, stay inside a building unless officials tell you to leave. Sometimes people are asked to leave an area before a storm strikes. If that happens, people will follow a safe route away from the area.

 CAUSE AND EFFECT How might a severe storm affect you?

Weather siren ▶

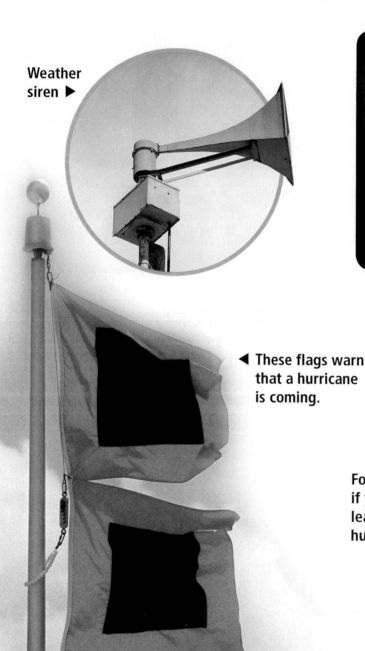

▲ Watch TV during severe weather to get directions about what to do.

◀ These flags warn that a hurricane is coming.

Follow signs like these if you are asked to leave an area when a hurricane is coming. ▶

EVACUATION ROUTE

1. CAUSE AND EFFECT Draw and complete each graphic organizer.

Falling rain passes through a layer of freezing air.	→ **A** _____ forms.
Water vapor in clouds turns directly to ice.	→ **B** _____ forms.
Winds begin to rotate over the sea at a speed greater than 119 kph (74 mph).	→ A **C** _____ forms.

2. SUMMARIZE Summarize this lesson by describing what causes these different kinds of weather: rain, snow, sleet, hail, tornado, hurricane.

3. DRAW CONCLUSIONS What affects the kind of precipitation that will fall?

4. VOCABULARY Write a weather report that uses at least four vocabulary terms from this lesson.

FCAT Prep

5. Read/Inquire/Explain Explain how weather is related to the water cycle.

6. Which of the following is **not** a kind of precipitation?
A. air   **C.** rain
B. hail   **D.** sleet

Links

Writing

Narrative Writing
Suppose that you're a drop of water in a cloud. Write a **story** that describes what you experience as you continue your travel through the water cycle.

Math

Measure Temperature
Measure the outdoor temperature. Based on the temperature you found, what kind of precipitation is most likely to fall now in your area?

Health

Weather and Health
Make a booklet that shows what to do to stay safe during severe weather, such as tornadoes, thunderstorms, and hurricanes.

 For more links and activities, go to **www.hspscience.com**

How Do Land Features Affect the Water Cycle?

Fast Fact

Thunderstorms in a Row When cold air over the ocean meets warm air over the land, squall lines can form. A squall line is a long line of moving thunderstorms. Squall lines can stretch across the land for hundreds of kilometers! In the Investigate, you will observe how land and water heat up.

Heating Land and Water

Materials
- **2 small plastic or foam cups**
- **water**
- **2 thermometers**
- **stopwatch**
- **dark soil or sand**
- **light source with 100-W bulb or greater**

Procedure

1. Fill one cup with dark soil or sand. Fill the second cup with water. Place a thermometer upright in each cup.

2. Time one minute, using the stopwatch. Then measure and record the temperatures of the two cups.

3. Remove the thermometer after every measurement. Place the cups under the light. Make sure that both cups get an equal amount of light.

Step 3

4. After the cups have been under the light for 5 minutes, measure and record their temperatures. Repeat this step 3 times.

5. Turn the lamp off. Time 5 minutes, and then measure and record the temperatures of the cups. Repeat this step twice.

Step 4

Draw Conclusions

1. Describe how the soil and water heated differently. How did they cool differently?

2. **Inquiry Skill** Scientists use what they observe to form a hypothesis. Use your observations from this investigation to hypothesize how the weather on Earth would be different if Earth's surface were mostly land instead of mostly water.

Investigate Further

Does wet soil heat differently from dry soil? Conduct an experiment to find out.

SC.D.1.2.3.4.1 water cycle
SC.H.1.2.5.4.1 using models
SC.H.2.2.1.4.2 patterns in nature

297

Reading in Science

LA.E.2.2.1 cause and effect
SC.D.1.2.3.4.1 water cycle
SC.H.2.2.1.4.2 patterns in nature

VOCABULARY
sea breeze p. 298
land breeze p. 298
rain shadow p. 300

SCIENCE CONCEPTS
▶ how temperature affects the water cycle
▶ how landforms affect the water cycle

(Focus Skill) **READING FOCUS SKILL**
CAUSE AND EFFECT Look for ways that landforms affect the water cycle.

Sea Breezes and Land Breezes

Have you ever been to the beach on a hot day? It might be so hot that your feet burn when you walk on the sand. But when you go into the water, you quickly cool off. That's because the water is cooler than the sand.

Land heats up much more quickly than water. Land also cools down more quickly than water. Because of this, the temperature of the air over land is almost always different from the temperature of air over nearby water. During the day, the air over water is cooler than the air over land. The hot air over a beach is pushed upward by the cool air moving in from over the water. This causes a sea breeze. A **sea breeze** is a breeze moving from the water to the land. During the night, the land becomes cooler than the water. This causes a land breeze. A **land breeze** is a breeze moving from the land to the water.

 CAUSE AND EFFECT What causes a land breeze?

Warm air is pushed upward as cool air moves into its place. During the day, the air over land is warmer than the air over water, which causes a sea breeze.

During the evening, the air over water is warmer than the air over land, which causes a land breeze.

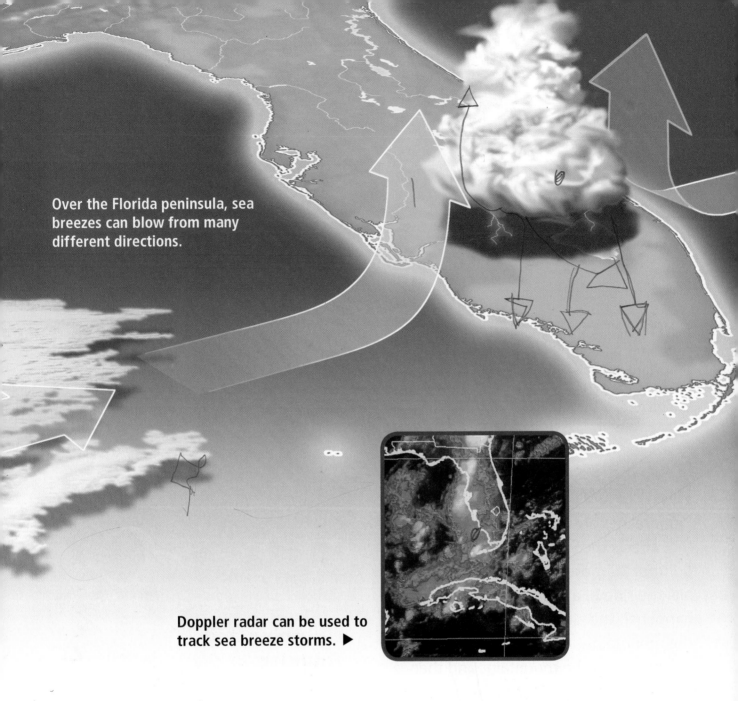

Over the Florida peninsula, sea breezes can blow from many different directions.

Doppler radar can be used to track sea breeze storms. ▶

Sea Breeze Storms

You learned in Lesson 1 that when water vapor cools, it condenses to form precipitation. Sometimes, cool sea breezes push clouds toward the shore. The clouds can then produce storms over the land. These storms are called sea breeze storms.

A peninsula is a piece of land that is surrounded by water on three sides. Over a peninsula like Florida, sea breezes can come in from the east and from the west. The collision of the two sea breezes causes the air to become unstable. If the two bodies of air have a lot of water vapor, a very strong sea breeze storm could form over the center of the peninsula. This type of sea breeze storm happens often in Florida during the summer.

 CAUSE AND EFFECT What causes a sea breeze storm?

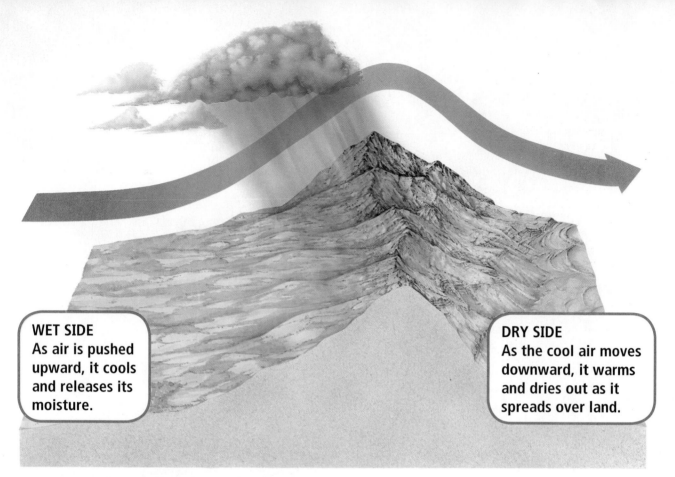

WET SIDE
As air is pushed upward, it cools and releases its moisture.

DRY SIDE
As the cool air moves downward, it warms and dries out as it spreads over land.

Rain Shadows

Shorelines are not the only landform that affects the water cycle. Mountains do, too. Suppose a moving body of air hits the side of a mountain range. What happens? The air can't move through the mountains. Instead, the air is pushed up the side of the mountains and then over them. As the air moves up, it cools. The water vapor in the cooler air condenses and brings rain to that side of the mountains. By the time the air reaches the other side, the air is dry. So, it doesn't rain on the other side. This causes a rain shadow. A **rain shadow** is the area on the far side of a mountain range that gets little or no rain or cloud cover.

 CAUSE AND EFFECT What is the effect of a rain shadow?

Insta-Lab

Lightning and Thunder

The next time a thunderstorm is in your area, watch for lightning. When you see the lightning, start counting, "One-Mississippi, two-Mississippi, ..." and so on. When you hear the thunder, stop counting. For every three seconds you count, the thunderstorm is about one kilometer from you. How far away is the thunderstorm?

1. CAUSE AND EFFECT Copy and complete this graphic organizers.

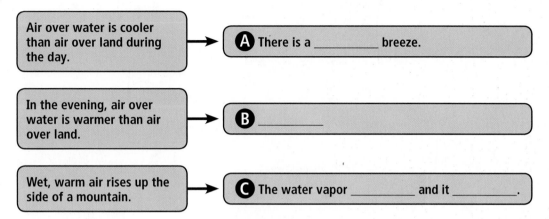

Air over water is cooler than air over land during the day. → **A** There is a _____ breeze.

In the evening, air over water is warmer than air over land. → **B** _____

Wet, warm air rises up the side of a mountain. → **C** The water vapor _____ and it _____.

2. SUMMARIZE Write a paragraph summarizing the lesson. Start with this sentence: The water cycle is affected by landforms.

3. DRAW CONCLUSIONS Will sea breeze storms happen more often in warm places or cool places? Explain.

4. VOCABULARY Explain the difference between a land breeze and a sea breeze.

FCAT Prep

5. Read/Inquire/Explain Explain why a mountain may be green on one side and desertlike on the other.

6. How does warm air move?
- **A.** It falls.
- **B.** It is pushed upward.
- **C.** It spins.
- **D.** It stays still.

Links

Writing

Expository Writing

Suppose that you are an early explorer of a mountain range that experiences the rain shadow effect. Write a **journal** describing your explorations of the range.

Math

Solve Problems

A sea breeze storm is moving across Florida from the northeast to the southwest at 23 km/hr. How long does the storm take to reach Tampa if it started above Orlando, which is 137 km away?

Physical Education

Water Sports

Many water sports, such as sailing, make use of sea breezes. Choose a sport that uses sea breezes, and write a simple how-to guide for this sport.

For more links and activities, go to www.hspscience.com

How Can Weather Be Predicted?

Fast Fact

A Winter Wonderland Ice storms deposit massive amounts of ice over everything. In fact, during a severe ice storm about 45,000 kilograms (99,000 lb) of ice can pile up on a 15-meter (50-ft) pine tree! In the Investigate, you will make and use a weather instrument used to help predict weather.

Making a Barometer

Materials
- plastic jar
- safety goggles
- wooden craft stick
- scissors
- large rubber band
- large index card
- large round balloon
- tape
- ruler

Procedure

1. **CAUTION: Wear safety goggles.** Be careful when using scissors. Use the scissors to cut the neck off the balloon.

2. Have your partner hold the jar while you stretch the balloon over the open end. Secure the balloon with the rubber band.

3. Tape the craft stick to the top of the balloon. More than half of the craft stick should extend beyond the jar's edge.

4. On the blank side of an index card, draw a line and label it *Day 1*. Tape the card to a wall. The line should be at the same height as the stick on your barometer. Next to it, record the current weather.

5. Air pressure is the force of air pressing down on Earth. Measure air pressure by marking the position of the wooden stick on the index card for the next four days. Label the marks *Days 2–5*. Record the pressure and weather each day.

Draw Conclusions

1. How did the air pressure change? What might cause changes in air pressure?

2. **Inquiry Skill** Scientists use instruments to measure weather data. Infer how a barometer works.

Step 3

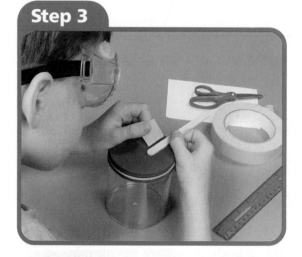

Step 4

Investigate Further

Track changes in air pressure and weather for five more days. What can you infer is the relationship between air pressure and type of weather?

SC.D.1.2.3.4.1 water cycle
SC.H.1.2.3.4.1 working collaboratively
SC.H.1.2.5.4.1 using models

Reading in Science

LA.E.2.2.1 cause and effect
SC.D.1.2.3.4.1 water cycle
SC.H.2.2.1.4.2 patterns in nature

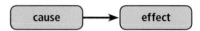

VOCABULARY
air mass p. 304
cold front p. 306
warm front p. 306
barometer p. 310
anemometer p. 310

SCIENCE CONCEPTS
▶ what makes an air mass
▶ how to read a weather map

READING FOCUS SKILL

CAUSE AND EFFECT Look for the causes of changes in weather.

| cause | → | effect |

Air Masses

Have you ever wondered why the weather can be sunny one day and rainy the next? Movements of air masses cause weather changes. An **air mass** is a large body of air. All of the air in an air mass has a similar temperature and moisture level. Moisture level means the amount of water that is in air.

The map shows where the air masses that affect North America form. Cool air masses are in blue. Warm air masses are in red. ▼

The temperature and moisture level of an air mass depend on where the air mass formed. Air masses that form over land are dry. Air masses that form over water have a lot of moisture in them. In the United States, cold air masses come from the north. Warm air masses come from the south.

The temperature and moisture level of an air mass affect the kind of weather the air mass brings. Cold, wet air masses can bring snow to an area. But cold, dry air masses can bring cool weather

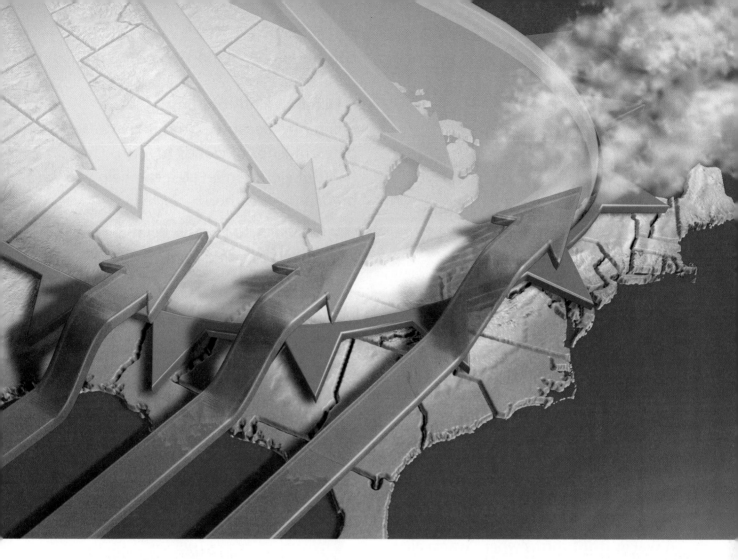

▲ Air masses do not mix very much with each other. Instead, they stay separate as they move.

with little or no precipitation. Warm air masses with a lot of moisture usually bring precipitation. But warm, dry masses can bring warm weather with little or no precipitation.

As air masses move, they tend to stay separate from each other. That's because warm air is lighter than cold air. When they come in contact with each other, warm air masses are pushed upward and cold air masses sink.

 CAUSE AND EFFECT What causes the weather to change?

Making an Air Mass

Fill a cup halfway with ice cubes. Wait five minutes. With one hand, pour chilled water into the cup. Hold the other hand over the cup as you pour the water. What do you feel? If the air you felt were an air mass, how would you describe it? In a cold front, the air is colder behind the front than ahead of it.

Fronts

When air masses move, they come into contact with other air masses. The border between one air mass and another is called a front. Most storms happen at fronts.

There are two main types of fronts: cold fronts and warm fronts. A **cold front** forms where a cold air mass moves under a warm air mass. This causes the warm air mass to move upward. As the warm air mass moves up, it begins to cool. Remember that water vapor condenses when it cools. The condensing water vapor in the upward-moving air mass forms clouds. It might begin to rain along the front. Thunderstorms will often develop. Also, the air temperature will become cooler as the cold air mass moves forward.

A **warm front** forms where warm air moves over cold air. The warm air slides up over the cold air as it moves forward. Warm fronts generally move slowly. Because of this, warm fronts bring steady rain instead of thunderstorms. Warm fronts are then followed by clear, warm weather as the warm air mass moves over the area.

Fronts do not always move. A front that stays in one place for many days is called a stationary front. Stationary fronts happen when the two air masses along a front do not have enough energy to move. The weather along a stationary front is often cloudy and wet. This kind of front can leave many inches of snow or cause flooding rains.

For this reason, stationary fronts can be dangerous.

Different kinds of fronts move differently. Because of this, they cause different kinds of clouds to form. The types of clouds in an area can help you predict the weather.

 CAUSE AND EFFECT What are the effects of a cold front?

▲ In a warm front, the air is warmer behind the front than ahead of it.

In a cold front, the air is colder behind the front than ahead of it. ▼

Stratus clouds often occur along warm fronts.

Stratus clouds can develop into nimbostratus clouds. Nimbostratus clouds bring light rain or snow showers. ▶

◀ CUMULUS CLOUDS
Cumulus (KYOO•myuh•luhs) clouds are common on clear, warm days.

Cumulus clouds can develop into cumulonimbus, or thunderstorm, clouds. ▶

CIRRUS CLOUDS
Cirrus (SIR•uhs) clouds usually indicate cool, fair weather.

307

Weather Maps

Have you ever used a street map to find a friend's house? Have you ever used a trail map while hiking? Another kind of map you can use is a weather map. A weather map helps you know what the weather is like in an area.

Weather maps use symbols to show the weather. A sun symbol means it is sunny in the area. A symbol of a cloud with rain means it is raining in the area.

Fronts are also shown on weather maps. The symbol for a warm front is a red line with half circles along it. A blue line with triangles shows a cold front.

Many weather maps show temperature. Sometimes the temperature is written on the map. In the United States, the temperature is given in degrees Fahrenheit. Almost all other countries give the temperature in degrees Celsius. When the temperature is not written on the weather map, it may be shown using colors. When an area is warm, it will be colored red (very hot), orange (warm), or yellow (mild).

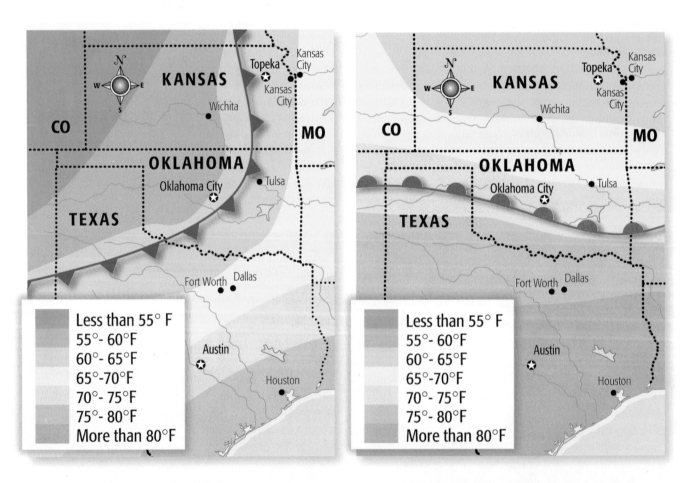

▲ A line with triangles is the symbol for a cold front. The triangles point in the direction of movement.

▲ A line with half circles is the symbol for a warm front. The half circles point in the direction the front is moving.

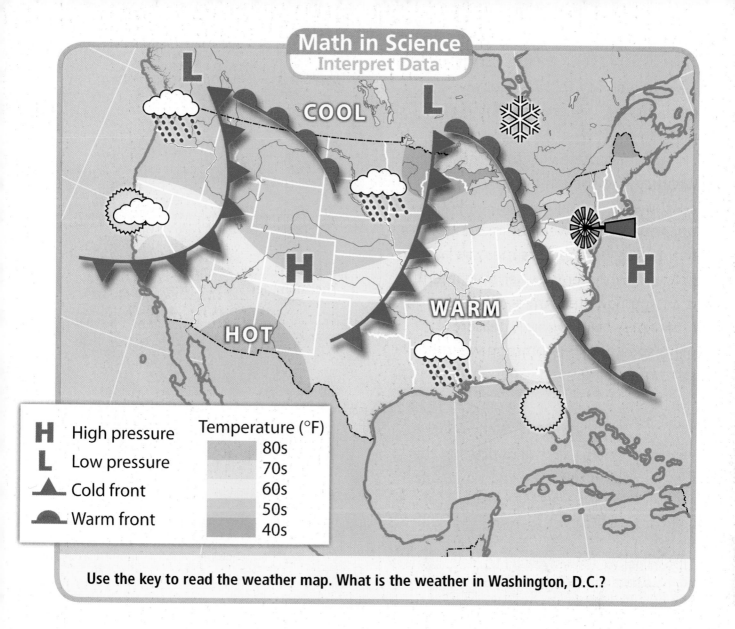

COOL

L

L

HOT

H

WARM

H

H	High pressure	Temperature (°F)
L	Low pressure	80s
▲	Cold front	70s
		60s
◓	Warm front	50s
		40s

Use the key to read the weather map. What is the weather in Washington, D.C.?

When an area is cold, it will be colored green (cool) or blue (very cold).

Other information you may see on a weather map includes wind speed and direction, air pressure, and the highest and lowest temperature in an area for that day.

Where does all the information on a weather map come from? Weather information is collected at thousands of weather stations across the country. A weather station is a place that has

many different instruments that measure weather. The information from the weather stations is reported to the National Weather Service (NWS). The NWS then studies the weather data from all the weather stations. Each day, the NWS makes weather maps based on the information collected at all the weather stations.

 CAUSE AND EFFECT How would the weather map above look if a warm front were moving through Florida?

Measuring Weather

When you say that it is hot or cold outside, you are describing one part of weather—the temperature. The most accurate way to describe weather is to use data from weather instruments. In the Investigate, you built one kind of weather instrument—a barometer. **Barometers** measure air pressure. Another weather instrument is an anemometer. **Anemometers** (an•uh•MAHM•uht•uhrz) measure wind speed. Other common weather instruments are wind vanes and rain gauges.

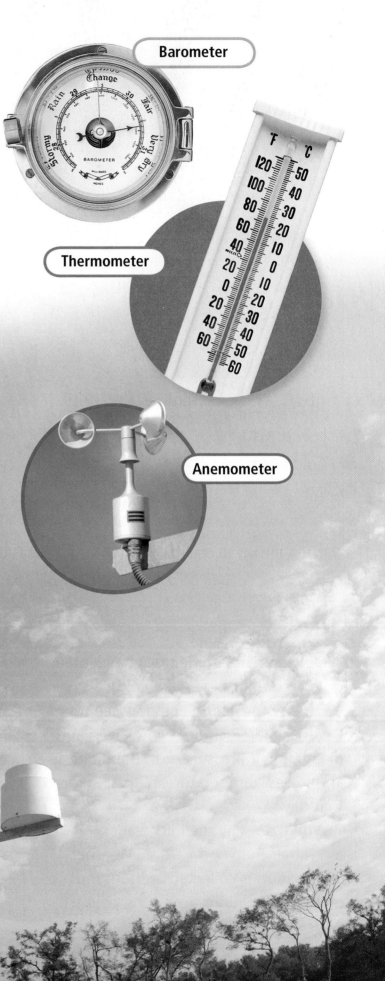

Barometer

Thermometer

Anemometer

 Focus Skill **CAUSE AND EFFECT** While reading a thermometer, you notice that the temperature has fallen throughout the day. What might be causing this?

This school weather station collects data for students. The data is shared with other schools. ▶

1. CAUSE AND EFFECT Copy and complete the following graphic organizer.

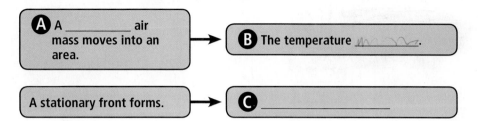

A A _____ air mass moves into an area. → **B** The temperature _____.

A stationary front forms. → **C** _____

2. SUMMARIZE Write a paragraph explaining how air masses, fronts, and the water cycle are related.

3. DRAW CONCLUSIONS Why might it have been more difficult to predict weather years ago?

4. VOCABULARY Use each vocabulary term in the lesson in a sentence.

FCAT Prep

5. Read/Inquire/Explain You hear on the radio that a cold front is headed toward your town. What type of weather can you expect?

6. Which of the following instruments measures wind speed?
- **A.** anemometer
- **B.** barometer
- **C.** rain gauge
- **D.** thermometer

Links

Writing

Narrative Writing
Use what you have learned in this chapter to write a short **poem** about weather and the water cycle. Use these terms in your poem: *air mass, front, rain, clouds.*

Math 9÷3

Subtract Decimals
Suppose you record a rainfall of 0.3 cm in the gauge in the morning. You don't empty the gauge. In the afternoon, the gauge reads 1.5 cm. How much new rain fell?

Language Arts

Be a Weather Forecaster
Make up a weather map of your state. Present your forecast to the class. Be sure to use the correct vocabulary for the weather you are describing.

 For more links and activities, go to www.hspscience.com

INTO THE EYE OF THE STORM

Hurricane Charley occurred in August 2004. Normally, during such a deadly storm, many people run, drive, or fly away as fast and as far as possible. One flight crew working for the National Weather Service, however, flew into (yes, into) the storm. Called Hurricane Hunters, they actually flew a plane into the center of Charley.

Hurricanes are powerful, whirling storms that form over warm oceans and cause torrential rains and heavy winds. The eye of a hurricane is the calm center of the storm. The eye has little wind and few clouds. Swirling around the eye are heavy winds.

Hurricane Hunters fly directly into the eye of a hurricane—not above it. The reason is that a hurricane can be more than 15,000 meters (50,000 ft) high, and the planes can fly only as high as 9000 meters (30,000 ft).

312

Hurricanes are rated on a scale of 1 to 5. The ratings are based on a storm's wind speed and potential for destruction.

CATEGORY 1	**74 to 95 miles per hour (mph)** Minor damage to trees and shrubs; minor flooding
CATEGORY 2	**96 to 110 mph** Some trees and signs blown down; some flooding; no major damage to buildings; some evacuations
CATEGORY 3	**111 to 130 mph** Some large trees and signs destroyed; some damage to small buildings; some evacuations
CATEGORY 4	**131 to 155 mph** Extreme damage to buildings; major beach erosion; evacuations up to 2 miles from shore
CATEGORY 5	**Greater than 155 mph** Severe damage to buildings; some small buildings knocked down; evacuations up to 10 miles from shore

A Hurricane Hunter drops a tube into the eye of a storm.

As the plane "punched through" the eye wall of Charley, crew members experienced a rocky ride. The eye wall is a solid ring of thunderstorms around the eye. The strongest winds and heaviest rains are located here.

The plane contains equipment that records weather. In the eye of the storm, Hurricane Hunters released small tubes attached to parachutes. Each tube was about the size of a can of tennis balls. The tubes sent information about wind speed, power, and moisture back to the crew.

Accurate Forecasting

As part of their job, Hurricane Hunters help forecasters rate storms. Hurricanes are rated on a scale of 1 to 5.

A storm's rating is based on wind speed and potential for damage. Before hitting land, Charley was a Category 4 storm.

Charley packed winds of up to 230 kilometers (145 mi) per hour by the time it hit land. The storm first walloped Jamaica and Cuba before slamming into Florida.

Hurricane Charley left about a million Florida households without electricity. The storm destroyed or severely damaged at least 16,000 homes and left thousands of residents without running water.

THINK ABOUT IT

1. Why is it important that forecasters accurately predict the path of a hurricane?
2. How do you think hurricanes can cause flooding on land?

Find out more! Log on to **www.hspscience.com**

SCIENCE Spin™ from WEEKLY READER®

People

SC.D.1.2.3.4.1
water cycle
SC.H.3.2.1.4.1
technologies,
costs/benefits

Saving the Earth

Earth Day encourages kids around the world to take action. From cleaning up local parks to testing local water, kids help the Earth on Earth Day, which is held on April 22.

But eleven-year-old Michaela Piersanti from New Haven, Connecticut, thinks the environment needs to be protected all year long, not just on Earth Day.

Although the event is important to millions of kids like Michaela, more needs to be done. "We need to keep the Earth clean," Michaela said. "If we pollute, it can make animals sick and possibly kill them."

Water for Life

A big part of Earth Day is making people aware of water pollution. In fact, the theme of a recent Earth Day was "Water for Life."

That theme was chosen because more than 1 billion people around the world do not have clean drinking water. Water gets polluted from sewage, factories, and chemicals. Pollution harms the plants and animals that live in the water. It also makes drinking water unsafe.

HELP!

SAVE THE EARTH

You Can Do It!

Make a Rain Gauge

Materials
- 1-L clear plastic bottle
- scissors
- plastic ruler
- masking tape

Procedure

1. **CAUTION: Be careful when using scissors. Remove the cap from the bottle, and have an adult cut the top off the bottle.**

2. Tape the ruler to the outside of the bottle. The zero mark should be at the bottom of the bottle.

3. Turn the bottle top over so that it will act like a funnel, and put it inside the bottle bottom.

4. Put the rain gauge out in the open, but away from any roof edges or trees.

5. After it rains, measure the rainfall, and empty the bottle.

Draw Conclusions

How much rainfall did you measure? How did measuring rainfall help you describe weather?

Design Your Own Investigation

Weather and the Seasons

How does weather in your area change from season to season? Design an investigation in which you use various weather instruments to measure weather over the course of a year. Record data regularly. Use your data to compare measurements such as average daily temperature, wind speed and direction, and amount of precipitation among the different seasons. Then draw graphs that show how weather in your area changes over the year.

Review and FCAT Preparation

Vocabulary Review

Use the terms below to complete the sentences. The page numbers tell you where to look in the chapter if you need help.

precipitation p. 282   **land breeze** p. 298

water cycle p. 282   **air mass** p. 304

evaporation p. 284   **warm front** p. 306

condensation p. 285   **barometer** p. 310

hurricane p. 292   **anemometer** p. 310

1. A breeze moving from the land to the sea is a _____.

2. A large tropical storm with high wind speeds is called a _____.

3. Air pressure is measured with a _____.

4. A gas changes to a liquid during the process of _____.

5. A large body of air is called an _____.

6. Water that falls to Earth from the air is known as _____.

7. A liquid changes to a gas during the process of _____.

8. Warm air pushes forward and moves over cold air along a _____.

9. Wind speed is measured with an _____.

10. The movement of water through the environment is known as the _____.

Check Understanding

Write the letter of the best choice.

11. In the water cycle, what happens before water condenses in clouds?
    A. Water dissolves salt.
    B. Water evaporates.
    C. Water falls as precipitation.
    D. Water vapor changes to a gas.

12. Look at the diagram below. What is shown?
    F. evaporation
    G. groundwater formation
    H. cirrus clouds
    I. sea breeze

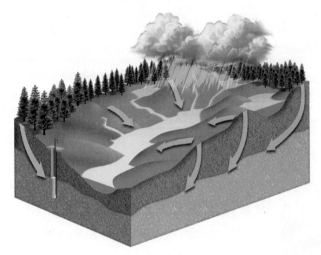

13. What type of precipitation is shown in the picture?

A. hail   **C.** sleet
B. rain   **D.** snow

14. Landforms such as mountains affect the water cycle.

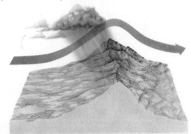

What is it called when one side of a mountain is dry?

F. a land breeze   **H.** a sea breeze
G. a rain shadow   **I.** a tornado

15. There is a stationary front over Centerville. What kind of weather is Centerville most likely having?

A. a few hours of drizzly rain
B. a few hours of thunderstorms
C. clear weather
D. several days of rain or snow

16. How would an air mass that forms over the Gulf of Mexico most likely be described?

F. cold and dry
G. cold and moist
H. warm and dry
I. warm and moist

Inquiry Skills

17. You **observe** clouds forming on a warm, sunny day. What can you **infer** is happening in the atmosphere? What may happen later in the day?

18. Suppose you plan to **measure** weather conditions over the next week. What will you measure, and what equipment will help you?

READ INQUIRE EXPLAIN Read/Inquire/Explain

19. Look at the weather map below. Describe the weather in Miami.

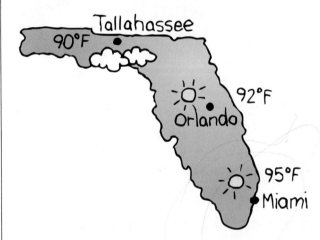

20. Tonya watches the weather report every day for a week. Each day, the average temperature is the same, and the air pressure doesn't change.
Part A Explain what might be happening to cause the weather in Tonya's town.
Part B How would the weather change if a warm front came through the area?

Lesson 1 **What Are Natural Resources?**

Lesson 2 **How Do Living Things Use Resources?**

Lesson 3 **What Is Conservation?**

Vocabulary

FCAT-Tested
resource
renewable resource
nonrenewable resource
conservation

Other Terms
natural resource
energy resource
fossil fuel
mineral resource
preservation

What do YOU wonder?

At a height of 221 meters (726 ft), Hoover Dam, on the Colorado River, is as tall as a 70-story skyscraper. What resources do the dam and its lake provide?

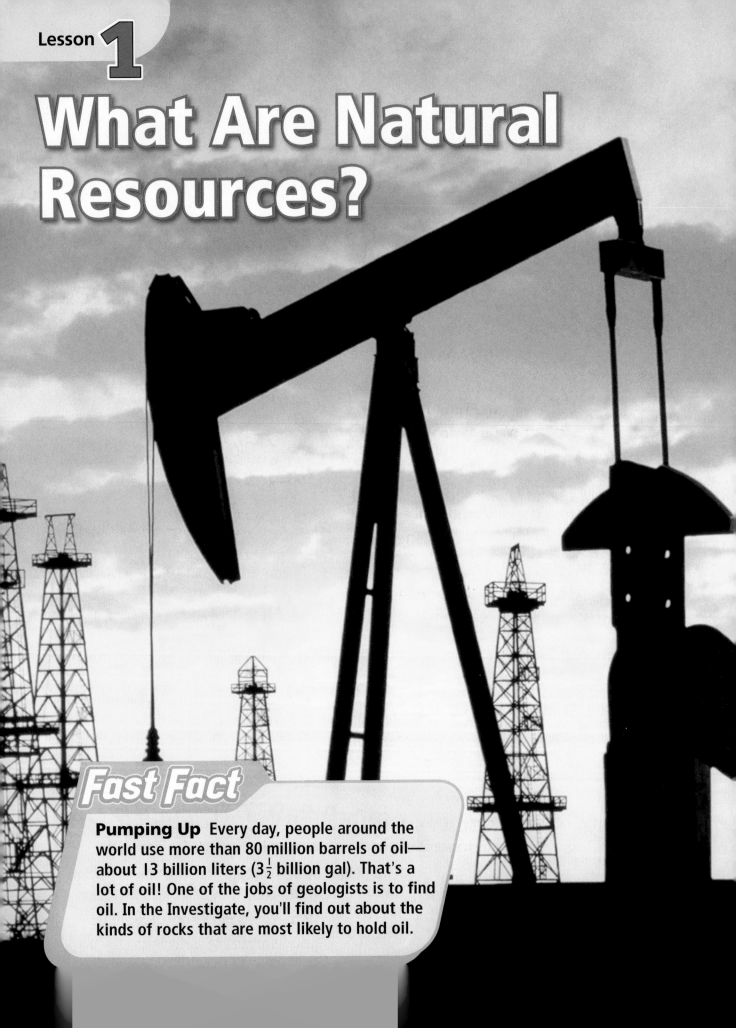

What Are Natural Resources?

Fast Fact

Pumping Up Every day, people around the world use more than 80 million barrels of oil—about 13 billion liters ($3\frac{1}{2}$ billion gal). That's a lot of oil! One of the jobs of geologists is to find oil. In the Investigate, you'll find out about the kinds of rocks that are most likely to hold oil.

What Kinds of Rocks Hold Oil?

Materials
- limestone
- mineral oil
- paper plates
- dropper
- shale
- sandstone
- clock

Procedure

1. Place the rock samples on separate paper plates. Observe each rock. Predict which one will hold oil best.

2. Fill the dropper with mineral oil. Put five drops of oil on the limestone sample.

3. Observe and record the time it takes for the five drops of oil to soak into the sample.

4. Continue adding oil, counting the drops, until the sample soaks up no more oil. Use numbers to record how many drops the rock holds.

5. Repeat Steps 2-4 using the other rock samples.

Step 2

Step 5

Draw Conclusions

1. Which rock soaked up the first five drops of oil the fastest? How long did that take?

2. Which rock can hold the most oil? How did you draw your conclusion?

3. **Inquiry Skill** Scientists often use numbers to compare things. How did you use numbers to compare in this Investigate?

Investigate Further

Geologists search for deposits of petroleum, from which oil is produced. Plan an investigation to determine which rocks would be good sources of petroleum.

VOCABULARY
resource p. 322
natural resource p. 322
energy resource p. 323
fossil fuel p. 324
mineral resource
   p. 326

SCIENCE CONCEPTS
▶ what resources are
and how they are
used
▶ what fossil fuels are
and how they are
used

Focus Skill

READING FOCUS SKILL

MAIN IDEA AND DETAILS
Look for details about why
resources are important.

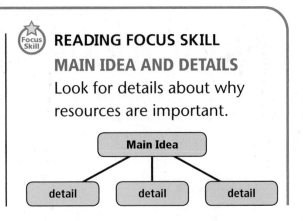

Natural Resources

The gasoline that goes into cars comes
from a resource. So does the material
used to make cans. A **resource** is any
material that people use to satisfy a
need, such as food, shelter, or fuel.

Earth is the source of most resources
that living things depend on. Many
resources are **natural resources**, or
those that are found in nature and not
made by people. Soil is just one natural
resource that living things depend on.
Farmers need soil to plant crops. People
and animals eat the plants that grow
in soil.

Another important natural resource is
water. Oceans provide homes and food
to many living things. Fresh water—
including lakes, ponds, rivers, and
streams—also provides homes and food
to living things. People need clean, fresh
water to drink, as well.

**Farms take up about 43 percent of the
land in the United States. The average
farmer in the United States provides
enough food for 130 people. ▼**

Forests are another important natural resource. People use wood for building houses and for making furniture. People use trees to make paper, too.

People also depend on resources for energy. An **energy resource** is a resource used to produce electricity, heat, or light. Most energy resources are natural resources. Some of these, such as oil and coal, are burned to produce electricity. Oil is also used to make gasoline for cars, plastic for containers, and even fibers for clothes. Some people burn wood for heat. People can also get energy from the wind, from moving water, and from sunlight.

 MAIN IDEA AND DETAILS What are three natural resources that people depend on?

▲ More than half of the wood harvested in the world is burned for fuel.

◀ People use water for drinking, for washing, for preparing food, and for irrigating crops and lawns. Each person in the United States uses about 380 liters (100 gal) of water every day.

323

Fossil Fuels

You may think of fossils only as dinosaur bones in museums. But fossils are important to everyone. Coal, natural gas, and oil are natural resources known as **fossil fuels**. They formed from the remains of plants and animals that lived millions of years ago.

Fossil fuels are energy resources. Burning fossil fuels releases energy that first came from the sun. Ancient plants used the sun's energy to make food.

Animals ate the plants. When the plants and animals died millions of years ago, they piled up in layers under water or mud. Over many years, the matter in their decayed bodies slowly turned into *petroleum* (crude oil), coal, and natural gas. Today, petroleum is the world's most-used fossil fuel. Petroleum products fuel cars, planes, and ships. Coal is mostly used to make electricity. Natural gas is used for heating homes and businesses.

 MAIN IDEA AND DETAILS Why are coal and oil called fossil fuels?

Science Up Close

Coal Formation

Step 1

Millions of years ago, plants died and fell to the bottom of swamps. Under the water and mud, there was little oxygen to help the process of decay. Over time, the partially decayed remains became peat. Some people use peat as a fuel.

For more links and activities, go to **www.hspscience.com**

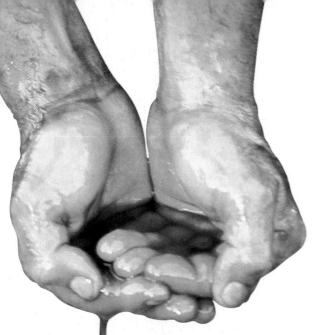

Insta-Lab

Drilling for Oil

Put a layer of clay at the bottom of a clear plastic cup. Add layers of rice, gummi worms, and sand. Push a straw through the layers, and pull it out. How is this similar to the way an oil driller finds oil?

▲ Petroleum is also called crude oil. It varies in color from clear to black, depending on where it was found.

Step 2

Over time, the decaying plants were buried deeper. The pressure on them changed the remains. Water and other substances were forced out, leaving mostly carbon.

Step 3

After even more time, the remains became coal. They were buried deeper, and the greater pressure changed them more.

Step 4

With even higher temperature and pressure, the coal became almost all carbon. The result was a hard form of coal, anthracite, that is a valuable fuel.

Anthracite

325

Mineral Resources

You use mineral resources every day. For example, the salt you put on food is a mineral resource. So is the copper in pipes that carry the water you drink. The silver in a ring is a mineral resource, too. A **mineral resource** is a natural resource that comes from minerals found on or beneath Earth's surface.

Few mineral resources are ready to use as they are found. For example, a lump of silver ore is not something you'd want in a ring. The ore must be processed to separate the silver from the other materials that are also found in the ore. Only then can the silver be used to make jewelry.

Even after some mineral resources are separated, they're combined with materials that make them more useful. Iron, for example, is combined with carbon and other materials in a hot furnace to make steel. Steel is stronger than iron. Steel makes tall buildings strong. It also makes strong parts for cars and ships.

MAIN IDEA AND DETAILS What are two places where minerals are found?

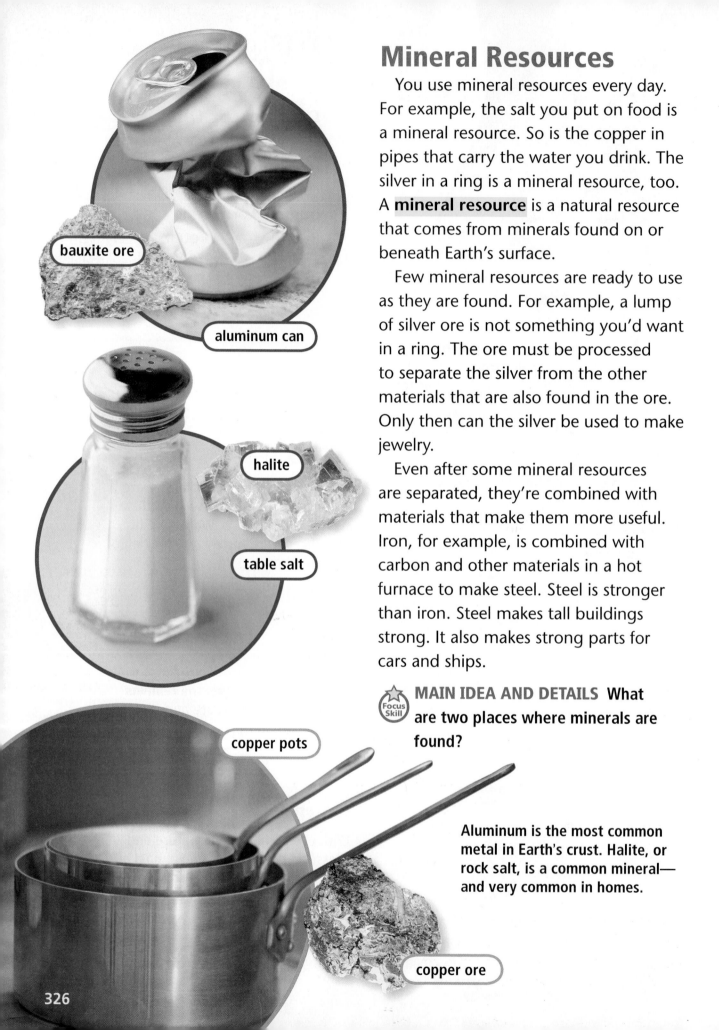

bauxite ore

aluminum can

halite

table salt

copper pots

Aluminum is the most common metal in Earth's crust. Halite, or rock salt, is a common mineral—and very common in homes.

copper ore

1. MAIN IDEA AND DETAILS Draw and complete this graphic organizer.

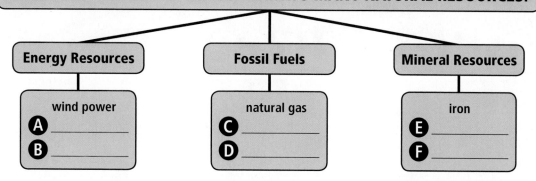

MAIN IDEA: LIVING THINGS USE EARTH'S MANY NATURAL RESOURCES.

Energy Resources

wind power
A _____
B _____

Fossil Fuels

natural gas
C _____
D _____

Mineral Resources

iron
E _____
F _____

2. SUMMARIZE Write a sentence that tells the most important information in this lesson.

3. DRAW CONCLUSIONS What are two ways that fossil fuels are different from other energy resources?

4. VOCABULARY Explain in a sentence what a mineral resource is.

FCAT Prep

5. Read/Inquire/Explain
Describe how resources are used in a car.

6. Which of these is a resource used to produce energy?
A. coal **C.** iron
B. copper **D.** soil

Links

Writing

Expository Writing
Suppose your community didn't have any fossil fuels. How would you get energy? Where in your community could you find energy resources? Write a **description** of these resources.

Math

Estimate Solutions
Each person in the United States uses about 11 liters of oil in a day. How many liters of oil is that in a year? Round to the nearest thousand.

Social Studies

Resource Revolution
There was a time when people didn't use so many resources. Find out about the Industrial Revolution. Why did the Industrial Revolution lead to a rise in the use of resources? Write a short report explaining this.

For more links and activities, go to www.hspscience.com

How Do Living Things Use Resources?

Fast Fact

Back to Nature An average lawn needs about 38,000 liters (10,000 gal) of water a year. Using native plants, which are adapted to the area, along with plants that don't need a lot of water, can cut outdoor water use by 50 percent. In the Investigate, you will explore many of the ways that you use resources such as water.

Using Resources Every Day

Materials • clipboard • pencil • paper

Procedure

1. Copy the table shown on this page.

2. Work with a partner to gather data. Walk around your classroom. When you find an item that belongs on the list, record the item.

3. Make a check mark under the name of the natural resource that item comes from. Some items may come from more than one type of resource. A pencil made of wood and the mineral graphite is one example of this. Remember that plastics are made from petroleum. Examples of resources that belong in the *Other* category are water and plants.

Item	Wood	Petroleum	Rocks and Minerals	Other

Draw Conclusions

1. Interpret the gathered data. Which type of natural resource do you use most often at school? Why do you use this resource the most?

2. **Inquiry Skill** Scientists use information they have gathered to predict. How would your life be different without petroleum products in the classroom?

Step 2

Rain Forests of the World

Investigate Further

Make another copy of the chart on this page. Then gather data about resources you use at home. Compare your results at home with the results from school. Do you use resources differently when you're at home?

VOCABULARY
preservation p. 334

SCIENCE CONCEPTS
► how people use and misuse natural resources
► how people can save natural resources

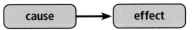 **READING FOCUS SKILL**
CAUSE AND EFFECT Look for the effects of misusing resources.

cause ⟶ effect

Use of Resources

People use many natural resources to meet their needs. People need water to drink. They need soil to grow food, and trees for wood to build homes. People need petroleum products to heat their homes and to run their cars.

People also need water to raise crops and to produce electricity. Factories need water to make products such as steel and cloth.

Because of these needs for water, people collect and store it. Some communities build lakes called *reservoirs* (REZ•er•vwahrz). Reservoirs store water until people need it. In some places where there isn't enough fresh water, people build factories to take the salt out of seawater or ocean water so it's safe to drink.

If you look around, you can probably see several ways you use wood. Is

▼ Water is used for many, many things. People need it to live. They also use it for such things as washing clothes, washing dishes, or washing their cars.

your pencil made of wood? Does your classroom have wooden chairs and desks? Wood is an important resource.

Because of the need for wood, companies grow and harvest trees. About one-fifth of the land in the United States has forests that can be used for lumber. Companies that own or use that land cut down the trees and then plant more trees for future use.

Petroleum is widely used around the world. People use petroleum products for many things, from gasoline to plastics. Because of these needs, companies around the world find and collect oil. After the crude oil is collected it is sent to factories that change it into more useful forms.

 CAUSE AND EFFECT Why do communities collect and store water?

People use natural resources for many things. Wood is used to build houses. Many of the foods people eat are natural resources. In the twentieth century, scientists discovered how to make plastics from petroleum.

Misuse of Resources

People are sometimes careless with resources. When that happens, the supply of resources can be reduced. Misuse of resources can cause problems for Earth and for all living things.

For example, the supply of trees can run low when people cut down an old forest and don't plant new trees to replace what they have cut. This kind of harvesting is called *deforestation* (dee•fawr•ist•AY•shuhn), and it destroys habitats. Another effect of deforestation is soil loss. Soil loss happens when there aren't enough trees to stop soil from washing away. Then nothing can be planted in that area.

Careless mining also causes problems. Some miners use poisonous chemicals to separate minerals after removing ores from the ground. Those poisons may get into streams. The result can be polluted water that's harmful to plants and animals living in it and that's unsafe to drink.

People may also waste some resources. There once seemed to be no end to the fish in the ocean. This is not the case today. When people

Deforestation like this is less common in the United States today. This way of harvesting is harmful to the land and living things.

Water Use in the United States

This graph shows the main uses of water in the United States. What is most water used for in the United States? Why do you think this is?

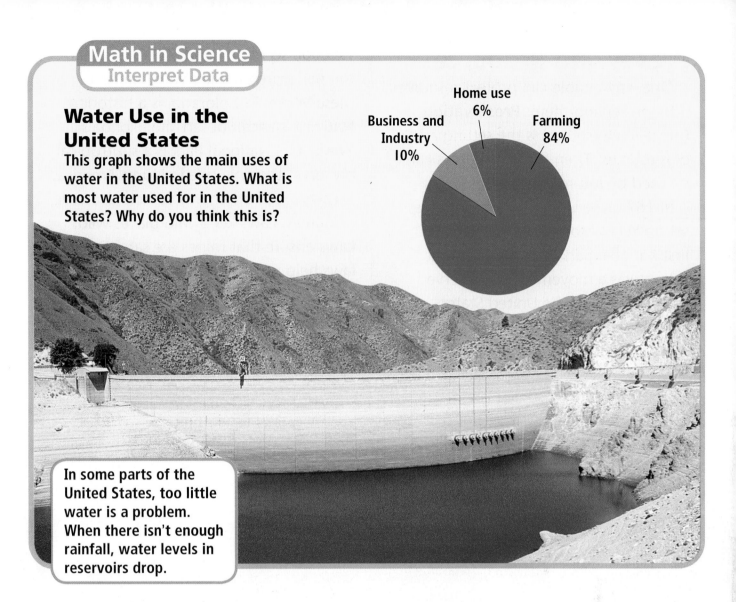

Home use 6%

Business and Industry 10%

Farming 84%

In some parts of the United States, too little water is a problem. When there isn't enough rainfall, water levels in reservoirs drop.

take too many fish out of the ocean, the chances of survival become smaller for those species. This is *overfishing.* People who make their living by fishing might lose their jobs if there are too few fish.

Some farmers are careless with the soil they use. When soil is poor, crops don't grow well. Soil that isn't protected may blow away. Most farmers now plant a "cover crop" on land they aren't using for their main crops. A cover crop keeps soil from blowing away and keeps the soil rich.

 CAUSE AND EFFECT What can be a result of careless mining?

The Water We Use

Use a large clear plastic cup. From the bottom, measure 8.4 cm up the side of the cup, and make a mark. Measure 1 cm more, and make a mark. Measure 0.6 cm more, and make another mark. Pour water up to each mark. What does each mark stand for?

Preserving Resources

One way people can protect resources is by preserving them. **Preservation** (prez•er•VAY•shuhn) is the setting aside of resources. Then those resources can be used by future generations.

In 1872, the United States Congress set up Yellowstone National Park as the first national park. The result of that action was a movement to preserve special places in the United States.

Today, the National Park Service looks after 324,000 sq km (about 125,000 sq mi) of land. The areas that the parks preserve are very different. Mesa Verde, in Colorado, is a historic Native American desert site. Florida's Everglades National Park is a subtropical preserve, the only one in North America.

Laws are another way to help preserve resources. Laws keep wild places wild. Laws ensure that mines are safe. Other laws help protect the air and water.

 CAUSE AND EFFECT What is one effect of the Everglades being made a national park?

▼ Many places have restrictions or laws to help preserve resources such as water.

Everglades National Park has both salt water and fresh water. Its wildlife includes wild turkeys, alligators, and cougars.

1. CAUSE AND EFFECT Copy and complete this graphic organizer.

| People need water, food, houses. | → | People use natural resources. |

A _____ → Natural resources are damaged.

People do not misuse resources. → **B** _____

2. SUMMARIZE Write a summary telling ways people use, misuse, and preserve resources.

3. DRAW CONCLUSIONS Why should people be careful not to overfish an area?

4. VOCABULARY Use the word *preservation* in a sentence about national parks.

FCAT Prep

5. Read/Inquire/Explain How might underground mining affect plants and animals in an area?

6. Which is an example of resource misuse?
   A. deforestation
   B. water storage
   C. processing ore
   D. planting cover crops

Links

Writing

Expository Writing
Write a brochure about a national park. First, research the park. Then, **describe** what the park is like, and tell why visitors would want to vacation there.

Math

Make a Line Graph
On average, the United States used 75 million liters of oil a day in 2000, 74 million liters in 2001, 75 million in 2002, and 76 million in 2003. Make a line graph to show this data.

Music

Song
Listen to a recording of the song "This Land Is Your Land," by Woody Guthrie. As you listen, keep track of the resources mentioned in the verses of the song.

 For more links and activities, go to www.hspscience.com

What Is Conservation?

Fast Fact

Trash to Art Some artists make art from old metal, bottle caps, plastic bags, junk mail, rubber tires, or lint from a dryer! This artist has found a new way to reuse old things. In the Investigate, you will make new paper from old paper.

Making Paper

Materials
- newspaper
- water
- blender
- plastic tubs
- clean cotton cloths
- wire screen
- plastic wrap
- several heavy books

Procedure

1. Your teacher will prepare a mixture of newspaper and water in a blender. Pour the blended mixture into a clean tub until the tub is one-fourth full.

2. Lay a damp cloth on a flat, waterproof surface. Slide the screen under the mixture in the tub. Pick up the screen, and press the wet newspaper to squeeze out the extra water.

3. Carefully flip the screen onto the cloth. Press it down firmly. Remove the screen.

4. Lay a dry cloth on top of the mixture. Cover the cloth with plastic wrap. Stack books on the plastic wrap.

5. After 24 hours, remove the books and cloths. Place the newly made paper on a dry cloth to dry.

Draw Conclusions

1. How does the paper you made compare with ordinary newspaper?

2. **Process Skill** What other types of paper could you experiment with to see if they would also be good for recycling into new paper?

Step 1

Step 2

Investigate Further

Try adding lint from a dryer or using different types of paper to affect the quality of your paper. Then draw conclusions about how different materials change the paper.

Reading in Science

SC.B.2.2.3.4.1 fossils fuels; SC.B.2.2.2.4.1 energy conservation; SC.B.2.2.2.4.2 nonrenewable energy sources, SC.D.2.2.1.4.1 conservation of natural resources; SC.D.2.2.1.4.2 misusing natural resources; LA.A.2.2.7 compare and contrast

VOCABULARY
renewable resource
    p. 338
nonrenewable resource
    p. 340
conservation p. 342

SCIENCE CONCEPTS
▶ what renewable resources are
▶ what nonrenewable resources are
▶ what conservation is

 READING FOCUS SKILL
COMPARE AND CONTRAST
Look for ways in which resources are alike and different.

[alike]——[different]

Renewable Resources

Many of the resources that people use and that help them meet their needs come from nature. Some resources can be replaced easily, while others can't. A **renewable resource** is one that can be replaced within a human lifetime.

One example of a renewable resource is solar energy. You feel solar energy when the sun warms you. Solar power systems collect that energy. Some of those systems change solar energy into electricity. In other solar power systems, the sun's energy heats water that people use for cooking, for washing, or for heating homes.

Another renewable resource is wood. Within a human lifetime, trees can grow to replace those that people use. Companies cut down trees to make lumber, paper, and furniture. They then plant small trees that grow to replace the ones that were cut down.

The tree in the first picture was planted to replace a tree that was cut down. The trees in the second picture will be harvested one day. They will be used for lumber and paper.

That way, a forest can remain a home for animals and plants.

Have you ever seen tall windmills turning on the top of a windy hill? Those windmills are turbines. They are part of a wind farm. As you may have guessed, wind is also a renewable resource. The turbines are connected to electric generators (JEN•er•ayt•erz). The generators change wind power into the electricity that powers people's homes.

Some companies are making new fuels to replace fossil fuels. One of these fuels is biodiesel (BY•oh•dee•zuhl). People make biodiesel from renewable sources such as vegetables. Soybean oil, for example, can be used to make biodiesel. Certain types of engines can use the biodiesel as fuel.

 COMPARE AND CONTRAST How are renewable resources alike?

▼ Farmers have used windmills for hundreds of years, although they didn't look like the one below.

▲ Long ago, people burned vegetable oil for light, but using biodiesel for vehicles is new.

These solar panels use energy from the sun to heat water. ▼

339

Nonrenewable Resources

Renewable resources can be replaced in a human's lifetime, but nonrenewable resources can't be. **Nonrenewable resources**, such as fossil fuels, are resources that have taken millions of years to form.

Fossil fuels have many good uses. Fossil fuels are less expensive than most other forms of energy. People use fossil fuels because they work well to provide power, heat, and light. Many people have jobs mining fossil fuels.

However, there are also problems with fossil fuels. Because they are nonrenewable, there will be no more fossil fuels after they have all been used. Also, when fossil fuels burn, they give off harmful substances. Those substances can mix with water in the air and form acid rain, which harms trees and ruins buildings.

 COMPARE AND CONTRAST What problems do fossil fuels cause?

Oil is a vital resource. However, oil spills kill birds, fish, and other wildlife. Oil spills are very hard to clean up and can having lasting effects on the environment.

Acid rain can destroy sculptures as well as buildings. These photographs show what damage acid rain caused to a statue over a period of about 50 years.

Before

After

Strip mining, which removes layers of land to reach minerals, leaves bare and ugly places where most plants can't grow.

Insta-Lab

The Problem with Acid

CAUTION: Wear safety goggles. Place vinegar, an acid, in one glass and water in another. Drop a piece of chalk into each glass. Watch each glass for two minutes. What happens? How is what happens to the chalk in vinegar similar to what happens when acid rain falls on statues?

Conservation

You can help the environment by conserving resources. **Conservation** (kahn•ser•VAY•shuhn) is the careful use and protection of Earth's natural resources. Conservation can help save nonrenewable resources. Conserving Earth's nonrenewable resources can also decrease pollution. Here are three ways to conserve resources every day.

One way to conserve is to *reuse.* For example, you can reuse shopping bags instead of getting new ones every time you shop.

A second way to conserve is to *reduce.* When you reduce, you use less. For example, when you choose a cereal in just a plastic bag, you use less of the resources needed to package products.

A third way to conserve resources is to *recycle.* Recycling is making new products from old ones. You can recycle paper, glass, aluminum cans, plastic, and cardboard.

⭐ **COMPARE AND CONTRAST** How are recycling, reducing, and reusing materials all alike?

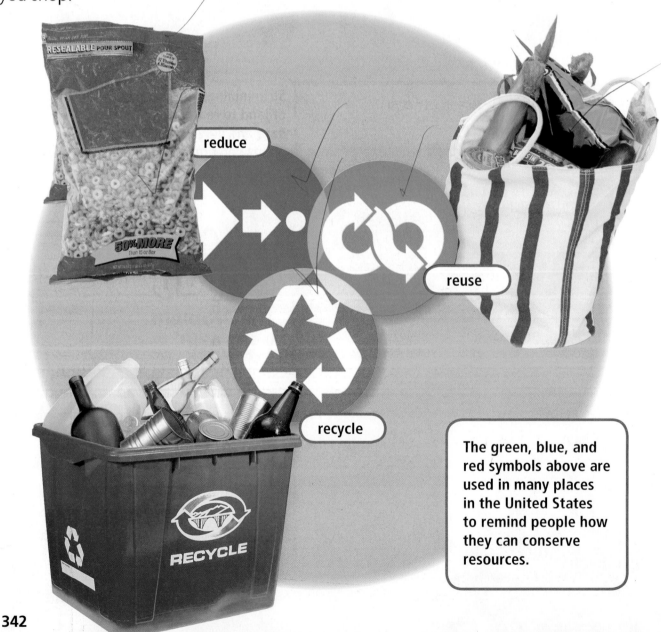

reduce

reuse

recycle

The green, blue, and red symbols above are used in many places in the United States to remind people how they can conserve resources.

1. COMPARE AND CONTRAST Copy and complete this graphic organizer.

Nonrenewable resources cannot be replaced in a human lifetime. Examples: coal

A _____

B _____

People use all of these resources to meet their needs.

Renewable resources can be replaced in a lifetime. Examples: trees

C _____

D _____

2. SUMMARIZE Write a short summary of this lesson.

3. DRAW CONCLUSIONS Why do scientists want to develop fuels that people can use in place of fossil fuels?

4. VOCABULARY Use the word *conservation* in a sentence to explain its meaning.

FCAT Prep

5. Read/Inquire/Explain Name ways you can use nonrenewable and renewable resources to dry wet clothes.

6. What causes acid rain?
- **A.** burning fossil fuels
- **B.** wind
- **C.** renewable resources
- **D.** solar power

Links

Writing

Write to Persuade
Write a slogan to **persuade** people that they should reduce, reuse, and recycle. If you like, set your slogan to music.

Math

Solve a Problem
Recycling aluminum cans can earn a dollar a kilogram. How many kilograms of cans do 25 students need to recycle to earn enough for a trip that costs $35 per student?

Art

New Art from Old Things
Look at the photograph at the beginning of this lesson. Then make your own art from things you might otherwise throw out.

 For more links and activities, go to www.hspscience.com

HOW Sweet IT IS!

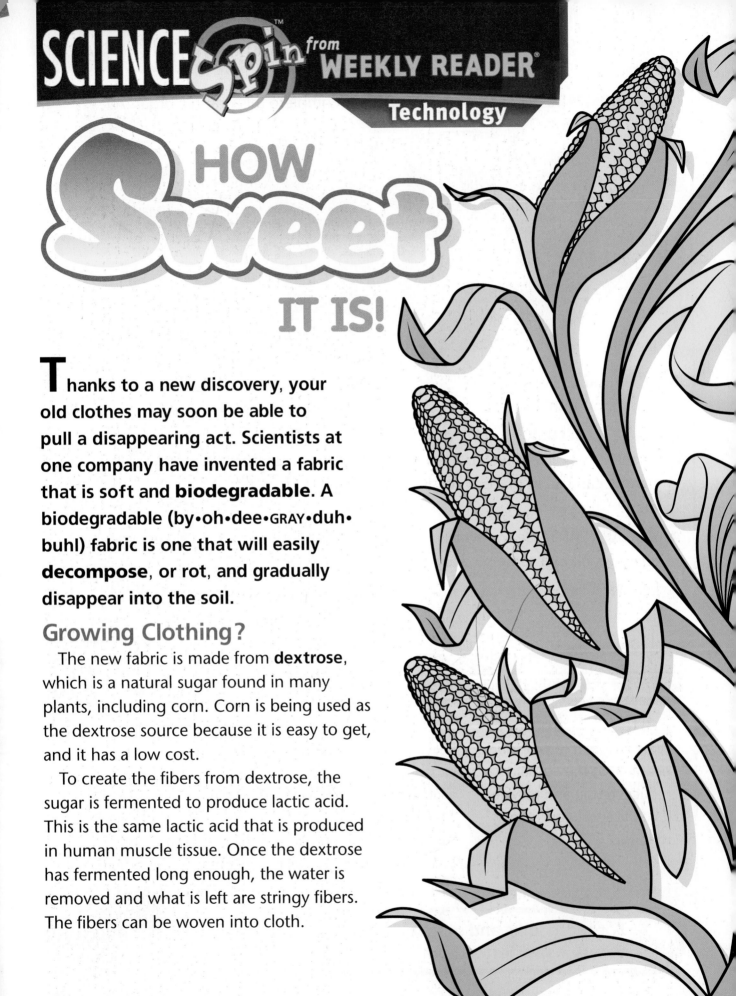

Thanks to a new discovery, your old clothes may soon be able to pull a disappearing act. Scientists at one company have invented a fabric that is soft and **biodegradable**. A biodegradable (by•oh•dee•GRAY•duh•buhl) fabric is one that will easily **decompose**, or rot, and gradually disappear into the soil.

Growing Clothing?

The new fabric is made from **dextrose**, which is a natural sugar found in many plants, including corn. Corn is being used as the dextrose source because it is easy to get, and it has a low cost.

To create the fibers from dextrose, the sugar is fermented to produce lactic acid. This is the same lactic acid that is produced in human muscle tissue. Once the dextrose has fermented long enough, the water is removed and what is left are stringy fibers. The fibers can be woven into cloth.

Clothing Breakdown

Manufacturers of biodegradable cloth say that by using renewable resources, such as corn, they are protecting the environment. That's because when such cloth is thrown away, it breaks down naturally within weeks, leaving no litter behind. Another benefit of biodegradable cloth, say manufacturers, is that they do not have to use as much oil to make products.

Scientists think the fabric will appeal to hikers with overloaded backpacks. "When you're done with a shirt, just dig a hole and bury it," explained one of the scientists who developed the fabric. "There are all sorts of bugs that will love to eat it up."

THINK ABOUT IT

1. Can you think of other uses for biodegradable products?

2. How might biodegradable cloth impact the amount of garbage we produce?

Find out more! Log on to
www.hspscience.com

SC.H.3.2.1.4.2 reporting on science
SC.H.3.2.3.4.1 impact of scientific discoveries
SC.H.3.2.4.4.1 solving problems/new ideas

SC.D.1.2.3.4.1 water cycle, SC.D.2.2.1.4.1 conservation of natural resources, SC.H.2.2.1.4.2 patterns in nature

Teaching About Groundwater

Groundwater is water that is found underground in the cracks in soil, sand and rock. It is used for drinking water by about half of the people in the United States.

Keeping groundwater clean is important, says Allyson Lien. She should know. She recently won the President's Environmental Youth Award for her work teaching people about the importance of groundwater.

One of the things she did was to build models that show kids how groundwater moves underground.

A government official gave Allyson's work high marks. She said that Allyson helped to get young people involved in protecting natural resources.

You Can Do It!

Materials
- shallow cardboard box
- aluminum foil
- scissors
- tape
- 2 drinking straws
- cheese

Quick and Easy Project

Solar Cooker

Procedure

1. Line the inside bottom and sides of the box with aluminum foil. Tape down the foil.

2. Cut around the top of the box to make a lid. Leave one side attached. Cover the inside of the lid with aluminum foil. Tape the foil to the lid.

3. Prop up one side of the lid with the straws.

4. Place the cooker so the sun's rays shine inside. Put the cheese inside.

Draw Conclusions
Why does the solar cooker get hot and melt the cheese? How is the solar cooker like cookers that use other energy sources?

Design Your Own Investigation

Reduce, Reuse, Recycle

Many people don't think about how they can conserve resources. Take notes for several days about how your class or school uses resources. Then design ways to reduce, reuse, or recycle those resources. Make a chart to keep track of how well your ideas work.

Review and FCAT Preparation

Vocabulary Review

Use the terms below to complete the sentences. The page numbers tell where to look in the chapter if you need help.

fossil fuel p. 324
mineral resource p. 326
preservation p. 334
renewable resource p. 338
nonrenewable resource p. 340
conservation p. 342

1. A resource that can be replaced in a human lifetime is a _____.

2. Protecting an area is _____.

3. The careful use and protection of natural resources is _____.

4. An energy source that came from organisms that lived millions of years ago is a _____.

5. Salt is a _____.

6. A resource that can't be replaced in a human lifetime is a _____.

Check Understanding

Write the letter of the best choice.

7. **COMPARE AND CONTRAST** How are plastic and gasoline similar?
   A. Both are easy to recycle.
   B. Both are made from petroleum.
   C. Both are ways to reuse minerals.
   D. Both are made of recycled materials.

8. **CAUSE AND EFFECT** What can be an effect of a farmer's not taking care of the land?
   F. pollution
   G. loss of soil
   H. reuse of wood products
   I. extra use of mineral resources

9. What does this illustration show?

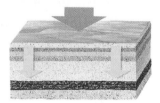

   A. how coal is formed
   B. how drillers find oil
   C. how minerals are mined
   D. why some resources are renewable

10. Which is an example of misuse of natural resources?
   F. farming   H. deforestation
   G. solar power   I. wind power

11. Which item shown is an example of a renewable resource?

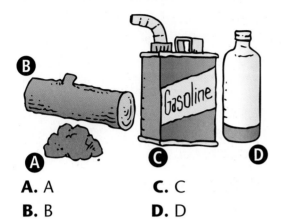

A. A   **C.** C
B. B   **D.** D

12. From which did fossil fuels form?
  F. petroleum
  G. fresh water
  H. the pressure of crude oil
  I. plants and animals

13. Which describes what soil is?
  A. a fossil fuel
  B. an energy resource
  C. a natural resource
  D. a resource that forms during a human lifetime

14. Where would laws most likely protect land from mining?
  F. a farm field
  G. private land
  H. a national park
  I. the top of a mountain

15. An aluminum can is made from used aluminum. What is this an example of?
  A. recycling   **C.** repairing
  B. reducing   **D.** reusing

16. Which problem could careless underground mining cause?
  F. acid rain   **H.** conservation
  G. polluted air   **I.** unhealthful water

Inquiry Skills

17. How can scientists **use numbers** to know how much people are recycling?

18. How can **interpreting data** help a scientist find out if air pollution laws are working?

Read/Inquire/Explain

19. Give examples of how people could reduce, reuse, and recycle resources.

20. Maurice knows that he and his family use energy resources every day, but he isn't sure where energy resources come from.
Part A Explain to Maurice how most energy resources on Earth come from the sun.
Part B Explain to Maurice the benefits of and problems with the use of petroleum and wind power.

Sunshine State Standards
SCIENCE STRAND E

Earth and Space

The chapters in this unit address these Grade Level Expectations from the Florida Sunshine State Standards.

Chapter 10

Planets and Other Objects in Space

SC.E.1.2.1.4.1   knows that the tilt of the Earth causes the change of seasons, length of day, and the amount of energy available.

SC.E.1.2.2.4.1   understands the cause of the phases of the Moon (for example, the movement patterns of the Earth and Moon relative to the Sun).

SC.E.1.2.3.4.1   knows how the energy of the Sun can be captured as a source of heat and light on Earth (for example, plants, solar panels).

SC.E.1.2.4.4.1   knows characteristics of Jupiter, Saturn, Uranus, Neptune, and Pluto.

SC.E.2.2.1.4.1   understands that the Sun is a medium-sized star located near the edge of a galaxy containing billions of other stars, which in turn is one of the innumerable galaxies in the Universe.

The investigations and experiences in this unit also address many of the Grade Level Expectations in Strand H, The Nature of Science.

Science in Florida

Cape Canaveral

NASA

Dear Calvin,
I had as much fun at Kennedy Space Center today as we did at summer camp last year. My class learned all about NASA and how they explore the universe. The postcard I bought shows the vehicle assembly building where they get the space shuttle ready to launch. The VAB is 52 stories tall and towers above everything else at the space center.
Hope you're having fun too,
Paulo

The Sunshine State

USA

FCAT Writing

Writing Situation
Think about what it would be like to go into space on the space shuttle. Write a story about being in space.

Experiment!

Build a Model Solar System Our solar system is made up of nine unique planets. It takes Earth 365.26 days, which we call one year, to travel around the sun. Do the other planets take the same amount of time to orbit the sun? To find out, build a model of the solar system, and test your hypothesis.

10 Planets and Other Objects in Space

Vocabulary

FCAT-Tested	Other Terms
axis	orbit
moon	comet
phases	constellation
solar system	galaxy
planet	universe
star	
sun	

What do **YOU** wonder?

On a clear night away from city lights, about 3,000 stars are visible. Why can we see these objects only at night? What other objects can be seen in the night sky?

How Do Earth and Its Moon Move?

Fast Fact

Sun, Moon, and Myths To the ancient Romans, Diana was the goddess of the moon. They honored Apollo as the sun god. The ancient Romans believed that their gods caused day and night and brought about changes in weather and seasons. In the Investigate, you will learn more about what really causes the seasons on Earth.

Seasons and Sunlight

Materials
- small 60-watt table lamp
- ruler
- graph paper
- black construction paper

- thermometer

Procedure

1. Work with a partner. Shine the lamp straight down from a height of 30 cm onto a sheet of graph paper. Draw an outline of the lit area, and label it Step 1.

2. Repeat Step 1 with a new sheet of graph paper, this time placing the lamp at an angle. Label this outline Step 2.

3. Shine the lamp straight onto a sheet of black paper. After 15 minutes, measure the temperature of the paper in the lit area. Record the temperature on the sheet of graph paper labeled Step 1.

4. Now use another sheet of black paper, and angle the light as you did in Step 2. Again, measure the temperature of the lit area after 15 minutes. Record the temperature on the sheet of graph paper labeled Step 2.

Step 1

Step 4

Draw Conclusions

1. How did the area covered by the light change? How did the temperature in that area change? Explain why these changes occurred.

2. **Inquiry Skill** How could scientists measure the effect that the sun has on seasons?

Investigate Further

Try your experiment on the real thing! Choose a sunny spot outdoors, and measure and record its temperature throughout the day. Why do you think it changes?

SC.E.1.2.1.4.1 changing seasons, **SC.H.1.2.3.4.1** working collaboratively, **SC.H.1.2.5.4.1** using models

Reading in Science

VOCABULARY
axis p. 356
orbit p. 356
moon p. 358
phases p. 358

SCIENCE CONCEPTS
▶ why there are seasons on Earth
▶ why the moon appears to change shape

Focus Skill **READING FOCUS SKILL**
SEQUENCE Events in a sequence happen in a certain order.

Earth's Tilt and the Seasons

Night follows day. Spring follows winter. The changes of night and day, as well as the seasons, occur because of the ways Earth moves.

Earth moves in two ways. Earth rotates, or spins, on its axis. An **axis** is an imaginary line through both poles. It takes about 24 hours for Earth to completely rotate on its axis. The second way Earth moves is by orbiting, or revolving around, the sun. The path of one object in space around another object is its **orbit**.

As Earth orbits the sun, part of it is tilted toward the sun. That part of Earth takes in more energy from the sun. This energy is in the form of heat. The part of Earth that is tilted away from the sun takes in less energy from the sun.

In this illustration, Earth's tilt is causing the sun's rays to shine more directly on the Northern Hemisphere than on the Southern Hemisphere. So the Northern Hemisphere has summer.

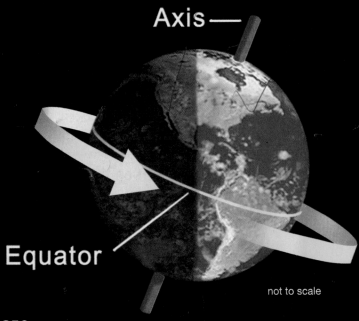

Axis—

Equator

not to scale

356

1 The summer *solstice* (SAHL•stis), about June 21 in the Northern Hemisphere, is the day of the year that has the most hours of daylight. **3** The winter solstice, about December 21, is the day that has the most hours of darkness.

2 On the autumn *equinox* (EE•kwih•nahks), about September 21, and the **4** spring equinox, about March 21, the hours of daylight and darkness are the same. These dates mark the beginning of autumn and of spring.

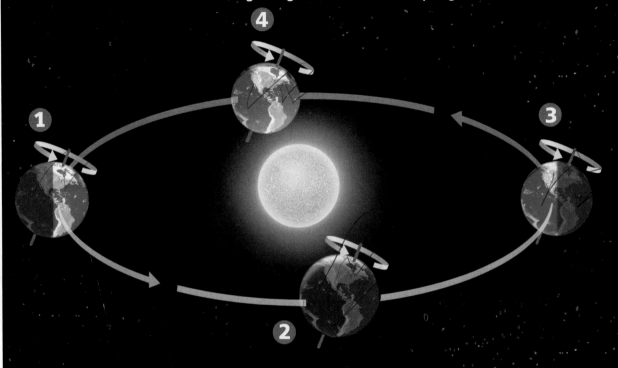

During June, July, and August, the Northern Hemisphere of Earth is tilted toward the sun and the Southern Hemisphere is tilted away. The sun's rays shine more directly on the Northern Hemisphere, which has summer, than on the Southern Hemisphere, which has winter. As Earth continues its orbit, the Northern Hemisphere is tilted away from the sun, causing winter. The Southern Hemisphere is tilted toward it, causing summer. This cycle continues as Earth orbits the sun.

 SEQUENCE What happens next after the Northern Hemisphere has been tilted away from the sun?

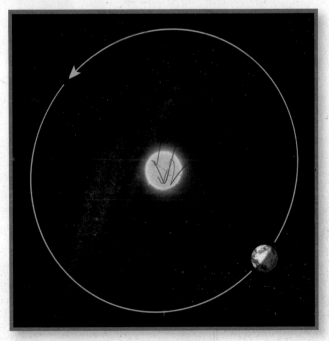

▲ Earth's orbit around the sun is almost a perfect circle.

Moon Phases

The **moon** is a small planetlike body that orbits Earth, rather than the sun. As Earth orbits the sun, the moon orbits Earth.

The moon appears to shine, but the light you see is actually reflected light from the sun. As the moon orbits Earth, different amounts of its lit surface can be seen. That's why the moon seems to have different shapes, or **phases**.

The phases of the moon follow the same pattern about every $29\frac{1}{2}$ days. On one of those days, all of the lit side of the moon can be seen from Earth. When this happens, we say there is a full moon. Then, as the days pass and the position of the moon changes, from Earth we see less of the lit side. Finally, we see none of the lit side at all. On that night, the moon is called a new moon.

 SEQUENCE What phase of the moon happens after we see less and less of the moon at night?

During the first half of the moon's cycle, the amount of the lit side of the moon seen from Earth *waxes*, or increases.

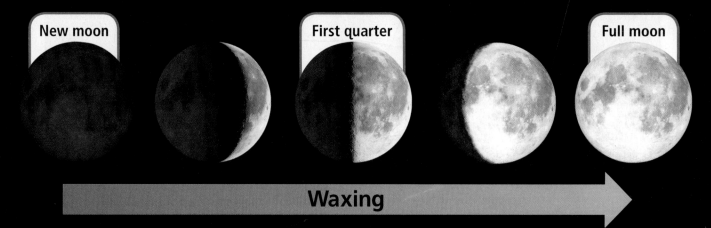

New moon | First quarter | Full moon

Waxing

During the second half of the moon's cycle, the amount of the lit side of the moon seen from Earth *wanes*, or decreases. Then the cycle begins again.

Full moon | Third quarter | New moon

Waning

One half of the moon is always being lit by the sun. Whether people can see all, some, or none of the lit side depends on the positions of the moon and Earth.

During the new moon phase, the lit side of the moon can't be seen from Earth.

The full moon phase occurs about 15 days after the new moon phase.

New Moon To Full Moon

When the moon's orbit brings it between Earth and the sun, its lit side can't be seen from Earth. This phase is called the new moon. Later in the month, when Earth is between the moon and the sun, we see the sun's light reflected from one whole side of the moon. When this happens, we see a full moon.

Insta-Lab

Sun, Moon, and Earth

Model the moon phases in a dark room. Use a flashlight for your "sun" and two balls for your "moon" and "Earth." Shine the sun toward Earth, and move the moon around Earth. What causes changes in how much of the moon's lit side can be seen from Earth?

For more links and activities, go to www.hspscience.com

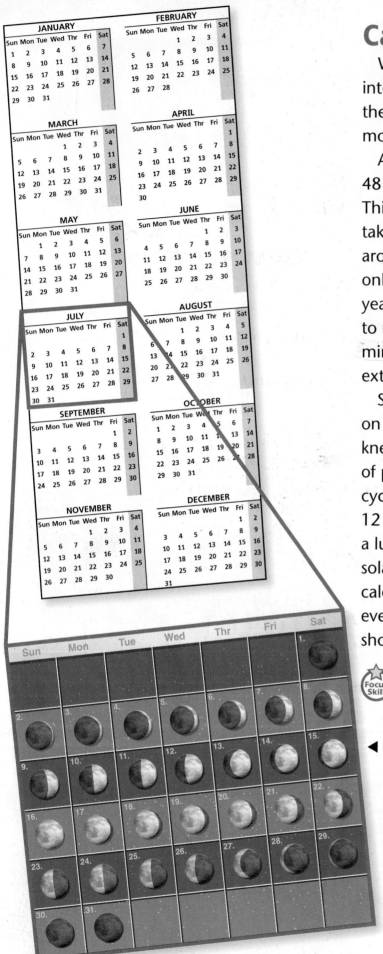

Calendars

We use calendars to divide time into days, months, and years. All of these units of time are based on the movements of Earth.

A solar year is 365 days, 5 hours, 48 minutes, and $45\frac{1}{2}$ seconds long. This is based on the amount of time it takes Earth to make one complete orbit around the sun. Today's calendars have only 365 days in a year. So every four years, an extra day is added in February to make up for the extra hours and minutes in a solar year. Years with an extra day are called leap years.

Some ancient people based months on the movements of the moon. They knew that the moon completes a cycle of phases in about $29\frac{1}{2}$ days. Each cycle was considered a month, and 12 months made a lunar year. However, a lunar year is $11\frac{1}{2}$ days shorter than a solar year. Some cultures that use lunar calendars add a month to their calendar every few years to make up for the shorter lunar year.

Focus Skill **SEQUENCE** **What occurs after three years have 365 days each?**

◀ **Most calendars are based on the solar year. Many also show the phases of the moon, which don't happen on the same day each month.**

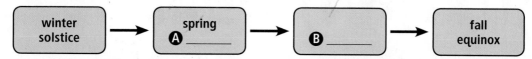

Focus Skill

1. SEQUENCE Copy and complete this graphic organizer.

| winter solstice | → | spring **A** _____ | → | **B** _____ | → | fall equinox |

2. SUMMARIZE Explain how the position and movement of Earth cause the seasons.

3. DRAW CONCLUSIONS If Earth took 500 days instead of 365 to orbit the sun, how would the seasons be different? Why?

4. VOCABULARY Use *axis* in a sentence that explains its meaning.

FCAT Prep

5. Read/Inquire/Explain How would day and night be different if Earth's axis were not tilted?

6. If you live in the Southern Hemisphere, what season do you have in August?

  A. spring   **C.** fall

  B. summer **D.** winter

Links

Writing

Expository Writing
Suppose a friend from the Southern Hemisphere plans to visit you in December. Write a **letter** explaining what kind of clothes to pack and why.

Math

Use Data
A normal year has 365 days. In a normal year, on average, how many days are in a month? How many days, on average, are there in each season?

Social Studies

Different Calendars
Research and report on a calendar other than the one you use. It can be an ancient calendar or one that is used today in a different part of the world.

For more links and activities, go to
www.hspscience.com

How Do Objects Move in the Solar System?

Rings Around a Planet Saturn's rings have fascinated sky gazers since the astronomer Galileo (gal•uh•LAY•oh) first saw them in 1610. We've learned that the rings are made of rock, gas, and ice. Saturn is millions of kilometers from Earth. In the Investigate, you will make a model to help you understand that distance.

Distances Between Planets

Materials • **4-m length of string** • **tape measure**
  • **9 markers of different colors**

Procedure

① Copy the table.

② At one end of the string, make a large knot. This knot will stand for the sun as you make your model.

③ An AU (astronomical unit) is Earth's average distance from the sun. In your model, 10 cm will represent 1 AU. Use the tape measure to measure Earth's distance from the knot that represents the sun. Use a marker to mark this point on the string. Record on the table which color you used for Earth by placing a small dot with the marker next to the planet name.

④ Complete the Scale Distance column of the table. Repeat Step 3 for each planet. Use a different color for each planet.

Planet Data

Planet	Average Distance from the Sun (km)	Average Distance from the Sun (AU)	Scale (cm)	Planet's Diameter (km)
Mercury	58 million	$\frac{4}{10}$	4	4876
Venus	108 million	$\frac{7}{10}$	7	12,104
Earth	150 million	1		12,756
Mars	228 million	2		6794
Jupiter	778 million	5		142,984
Saturn	1429 million	10		120,536
Uranus	2871 million	19		51,118
Neptune	4500 million	30		49,532
Pluto	5900 million	39		2274

Step 3

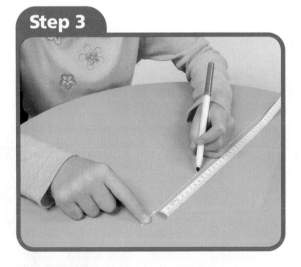

Draw Conclusions

1. In your model, how far away from the sun is Mercury? How far away is Pluto?

2. Why do scientists use AUs to measure distances in the solar system?

3. **Inquiry Skill** How does it help to use numbers instead of using real distances?

Investigate Further

Use a calculator to make a model of planet diameters. Use 1 cm to represent Earth's diameter. Then divide the other planets' diameters by Earth's. Make a scale drawing.

Reading in Science

VOCABULARY
solar system p. 364
planet p. 364
comet p. 368

SCIENCE CONCEPTS
▶ what makes up our solar system
▶ what the inner and outer planets are

READING FOCUS SKILL
COMPARE AND CONTRAST
Look for phrases such as *by contrast* and *in common*.

alike ——— different

Our Solar System

A **solar system** is a group of objects in space that orbit a star in the center, plus the star itself. The sun is the star in the center of our solar system. Everything else in the solar system is small compared to the sun.

Our solar system contains a variety of objects. These include planets and moons as well as asteroids, which are small and rocky. A **planet** is a large object that orbits a star. A moon is a smaller object that orbits a planet.

In our solar system, there are nine planets. Often, scientists group them as the inner planets, which are closer to the sun, and the outer planets, which are farther from the sun. These groups of planets are separated by a ring of asteroids that orbit the sun between Mars and Jupiter.

COMPARE AND CONTRAST **How are moons and planets similar and different?**

The sun is the largest object in our solar system. The next-largest objects are the nine planets that orbit the sun.

Mercury
Venus
Earth
Mars
Jupiter
Saturn
Uranus
Neptune
Pluto

Mercury is about the size of Earth's moon and is covered with craters. Although it's the planet closest to the sun, it's still about 58 million kilometers (36 million mi) from the sun.

The Inner Planets

The inner planets are those closest to the sun. They are Mercury, Venus, Earth, and Mars. These planets are alike in many ways. They all have rocky surfaces and are smaller than most of the outer planets. Also, none of the inner planets has more than two moons.

There are also differences among the inner planets. For example, it can be 450°C on Mercury—hot enough to melt lead—while Mars's temperature never gets higher than 20°C.

Earth is the most unusual inner planet. Only Earth has liquid water on its surface and a large amount of oxygen in the atmosphere. This water and oxygen help support life on Earth.

COMPARE AND CONTRAST How are the inner planets similar?

Mars is called the Red Planet because it looks fiery red from Earth. Mars is small—its diameter is only half of Earth's. It has huge dust storms that can last for months. Scientists think that at one time, Mars may have had liquid surface water.

Venus is about the same size as Earth. Venus is the third-brightest object in Earth's sky—only the sun and the moon appear brighter. Clouds of sulfuric (suhl•FYUR•ik) acid make the planet difficult to study from Earth. This radar image shows a surface made up of volcanoes, mountain ranges, highland regions, craters, and lava plains.

Earth is the largest of the inner planets. It's the only planet known to have life and the only one whose surface is mostly water. Earth's distance from the sun helps the planet maintain a temperature that supports life.

The Outer Planets

Beyond Mars, on the far side of the asteroid belt, are the outer planets. They are Jupiter, Saturn, Uranus, Neptune, and Pluto.

Four of the outer planets—Jupiter, Saturn, Uranus, and Neptune—have many similarities. These four planets are huge and made mostly of gases. These planets are often called the gas giants. They all have many moons, and they all are surrounded by rings that are made of dust, ice, or rock.

Pluto is unlike the other outer planets. It is by far the smallest planet in the solar system. It is smaller than Earth's moon. Pluto is the only outer planet that's not made mostly of gases. Instead, it has a rocky surface. Scientists think the surface is covered by frozen gases. Pluto wasn't discovered until 1930. The other planets were discovered much earlier.

 COMPARE AND CONTRAST How are the gas giants different from Pluto?

Jupiter—the largest planet in our solar system—has a diameter that's more than 11 times the diameter of Earth. Jupiter has at least 63 moons. For more than 300 years, a gigantic hurricane-like storm called the Great Red Spot has raged on Jupiter.

Saturn has rings that are visible from Earth through a telescope. Saturn has at least 31 moons. Its atmosphere is mostly hydrogen and helium. Like the other gas giants, Saturn has no known solid surface.

Length of a Year

On any planet, a year is the length of time it takes that planet to orbit the sun. Here is a list of how long a year is on some planets in our solar system, compared to a year on Earth.

Planet Years

Planet	Length of Year (in Earth years)
Mars	1.9
Jupiter	11.9
Saturn	29.5
Neptune	165
Pluto	249

If a person has just turned 60 on Earth, about how old is he or she in Saturn years?

Tiny Pluto has a rocky surface covered with nitrogen ice and small amounts of methane and carbon dioxide ices. Its atmosphere is mostly nitrogen. Pluto's moon is almost as large as Pluto itself. From the surface of Pluto, the sun looks like any other bright star in the sky.

Neptune's atmosphere is mainly hydrogen and helium. It is one of the windiest places in the solar system. Winds can reach 2000 kilometers per hour (1200 mi/hr). Neptune has at least 13 moons.

Uranus is another gas giant. Uranus rotates on its side as it orbits the sun. Scientists think this may be the result of a collision with an object the size of Earth. Uranus has at least 27 moons.

Insta-Lab

Planet Sizes

Compare the approximate sizes of planets. Use a marble to represent Pluto, a table tennis ball to represent Earth, and a basketball to represent Jupiter. Which of the three balls would best represent the size of Venus?

Other Objects in the Solar System

There are objects besides planets orbiting the sun. Two types of such objects are asteroids and comets. Although both orbit the sun, comets and asteroids are very different.

Asteroids are bits of rock and metal. Most are less than 1 kilometer (0.6 mi) across. The largest known asteroid is about 1000 kilometers (620 mi) in diameter. Most asteroids orbit the sun in a belt between Mars and Jupiter.

By contrast, a **comet** is a ball of rock, ice, and frozen gases. Most comets are less than 10 kilometers (6 mi) across, but the tails can be as much as 100,000 kilometers (62,000 mi) long. As a comet's orbit brings it close to the sun, the sun's heat may turn some of the frozen matter into gas. That gas, and dust that rises with it, then looks like a fiery tail and may be visible from Earth.

COMPARE AND CONTRAST What do comets and asteroids have in common?

Some comets, like Halley's comet, become well known because their orbits bring them close to Earth.

◄ This is the asteroid Gaspra. Asteroids are harder to see from Earth than comets. A 1991 space probe took the first close-up pictures of an asteroid.

1. COMPARE AND CONTRAST Copy and complete this graphic organizer. Write differences and similarities of the inner planets and the gas giants.

Inner Planets

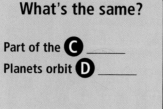

What's different?

Close to **A** _____
Small with rocky surfaces
No more than **B** _____ moons

What's the same?

Part of the **C** _____
Planets orbit **D** _____

Outer Planets

What's different?

E _____ from the sun
Have many **F** _____
Rings of dust, ice, and rock
Large except for **G** _____

2. SUMMARIZE Write two sentences that tell the most important information in this lesson.

3. DRAW CONCLUSIONS Why do you think life hasn't been found on any of the other planets in the solar system?

4. VOCABULARY Write a definition for *solar system.*

FCAT Prep

5. Read/Inquire/Explain
Suppose you look into the sky and see a comet. What can you conclude about the comet?

6. What separates the inner planets from the outer planets?

A. asteroid belt   **C.** Earth
B. comets   **D.** Venus

Links

Writing

Narrative Writing

Research a planet other than Earth. Write a travel guide that could be used by people who might visit that planet. Tell about the sights they would see or what a typical day might be like.

Math

Make a Bar Graph

Use the table in the Investigate to find the diameters of the planets in our solar system. Make a bar graph that compares their diameters.

Literature

Planet Fiction

Read a short story about life on another planet or about space travel. Decide whether the story could really happen. Report to the class on what you read.

 For more links and activities, go to www.hspscience.com

What Other Objects Can Be Seen in the Sky?

Fast Fact

Deep Space Images from the Hubble Space Telescope show distant objects in detail. They show space objects, such as the Omega Nebula, that are very far from Earth. In the Investigate, you will make your own telescope.

Make a Telescope

Materials
- modeling clay
- I thin (eyepiece) lens
- small-diameter cardboard tube
- I thick (objective) lens
- large-diameter cardboard tube

Procedure

1. Use the clay to fasten the thin lens in one end of the small tube. Set the lens as straight as possible, taking care not to smear the middle of the lens with clay.

2. Repeat Step 1, using the thick lens and the large tube. Slide the open end of the small tube into the large tube. You have just made a telescope.

3. Hold your telescope up, and look through each lens. CAUTION: **Never look directly at the sun.** Slide the small tube into and out of the large tube until what you see is in focus. How do objects appear through each lens? Record your observations.

Draw Conclusions

1. What did you observe as you looked through each lens?

2. Inquiry Skill Astronomers are scientists who study objects in space. Astronomers use telescopes to observe objects that are far away. How would you plan and conduct a simple investigation to observe Earth's moon?

Step 1

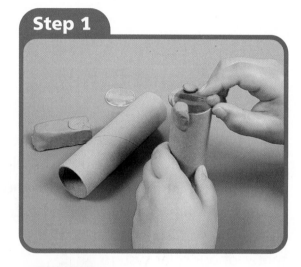

Step 2

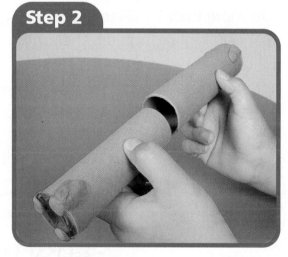

Investigate Further

Use your telescope to observe the moon at night. List details you can see by using your telescope that you can't see by using only your eyes.

Reading in Science

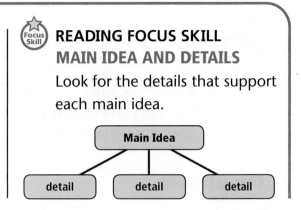
SC.E.2.2.1.4.1 sun size and location
LA.A.2.2.1 main idea and details

VOCABULARY

star p. 372

sun p. 372

constellation p. 374

galaxy p. 374

universe p. 374

SCIENCE CONCEPTS

▶ what stars and galaxies are

▶ what constellations are

READING FOCUS SKILL

MAIN IDEA AND DETAILS

Look for the details that support each main idea.

```
            ┌─────────────┐
            │  Main Idea  │
            └─────────────┘
           /       |        \
   ┌────────┐ ┌────────┐ ┌────────┐
   │ detail │ │ detail │ │ detail │
   └────────┘ └────────┘ └────────┘
```

The Sun and Other Stars

You have probably looked up at the stars in the night sky and noticed their different sizes and colors. You may know that a **star** is a huge ball of superheated gases. The **sun** is a star that is at the center of our solar system.

At more than 1 million kilometers (621,000 mi) in diameter, the sun is the largest object in the solar system. It is the source of most of the energy on Earth—without it life could not exist.

From Earth, the sun looks like a ball of light. Like other stars, it is made up of gases, mostly hydrogen and helium.

The sun sometimes has dark spots called sunspots on its surface. They do not give off as much light and heat energy as the rest of the sun's surface. The red streams and loops are solar flares, gases that shoot out from the sun. These hot fountains of gas often begin near a sunspot and extend tens of

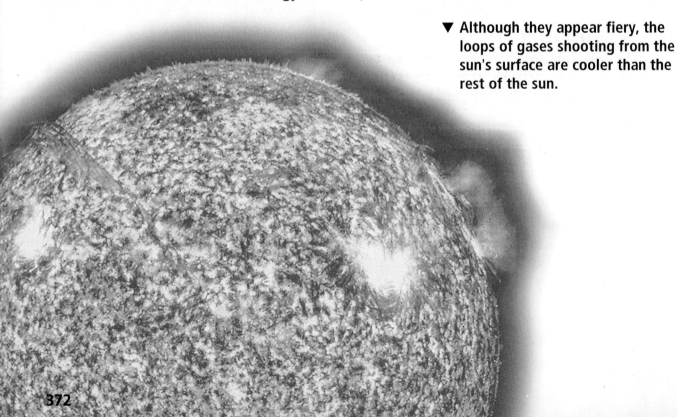

▼ Although they appear fiery, the loops of gases shooting from the sun's surface are cooler than the rest of the sun.

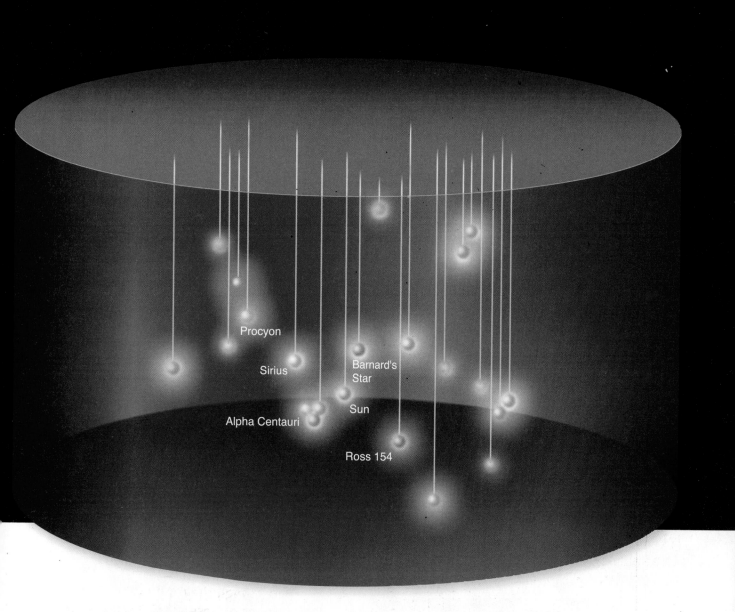

▲ This map shows the positions of the 20 nearest stars. The three closest to our solar system make up Alpha Centauri (AL•fuh sen•TAW•ry). From Earth, Alpha Centauri looks like one star.

thousands of kilometers into space. Both sunspots and solar flares last only a few days.

Stars' colors tell us about the stars' temperatures. Red stars are the coolest and blue the hottest. The sun, a medium-size yellow star, is between the hottest and the coolest.

Stars go through stages. They form from clouds of spinning dust and gas, which gravity squeezes. When the mass is squeezed enough, changes take place that form a star. The mass of the star then begins to change into light and heat. Over billions of years, most of the mass of the star is converted to light and heat.

 MAIN IDEA AND DETAILS What does a star's color tell about the star?

Groups of Stars

Have you ever seen the Big Dipper in the night sky? The Big Dipper belongs to a group of stars called Ursa Major. These stars form a **constellation**, a group of stars that form an imaginary picture in the sky. In ancient times, people often gave names to these imaginary star pictures. Constellations are helpful to people because their patterns serve as landmarks in the night sky. For hundreds of years, sailors have used them to find their way.

Have you seen a bright band of stars on a clear summer night? If so, you were looking at the Milky Way, the galaxy in which our solar system lies. A **galaxy** is a huge system of gases, dust, and stars.

Galaxies contain billions of stars. Our sun is on the edge of the Milky Way galaxy. Constellations are made up of stars in our own galaxy. The Milky Way is only one of the millions of galaxies in the universe. The **universe** is everything that exists in space.

There are many galaxy shapes. The Milky Way is a spiral (SPY•ruhl) galaxy. A barred spiral galaxy has two main arms. Some galaxies look like balls or eggs. Other galaxies have no regular shape.

 MAIN IDEA AND DETAILS What are two ways in which people classify groups of stars?

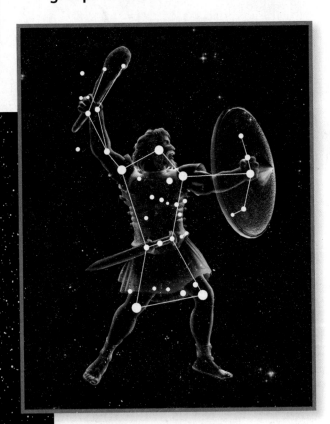

▲ This is a drawing of Orion, a hunter in Greek myths.

◄ This is how the constellation Orion appears in the night sky.

This barred spiral galaxy has two main arms branching out from it.

This photo, taken by the Hubble Space Telescope, shows some of the many galaxies in the universe.

Insta-Lab

Make a Constellation Model

Use a pencil point or toothpick to poke a "constellation" in a piece of aluminum foil. Use a rubber band to fasten the foil to the end of a paper towel tube. Look through the tube to see your constellation. Turn the tube while you look through it. What planetary motion are you modeling when you turn the tube?

Seasonal Star Positions

Each day, the sun appears to rise in the east, move across the sky, and set in the west. The same is true for stars at night. However, what is actually moving is Earth.

The positions of the stars appear to change with the seasons, too. In winter, you may see Orion clearly in the night sky. A few months later, Orion may no longer be visible.

This, too, is due to Earth's movement. As Earth revolves around the sun, we see different parts of space at different times of the year.

To see Orion in the same place you saw it last winter, you must wait until next winter. It will be visible again when Earth reaches that part of its orbit of the sun.

Where you live determines the constellations you will see. In the Northern Hemisphere, people see different sets of constellations from those people see in the Southern Hemisphere. People who live near the equator can see some constellations of both hemispheres.

 MAIN IDEA AND DETAILS Explain why constellations seem to change their locations.

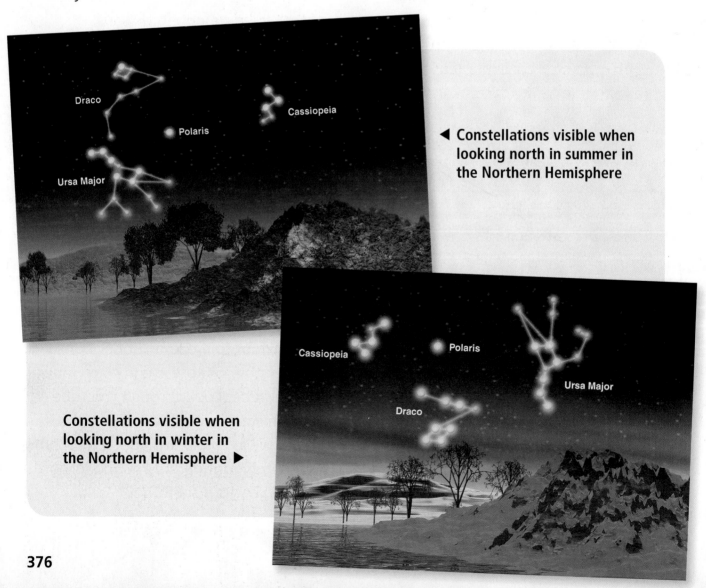

◀ Constellations visible when looking north in summer in the Northern Hemisphere

Constellations visible when looking north in winter in the Northern Hemisphere ▶

Focus Skill

1. MAIN IDEA AND DETAILS Copy and complete this graphic organizer. Write two supporting details for each main idea about stars.

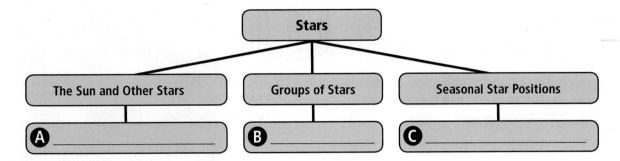

Stars

The Sun and Other Stars — A _____

Groups of Stars — B _____

Seasonal Star Positions — C _____

2. SUMMARIZE Write a sentence or two to tell the important facts you learned about stars.

3. DRAW CONCLUSIONS If the sun were a red star or a blue star, how would it be different?

4. VOCABULARY Use the terms *star, galaxy,* and *universe* in a sentence about objects in space.

FCAT Prep

5. Read/Inquire/Explain How were constellations useful to sailors long ago? When might they be useful to sailors today?

6. Which **best** describes the sun?
   A. small star   **C.** large star
   B. medium-size star   **D.** very large star

Links

Writing

Expository Writing

Choose a constellation in the illustration of the winter sky. Write a **paragraph** explaining how to find it on a winter night.

Math

Multiply AUs

Earth is 150 million km from the sun. Scientists refer to this distance as 1 AU, or 1 astronomical unit. Neptune is 30 AUs from the sun. How many km is that?

Social Studies

Careers in Space

The United States began to explore space in the 1960s. Research space-related careers, and report to the class.

 For more links and activities, go to www.hspscience.com

WATER WORLD

Over the years, many people have dreamed of going to Mars. The day when travel to Mars is possible is coming closer. Robot spacecraft have already traveled there. Those spacecraft have made many amazing discoveries.

One of the most recent spacecraft to journey to the fourth rock from the sun is *Mars Odyssey*. Photos taken by *Mars Odyssey* show that Mars has water. Because it is very cold on Mars, the water is frozen. Most of the water is frozen under the surface of Mars.

Lots of Lakes

Even though lots of ice crystals are mixed in with the Martian soil, Mars doesn't have as much water as Earth. Mars has buried lakes of water, not buried oceans of water. In fact, some scientists think that if you could collect all the water on Mars, it would fill a lake about twice the size of Lake Michigan.

There is evidence that some of the frozen water locked under the surface of Mars might melt every once in a while. Some of the water is only 46 centimeters (18 in.) below the surface. Molten rock deep beneath the surface of Mars might heat the ice. The water may then flow onto the surface.

A Grand Canyon?

Photos taken by *Mars Odyssey* show long, dark streaks on the walls of some canyons. The streaks might indicate areas where water recently flowed down the canyon walls.

Not all scientists agree, however. Many scientists say wind blowing across Mars caused the streaks. Scientists have long known about powerful wind storms on Mars. Some of those storms blow across the surface for months at a time.

Even if liquid water and life do not exist on Mars today, many scientists still want to explore the red planet. "I'm interested in Mars because it's probably the most fascinating planet in the solar system besides Earth, and probably the only one that could have ever supported other forms of life," said one NASA scientist.

THINK ABOUT IT

1. What would life on Earth be like if Earth had as little water as there is on Mars?
2. How have satellites helped us learn about other planets?

Some scientists say these dark lines were caused by streams of water flowing down a canyon wall.

Frozen carbon dioxide covers the North Pole of Mars.

The *Mars Odyssey* spacecraft studies Mars. Photos by the spacecraft show that ice exists on Mars.

Spin-In

Find out more! Log on to
www.hspscience.com

SC.H.1.2.1.4.1 scientists publish, enabling repetition,
SC.H.3.2.4.4.1 solving problems/new ideas

Moonstruck

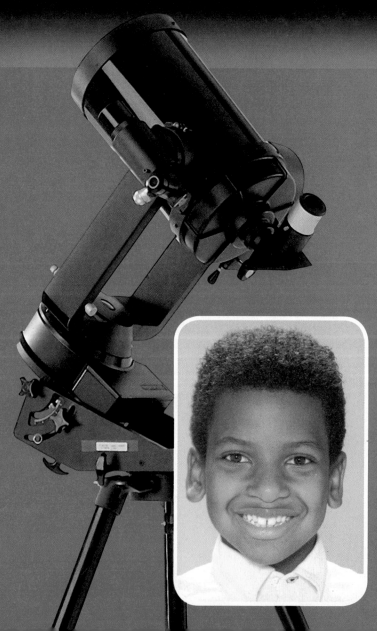

Recently, Christopher Ray Clark carried his telescope into his backyard. He set it up and pointed it skyward. Then, he saw an amazing sight.

As Christopher looked at the nighttime sky, he saw a total lunar eclipse. Christopher saw a shadow slowly move across the moon. The moon had a red color when the shadow completely covered it. The eclipse lasted for a few hours.

A total lunar eclipse occurs when the moon passes through Earth's inner shadow, called the **umbra**. As the moon passes through the umbra, Earth blocks all direct sunlight from reaching the moon. A small amount of red light makes it through Earth's atmosphere, making the moon appear red or orange.

You Can Do It!

Materials
- small ball of clay
- pencil, ruler
- 15-cm x 20-cm cardboard

Quick and Easy Project

Tell Time by Using the Sun

Procedure

1. On the cardboard, draw a half circle with a 7-cm radius. Put the clay in the center of the straight side.
2. Stand the pencil in the clay with the point up. You have made a sundial.
3. Put your sundial on a sunny windowsill, with the straight side along the window. Every hour, mark the pencil's shadow on the cardboard. Write the time at the mark.
4. On the next sunny day, use your sundial to tell time.

Draw Conclusions
How does your sundial work? Would it work in any sunny window? Why or why not?

Design Your Own Investigation

Make a Spiral Galaxy

A spiral galaxy gets its shape from many orbiting stars. Use a paper punch to punch out many "stars" from construction paper. Fill a large bowl halfway with water. Pour the stars into the water. How can you make them form a "spiral galaxy"? How does what you do show what happens in space?

Vocabulary Review

Use the terms below to complete the sentences. The page numbers tell you where to look in the chapter if you need help.

axis p. 356	**comet** p. 368
orbit p. 356	**star** p. 372
moon p. 358	**sun** p. 372
solar system p. 364	**galaxy** p. 374
planet p. 364	**universe** p. 374

1. The star at the center of our solar system is the _____.

2. The path an object takes around another object is its _____.

3. A star and a group of objects that orbit it make up a _____.

4. The imaginary line through both poles of a planet is its _____.

5. A small mass of rock, ice, and frozen gases that orbits the sun is a _____.

6. A large object that orbits a star is a _____.

7. An enormous ball of superheated gases in space is a _____.

8. Everything that exists in space is part of the _____.

9. A large system of stars, dust, and gas is a _____.

10. A natural object that orbits a planet is a _____.

Check Understanding

Write the letter of the best choice.

11. MAIN IDEA AND DETAILS Which detail is true of the sun?

    A. It's a ball of hydrogen and helium.

    B. It's a ball of oxygen and hydrogen.

    C. It's a ball of helium and phosphorus.

    D. It's a ball of carbon dioxide and oxygen.

12. COMPARE AND CONTRAST How are asteroids and comets different?

    F. Asteroids are much smaller than comets.

    G. Comets orbit the sun, while asteroids orbit Earth.

    H. Comets are made up of rock, ice, and frozen gases, while asteroids are made up of rock and metals.

    I. Asteroids are pieces of Earth, while comets are pieces of the sun.

13. Which **best** describes the sun's location in the universe?

   A. near the barred spiral galaxy

   B. at the edge of the solar system

   C. at the edge of a galaxy called the Milky Way

   D. in the center of a galaxy called Alpha Centauri

14. Samantha must label this diagram of the sun.

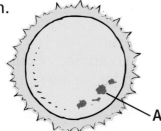

Which label should she use to identify area A?

   F. bits of rock   **H.** spinning dust

   G. oxygen   **I.** sunspot

15. What are the gas giants?

   A. comets

   B. stars in the Milky Way

   C. four of the five outer planets

   D. the sun and Alpha Centauri

16. What does this illustration **best** show?

   F. why Earth rotates

   G. why planets orbit the sun

   H. why the moon has phases

   I. why Earth has seasons

Inquiry Skills

17. You **used numbers** to understand distances in space. What other ideas in this chapter did using numbers help you understand?

18. How could **measuring** the orbit of a comet help scientists understand when it will next be visible from Earth?

Read/Inquire/Explain

19. Why are there phases of the moon?

20. Suppose that you have been asked to do a presentation about our solar system. You are to present information about the planets and show where they are located in space.

Part A Make a labeled drawing of the solar system. Include the nine planets and the sun.

Part B Write a paragraph that explains how the inner planets and the outer planets are different.

Processes of Life

The chapters in this unit address these Grade Level Expectations from the Florida Sunshine State Standards.

Chapter 11 Cells

SC.F.1.2.1.4.1 knows that complex animals have specialized organs to carry out life processes.

SC.F.1.2.4.4.1 knows that living things are composed of cells.

SC.F.1.2.4.4.2 knows that processes needed for life are carried out by the cells.

Chapter 12 The Human Body

SC.F.1.2.1.4.2 knows the major organ systems of the human body.

SC.F.1.2.1.4.3 understand the functions of various body systems.

The investigations and experiences in this unit also address many of the Grade Level Expectations in Strand H, The Nature of Science.

LIFE SCIENCE

Science in Florida

Gainesville

The Sunshine State

USA

Dear Corey,

My cousin is going to the University of Florida and is studying to become a nurse. She gave me a tour of the Shands Teaching Hospital. She listened to me breathe with her stethoscope and let me listen to my own heartbeat. I think I want to be a doctor when I grow up!

Talk to you soon,

Constance

FCAT Writing

Writing Situation

Think about the last time you went to the doctor. Explain why it is important to go to the doctor.

Experiment!

Lung Capacity No two people are exactly the same. One difference among people is lung capacity, or the amount of air the lungs can hold. Are the lungs of males the same size as the lungs of females? Do your lungs get larger as you get taller? Plan and conduct an experiment to find out.

11 Cells

Lesson 1 What Are Cells?

Lesson 2 What Do Cells Do?

Lesson 3 How Do Cells Work Together?

Vocabulary

FCAT-Tested
tissue
organ

Other Terms
cell
cell membrane
nucleus
cell wall
red blood cell
white blood cell
neuron

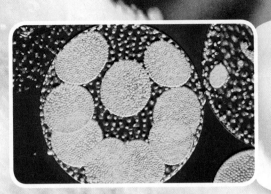

This water-skier is sharing the water with millions of plantlike organisms, such as the beautiful *volvox* colony shown. What do you think the water-skier and the volvox colony have in common?

What Are Cells?

Fast Fact

Eggceptional This enormous ostrich egg holds about 77 times as much as the chicken egg. But each is only a single cell! In the Investigate, you'll model a cell.

Make a Model Cell

Materials
- large shell pasta or wagon-wheel pasta
- zip-top plastic bag
- small tube-shaped pasta
- paper towel
- small round pasta
- plastic spoon
- gelled gelatin

Procedure

1. Place one piece of large pasta into the bag. The bag is a model of the membrane that surrounds the cell. The pasta is the cell's nucleus. The nucleus controls the cell's activities.

2. Add pieces of the other pasta shapes. The tube-shaped pasta stands for the structures that release energy for the cell. The round pasta stands for cell storage areas.

3. Carefully spoon some gelatin into the bag until the bag is about two-thirds full. The gelatin represents the jellylike material that fills the space in a cell.

4. Seal the bag. Place it on a paper towel on your desk or table.

Draw Conclusions

1. Observe your model. What cell part makes up most of your model?

2. **Inquiry Skill** Scientists often use models to understand complex structures. Draw conclusions about cells, based on your model. What does your model NOT tell you?

Step 1

Step 2

Investigate Further

Make a drawing of your cell model, and label each part. Compare your drawing to the pictures in this lesson.

VOCABULARY

cell p. 390
cell membrane p. 391
nucleus p. 391
cell wall p. 392

SCIENCE CONCEPTS

▶ that living things are made up of cells
▶ how cells carry out tasks

READING FOCUS SKILL

MAIN IDEA AND DETAILS
Look for details about the jobs that different parts of cells carry out.

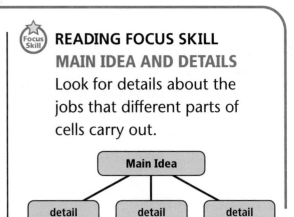

Cells as Building Blocks

Think about your school. It may be a large building, but it is made of smaller parts. It may be made of bricks or cement blocks and many pieces of wood, metal, and glass.

Living things are also made up of smaller parts. The building blocks of life are called cells. A **cell** is the basic unit of all living things.

All living things are made up of cells. Some living things, such as bacteria, are one-celled organisms. Others are made up of many cells. Each cell carries out all the activities needed for it to stay alive. All the cells work together. They combine to form a larger living thing and to keep it alive.

The parts of your school work together to keep it running well. For

◀ This magnolia tree is full of leaves. The leaves are made of cells.

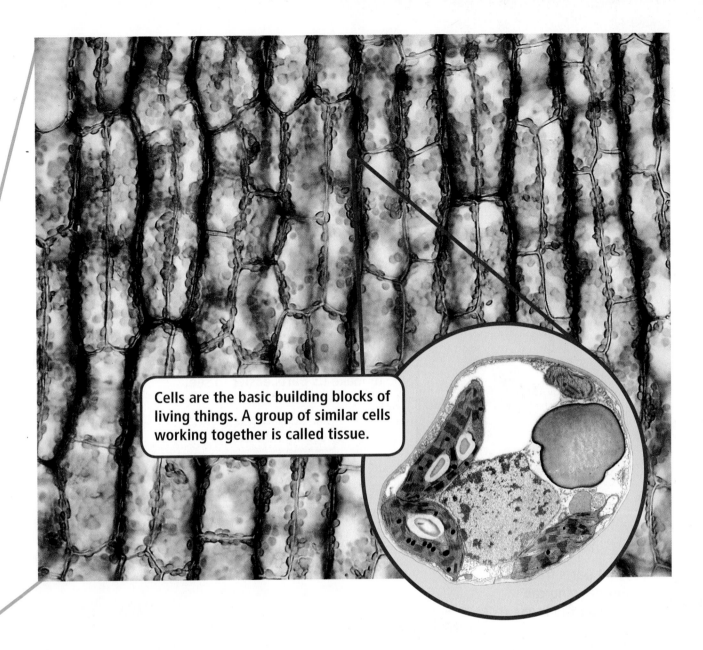

Cells are the basic building blocks of living things. A group of similar cells working together is called tissue.

example, a furnace heats the school. Wires carry electricity to run the lights. Pipes bring water for drinking and washing. Together, the parts make the school work. Cells, too, are made of parts that do different jobs. Some cells, such as bacteria, have few parts. Plant and animal cells are more complex and have more parts.

All cells are surrounded by a thin covering, or **cell membrane**, which holds the cell together. All cells are filled with jellylike *cytoplasm* (SYT•oh•plaz•uhm). In plant and animal cells, special parts float in the cytoplasm. For example, *vacuoles* (VAK•yoo•ohlz) are parts that store food and water. *Mitochondria* (myt•oh•KAHN•dree•uh) are parts that release energy.

Both plant and animal cells also have a nucleus. The **nucleus** is the cell's control center.

 MAIN IDEA AND DETAILS What parts do all cells have?

Plant Cells

All cells are alike in some ways, but they are not identical. Cells differ in size and shape. Plant cells and animal cells have different parts.

The outermost part of an animal cell is the cell membrane. Plant cells have a cell membrane, too, but it's surrounded by a tough wall. This **cell wall** makes the cell stiff and helps support the whole plant.

Many plant cells have another cell part that animal cells do not have. *Chloroplasts* (KLAWR•uh•plasts) float in the cytoplasm. Chloroplasts are filled with a green pigment, or colored matter, called *chlorophyll* (KLAWR•uh•fil). Chlorophyll lets plants use energy from the sun to change water and carbon dioxide into food.

 MAIN IDEA AND DETAILS What cell parts are found in plant cells but not in animal cells?

◀ This is a plant cell magnified many times. It has been dyed to make its parts easier to see.

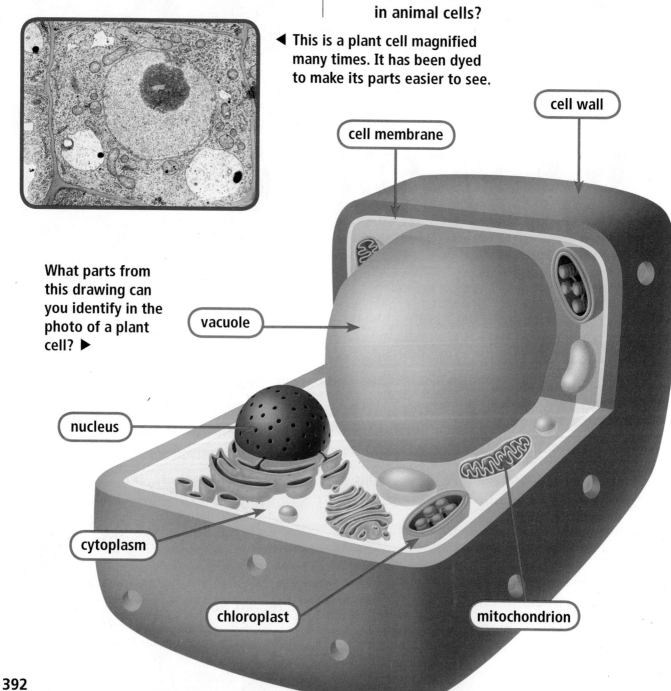

What parts from this drawing can you identify in the photo of a plant cell? ▶

cell wall

cell membrane

vacuole

nucleus

cytoplasm

chloroplast

mitochondrion

Animal Cells

As you know, a plant cell is surrounded by a stiff cell wall. Animal cells have only a cell membrane. This thin covering keeps the contents of the cell together. It is the "gatekeeper." It controls all materials that enter and leave the cell.

Animal cells are different from plant cells in another way. They have more storage areas, called vacuoles, in the cytoplasm. Some vacuoles store materials that the cell needs, such as food and water. Other vacuoles store wastes until they can be removed from the cell.

 MAIN IDEA AND DETAILS What structures do animal cells have that plant cells also have?

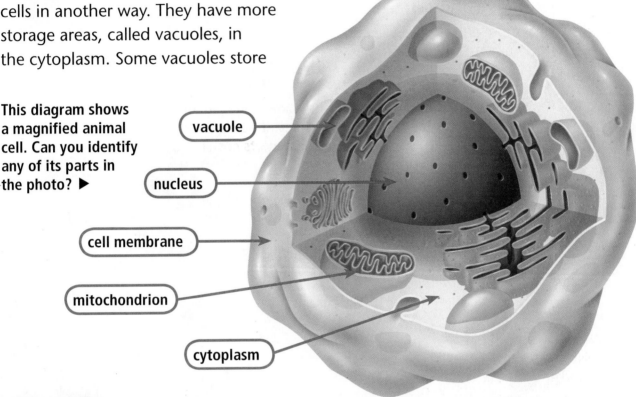

This diagram shows a magnified animal cell. Can you identify any of its parts in the photo? ▶

- vacuole
- nucleus
- cell membrane
- mitochondrion
- cytoplasm

Make a Model

Blow up a balloon half way. Suppose that it is an animal cell. What part of the cell does the balloon represent? Create a "plant cell" by blowing up the balloon inside a cup. What does the cup stand for?

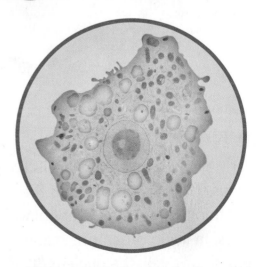

▲ This is an actual animal cell as seen under a microscope. It has been enlarged and dyed so it is easier to see.

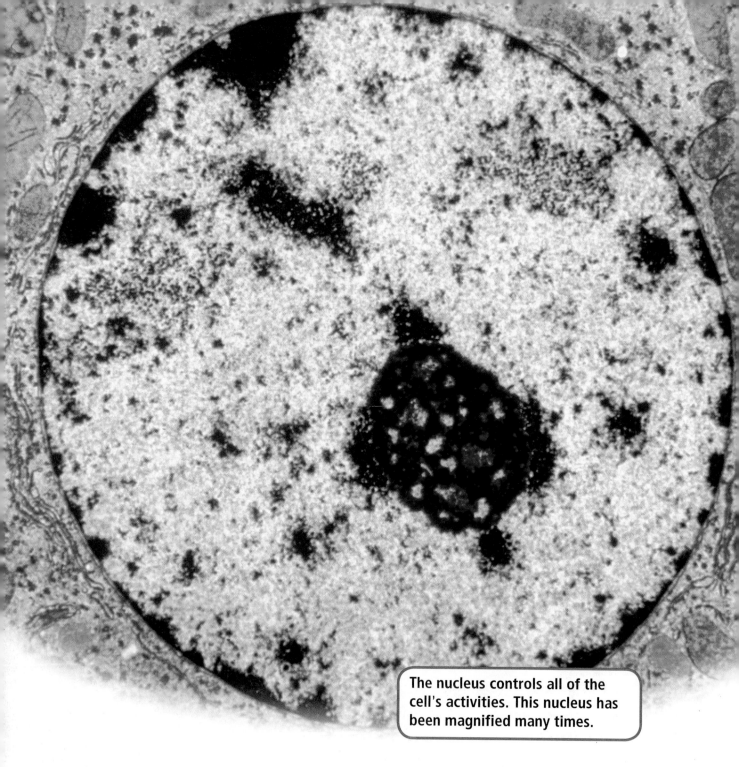

The nucleus controls all of the cell's activities. This nucleus has been magnified many times.

The Nucleus

Nearly all plant and animal cells have a nucleus. The nucleus contains the information that controls everything the cell does. In living organisms made up of more than one cell, the nucleus "tells" the cell how to work with other cells to keep the organism healthy.

Just as one cell is separated from others by its cell membrane, the nucleus is separated from the cytoplasm by a membrane. Small openings in the nuclear membrane let materials in and out of the nucleus.

 MAIN IDEA AND DETAILS What is the job of the nucleus?

1. MAIN IDEA AND DETAILS Draw and complete this graphic organizer about cell parts and what they do.

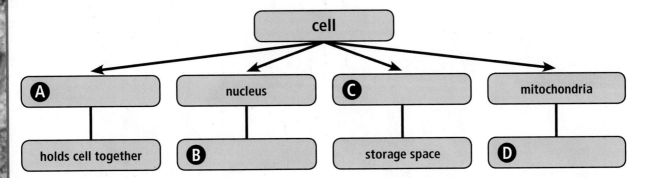

cell

A — holds cell together

nucleus — B

C — storage space

mitochondria — D

2. SUMMARIZE Use your graphic organizer to write a summary about the jobs of the different parts of a cell.

3. DRAW CONCLUSIONS How are chloroplasts important to plant cells?

4. VOCABULARY Use lesson vocabulary and ideas to create a crossword puzzle.

FCAT Prep

5. Read/Inquire/Explain Plant and animal cells both have vacuoles that store food. When might these vacuoles be useful?

6. Which cell part is found only in plant cells?

A. cell membrane   **C.** nucleus
B. cell wall   **D.** vacuole

Links

Writing

Narrative Writing

Take an imaginary journey into a cell. Write a trip diary that **describes** what you find on your travels. Present your trip diary to your class.

Math

Use a Rule

Blood contains 1 white blood cell for every 600 red blood cells. If a sample of blood has 3,000 red blood cells, how many white blood cells does it have?

Art

Pigments

Chlorophyll is the green pigment that helps plants make food. Use an encyclopedia to find out which pigments are used to make paints.

 For more links and activities, go to **www.hspscience.com**

What Do Cells Do?

Fast Fact

A Safety Net The material in this photograph is called *fibrin*. Strands of fibrin help heal torn blood vessels by sealing them with a netlike web. You'll learn about other parts of blood in the Investigate.

Blood Cells

Materials
- Microslide Viewer
- Slide A—red blood cells
- Slide B—white blood cells
- Slide C—platelets

Procedure

1. Make a table like the one shown.

2. Use the Microslide Viewer to carefully observe the cells on Slide A.

3. Take notes to describe what one of the cells looks like. What cell parts can you see?

4. Record your observations in the table. You can use words or drawings.

5. Repeat Steps 2–4 for Slides B and C.

Slide	Cell Parts	Observations
red blood cells		
white blood cells		
platelets		

Step 2

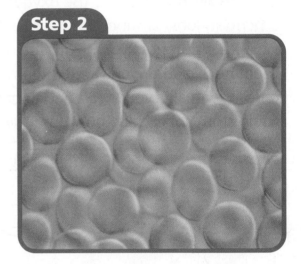

Draw Conclusions

1. Describe each part of blood. How are the parts alike? How are they different?

2. **Inquiry Skill** Many scientists use microscopes in their work. What does a microscope do that makes it possible to observe and compare the different parts of blood?

Investigate Further

Observe prepared slides of different kinds of cells. Compare them with the cells you observed.

VOCABULARY
red blood cell p. 398
white blood cell p. 400
neuron p. 402

SCIENCE CONCEPTS
▶ how cells carry oxygen, protect your body, and sense information

READING FOCUS SKILL
MAIN IDEA AND DETAILS
Look for details about the jobs that cells do.

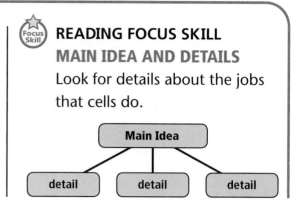

Getting Oxygen

Every cell in your body needs oxygen from the air to work. Cells use oxygen to perform jobs, or functions, that keep you alive. Without oxygen, your muscles would not do what you wanted them to do. Eventually, your heart and brain would stop working. So how does the oxygen that you inhale reach each cell? Your body has a delivery system—your blood!

Every **red blood cell** is part of the system that delivers oxygen to all cells. Red blood cells are your body's "delivery trucks."

The journey begins in the lungs. There, red blood cells pick up oxygen. Then the oxygen-rich cells travel to the heart. The heart pumps the blood all through the body.

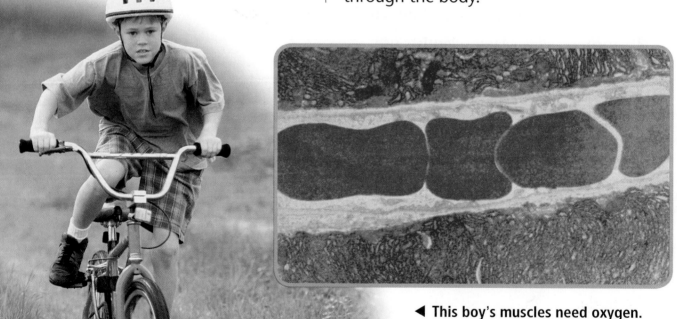

◀ This boy's muscles need oxygen. Red blood cells, such as the ones above, carry oxygen from the air that the boy breathes to every cell in his body.

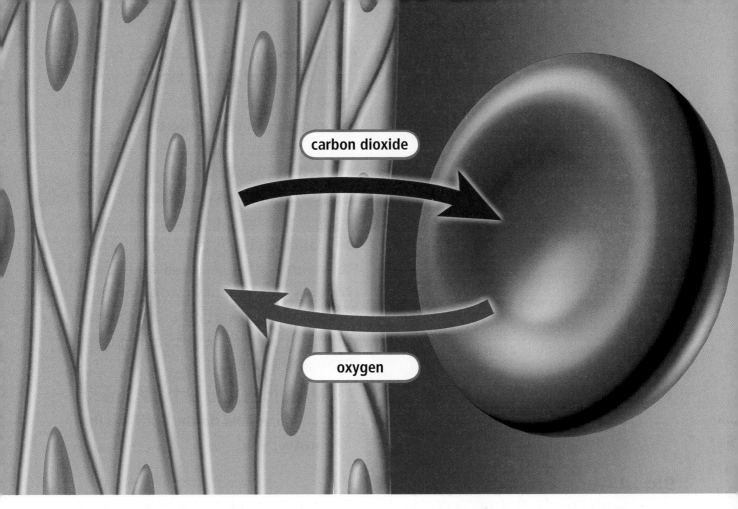

carbon dioxide

oxygen

From your heart, your blood travels along the "highways" of your blood vessels. Flexible red blood cells can fit inside any blood vessel, including tiny capillaries.

Oxygen-rich red blood cells travel to every body cell. Oxygen molecules can pass through the walls of capillaries. Then they slip through the cell membrane. The cell uses the oxygen to perform its functions.

In addition to delivering oxygen, the red blood cells pick up a waste gas, *carbon dioxide*. They carry it to the lungs, where it is exhaled, or breathed out of the body.

 MAIN IDEA AND DETAILS How do the cells of the body get the oxygen they need?

▲ Oxygen moves from the red blood cell across the capillary wall into the muscle cells. The waste gas—carbon dioxide—moves in the opposite direction.

Breathing Rates

Count the number of breaths you take in one minute. Then jog in place for 30 seconds. Right after, count your breaths for one minute. How do your breathing rates compare?

Protecting the Body

Have you skinned a knee and had the wound form a scab? Your body has an amazing power to heal itself. Different types of white blood cells help protect and heal your body. Each of these **white blood cells** does its part to defend you from illness and to help you heal after an injury.

White blood cells protect you from germs in different ways. When germs that cause a cold enter your body, some white blood cells attack and kill the germs. Others make *antibodies*.

Antibodies are like tags that identify certain kinds of germs. When germs of those kinds enter your body again, white blood cells can recognize them.

After an injury, white blood cells spring into action. Some surround germs and destroy them. Small cell fragments called *platelets* release chemicals. This causes long, sticky threads of *fibrin* to form. Fibrin forms a net that seals the broken blood vessels. Bleeding stops, and a scab forms. The scab acts as a wall to protect your body so that germs cannot enter through the cut.

 MAIN IDEA AND DETAILS After an injury, how do the body's cells protect you?

Math in Science
Interpret Data

Blood Components

The graph below shows the different parts of blood. Which part makes up the greatest part of blood? Which makes up the least? What do you think happens to the type of cells with the lowest number when the body needs protection?

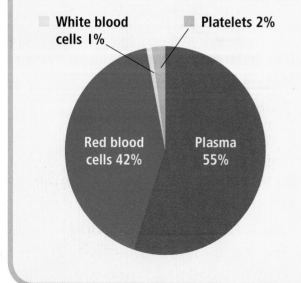

White blood cells 1%

Platelets 2%

Red blood cells 42%

Plasma 55%

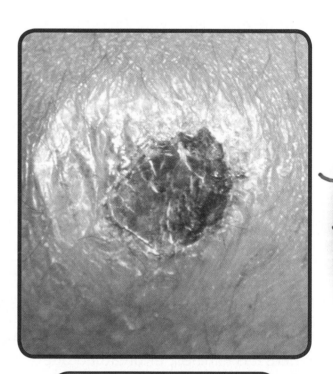

This scab started as a *clot* formed by platelets.

White Blood Cells to the Rescue!

There are many different kinds of white blood cells. Each protects your body in a different way. Here, two kinds are shown.

▲ Macrophages (MAK•roh•fayj•uhz), the largest blood cells, travel in the blood, destroying germs. Macrophages make a substance that activates T-cells.

◄ Some T-cells guide other white blood cells to protect the body. Some T-cells kill and remove germs.

For more links and activities, go to **www.hspscience.com**

Sensing Information

Some cells help the body get the oxygen it needs, and others fight infection. Still others help the body sense information about its surroundings.

Your skin is filled with tiny nerve cells, called **neurons**. These neurons give your brain information about the world around you. For example, when you touch a hot pan, how does your body know to pull your hand back?

First, your fingertips touch the pan, and *sensory receptors* in your skin are stimulated. A message travels along sensory neurons to the *spinal cord*—a thick rope of nerve tissue inside your backbone. A message travels from the spinal cord to the muscles of your arm. You quickly pull your hand away.

Your brain does not control this kind of response, but it processes most sensory information. Stroking an animal's fur stimulates the sensory receptors. This sends a message to the brain. The brain "reads" the message and sends a signal back to the hand, "telling" you that the fur is soft.

★ **Focus Skill** **MAIN IDEA AND DETAILS How does your skin sense information about your surroundings?**

touch receptor

How does this boy know that the puppy's fur is soft?

1. MAIN IDEA AND DETAILS Draw and complete this graphic organizer.

Type of Cell	Job
A _____	Carrying oxygen
Neuron	**B** _____
C _____	Protecting the body

2. SUMMARIZE Use your graphic organizer to summarize the way cells do different jobs for the body.

3. DRAW CONCLUSIONS How might an injury to the spinal cord affect the way the body senses information?

4. VOCABULARY Use your own words to write a definition for each of the vocabulary terms.

FCAT Prep

5. Read/Inquire/Explain How does exercise affect your body's need for oxygen?

6. Which of these helps protect the body by stopping bleeding?

A. red blood cell   **C.** neuron

B. white blood cell   **D.** platelet

Links

Writing

Narrative Writing

Imagine that red blood cells are like trucks. Write a **story** describing their journey along the "highways" in your body.

Math

Calculate

Suppose that 100 red blood cells are replaced every 120 days. How many red blood cells will have been replaced by new ones after 360 days?

Health

Vaccinations

Research the history of vaccines. Make a time line to show what you learned.

 For more links and activities, go to **www.hspscience.com**

How Do Cells Work Together?

Fast Fact

Collagen Connection These fibers are made up of *collagen* (KAHL•uh•juhn), a material that helps give skin its shape. When this strong material is heated, it becomes wobbly gelatin! You'll look at skin's function in the Investigate.

The Job of Skin

Materials   • apple   • hand lens   • plastic knife

Procedure

1 Make a table like the one shown.

2 Carefully observe the appearance of the apple skin with the hand lens. Record your observations in the table.

3 Using the plastic knife, carefully remove a bit of peel, or skin, from the apple. With the hand lens, closely observe the flesh inside the apple. Record your observations in the chart.

4 Allow the apple to sit for about an hour. Then observe the flesh with the hand lens. Has it changed? If so, how? Record your observations in the chart.

Draw Conclusions

1. Compare and contrast the appearance of the apple before you removed the skin, immediately after, and one hour after.

2. Inquiry Skill The cells of the apple skin work together. Draw a conclusion about the skin's job.

	Appearance
Apple with skin	
Apple without skin	
Apple without skin after 1 hour	

Step 3

Investigate Further

Keep your apple for about a week. Observe how it changes. How does a break in the skin affect the entire apple?

VOCABULARY
tissue p. 406
organ p. 408

SCIENCE CONCEPTS
▶ how cells of similar types form tissue
▶ how tissues of different types form organs that do specific jobs

READING FOCUS SKILL

MAIN IDEA AND DETAILS
Look for details about how cells work together.

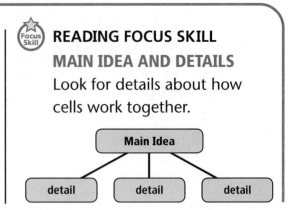

Tissues

Have you ever looked closely at the fabric that makes up your clothing? In the larger picture below, you can see a whole piece of cloth. You can also see that the fabric is made of smaller threads that are alike. They work together to make the fabric.

▼ Like body tissue, this fabric is made of many smaller parts working together.

Living things are made up of a kind of "fabric," too. Tissue is that fabric. A closer look shows that **tissue** is made of a group of cells of similar types working together. Each kind of tissue has its own job.

In the Investigate, you observed an apple's skin. The skin is a kind of tissue. It is made of cells that are similar. These cells work together to do the same job. They protect the apple.

There are four basic kinds of tissue in your body. You have skin tissue. You also

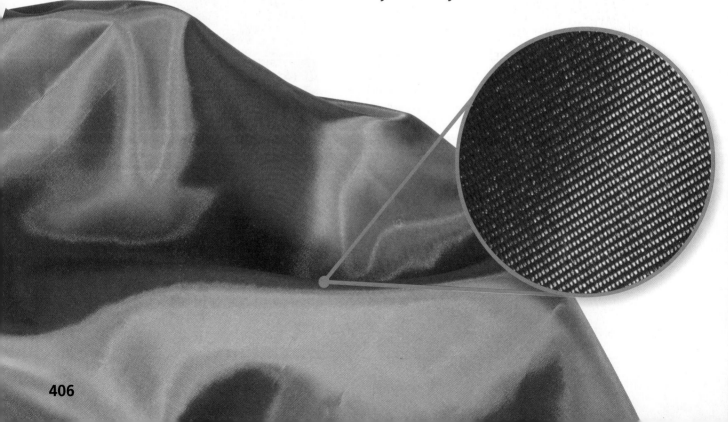

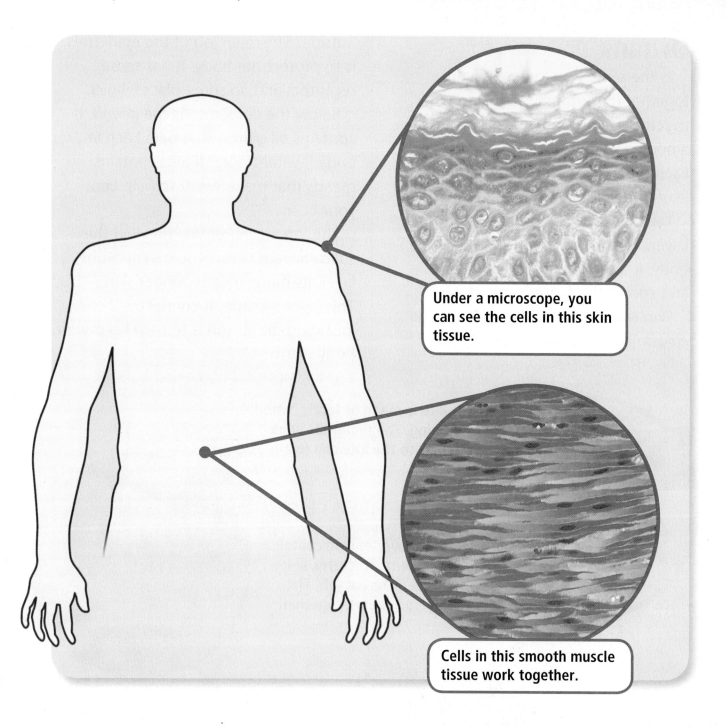

Under a microscope, you can see the cells in this skin tissue.

Cells in this smooth muscle tissue work together.

have muscle tissue, nerve tissue, and connective tissue.

Skin tissue is made of skin cells. Your skin protects your body. What makes up other types of tissue? Muscle cells make up muscle tissue. Neurons and related cells make up nerve tissue.

Connective tissue gives your body support. It includes the bones in your skeleton. It also includes the ligaments that hold joints together. Can you infer what kind of cells make up bone tissue?

Kinds of tissue join together to perform different jobs. Tissues form your bones, your heart, and your stomach, for example.

 MAIN IDEA AND DETAILS How are cells related to tissue?

Organs

In the same way that cells work together to form tissues, tissues work together to form organs. An **organ** is a body part that does a particular job. Each organ in your body is made of at least two kinds of tissue.

Your skin is your body's largest organ. Layers of skin tissue cover and line the body. It also contains muscle, nerve, and connective tissue.

Skin is divided into three layers. The *epidermis* (ep•uh•DER•mis) is on the outside. The main job of the epidermis is to protect the body. It has sense receptors and, in some places, hairs.

Below the epidermis is the *dermis*. It contains oil glands that help keep your body "waterproof." It also contains glands that make sweat to help cool your body.

The inner layer of skin is called the *subcutaneous* (sub•kyoo•TAY•nee•uhs) layer. Its name means "under skin." This layer is made of connective tissue, including fat. Its job is to help keep your body warm.

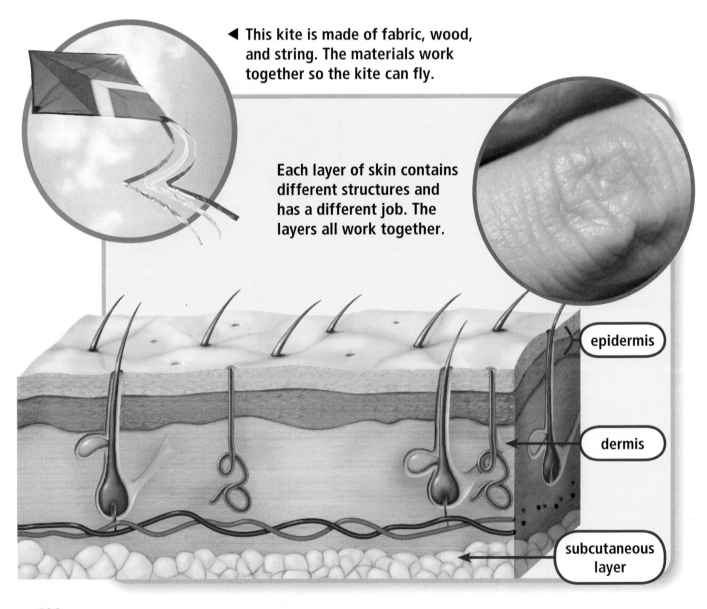

◀ This kite is made of fabric, wood, and string. The materials work together so the kite can fly.

Each layer of skin contains different structures and has a different job. The layers all work together.

epidermis

dermis

subcutaneous layer

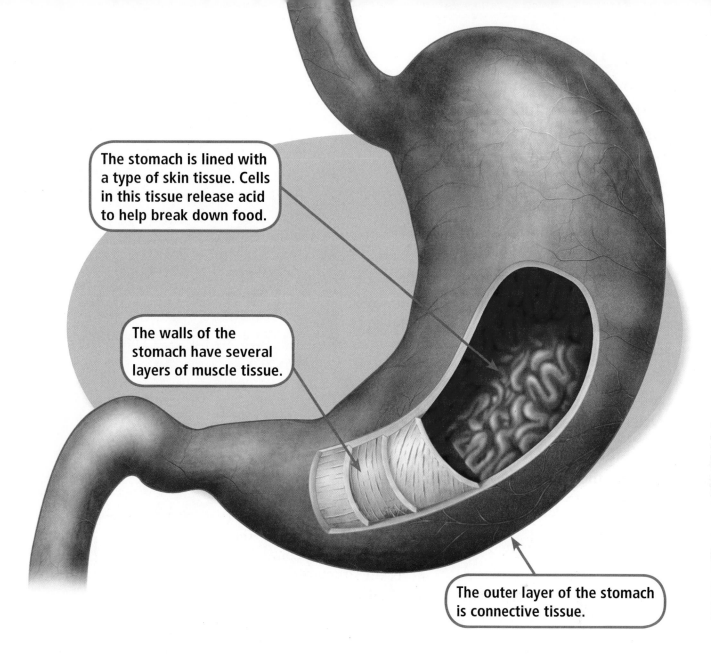

The stomach is lined with a type of skin tissue. Cells in this tissue release acid to help break down food.

The walls of the stomach have several layers of muscle tissue.

The outer layer of the stomach is connective tissue.

Like other organs, the stomach is made of more than one kind of tissue. The outside of the stomach is made of connective tissue. The muscular walls squeeze and relax to mix the food with digestive juices. This breaks down the food.

The inner part of the stomach is lined with a type of skin tissue. Some of the cells in this tissue make digestive juices.

 MAIN IDEA AND DETAILS How are organs related to tissues?

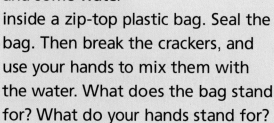

Model Stomach

Place two crackers and some water inside a zip-top plastic bag. Seal the bag. Then break the crackers, and use your hands to mix them with the water. What does the bag stand for? What do your hands stand for?

409

Systems

Groups of organs that work together to do major jobs for the body are systems. The human body has ten body systems. For example, bones work together and make up the skeletal system. Muscles work together and make up the muscular system. The organs that work together to digest the food you eat make up the digestive system. Your hair, skin, and nails extend from or cover your body. They make up the *integumentary* (in•teg•yoo•MEN•ter•ee) system. You will learn more about these body systems in the next chapter.

 MAIN IDEA AND DETAILS **What are the jobs of four human body systems?**

The skeletal system is made up of bones.

The digestive system— including the mouth, esophagus, stomach, and intestines—breaks down food and absorbs nutrients.

The muscular system works with the skeletal system and also helps many internal organs work.

The integumentary system—including skin, nails, and hair—covers and protects the body.

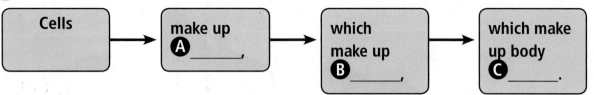

1. MAIN IDEA AND DETAILS Draw and complete this graphic organizer.

| Cells | → | make up **A**_____, | → | which make up **B**_____, | → | which make up body **C**_____. |

2. SUMMARIZE Use your graphic organizer to state the main idea of the lesson.

3. DRAW CONCLUSIONS Why are organs made of different tissues?

4. VOCABULARY Write clues for the vocabulary terms. Make a word search by hiding the terms in a grid of letters. Challenge a classmate to find the terms by solving the clues.

FCAT Prep

5. Read/Inquire/Explain How are cells, tissues, organs, and systems alike?

6. Which is **not** a kind of tissue?
- **A.** cell
- **B.** bone
- **C.** muscle
- **D.** nerve

Links

Writing

Persuasive Writing
Review each type of tissue. Which do you feel is the most important for life? Write a **paragraph** to persuade others to accept your view. Share your argument with the class.

Math

Make a Bar Graph
The brain is an organ. Research the brain sizes of several different mammals, and construct a bar graph showing their relative sizes.

Health

Organ Transplants
Sometimes when organs do not do their jobs well, doctors can replace them. Investigate which organs can be replaced with transplanted ones. Present your findings as a poster to educate people about organ transplants.

For more links and activities, go to **www.hspscience.com**

Seeing With

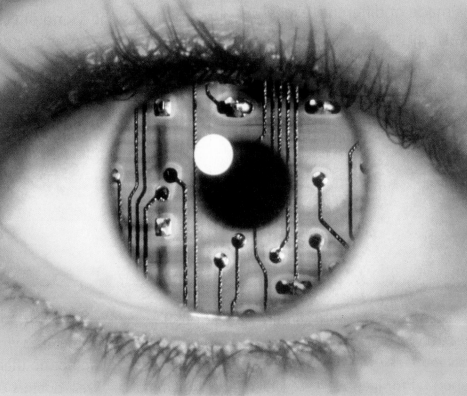

Bionic Eyes

Imagine if one day computer chips could be placed inside your eyes. What do you think the chips might help you to do? Maybe you could see through walls. Or would you be able to use your eyes to zoom in on tiny objects? Well, doctors today may not be able to give you super sight, but they are using computer chips to help blind people to see.

A Chip in the Eye

Inventing mechanical devices to replace tissues, organs, or body parts is called bionics. Scientists have been developing bionic body parts for many years. But in the last 20 years, they have started using computer chips to make bionic devices even better.

Seeing Again

Six people were in the first group to allow doctors to put chips in their eyes.

The patients say the computer chips have helped them to see better.

Before the operation, one patient could only see objects up to a few feet away. After the operation, he said he could see a flock of geese flying through the sky.

Another patient who saw only darkness before the operation can now see light and shadows. "Someone came along and developed this little thing to put in your eye, and suddenly I can see more light," he said. "None of us had expectations that we'd be able to see someone's face or read a book."

THINK ABOUT IT

1. Why do you think the computer chip is placed in the back of the eye?

2. What does the lens at the front of the eye do?

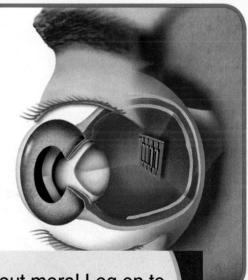

To place a computer chip in an eye, a doctor makes a tiny pocket in the retina at the back of the eye. The retina is like a movie screen. The lens at the front of the eye focuses light on the retina.

The computer chip is placed inside the tiny pocket in the retina. The chip is about the size of a pinhead and thinner than a human hair. The chip senses light and helps a person to see.

Find out more! Log on to
www.hspscience.com

SC.H.3.2.1.4.1 technologies, costs/ benefits

Lydia Villa-Komaroff

Lydia Villa-Komaroff grew up in a big family in New Mexico. When Villa-Komaroff was five, her father brought home a set of encyclopedias. He told her that all she needed to know was in those books.

She must have listened to her dad because Villa-Komaroff grew up to be one of the top scientists in her field. She has made many important discoveries in the field of biology.

Her most important discovery was in 1978 when she proved that bacterial cells could be changed to make **insulin**. Insulin is important in treating diabetes. People with diabetes need insulin to live. Villa-Komaroff's discovery made it easier and cheaper to get insulin.

Career   Biologist

When a drug company develops a new drug, biologists usually take part in the important first steps. Biologists study living things and how those things interact with their environments. These scientists work on a wide range of projects, including developing new drugs, increasing crop yields, and protecting the environment.

You Can Do It!

Quick and Easy Project

Your Skin's Oil Glands

Materials
- clear plastic cup
- vegetable oil
- water

Procedure

1. Pour a small amount of oil into the cup. The oil represents the oil made by glands in your skin. **CAUTION: Wipe up spills immediately so that you don't slip or fall.**

2. Slowly pour water into the cup. Wait a few minutes.

3. Observe what happens to the oil and water. Record your observations.

Draw Conclusions
What job does the oil produced by the skin do?

Design Your Own Investigation

Make a Model

How do the skin's sweat glands cool your body? Make a model to show the process. How well does your model work? Plan and carry out an experiment to test it.

Vocabulary Review

Use the terms below to complete the sentences. The page numbers tell you where to look in the chapter if you need help.

cell p. 390
cell membrane p. 391
nucleus p. 391
cell wall p. 392
red blood cell p. 398
white blood cell p. 400
tissue p. 406
organ p. 408

1. The stiff outermost covering of a plant cell is the _____.

2. The part of blood that transports oxygen to all of the body's cells is the _____.

3. Different tissues working together to carry out a specific job for the body make up an _____.

4. The basic unit of structure and function in living things is the _____.

5. A cell that helps protect the body is the _____.

6. The structure that directs all of the cell's activities is the _____.

7. The outermost layer of an animal cell is the _____.

8. Cells of similar kinds that work together to carry out a job for a living thing form _____.

Check Understanding

Write the letter of the best choice.

9. What kind of cell is shown?

   A. animal
   B. bone
   C. plant
   D. skin

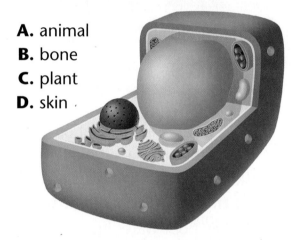

10. Which sequence shows how your body is organized?

   F. cells—organs—organ systems—tissues
   G. tissues—cells—organs—organ systems
   H. organ systems—tissues—organs—cells
   I. cells—tissues—organs—organ systems

11. Which part of blood helps bleeding stop?
   A. macrophage
   B. platelet
   C. red blood cell
   D. white blood cell

12. What is the job of these threadlike strands?

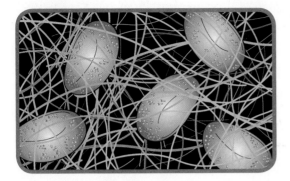

  F. to kill germs

  G. to move muscles

  H. to form a scab

  I. to carry oxygen

13. **MAIN IDEA AND DETAILS** Which cell part releases energy that the cell needs?

  A. chloroplast

  B. mitochondrion

  C. nucleus

  D. vacuole

14. **MAIN IDEA AND DETAILS** Which kind of white blood cell can either guide other white blood cells or kill and remove germs?

  F. B-cell   **H.** platelet

  G. macrophage   **I.** T-cell

15. Which statement about macrophages is **not** true?

  A. They destroy germs.

  B. They travel through the body's blood vessels.

  C. They activate T-cells.

  D. They are the smallest blood cells.

16. What is the outer layer of this organ called?

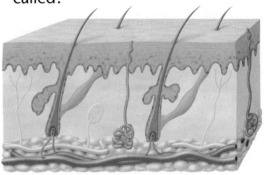

  F. dermis

  G. epidermis

  H. integumentary

  I. subcutaneous layer

Inquiry Skills

17. **Compare** plant and animal cells. What are the differences?

18. You know that people need more oxygen when they are active. **Draw conclusions** about why this is so.

Read/Inquire/Explain

To better understand how cells work, compare them with familiar things.

19. How is the nucleus of a cell like your brain?

20. **Part A** Explain how the parts of a cell are like the members of a sports team.

Part B Which part of a cell is like the coach of the team? Why?

Chapter 12

The Human Body

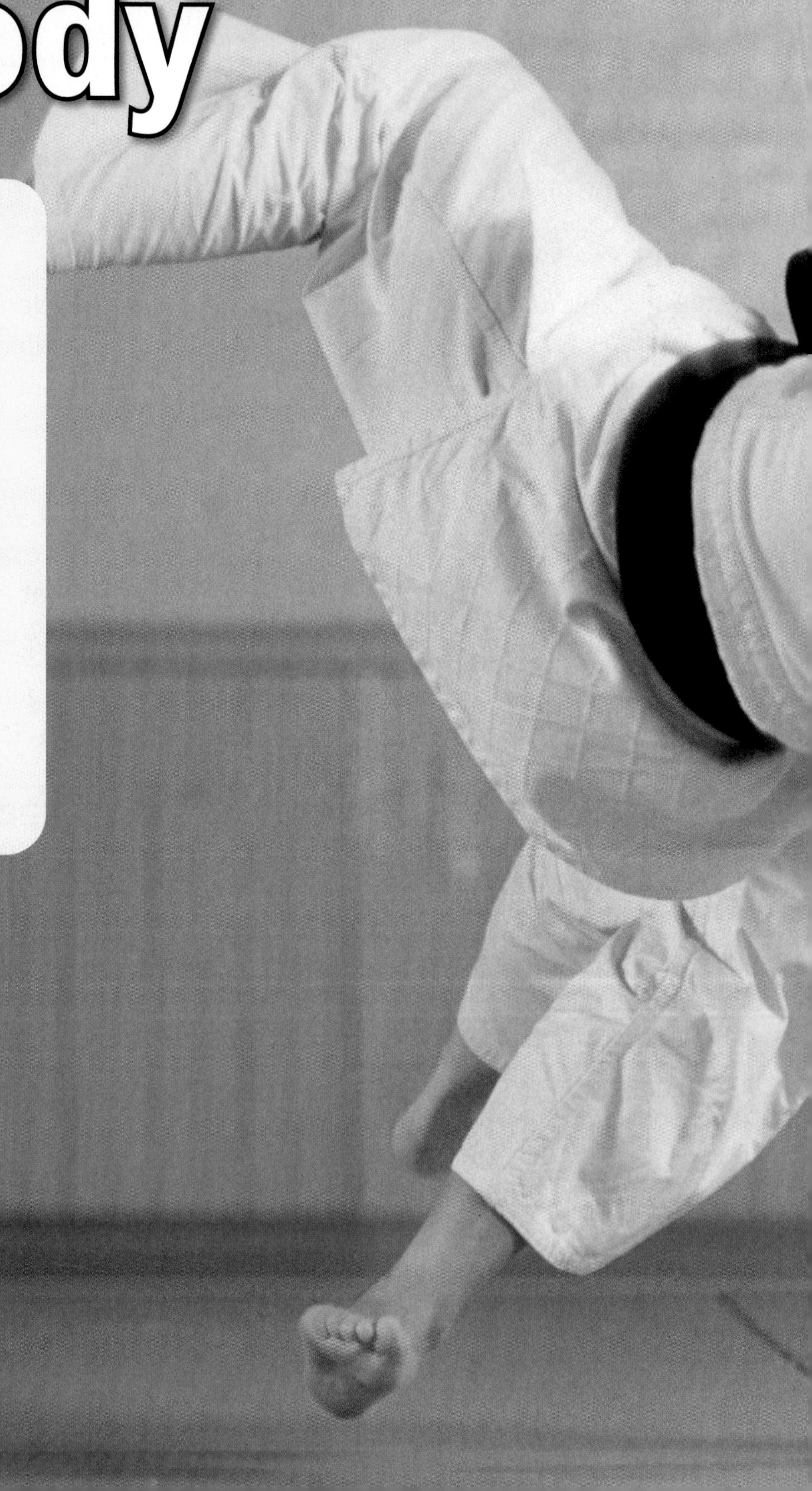

Vocabulary

bone
joint
muscle
diaphragm
artery
capillary
vein
spinal cord
esophagus
stomach

What do YOU wonder?

These two women are practicing judo, a Japanese martial art. Judo strengthens the heart and helps it send oxygen to muscles. What other body systems are used when practicing judo?

How Do the Skeletal and Muscular Systems Work?

Fast Fact

Amazing Feats Men and women all over the world compete to find out who is the strongest by pulling such huge and heavy objects as airplanes and trucks. In the Investigate, you'll make a model of how bones and muscles move to help us do amazing things!

WSM 2002

A Model Arm

Materials   • **2 rulers**   • **masking tape**   • **2 long balloons**

Procedure

1. Lay the two rulers end to end. Leave about a 5-mm gap between them. Use tape to make a hinge. Label the rulers *upper arm* and *lower arm.*

2. Blow up each balloon about halfway. The balloons represent arm muscles.

3. Cut four pieces of tape. Tape one end of a balloon to the top of the upper arm. Tape the other end of the balloon to the top of the lower arm, near the hinge.

4. Tape one end of the other balloon to the back of the upper arm, at the top. Make sure the lower arm is bent only a little in relation to the upper arm. Then tape the free end of the balloon to the lower arm, near the hinge.

5. Bend and straighten the model arm. Observe the way each part moves.

Step 1

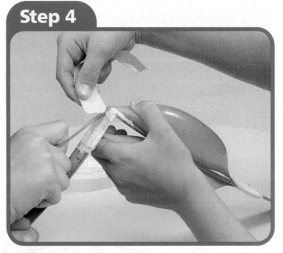

Step 4

Draw Conclusions

1. How do the muscles help the arm move?

2. **Inquiry Skill** How is your model like a real arm? How is it different? Compare.

Investigate Further

Use the pictures in this lesson to identify the parts represented in your model. Which bone does each of the rulers represent? Which muscle does each balloon represent?

Reading in Science

SC.F.1.2.1.4.2 human organ systems
SC.F.1.2.1.4.3 body system functions; LA.A.2.2.1 main idea

VOCABULARY

bone p. 422
joint p. 422
muscle p. 424

SCIENCE CONCEPTS

► that bones support the body, protect organs, and make blood cells

► how muscles work with bones to move the body

► how bones meet at joints

READING FOCUS SKILL

MAIN IDEA AND DETAILS

Look for details about how the skeletal and muscular systems work.

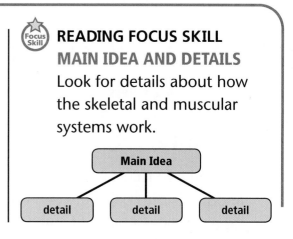

Skeletal System

Have you ever seen a skeleton? A skeleton may look weird, but the bones of the human body work together to do some very important jobs. Bones support your body and give it shape. They help you move, and some bones make blood cells. They also protect the organs inside your body. Your skull, for example, protects your brain from injury. Your ribs protect your heart and lungs.

A **bone** is a hard organ made up of connective tissue. The outer part is hard, smooth, and strong. This part helps your bones support your body. It gives your body its shape. The bone is lined with spongy bone tissue, which has many open spaces. The center of many bones has marrow that makes red blood cells.

A place where your bones meet is called a **joint**. At a joint, muscles and bones work together to move a part of your body. Some joints open and close, like the hinges of a door. Your knees work this way. Other joints move in different ways.

MAIN IDEA AND DETAILS What jobs do bones do for your body?

The hard outer part of a bone gives it strength. The marrow inside the bone makes new blood cells. ►

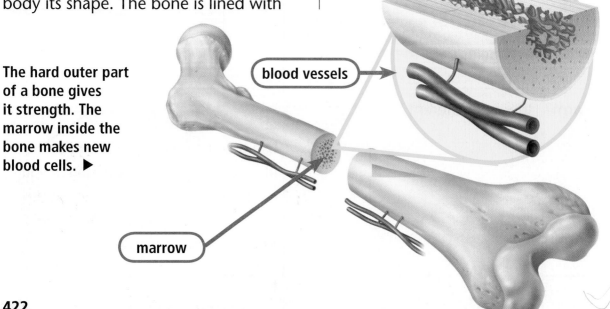

blood vessels

marrow

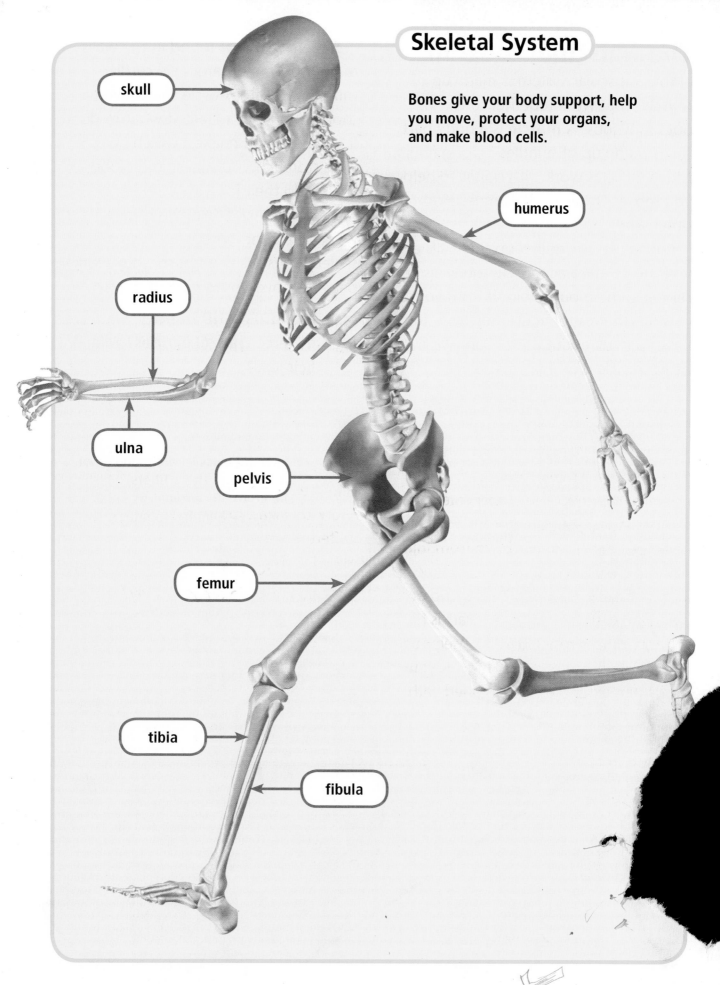

Skeletal System

skull

Bones give your body support, help you move, protect your organs, and make blood cells.

humerus

radius

ulna

pelvis

femur

tibia

fibula

The Muscular System

Your muscular system is made up of muscles that work together to carry out many jobs. A **muscle** is a body part that's made up of bundles of long fibers. Many muscles work with bones to help you move. Other kinds of muscle do other work.

Cardiac muscle makes up the walls of your heart. Cardiac muscle squeezes and relaxes to help pump blood from your heart to the rest of your body. You don't have to think about this action—your heart muscle works on its own.

Smooth muscle is found in the walls of your body's organs. Like cardiac muscle, smooth muscle works even though you don't "tell" it what to do. It squeezes and relaxes, which helps your stomach, intestines, and blood vessels do their jobs.

Skeletal muscles help you move. They work by pulling on bones. Because skeletal muscles can't push, they work in pairs to move bones back and forth.

 MAIN IDEA AND DETAILS **What are the three types of muscles? What are their jobs?**

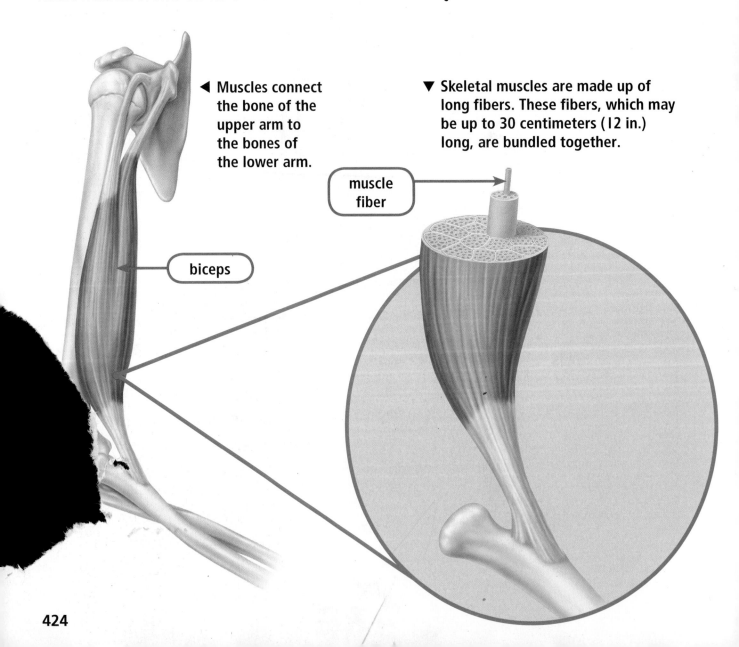

◀ Muscles connect the bone of the upper arm to the bones of the lower arm.

biceps

▼ Skeletal muscles are made up of long fibers. These fibers, which may be up to 30 centimeters (12 in.) long, are bundled together.

muscle fiber

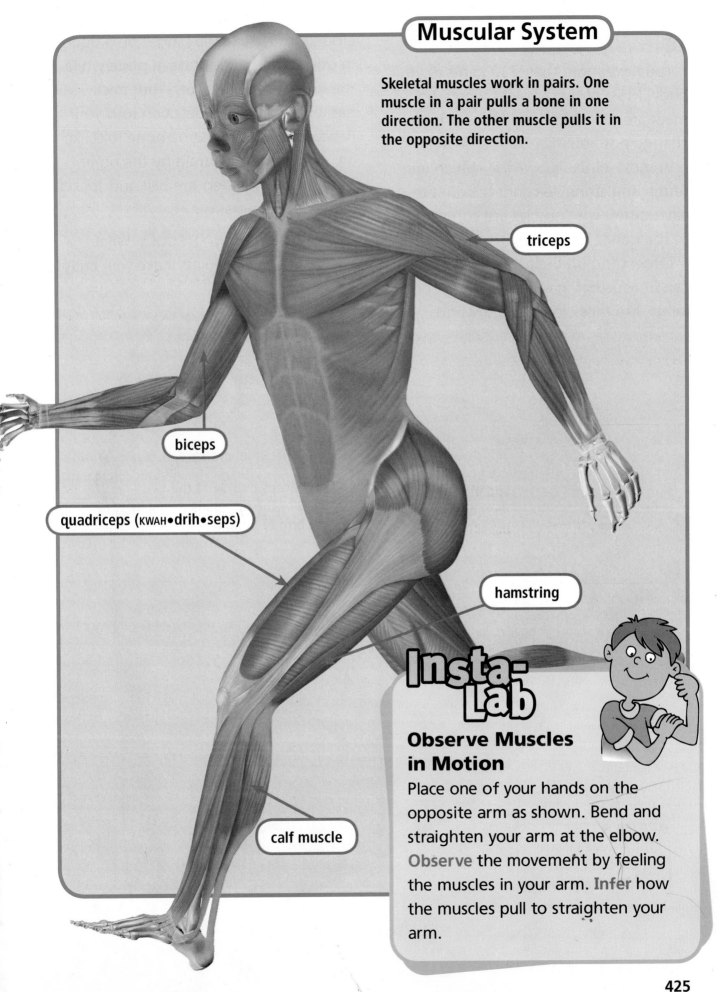

Muscular System

Skeletal muscles work in pairs. One muscle in a pair pulls a bone in one direction. The other muscle pulls it in the opposite direction.

triceps

biceps

quadriceps (KWAH•drih•seps)

hamstring

calf muscle

Insta-Lab

Observe Muscles in Motion

Place one of your hands on the opposite arm as shown. Bend and straighten your arm at the elbow. Observe the movement by feeling the muscles in your arm. Infer how the muscles pull to straighten your arm.

Joints

You have more than 230 joints in your body. Most of these places where bones meet are movable. They let your body change position.

In most joints, *ligaments*—which are tough and stringy—connect bones to each other. The muscles are connected to the bones by *tendons*.

Depending on their shape, bones can fit together in different ways. Some joints, like those in your knees and elbows, move like the hinges on a door. In others, one bone stays in place while the other turns, or *pivots*. Your neck has a pivot joint that lets you turn your head. In other joints, one bone rolls like a ball in a socket formed by the other bone. Your shoulders are ball-and-socket joints.

 MAIN IDEA AND DETAILS What is a joint? How do joints move your body?

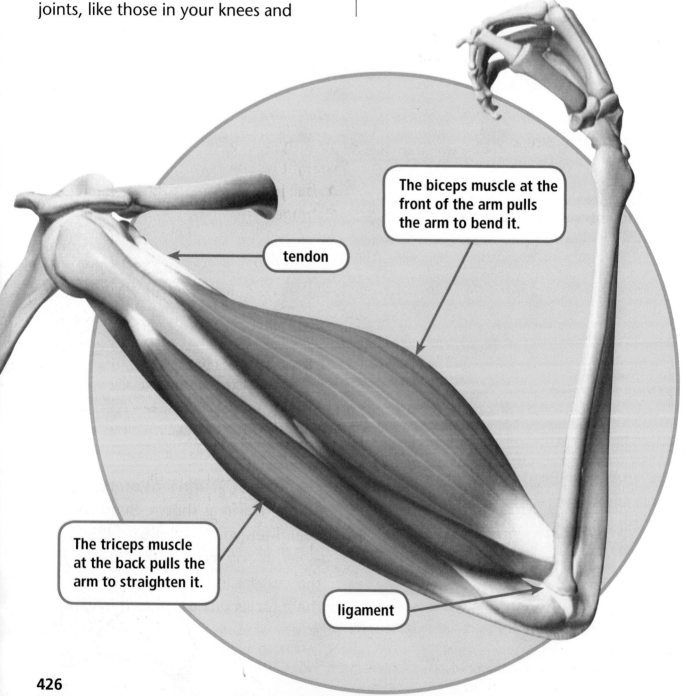

tendon

The biceps muscle at the front of the arm pulls the arm to bend it.

The triceps muscle at the back pulls the arm to straighten it.

ligament

1. MAIN IDEA AND DETAILS Draw and complete this graphic organizer.

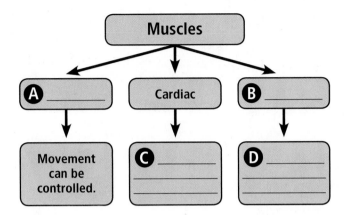

Muscles

A _____   Cardiac   B _____

Movement can be controlled.   C _____   D _____

2. SUMMARIZE Use your graphic organizer to write a summary of what you learned about muscles.

3. DRAW CONCLUSIONS Why isn't the heart made up of smooth muscle like other organs in your body?

4. VOCABULARY Use the lesson vocabulary to write a sentence about how the body moves.

FCAT Prep

5. Read/Inquire/Explain In what ways do the skeletal and muscular systems work together?

6. What type of joint bends and straightens the knee?
   A. ball joint   **C.** pivot joint
   B. hinge joint   **D.** socket joint

Links

Writing

Narrative Writing
Suppose you take a long hike. Write a **story** describing the hike from the point of view of your muscles. How would your skeletal muscles respond? What about your cardiac muscles?

Math

Multiply Whole Numbers
Count your heartbeats for 15 seconds. Multiply this number by 4 to see how many times your heart beats each minute. Multiply to find out how many times your heart beats in one hour.

Physical Education

Make a Plan
Experts say that you should exercise each day to stay healthy. What activities can you do each day to get 30 minutes of exercise? Make a plan.

 For more links and activities, go to **www.hspscience.com**

427

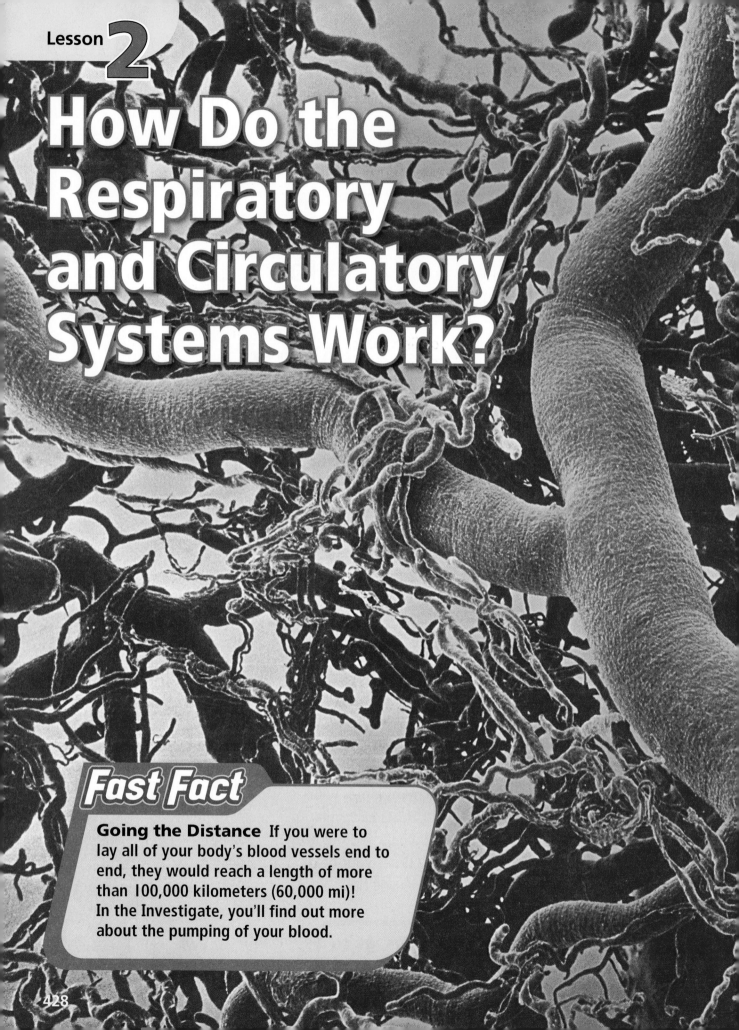

Lesson 2

How Do the Respiratory and Circulatory Systems Work?

Fast Fact

Going the Distance If you were to lay all of your body's blood vessels end to end, they would reach a length of more than 100,000 kilometers (60,000 mi)! In the Investigate, you'll find out more about the pumping of your blood.

Heart Rates

Materials • stopwatch, timer, or clock with second hand

Procedure

① Make a table like the one shown.

② While you're sitting, find the pulse on your wrist. Count the number of times your heart beats in 15 seconds. Use that number, multiplying it by 4, to find how often your heart beats in a minute while resting. Record the result on your table.

③ Stand up and march in place for 1 minute. As soon as you stop, find your pulse. Count your heartbeats for 15 seconds, and use the number to calculate the beats per minute. Record the result.

④ Rest for a few minutes, and then run in place for 1 minute. As soon as you stop, find your pulse. Count your heartbeats for 15 seconds. Then use the number to find the beats per minute. Record the result.

Activity	Heart Rate
Sitting	
After marching for 1 minute	
After running for 1 minute	

Step 2

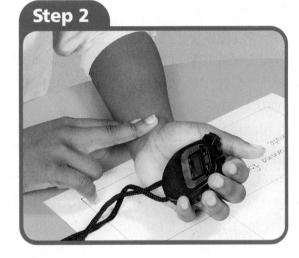

Draw Conclusions

1. Which activity increased your heart rate the least? Which increased it the most?

2. **Inquiry Skill** Plan an investigation to find out which activity elevates your heart rate for a longer time.

Investigate Further

How do you think exercise affects your breathing rate? Make a prediction, and design an experiment to find out.

VOCABULARY
diaphragm p. 430
artery p. 432
capillary p. 432
vein p. 432

SCIENCE CONCEPTS
▶ how the respiratory system works
▶ how the circulatory system carries oxygen and nutrients

 READING FOCUS SKILL
SEQUENCE Note the order of events of respiration and circulation.

The Respiratory System

Put your hand on your chest, take a deep breath, and let it out. Do you feel your chest rise and fall? This movement is caused by breathing. A muscle called the **diaphragm** (DY•uh•fram), located below your lungs, pulls air in to your body and then pushes it out again. The air that comes in contains the oxygen your body needs.

Air travels from your nose or mouth into the *trachea* (TRAY•kee•uh). The trachea branches into smaller and smaller tubes that lead into your lungs. There, the tubes end in tiny air sacs, and tiny blood vessels wrap around the air sacs. The air sacs and the blood vessels have thin walls that let gases move through them.

Oxygen that you inhale moves from the air sacs into the blood. Then blood moves to the heart. The heart pumps the blood that has lots of oxygen to all parts of the body. Blood cells also carry carbon dioxide, a waste product made in the body's cells, to the air sacs. Carbon dioxide leaves the body when you exhale, or breathe out.

 SEQUENCE How does oxygen get to the cells of the body?

Tiny blood vessels wrap around the air sacs in the lungs. Oxygen moves from the air sacs into the blood in these tiny vessels. ▶

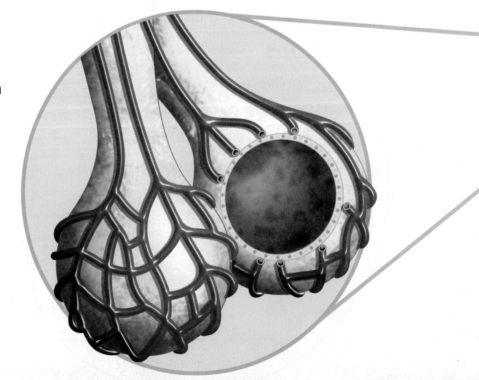

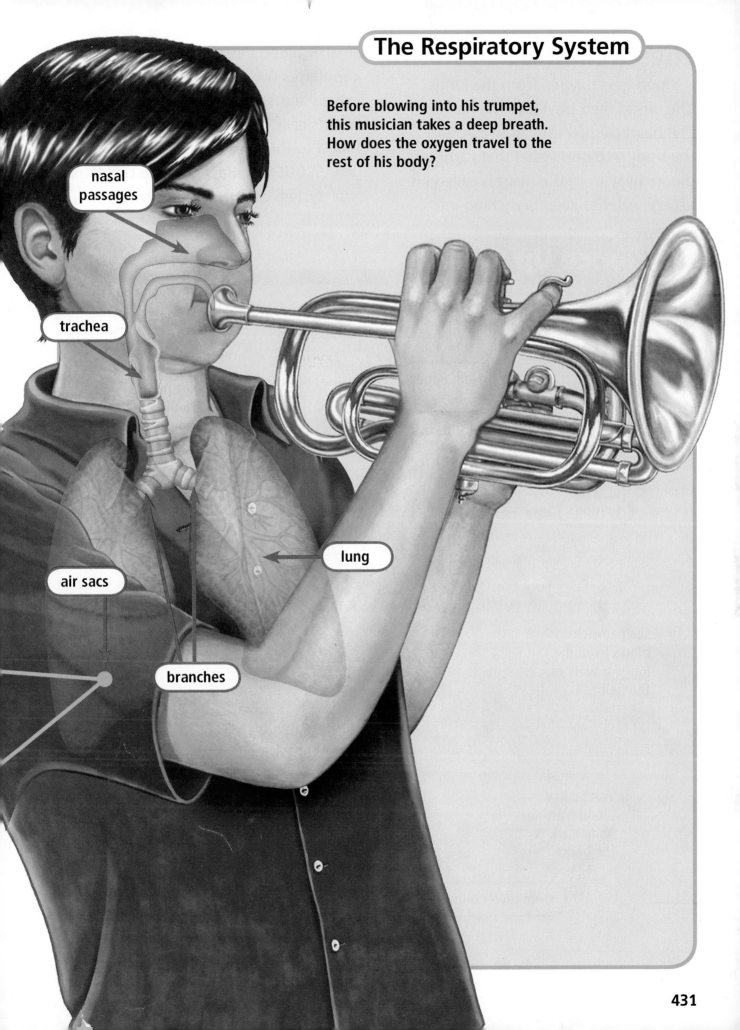

The Respiratory System

Before blowing into his trumpet, this musician takes a deep breath. How does the oxygen travel to the rest of his body?

nasal passages

trachea

lung

air sacs

branches

The Circulatory System

Blood gets oxygen from the lungs. The blood then travels to the heart. The heart pumps the blood through the body. A blood vessel that carries blood away from the heart is called an **artery**. Arteries keep branching into smaller blood vessels, until they become **capillaries** (KAP•uh•lair•eez). Oxygen moves across capillary walls to reach the body's cells. **Veins** are vessels that return blood to the heart.

 SEQUENCE How does the circulatory system get oxygen to each cell?

Science Up Close

The Heart

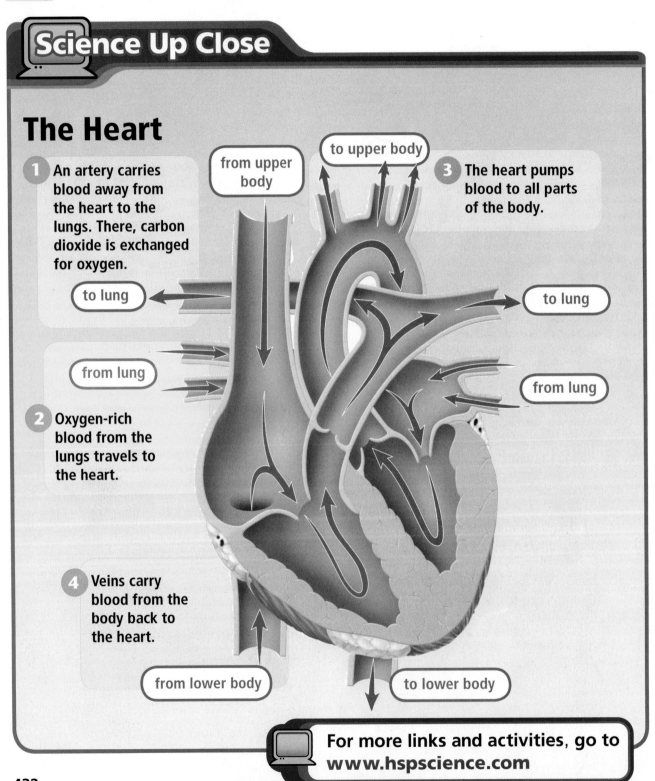

1. An artery carries blood away from the heart to the lungs. There, carbon dioxide is exchanged for oxygen.

from upper body

to upper body

3. The heart pumps blood to all parts of the body.

to lung

to lung

from lung

from lung

2. Oxygen-rich blood from the lungs travels to the heart.

4. Veins carry blood from the body back to the heart.

from lower body

to lower body

For more links and activities, go to www.hspscience.com

The Circulatory System

Blood is carried away from the heart through arteries. Blood returns to the heart through veins.

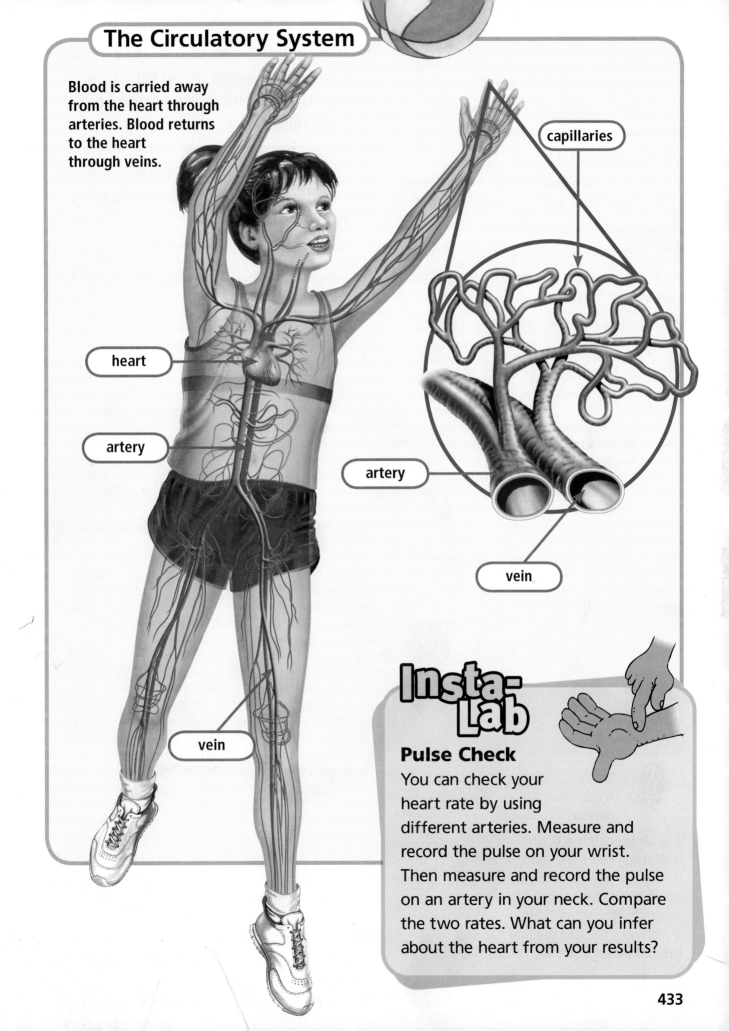

heart

artery

vein

capillaries

artery

vein

Insta-Lab

Pulse Check

You can check your heart rate by using different arteries. Measure and record the pulse on your wrist. Then measure and record the pulse on an artery in your neck. Compare the two rates. What can you infer about the heart from your results?

Blood

Can you guess what tissue is needed for both circulation and respiration? That tissue is *blood.* Blood is a liquid form of connective tissue.

There are different kinds of blood cells. They all travel in a liquid called *plasma.* Red blood cells are shaped like flattened spheres. Their shape allows them to bend and squeeze through tiny capillaries. This is important because red blood cells carry oxygen to all of the body's cells.

White blood cells protect the body from illness. When germs enter the body, white blood cells work to destroy them. Some white blood cells attack the germs, and some make proteins that work with attack cells to kill germs.

Platelets are colorless, sticky parts of the blood. Whenever you get a cut and bleed, you have torn a blood vessel. Platelets move to the cut and stick together to stop the bleeding.

 SEQUENCE **What happens when a blood vessel is cut?**

White blood cells protect the body from sickness.

The straw-colored liquid is plasma. The dark layer below the plasma is made up of red blood cells. A layer of white blood cells is between the plasma and the red blood cells. ▶

When a blood vessel is cut, platelets stick together to form a clot. This stops the bleeding.

Red blood cells contain a protein called hemoglobin, which carries oxygen.

434

1. SEQUENCE Draw and complete this graphic organizer about respiration.

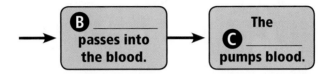

Air enters the nose or mouth. → It passes through the **A** _____. → It enters air sacs in the lungs. →

→ **B** _____ passes into the blood. → **C** The _____ pumps blood.

2. SUMMARIZE Use your graphic organizer to describe how the respiratory system and circulatory system work together.

3. DRAW CONCLUSIONS Why is it easy for oxygen to move from the air sacs to the blood?

4. VOCABULARY Use the vocabulary to construct a word puzzle.

FCAT Prep

5. Read/Inquire/Explain What would happen if blood entering the heart mixed with blood leaving it?

6. Which of these carry blood away from the heart?

A. air sacs   **C.** capillaries

B. arteries   **D.** veins

Links

Writing

Narrative Writing

Write a **story** describing the travels of a blood cell through arteries, capillaries, veins, and the heart.

Math

Multiply Whole Numbers

Count the number of times you breathe in one minute. Then **calculate** the number of breaths you are likely to take in one hour.

Health

Healthy Lungs and Heart

Use reference materials to investigate the relationship between exercise and a healthy heart and lungs. How does exercise help you?

For more links and activities, go to www.hspscience.com

How Do the Nervous and Digestive Systems Work?

Fast Fact

Brainy Bytes Most human brains weigh about 1400 grams (3 lb), but genius Albert Einstein's brain was much smaller. It weighed only 1230 grams (2.71 lb). In the Investigate, you'll find out how well your own brain detects the slightest touches.

The Sense of Touch

Materials • index card • ruler • tape • 8 toothpicks

Procedure

CAUTION: Toothpicks are sharp. Do not play with them. Use them only as directed.

1 Copy the table. Then predict which of the body parts that are named has the best sense of touch. Record your prediction.

2 Along one edge of the index card, make two marks 1 cm apart. Use the ruler. Tape a toothpick to each mark. The toothpicks should stick out 1 cm from the edge.

3 Repeat Step 2 for the other three edges of the index card. But space the toothpicks 2 cm, 5 cm, and 8 cm apart.

4 Look away while a partner *lightly* touches each pair of toothpicks to a body part named in the table. At each part, begin with the 1-cm distance and then try the greater distances in turn.

5 For each body part, predict the shortest distance at which you'll feel two separate toothpicks. When you do feel two, tell your partner. Record the distance.

Draw Conclusions

1. On which body part did you feel two toothpicks at the shortest distance?

2. **Inquiry Skill** Based on the results of this test, which body part would you infer has the best sense of touch? Explain.

Prediction:		
Distance Apart When Two Toothpicks Are First Felt		
Palm	Lower Arm	Upper Arm
Prediction			
Actual			

Step 4

Investigate Further

Use your results to predict which will be more sensitive, your fingertip or the back of your neck. Test your prediction.

SCIENCE CONCEPTS
▶ how the nervous system acts as the body's control system
▶ how the digestive system helps the body get energy and nutrients from food

 **READING FOCUS SKILL**
SEQUENCE Look for the order in which events happen.

The Nervous System

Has a doctor ever tapped on your knee with a small rubber mallet or checked your eyes with a light? Doctors use these tools to check the nervous system. The nervous system is very important. None of the other body systems could work without its help.

Your brain is the control center of your nervous system. There are billions of nerve cells in your brain. Signals from the brain direct your body's activities.

Your brain receives information from all parts of your body. Messages from your body travel along nerves to the spinal cord. The **spinal cord** is a bundle of nerve tissue that runs through your backbone to your brain. The brain acts on information it gets from the body. Then it sends messages back out through the spinal cord.

SEQUENCE How do messages from the body reach the brain?

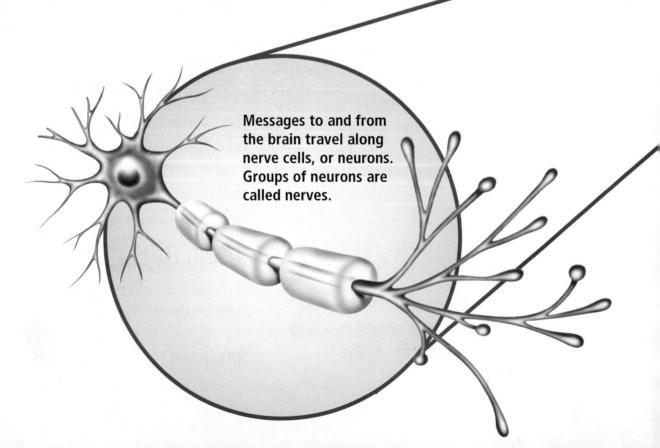

Messages to and from the brain travel along nerve cells, or neurons. Groups of neurons are called nerves.

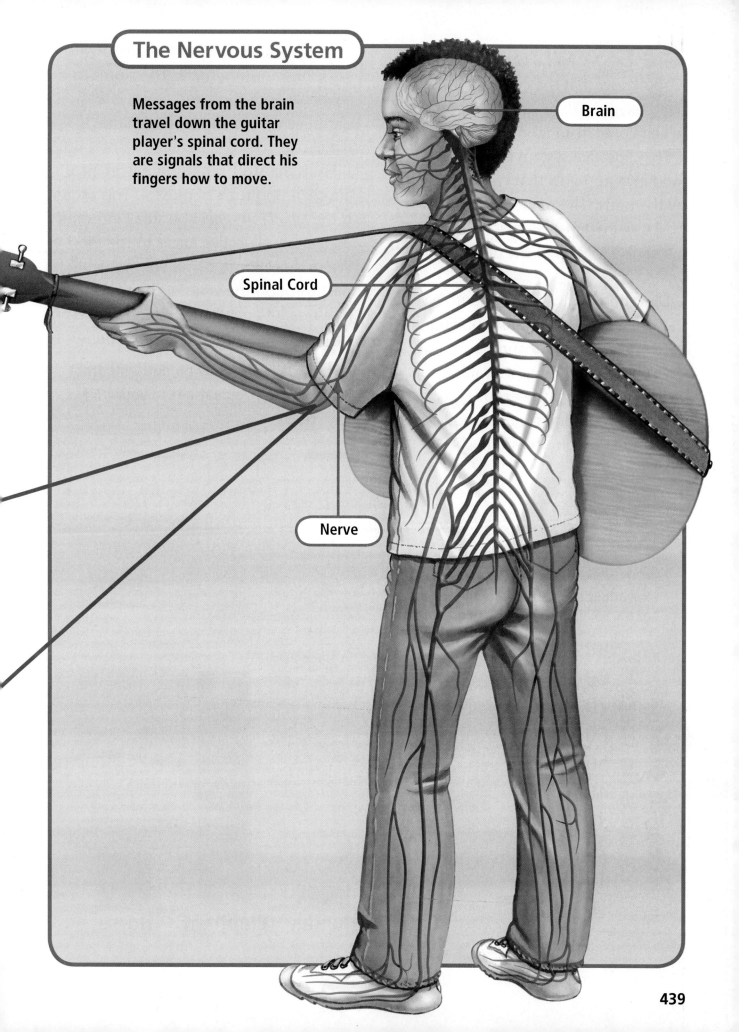

The Nervous System

Messages from the brain travel down the guitar player's spinal cord. They are signals that direct his fingers how to move.

Brain

Spinal Cord

Nerve

439

The Digestive System

You know that the cells of your body need oxygen. They also need nutrients, which come from food.

The digestive system breaks down food into nutrients that can be used by the body. The mouth, esophagus (ih•SAHF•uh•guhs), stomach, and small intestine are parts of the digestive system.

Digestion begins in the mouth. When you chew, your teeth grind up your food. Saliva softens it and begins to break it down. After you swallow, the food travels down the **esophagus**, a muscular tube that connects your mouth to the next organ, the stomach.

The **stomach** is a baglike organ with walls of smooth muscle. The stomach squeezes your food and mixes it with digestive juices. The food becomes almost liquid.

From the stomach, food passes into another long tube of muscle. This organ is the *small intestine.* The small intestine adds other digestive juices to the food. When digestion is complete, nutrients pass through the walls of the small intestine into capillaries. Blood carries the nutrients to each cell in the body.

 SEQUENCE How do nutrients from the food you eat get to your body's cells?

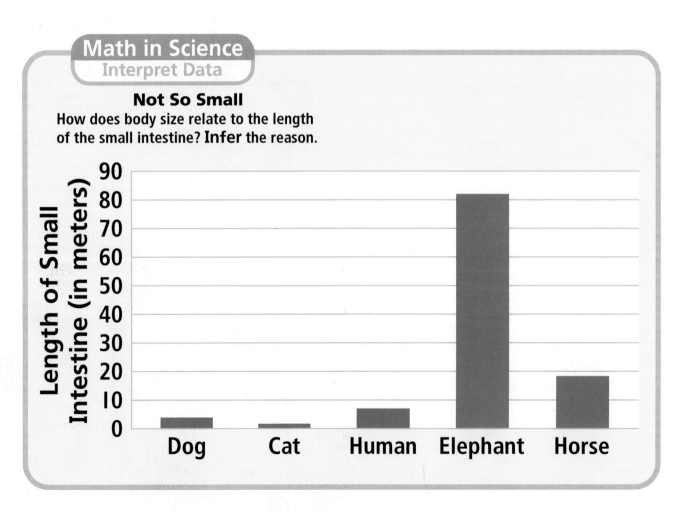

Math in Science
Interpret Data

Not So Small
How does body size relate to the length of the small intestine? **Infer** the reason.

Length of Small Intestine (in meters)

Dog Cat Human Elephant Horse

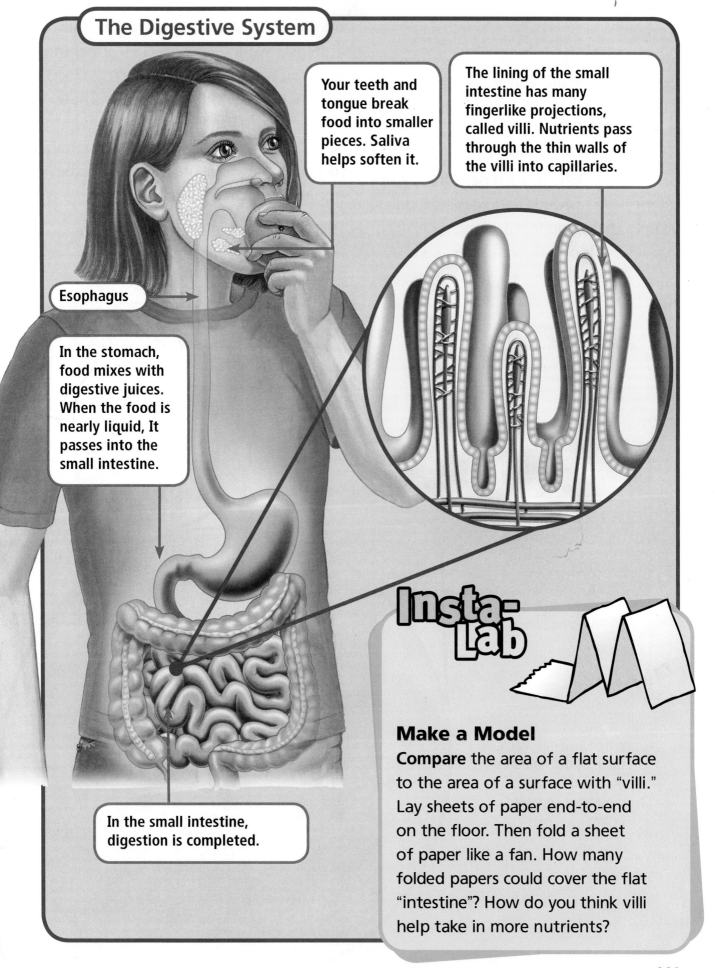

The Digestive System

Your teeth and tongue break food into smaller pieces. Saliva helps soften it.

The lining of the small intestine has many fingerlike projections, called villi. Nutrients pass through the thin walls of the villi into capillaries.

Esophagus

In the stomach, food mixes with digestive juices. When the food is nearly liquid, It passes into the small intestine.

In the small intestine, digestion is completed.

Insta-Lab

Make a Model
Compare the area of a flat surface to the area of a surface with "villi." Lay sheets of paper end-to-end on the floor. Then fold a sheet of paper like a fan. How many folded papers could cover the flat "intestine"? How do you think villi help take in more nutrients?

441

Taste

Your sense organs include your eyes, ears, nose, mouth, and skin. They send signals along nerves to your brain. The signals tell you about your surroundings.

Have you ever smelled something delicious cooking in a kitchen? If so, you might have noticed that pleasant food aromas make you feel hungry. When you taste a food's delicious flavor, you might notice that your senses of smell and taste work together. They affect the way you sense the food you eat.

Taste buds cover your tongue. These tiny sense organs allow you to sense different flavors. Taste buds send signals to your brain. Your brain interprets the signals as flavors.

 SEQUENCE How does your body sense taste?

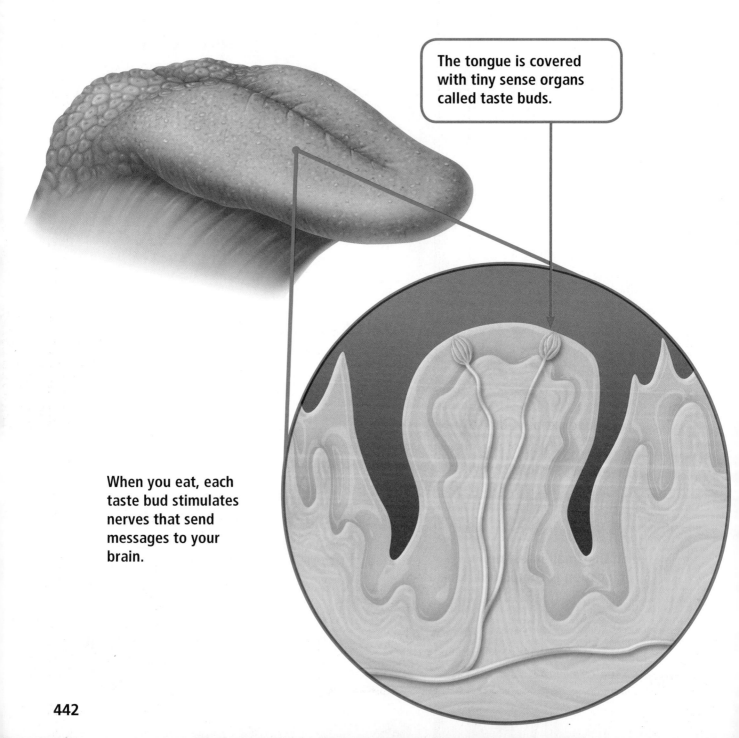

The tongue is covered with tiny sense organs called taste buds.

When you eat, each taste bud stimulates nerves that send messages to your brain.

1. **SEQUENCE** Draw and complete this graphic organizer about digestion.

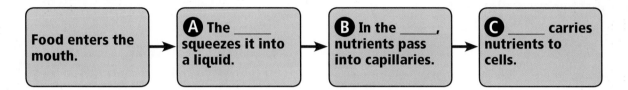

| Food enters the mouth. | → | **A** The _____ squeezes it into a liquid. | → | **B** In the _____, nutrients pass into capillaries. | → | **C** _____ carries nutrients to cells. |

2. **SUMMARIZE** Use your graphic organizer to write a paragraph about digestion.

3. **DRAW CONCLUSIONS** Suppose someone falls and lands hard on his or her back. Why shouldn't you move the person until help arrives?

4. **VOCABULARY** Write your own definition for each vocabulary term.

FCAT Prep

5. **Read/Inquire/Explain** How might a serious injury to the spinal cord affect the rest of the body?

6. Where do nutrients move from the digestive system to the circulatory system?

   A. esophagus   **C.** small intestine

   B. mouth   **D.** stomach

Links

Writing

Expository Writing

Think about some of your favorite foods. Which of the foods taste salty? Which taste sweet, sour, or bitter? Write a **description** of each of the tastes.

Math

Make a Bar Graph

Nerves can send messages back and forth at the amazing speed of 430 kilometers per hour (267 mi/hr). Find two things that travel faster and two that travel more slowly. Make a bar graph to **compare** the speeds.

Health

Good Taste

Read a book or another reference about taste and the body parts that help you taste. Then make a checklist of good health habits for keeping your sense of taste.

 For more links and activities, go to **www.hspscience.com**

Beauty QUEEN

Could a battered and forgotten face be the lost Queen Nefertiti?

Queen Nefertiti's name means "the beautiful one has come." It is not surprising that she was given such a name. Queen Nefertiti has long been admired for her swanlike neck and high cheekbones.

But Nefertiti was more than just a pretty face. She is believed to have been one of the most powerful women who ever lived. She ruled Egypt more than 3,000 years ago.

A Lost Queen

Mysteriously, no one knows how Queen Nefertiti died. Her remains have never been found—until now, perhaps.

A team of archaeologists led by Joann Fletcher uncovered three mummies in a tomb in Egypt. (Archaeologists are scientists who dig up ancient objects and study them to learn about the past.) Fletcher believes that one of the mummies is Queen Nefertiti.

Rebuilding the Mummy's Face

Modern science is helping Fletcher prove her idea and identify the face of the mummy. After X rays of the mummy were taken, scientists put together a computerized version of what the face would have looked like.

Mounting Evidence

Scientists are quick to point out that the computerized version of the face does not

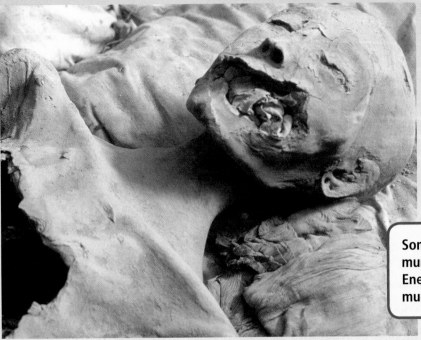

Some scientists believe that the mummy seen here is Nefertiti. Enemies may have smashed the mummy's face.

prove that the mummy is Queen Nefertiti. The re-created face, however, isn't the only clue to the past.

There are other pieces of the puzzle that make Fletcher's team think the mummy is Nefertiti. First, the mummy's hair had been shaved off. Nefertiti preferred a shaved head for health and cleanliness. A shaved head also helped her stay cool in Egypt's heat. Second, traces of a wig found next to the mummy matched the kind that Nefertiti would have worn.

In addition, the mummy's left earlobe was pierced twice. Statues of Nefertiti show her having a double-pierced ear. The mummy's forehead showed the mark of a tight-fitting band—a sign of royalty. Another clue was the mummy's bent arm, which was broken off. Royalty were usually buried with their arms bent.

Challenging the Evidence

Not all scientists are convinced that the mummy is Nefertiti.

"If the mummy is female and if it is royal, then you still do not necessarily have Nefertiti," one archaeologist told Time magazine.

Another scientist from Egypt expressed doubts that the mummy is even a female. He said that both men and women of that time could have double-pierced ears.

But Fletcher believes that she has found the long-lost queen and has returned Nefertiti to her rightful place in history.

THINK ABOUT IT

1. How do mummies help to tell us about how people lived in the past?
2. How was technology used to study the mummy?

The Face That Changed Egypt

Scientists used a computer to re-create a face (left) based on the skull of the mummy. It looks like a statue of Nefertiti (right).

Find out more! Log on to **www.hspscience.com**

SC.H.3.2.4.4.1 solving problems/new ideas
SC.H.3.2.3.4.1 impact of scientific discoveries

Robots to the Rescue?

Nadrian Seeman is a chemist. He wants to build tiny robots to battle diseases inside people. Seeman is trying to build tiny robots out of DNA. He is an expert in nanotechnology. He studies how to build devices from single atoms and molecules.

Seeman has built a tiny gadget called a "nanowalker." It can move from place to place. Seeman built the tiny robot out of fragments of DNA. DNA consists of instructions for life. The instructions control how living things look and function.

Career   Physical Therapist

When a person suffers a serious injury, he or she may be operated on by a medical doctor. After an operation many patients meet with a physical therapist. These experts know how a person's bones and muscles are connected. They help people recover from their injuries.

You Can Do It!

Quick and Easy Project

Model the Intestine

Procedure

1. Suppose that your fingers are like the villi in the small intestine.
2. Hold your left hand up, with the fingers together. Trace around the fingers of your left hand.
3. Spread the fingers of your left hand. Trace around the fingers of your left hand.

Draw Conclusions

How is the surface in the small intestine like one of the surfaces you traced? How does this help absorb food?

Design Your Own Investigation

Model Absorption

Particles of nutrients must be small to get through the villi and into the blood. Make a model to show this. You might use a surface such as a cloth and small and large particles in water.

Vocabulary Review

Use the terms below to complete the sentences. The page numbers tell you where to look in the chapter if you need help.

bone p. 422   artery p. 432

joint p. 422   vein p. 432

muscles p. 424   spinal cord p. 438

diaphragm p. 430   esophagus p. 440

capillary p. 432   stomach p. 440

1. A tiny, thin-walled blood vessel is a _____.

2. The bundle of nerve tissue that carries messages to and from the brain is the _____.

3. A hard organ that helps support and move the body is a _____.

4. A place where two bones meet is a _____.

5. The main muscle that controls the movement of air into and out of the body is the _____.

6. Smooth, cardiac, and skeletal are types of _____.

7. A blood vessel that carries blood away from the heart is an _____.

8. The muscular organ that makes food almost a liquid is the _____.

9. The tube between the mouth and the stomach is the _____.

10. A blood vessel that carries blood to the heart is a _____.

Check Understanding

Write the letter of the best choice.

11. **MAIN IDEA** What are these fingerlike projections in the small intestine?

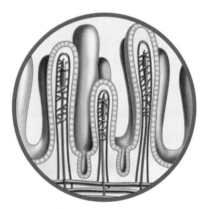

A. capillaries
B. epithelial tissue
C. nerves
D. villi

12. **SEQUENCE** What is the path that blood follows through the body, beginning at the heart?

F. heart, capillaries, arteries, veins, heart

G. heart, arteries, capillaries, veins, heart

H. heart, veins, capillaries, arteries, heart

I. heart, capillaries, veins, arteries, heart

13. How are taste and smell related?

    A. They use the same sense organ.

    B. They work together.

    C. They are both reflexes.

    D. They are not related.

14. What two organs run parallel to each other?

    F. stomach and esophagus

    G. esophagus and intestine

    H. eyes and ears

    I. spinal cord and esophagus

15. Which is the main sense being used to catch the ball?

    A. hearing

    B. sight

    C. smell

    D. taste

16. Which systems work together to provide the body's cells with nutrients?

    F. circulatory and digestive

    G. circulatory and respiratory

    H. respiratory and circulatory

    I. respiratory and excretory

Inquiry Skills

17. Compare digestion and respiration.

18. Draw and complete the graphic organizer to show the following **order** of events. A message from a touch receptor reaches the brain, which then directs a leg muscle to move. Use the completed graphic organizer to write down the complete sequence of this process.

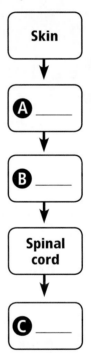

Skin

A ____

B ____

Spinal cord

C ____

Read/Inquire/Explain

19. How would unhealthy teeth or gums affect digestion?

20. Different body systems work together to keep us healthy.

Part A How are the digestive and circulatory systems related?

Part B Explain how the heart and lungs help each other provide oxygen to the body.

How Living Things Interact with Their Environment

LIFE SCIENCE

The chapters in this unit address these Grade Level Expectations from the Florida Sunshine State Standards.

Chapter 13 — Understanding Ecosystems

SC.G.1.2.6.4.1	knows that organisms are growing, dying, and decaying and that new organisms are being produced.
SC.G.1.2.7.4.1	knows that variations in light, water, temperature, and soil content are largely responsible for the existence of different kinds of organisms and population densities in an ecosystem.
SC.G.2.2.1.4.2	knows characteristics that allow members within a species to survive and reproduce.
SC.G.2.2.3.4.1	understands patterns of interdependency in ecological systems.
SC.G.2.2.3.4.3	understands that changes in an ecological system usually affect the whole system.

Chapter 14 — Energy Transfer in Ecosystems

SC.G.1.2.1.4.1	knows how plants and animals interact with one another in an ecosystem.
SC.G.1.2.1.4.2	understands the relationships among organisms in aquatic and terrestrial food chains.
SC.G.1.2.4.4.1	knows organisms that act as decomposers.
SC.G.1.2.4.4.2	understands the need for nutrients and minerals for living organisms.
SC.G.1.2.4.4.3	understands the process of decay.
SC.G.2.2.1.4.1	knows the kinds of organisms that lived in the past and compares them to existing species.
SC.G.2.2.3.4.2	understands that what benefits one organism may be harmful to other organisms.

The investigations and experiences in this unit also address many of the Grade Level Expectations in Strand H, The Nature of Science.

Science in Florida

Tallahassee

coral snake

Dear Uncle Rodney,

This morning I was playing in my back yard when I saw a snake in the bushes. When I jumped back, the snake slithered off in the other direction. The snake didn't want to bother me, and I definitely didn't want to bother the snake. Dad warned me that there are some venomous snakes in Florida that could bite me. Do you have snakes where you live?

   Love,

   Lucy

The Sunshine State

USA

FCAT Writing

Writing Situation
Suppose you see a snake while you are playing outside. Explain how you should react and what you should do.

Experiment!

Counting Species When people develop land and build new houses, the environment that was already there is changed. The animals living in the habitat must find new places to live. Is there a difference between natural habitats and habitats that humans have developed? Are there more types of living things in one of the two environments? Plan and conduct an experiment to find out.

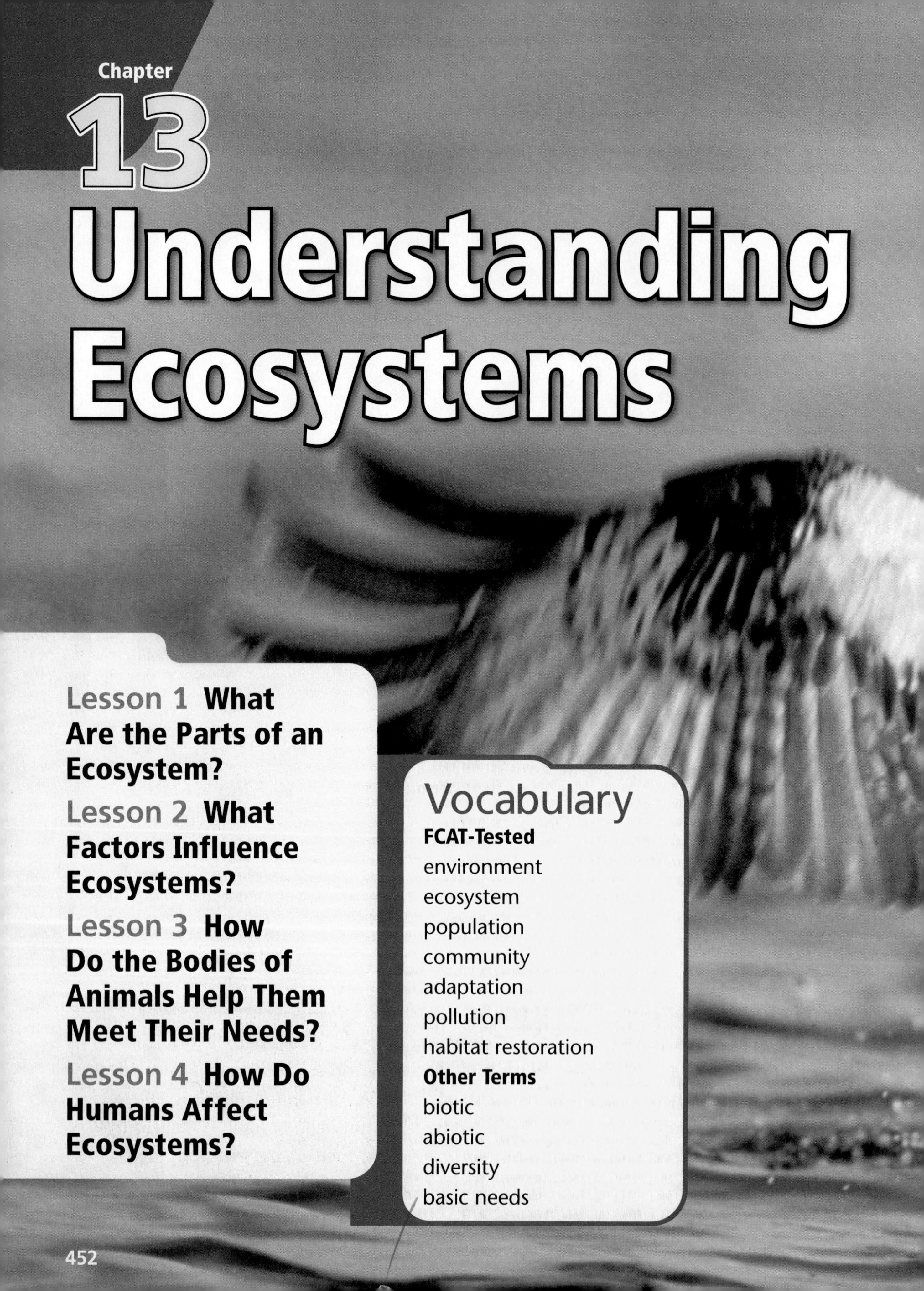

Chapter 13

Understanding Ecosystems

Vocabulary

FCAT-Tested

environment
ecosystem
population
community
adaptation
pollution
habitat restoration

Other Terms

biotic
abiotic
diversity
basic needs

What do YOU wonder?

This hawk has very sharp claws, called talons. Why don't birds such as sparrows have talons?

What Are the Parts of an Ecosystem?

Fast Fact

Silver Kings The tarpon in this photograph are not yet full-grown! These fish don't become adults until they are between 7 and 13 years old, when they can weigh more than 91 kilograms (200 lb). Tarpon live in salt water, but they can survive in a variety of ecosystems. In the Investigate, you will observe how sunlight affects plants in another ecosystem.

Modeling an Ecosystem

Materials
- gravel
- sand
- soil
- 6 small plants
- water in a spray bottle
- clear plastic wrap
- 2 empty 2-L soda bottles with tops cut off
- 2 rubber bands

Procedure

1. Pour a layer of gravel, a layer of sand, and then a layer of soil into the bottom of each bottle.

2. Plant three plants in each bottle.

3. Spray the plants and the soil with water. Cover the top of each bottle with plastic wrap. If necessary, hold the wrap in place with a rubber band.

4. Put one of the terrariums you just made in a sunny spot. Put the other one in a dark closet or cabinet.

5. After three days, observe each terrarium and record what you see.

Draw Conclusions

1. What did you observe about each of your ecosystems after three days? What part was missing from one ecosystem?

2. **Inquiry Skill** Scientists often learn more about how things affect one another by making a model. What did you learn by making a model and observing how its parts interact?

Step 2

Step 3

Investigate Further

What effect does sunlight have on seeds that have just been planted? First, write your hypothesis. Then plan an experiment to see if your hypothesis is supported.

SC.G.2.2.3.4.1 interdependency in systems
LA.A.2.2.1 main idea

VOCABULARY
environment p. 456
ecosystem p. 456
population p. 458
community p. 460

SCIENCE CONCEPTS
▶ how living and nonliving parts of an ecosystem interact
▶ what populations and communities are

READING FOCUS SKILL
MAIN IDEA AND DETAILS
Look for the parts that make up an ecosystem.

```
        Main Idea
     /      |      \
 detail   detail   detail
```

Ecosystems

Where do you live? You might name your street and town. You also live in an environment. An **environment** is all the living and nonliving things that surround you. The living things in your environment are people, other animals, and plants. The nonliving things around you include water, air, soil, and weather.

The parts of an environment affect one another in many ways. For example, animals eat plants. The soil affects which plants can live in a place. Clean air and clean water help keep both plants and animals healthy. All the living and nonliving things in an area form an **ecosystem** (EE•koh•sis•tuhm).

An ecosystem can be very small. It might be the space under a rock. That space might be home to insects and tiny plants. You might need a microscope to see some of the things living there.

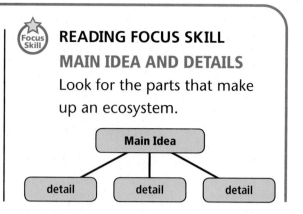
This prairie smoke plant grows well in the hot, dry climate of prairies and grasslands. ▼

Prairie dogs also live on the prairies and grasslands. ▼

Moose thrive in a coniferous, or evergreen, forest ecosystem.

The small ecosystem found under a rock has nonliving parts, too. They include pockets of air and the soil under the rock. You might find a few drops of water or maybe just damp soil. All ecosystems must have at least a little water.

The ecosystem under this rock has a climate. The *climate* in an area is the average weather over many years. Climate includes temperature and rainfall. The climate of an ecosystem depends on where the ecosystem is. If this rock is in Florida, its climate is warm and wet. If the rock is in Maine, its winters are icy.

An ecosystem can also be as large as a forest. A forest can provide many kinds of food and shelter. This ecosystem may include hundreds of kinds of plants and animals. Each organism finds what it needs in the forest.

Like all ecosystems, a forest has nonliving parts. They include water, air, soil, and climate. Later, you will read more about ways living and nonliving parts of an ecosystem affect one another.

 MAIN IDEA AND DETAILS **Name the two parts of an ecosystem, and give two examples of each part.**

This individual waterlily is part of a large population of waterlilies.

Individuals and Populations

One plant or animal is an *individual.* For example, one blueberry bush is an individual. One honeybee is an individual. One blue jay is an individual. You are an individual.

A group made up of the same kind of individuals living in the same ecosystem is a **population**. A group of blueberry bushes is a population. So is a hive of bees. So are all the blue jays living in one forest. So are all the people living in one city.

Robins might live in the same forest as the blue jays. Robins are a different kind of bird. That makes them a different population.

The members of a population might not live in a group. For example, frogs don't live in families. Still, a number of green tree frogs may live near the same pond. They belong to the same population. Bullfrogs might also live near that pond. They are a different population.

Many animals live in groups. People live in families. How many people are in your family? Wolves live in packs. A pack can have from 3 to 20 wolves. A wolf population may have several packs. The wolf population in Yellowstone National Park includes 19 packs.

Some populations can live in more than one kind of ecosystem. For instance, red-winged blackbirds often live in wetlands, but they are also found in other areas. Red-winged blackbirds can live in different ecosystems. If one ecosystem no longer meets the needs of these birds, they fly to another one.

Some populations can live in only one kind of ecosystem. One such animal is the Hine's emerald dragonfly. This insect can live only in certain wetlands. It can't survive in other places. Because this dragonfly can live only in specific places, its total number is very small.

Ecosystems are often named for the main population that lives there. For example, one kind of ecosystem forms where a river flows into the ocean. There, fresh water mixes with salt water. Many trees can't live in salty water. But mangrove trees have roots that allow them to get rid of the salt in the water.

When many mangrove trees live in a salty ecosystem, the area is called a *mangrove swamp.*

 MAIN IDEA AND DETAILS Name an individual and a population that are not mentioned on these two pages.

Insta-Lab

Eeek! Oh System!
Work with a partner to list some of the populations in your school ecosystem. Think about the building and the land around it. Then compare lists with other students. Did you list the same populations?

This individual male red-winged blackbird is part of a large population of blackbirds.

A population of red-winged blackbirds can include several million birds. Some of the birds fly 80 kilometers (50 mi) to find food.

Communities

You live in a community. Other animals and plants do, too. A **community** is all the populations that live in the same place.

Have you visited the Everglades National Park? Many different populations make up this community. The plants include mangrove trees, cypress trees, and saw grass. If you have been to the Everglades, you may know about the mosquitoes from getting bitten! The area has 43 kinds. And 50 kinds of butterflies live there.

Animals found in the Everglades community include alligators, bobcats, and raccoons. Bird-watchers like to visit the Everglades. They try to see some of the 350 kinds of land birds and 16 kinds of wading birds that live there.

In some ways, the Everglades is like all communities. The plants and animals there depend on one another. Some animals eat the plants. Other animals eat the plant eaters. The animals help spread the plants' seeds. The plants provide shelter for the animals.

 MAIN IDEA AND DETAILS Name three populations that might be found in a forest community.

▼ Many populations make up the communities in this cold taiga ecosystem. They include evergreen trees, moose, and many kinds of birds.

1. MAIN IDEA AND DETAILS Draw and complete this graphic organizer.

A pond ecosystem is made up of living and nonliving things.

Living Things
A _____
_____
_____

Nonliving Things
B _____
_____
_____

2. SUMMARIZE Write a summary of this lesson by using the lesson vocabulary words in a paragraph.

3. DRAW CONCLUSIONS Why do some ecosystems include more living things than other ecosystems?

4. VOCABULARY Use the lesson vocabulary words to create a matching quiz.

FCAT Prep

5. Read/Inquire/Explain How is a population different from a community?

6. Which word describes a group of cows standing together?
   A. community   **C.** individual
   B. ecosystem   **D.** population

Links

Writing

Expository Writing

You are a scientist planning an ecosystem on the moon. Write **two paragraphs** explaining what this ecosystem should include.

Math

Solve a Problem

The Everglades includes many "rivers of grass." The water in these rivers moves slowly, only 30 meters (100 ft) a day. How many meters would the water move in June? In February?

Social Studies

Ecosystems and People

Choose a group of people who live in an ecosystem different from yours. Find out how that ecosystem affects the people. Share what you learn in an oral or a written report.

For more links and activities, go to
www.hspscience.com

What Factors Influence Ecosystems?

That's Dry! This photograph shows the Atacama Desert in Chile. It's the driest place on Earth. Less than 0.01 centimeter (0.004 in.) of rain falls there every year. It hasn't rained in some parts of this desert for 400 years! In the Investigate, you will explore what happens when there is no rain.

Observing the Effects of Water

Materials
- 4 small identical plants in clay pots
- water
- large labels

Procedure

1. Use the labels to number the pots 1, 2, 3, and 4. Label pots 1 and 2 *watered*. Label pots 3 and 4 *not watered*.

2. Make a table like the one shown here. Draw a picture of each plant under Day 1.

3. Place all four pots in a sunny window.

4. Water all four pots until the soil is a little moist. Keep the soil of pots 1 and 2 moist during the whole experiment. Don't water pots 3 and 4 again.

5. Wait three days. Then observe and record how each plant looks. Draw a picture of each one under Day 4.

6. Repeat Step 5 twice. Draw pictures of the plants on Days 7 and 10.

	Day 1	Day 4	Day 7	Day 10
Plant 1 (watered)				
Plant 2 (watered)				
Plant 3 (not watered)				
Plant 4 (not watered)				

Step 4

Draw Conclusions

1. What changes did you observe during this Investigate? What do they tell you?

2. **Inquiry Skill** Scientists compare changes to determine how one thing affects another. How could you compare how fast the soil dries out in a clay pot with how fast it dries out in a plastic pot?

Investigate Further

How does covering a plant with plastic wrap affect the plant's need for water? Write your hypothesis. Then design and carry out an experiment to check your hypothesis.

Reading in Science

SC.G.2.2.3.4.1 interdependency in systems; **SC.G.1.2.7.4.1** variations affect ecosystems; **SC.G.2.2.3.4.3** changes in systems; **LA.E.2.2.1** cause and effect

VOCABULARY
biotic p. 464
abiotic p. 466
diversity p. 470

SCIENCE CONCEPTS
▶ how biotic and abiotic factors affect ecosystems
▶ how climate influences an ecosystem

READING FOCUS SKILL
CAUSE AND EFFECT
Look for ways in which factors affect ecosystems.

Living Things Affect Ecosystems

Do plants and animals need each other? Yes, they do! Plants and animals are living parts of an ecosystem. These living parts are **biotic** factors. *Bio* means "life." Biotic factors affect the ecosystem and one another in many ways.

For example, plants provide food for caterpillars, birds, sheep, and other animals. People eat plants every day—at least they should.

Plants also provide shelter for animals. For instance, many insects live in grasses. Squirrels make dens in trees. Your home likely contains wood from trees.

Animals help plants, too. When animals eat one kind of plant, it can't spread and take over all the available space. This gives other kinds of plants room to grow.

A gypsy moth can lay 1000 eggs or more. Most of the eggs hatch into hungry caterpillars like this one. ▶

A healthy tree isn't hurt when a few insects nibble on it.

Gypsy moth caterpillars can eat all the leaves on a tree. Bad weather or an attack by other insects may kill trees.

Animals help plants in other ways. Animal droppings make the soil richer. Earthworms help loosen the soil. Rich, loose soil helps plants grow.

At the same time, too many plant eaters can be harmful. A herd of hungry deer can eat enough leaves to kill a tree. A huge swarm of locusts can leave a field bare of plants.

You know that animals affect one another. For example, wolves eat rabbits. If the wolf population becomes too large, wolves can wipe out the rabbits. Then the wolves go hungry. Without the rabbits to eat them, the grasses spread.

In this case, an increase in wolves causes a decrease in rabbits. Fewer rabbits causes an increase in plants.

A change in plants can also cause a change in animals. If dry weather or disease kills the grasses, the rabbits starve. Then the wolves go hungry, too. Disease can also kill animals in an ecosystem.

Sometimes, a new kind of plant or animal changes an ecosystem. For example, people brought the skunk vine to the United States from Asia in 1897. For a time, they planted it as a crop. Now it grows wild. This smelly vine can grow 9 meters (30 ft) long! It crowds out other plants, and it can even grow underwater.

CAUSE AND EFFECT
Explain how an increase in plants could affect an ecosystem.

Math in Science
Interpret Data

food supply

number of deer

0 · 5 years · 10 years · 15 years · 20 years · 25 years

What happened to the population of deer as the food supply got smaller?

Tree leaves are a main source of food for deer. It takes 15 to 30 acres of land to provide enough food for one deer.

465

Nonliving Things Affect Ecosystems

Plants and animals are the living parts of an ecosystem. The nonliving parts include sunlight, air, water, and soil. The nonliving parts are **abiotic** factors. They are just as important as the biotic factors.

For example, a change in the water supply can affect all the living things in an ecosystem. Too little rain causes many plants to wilt and die. Animals must find other homes. Some may die.

An ecosystem with rich soil has many plants. Where the soil is poor, few plants grow. Few plants mean few animals in the ecosystem.

Air, water, and soil can contain harmful substances. They can affect all living things. You will learn more about this problem later in the chapter.

 CAUSE AND EFFECT How might a change in the water supply affect a rabbit?

Super Soil!
With a partner or a group, compare two different soil samples. How might each soil affect its ecosystem?

Nonliving Factors

Without the nonliving parts of an ecosystem, there would be no living parts.

Sunlight
Plants need sunlight to produce food. Where trees shade the ground, not many other plants can grow.

Water
Almost all living things need water. Plant roots absorb water, and animals drink it.

Soil
Most plants need soil to grow. The kind of soil in an ecosystem is one of the factors that determines which plants grow there.

For more links and activities, go to www.hspscience.com

Climate Affects Ecosystems

What is the climate like where you live? Is it warm and sunny, or is it cool and rainy? Maybe it's something in between.

Climate is an abiotic factor. It's a combination of other abiotic factors. Climate includes the amount of rainfall and sunlight in a region. It also includes the repeating patterns of the temperature of the air during the year.

Climate affects the soil. Some climates allow many plants to grow and help dead plants decay. Animals that eat the plants leave behind their droppings. The decaying plants and droppings make the soil richer.

Climate affects the kinds of plants and animals in an ecosystem. For example, warm, wet climates support tropical rain forests. Hot summers and cold winters result in temperate forests.

The frozen tundra suits the hardy caribou. The mosses they eat thrive there. Zebras could not survive in the tundra. They need the mild climate and tender grasses of the savanna.

 CAUSE AND EFFECT **What would happen to an ecosystem if its climate changed?**

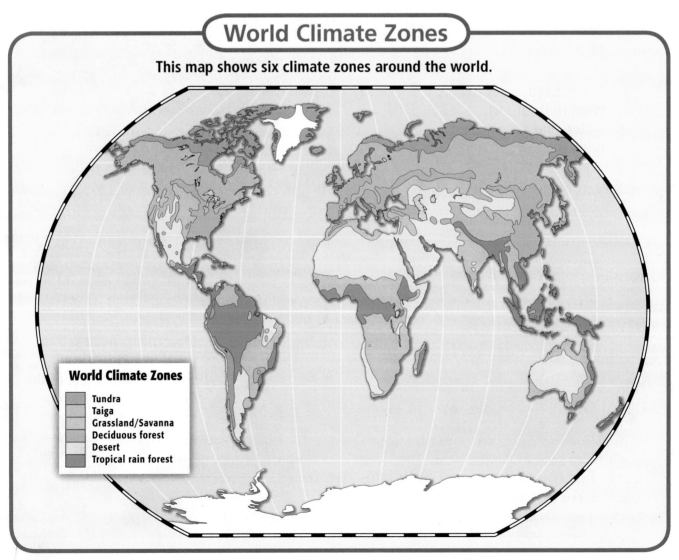

World Climate Zones

This map shows six climate zones around the world.

World Climate Zones
- Tundra
- Taiga
- Grassland/Savanna
- Deciduous forest
- Desert
- Tropical rain forest

Deciduous forests have four seasons. The trees, such as oaks and maples, lose their leaves in the fall. This helps them survive the cold winters.

Rain forests receive 2000 to 10,000 millimeters (7 to 33 ft) of rain each year! Tropical rain forests are near the equator.

The climate in the grassy savanna is nearly the same all year. The temperature stays between 18°C and 22°C (64°F and 72°F).

Deserts get only about 250 millimeters (10 in.) of rain a year. Plants there grow very quickly after a rain. Their seeds can survive for years as they wait for more rain.

The taiga covers more of Earth than any other kind of plant community. The taiga is mostly just south of the tundra and is very cold in winter. Most of its trees are evergreens.

The tundra has the coldest climate: −40°C to 18°C (−40°F to 64°F). *Tundra* means "treeless plain."

There are layers in a rain forest.

The *canopy* is the upper part of the trees. It is home to most rain-forest animals.

The next layer is the cool, dark *understory*. This layer is just right for plants that grow well in shade.

The bottom layer is the *forest floor*, where decaying matter provides food for plants.

Diversity

A rain-forest ecosystem provides many sources of food and shelter. That's why it has the most diversity of all of Earth's ecosystems. **Diversity** refers to the number of different kinds of living things.

In a rain forest, a wide range of plants and animals can find what they need to survive. Many kinds of monkeys live in the treetops. Snakes slip from branch to branch. Bright butterflies flit among the flowers. Frogs of many colors cling to tree trunks. Mushrooms and earthworms hide under decaying leaves. Some rain-forest plants have giant leaves. Other plants can't be seen without using a microscope.

Some ecosystems don't have much diversity. The tundra, for example, is very cold and dry. Much of its soil is frozen. Few living things can survive there.

How much diversity does the ecosystem where you live have?

CAUSE AND EFFECT What leads to a diversity of living things in an ecosystem?

Focus Skill

1. CAUSE AND EFFECT Draw and complete the graphic organizer.

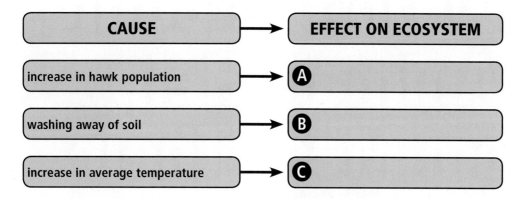

CAUSE	→	EFFECT ON ECOSYSTEM
increase in hawk population	→	**A**
washing away of soil	→	**B**
increase in average temperature	→	**C**

2. SUMMARIZE Use your completed graphic organizer to write a lesson summary.

3. DRAW CONCLUSIONS Which can exist without the other—biotic factors or abiotic factors? Explain your answer.

4. VOCABULARY Write a quiz-show-type question for each of the vocabulary words.

FCAT Prep

5. Read/Inquire/Explain How might flooding in their ecosystem affect some robins?

6. Which of these is an abiotic factor in an ecosystem?

A. ant   **C.** earthworm

B. decaying plant   **D.** sand

Links

Writing

Persuasive Writing

Write a **travel brochure** for a climate zone where few people vacation, such as the tundra or taiga. Tell your readers what interesting things they can see and experience there.

Math

Make a Graph

Find the average rainfall in five of the six world climate zones, including your own region. Then make a bar graph that compares the rainfalls.

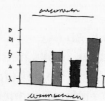

Literature

Learn More

Read a current nonfiction book about one of the world climate zones, such as the desert. After learning more about that climate zone, share what you know by making a display or a written report.

 For more links and activities, go to **www.hspscience.com**

How Do the Bodies of Animals Help Them Meet Their Needs?

Fast Fact

Big Beak! This toucan is an eye-catching sight! Its long, colorful beak looks heavy, but it's really very light. The long beak helps the toucan reach fruit at the ends of branches. In the Investigate, you will explore characteristics that help birds survive in their ecosystems.

Eating Like a Bird

Materials tools—
- 2 chopsticks or unsharpened pencils
- clothespin
- spoon
- pliers
- forceps

food—
- plastic worms
- cooked rice
- cooked spaghetti
- raisins
- birdseed
- peanuts in shells
- water in a cup
- small paper plates

Food	Best Tool (Beak)	Observations

Procedure

1. Make a table like the one shown here.

2. Put the tools on one side of your desk, and think of them as bird beaks. Put each kind of food on a paper plate.

3. Place one type of food in the middle of your desk. Try picking up the food with each tool (beak), and decide which kind of beak works best.

4. Test all the beaks with all the foods and with the water. Use the table to record your observations and conclusions.

Step 3

Draw Conclusions

1. Which kind of beak is best for picking up small seeds? Which kind is best for crushing large seeds?

2. **Inquiry Skill** Scientists experiment and then draw conclusions about what they have learned. After experimenting, what conclusions can you draw about why bird beaks are different shapes?

Investigate Further

Use a reference book about birds. Match the tools you used with real bird beaks. Make a hypothesis about how beak shape relates to food. Then read your book to find out if you are correct.

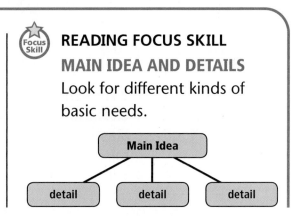

VOCABULARY

basic needs p. 474
adaptation p. 476

SCIENCE CONCEPTS

▶ what basic needs are shared by all living things

▶ how adaptations allow living things to meet their needs

READING FOCUS SKILL

MAIN IDEA AND DETAILS

Look for different kinds of basic needs.

> Main Idea
> detail · detail · detail

Basic Needs

What do you need to survive? You might want jeans in the latest style. You might want pizza for dinner every night. But you do not really need these things to survive.

All living things, from ants to tigers to you, have the same basic needs. These **basic needs** are food, water, air, and shelter.

Living things meet their needs in a variety of ways. Plants can make their own food, but they must have sunlight to do it. Most other living things depend on plants—or on animals that eat plants—for food.

Many animals, such as frogs and wolves, get their food by catching it. Some animals, such as vultures, wait until another animal has killed something. Then they eat the leftovers. Humans get most of their food by growing and raising plants and animals.

Plants get water from rain and from moist soil. Many animals drink water from streams and puddles, but some desert

Like every other living thing, a tiger needs water.

animals obtain enough water to survive from the foods they eat.

All animals must take in oxygen. Animals that live on land and some animals that live in water get oxygen from air. Other animals that live in water get oxygen from water.

Shelter can take many forms. Some insects live under rocks, while foxes make dens in hollow logs. Prairie dogs dig burrows in the ground, and eels hide in coral reefs. Delicate plants grow in protected places. People build homes of many sizes and shapes.

Hunger and thirst signal the need to eat and drink. Rain and cold tell many animals to find shelter. Meeting basic needs isn't always easy, but living things must do it to survive.

 MAIN IDEA AND DETAILS **How do you meet your basic needs?**

After beavers cut sticks and twigs from trees, they eat the leaves and bark. Then they use the sticks to build shelters. ▶

▼ The heron's long beak helps it catch frogs and fish in shallow water.

▲ Like other living things, this alligator needs air. It keeps its nostrils above water while it watches for food.

475

Adaptations

Plants and animals have adaptations that help them meet their needs. An **adaptation** is a body part or a behavior that a living thing gets from its parents, and which helps it to survive.

One adaptation is fur color. For example, during the summer, the snowshoe hare is rusty brown. This helps it blend with the ground. In the winter, the rabbit's fur turns white. This helps it blend with the snow. The color change helps the rabbit hide from enemies.

Instead of fur, fish and reptiles have scales. Their scales help protect them from injury and from drying out. Often, the color and pattern of their scales help them hide from enemies. A snake's scales help it slide along the ground to find food, water, and shelter.

Many frogs and lizards have long tongues that help them catch insects. Imagine how such a long tongue would look on a lion. Lions have other adaptations that help them catch their food, such as speed, strength, long claws, and sharp teeth.

You have explored differences in bird beaks. Different kinds of feet also help birds meet their needs. A robin's feet allow it to perch on a branch. An eagle's claws help it snatch up food, while a penguin's feet help it swim.

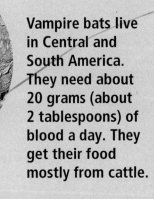

Vampire bats live in Central and South America. They need about 20 grams (about 2 tablespoons) of blood a day. They get their food mostly from cattle.

A vampire bat's tiny, razor-sharp teeth easily pierce the skin of its prey. It doesn't suck the blood. Instead, the bat laps it up with its tongue.

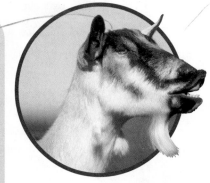

◄ A goat's teeth are adapted for the food it eats. Large and flat, these teeth are just right for grinding up grasses.

▼ Most goats eat grasses during the summer. During the winter, they eat hay, which is a dried grass. All these grasses require a lot of chewing.

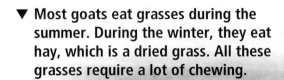

No one is sure how birds find their way from a summer home to a winter home. They might have an inner compass that guides them.

Birds often fly in a V formation. This adaptation helps them move through the air more easily. A group can fly farther in this formation than one bird can fly alone.

During a long, cold winter, food and water can be scarce. Animals need more shelter. Many have adapted to winter by migrating or hibernating.

Migration means "moving from a summer home to a winter home and back again." Gray whales' bodies allow them to swim 16,000 to 23,000 kilometers (10,000 to 14,000 mi) a year. They spend summer in the Arctic. In the fall, they swim to warmer waters. There, they give birth to their young.

Monarch butterflies migrate up to 4,800 kilometers (3,000 mi). As the weather cools, monarchs west of the Rocky Mountains fly to the west coast. Monarchs east of the Rockies fly to Mexico. There, they rest for the winter.

During *hibernation,* an animal's heart and breathing rates slow almost to a stop. Bats, ground squirrels, and woodchucks hibernate. Their bodies are adapted to survive for long periods on a tiny amount of food and oxygen.

Bears, skunks, and chipmunks sleep a lot. This helps them survive the cold winter months. Yet their body systems are still active. They are not hibernating.

 MAIN IDEA AND DETAILS What are three examples of adaptations?

All Thumbs
Use masking tape to tape your partner's thumb to his or her hand. Then ask your partner to write, pick up a pencil, eat, and so on. How is a thumb an adaptation?

Growth and Decay

All plants and animals follow a cycle of life. It begins with a fertilized egg. Sprouting, being born, or hatching come next. Then the seedling or baby grows into an adult. Adult living things reproduce in many ways. Some make seeds, some give birth to babies, and some lay eggs.

Living things are being born all the time. They are also dying and decaying. Fungi, insects, bacteria, and other plants help to decay, or decompose, dead organisms. The nutrients in a dead organism often become part of the soil. This makes the soil richer, which helps new plants to grow.

Living things can complete their life cycles only if they are able to meet all their basic needs. Adaptations help living things meet their basic needs.

If a plant or an animal can't meet its needs, it might die before it can reproduce. If this continues for every member of the species, this kind of living thing will no longer survive on Earth.

 MAIN IDEA AND DETAILS What parts make up the cycle of life?

◄ This tree fell years ago in the rain forest. As the log decayed, seeds blew onto it and sprouted. Now the dead tree is a "nurse log" for new trees. The new trees will grow in a row.

Adult trees stretch their roots around the nurse log and into the soil.

1. MAIN IDEA AND DETAILS Draw and complete this graphic organizer.

> Animals have adaptations to meet their needs.

> An adaptation to meet the need for food: **A** _____

> An adaptation to meet the need for water: **B** _____

> An adaptation to meet the need for shelter: **C** _____

2. SUMMARIZE Write a summary of this lesson. Begin with the sentence *All living things have basic needs.*

3. DRAW CONCLUSIONS Name three adaptations in behavior that some animals show during winter.

4. VOCABULARY Write a paragraph that includes a blank for each vocabulary term. Have a partner fill in the terms.

FCAT Prep

5. Read/Inquire/Explain Explain two ways that a body covering can help an animal meet its basic needs.

6. Which adaptation helps a robin catch a worm?

  A. sharp eyesight   **C.** perching feet
  B. feather coloring **D.** nest building

Links

Writing

Narrative Writing

Write a **story** about how a real animal in a forest uses an adaptation to meet its needs in some way. Make your story exciting!

Math

Solve a Problem

A deer must have about 20 acres of land to meet its need for food, water, and shelter. One square mile has 640 acres. How many deer could live on 2 square miles of land?

Art

Collage

Cut out magazine pictures, or use your own drawings, to make a collage of the basic needs of a person or a specific animal. Then display your work.

 For more links and activities, go to www.hspscience.com

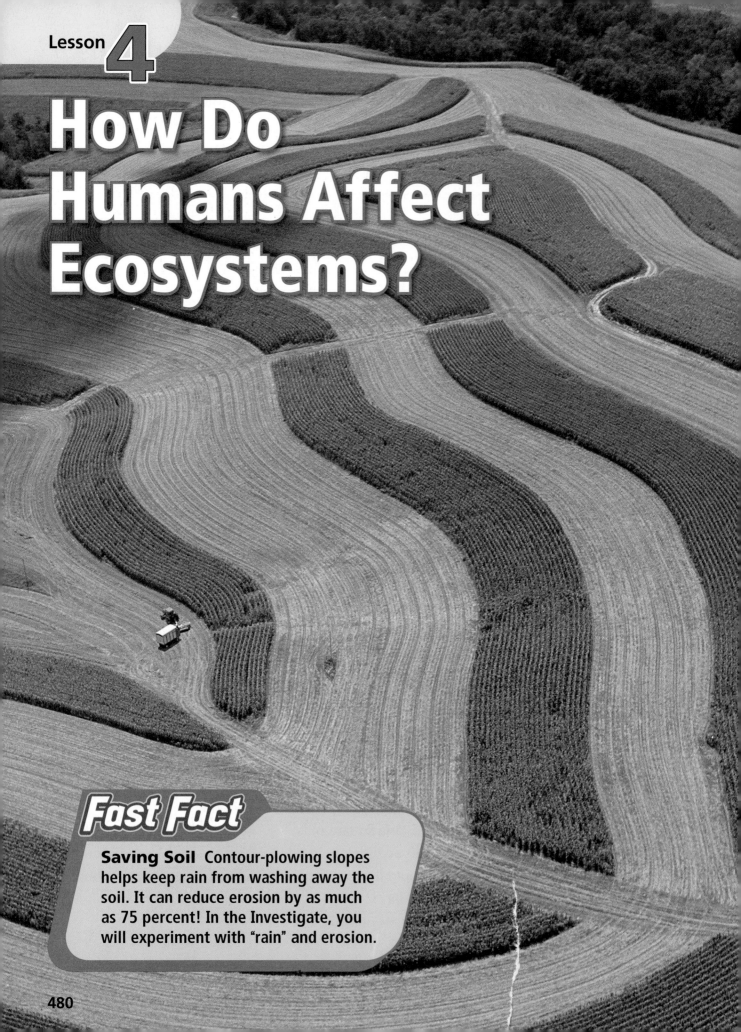

How Do Humans Affect Ecosystems?

Fast Fact

Saving Soil Contour-plowing slopes helps keep rain from washing away the soil. It can reduce erosion by as much as 75 percent! In the Investigate, you will experiment with "rain" and erosion.

Losing It: Observing Erosion

Materials
- marker
- soil and small rocks
- 2 paper cups
- water
- 2 clean plastic foam trays
- sharpened pencil
- measuring cup

Procedure

1. Use the marker to write *A* on one tray and on one paper cup. Write *B* on the second tray and on the second paper cup.

2. In each tray, make an identical slope out of soil and rocks.

3. Carefully use the pencil to make three small holes in the bottom of cup A. Make six larger holes in the bottom of cup B.

4. Record how the two slopes look now. Label your drawings *A* and *B.*

5. Hold cup A over the slope in tray A. Slowly pour 1 cup of water into the paper cup, and let it run down the slope. Record how the slope looks now.

6. Repeat Step 5, using cup B and tray B. Then record how the slope looks.

Draw Conclusions

1. At the end of the activity, compare the slopes. What did each cup represent?

2. **Inquiry Skill** An experiment is a careful, controlled test. What were you testing and what did you control in the activity?

Step 2

Step 5

Investigate Further

Try the same activity, using only rocks, using level soil, or using plants growing in the soil. Make a prediction about what will happen, and then do the activity to see if your prediction was accurate.

VOCABULARY
pollution p. 484
habitat restoration
  p. 485

SCIENCE CONCEPTS
▶ how humans use
  the resources in
  ecosystems
▶ the positive and
  negative ways
  humans affect
  ecosystems

 READING FOCUS SKILL
COMPARE AND CONTRAST
Compare positive and negative
effects that humans have on
ecosystems.

| alike | different |

Humans Within Ecosystems

Do you use any natural resources? You do if you breathe! Natural resources are the parts of ecosystems that humans use, including air.

What other natural resources do you use? Do you ever go to the seashore or a park? Those are natural resources. When you turn on a light, you use natural resources. Most electricity is produced by burning coal. Coal is a natural resource that is taken from under the ground.

Do you ride a bus to school? The fuel that makes the bus run is made from oil. Oil is a natural resource that is also taken from under the ground.

Minerals are natural resources, too. Iron, copper, and aluminum are examples of mineral resources.

Some natural resources can be replaced. Sunlight, air, and water are renewable resources. People can grow more trees and plant more crops.

▼ Natural resources
  include lakes, fresh
  air, and sunlight.

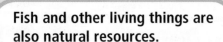
Fish and other living things are also natural resources.

More than 2000 years ago, people drank tea made from the bark of the white willow tree to help ease pain. In 1829, scientists discovered the chemical in the willow that reduces pain. They used it to make aspirin tablets.

Aspirin can be bought without a prescription. However, it is a powerful and valuable drug.

People have been growing wheat for 10,000 years.

Making bread is just one way wheat is used. This grain is also used in cakes, cookies, cereals, and pastas. Parts of the wheat plant are fed to cattle.

Some natural resources can't be replaced. They include coal, gas, and oil. After the supplies buried underground are used, these resources will be gone.

Humans use natural resources in many ways. People build homes and furniture from wood. They make bricks from clay, and glass from sand. They use iron to make steel, which they then use to make cars and many other things.

People raise crops to feed themselves and their animals. They use plants as medicines, too. Humans learned long ago that plants could help treat or cure some illnesses. More than 40 percent of the medicines used today originally came from plants.

For example, a medicine made from a plant called foxglove can help treat heart disease. Scientists use the bark of the Pacific yew tree to make a medicine to treat cancer.

Scientists have tested only 2 percent of all plants to see if they can be used as medicines. Who knows how many more medicines plants may provide?

 COMPARE AND CONTRAST Compare the supply of crops with the supply of coal.

Negative and Positive Changes

Humans make many negative changes in ecosystems. When people clear land for houses and shopping malls, they destroy habitats. As a result, the animals that lived there can no longer meet all their basic needs. They must move or die.

Farmers plow land to plant crops. Plowing loosens soil. That makes it easier for rain and wind to carry away the soil. Humans also cause some kinds of pollution. **Pollution** happens when harmful substances mix with water, air, or soil.

Storms washing chemicals off fields can cause water pollution. These chemicals flow into streams and rivers. Trash and waste from homes and businesses can also enter the water supply.

Much air pollution comes from burning gasoline. Fumes from car engines carry chemicals into the air. Factory smokestacks release more chemicals. Some of these chemicals form acid rain. Acid rain can burn trees and other plants. It can poison lakes and rivers.

Soil pollution can come from fertilizers and trash. Wastes, such as old paint and drain cleaners, can poison the soil.

Cars and other vehicles are a major source of air pollution in cities. This pollution causes smog and breathing problems.

Bicycles don't release pollution. They also provide a good way to get exercise.

Many laws are designed to prevent water pollution, but it still happens.

Water treatment plants remove harmful substances from water before it reaches people's homes. ▶

Without plant roots to hold soil in place, much of the soil can wash away.

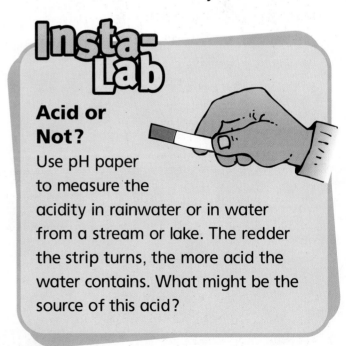

These people are helping prevent beach erosion by planting dune grasses.

Humans also make positive changes. Many groups are working to repair damage to ecosystems. They plant new trees and create new wetlands. They build parks over closed landfills. This process is **habitat restoration**.

People are also polluting less. For example, cars now have special devices on their tailpipes. These devices reduce the harmful gases that escape into the air. Factories now release fewer chemicals. They don't dump wastes into rivers and streams.

Many people now use natural ways to get rid of weeds and insects. They spread fewer chemicals on fields and lawns.

People also recycle paper, glass, metal, and plastic. Recycling uses less energy than making new products. That means less coal is burned. Burning less coal means less pollution.

People are learning other ways to help reduce pollution. Science is one way of finding solutions to the problems caused by pollution.

 COMPARE AND CONTRAST Which kind of pollution is most harmful—water, air, or soil? Why?

Insta-Lab

Acid or Not?

Use pH paper to measure the acidity in rainwater or in water from a stream or lake. The redder the strip turns, the more acid the water contains. What might be the source of this acid?

Planning for Change

Earth's human population keeps growing. People need more space for places to work and live. But before we build, we have to consider both abiotic and biotic factors. Some abiotic factors include the type of soil, the amount of rain, and the climate. A building set on soft soil will not stand. A home must be able to withstand the weather of the area where it is built.

Biotic factors can affect more than humans. Building new structures often means destroying wildlife habitats. Builders should plan new projects in ways that protect ecosystems. A building near a river must not pollute the water.

Even working close to a river can cause problems. Soil can wash into the water. Too much soil in the water can harm fish and plants.

Wetlands near the river must not be filled in. Wetlands help keep the water clean and provide homes for many plants and animals. Builders often leave or create ponds or pockets of forest. These habitats provide homes for some wildlife. Every ecosystem has a delicate balance. People must do their part to protect that balance.

 COMPARE AND CONTRAST **Compare a human and an animal seeking a new habitat. How are they the same?**

Construction must be carefully planned to protect natural ecosystems. ▶

◀ **Land-use planners must consider the biotic and abiotic factors in an ecosystem.**

1. COMPARE AND CONTRAST Draw and complete this graphic organizer.

Human Effects on Ecosystems

Negative Change: destruction of habitats

Positive Change: A

Negative Change: B

Positive Change: devices to reduce air pollution from cars

2. SUMMARIZE Write two sentences that tell what this lesson is mainly about.

3. DRAW CONCLUSIONS Why do humans affect natural ecosystems in negative ways?

4. VOCABULARY Make an acrostic for *pollution*. Each letter begins a sentence about that term.

FCAT Prep

5. Read/Inquire/Explain How can a weed killer used on a cornfield pollute a lake miles away?

6. Which of these is soil pollution likely to cause?
   A. air pollution   **C.** abiotic factors
   B. biotic factors   **D.** water pollution

Links

Writing

Persuasive Writing

Think of a way your community has had a negative effect on an ecosystem. Write a **letter** you might send to the editor of a local newspaper describing the problem.

Math

Comparing Gas Use

An older, larger car gets 10 miles per gallon of gasoline. A newer, smaller car gets 35 miles per gallon. How many fewer gallons would the newer car use on a 70-mile trip?

Health

Pollution and You

With a small group, research the health effects of water, air, or soil pollution. Then share what you learn in a written report, an oral presentation, or a poster.

 For more links and activities, go to **www.hspscience.com**

AQUARIUS
An Underwater Lab with a View

Many U.S. kids share their bedrooms with a brother or sister. Sharing a room can be a pain. Six scientists know it! They squeezed into a small underwater laboratory to study a coral reef. They worked and slept in the tiny space for ten days.

"I've been on missions where people snored," said Celia Smith, who led the mission in October. "You just kind of kick their bunk and try to get to sleep before they do."

This buoy supplies the *Aquarius* with fresh air and electricity.

▲ An aquanaut peers through a window in the *Aquarius* as another aquanaut swims around the laboratory.

The underwater lab is called *Aquarius.* It looks like a little yellow submarine.

The *Aquarius* was placed near the Florida Keys National Marine Sanctuary, a protected area of the ocean. Each year, several teams of scientists have lived in *Aquarius* for up to ten days at a time. The scientists who live and work in *Aquarius* are called aquanauts (AH•kwuh•nawts). The aquanauts study the nearby coral reef and the creatures that live in it.

A Room with a View

The latest team to visit *Aquarius* says the best part of living there is the view. They can see colorful fish swimming in the nearby reef. Smith said it's hard to tell, though, whether the aquanauts are watching the fish or the fish are watching the aquanauts.

The aquanauts spend as much time as they can on the reef studying sea life.

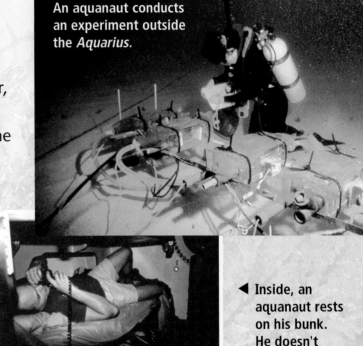

An aquanaut conducts an experiment outside the *Aquarius.*

◀ Inside, an aquanaut rests on his bunk. He doesn't have much room.

They can spend up to nine hours at one time outside the laboratory.

Smith likes to remind people that humans have barely begun to explore the oceans and need to learn more about life in the deep. "The really important thing for us to realize is how much we don't know about the oceans," she said.

THINK ABOUT IT

1. How might living underwater help scientists learn more about a coral reef ecosystem?
2. What might be the best thing about living underwater? What might be the worst thing?

IN THE DEEP

Aquarius is located about 19 meters (63 ft) deep in the ocean. It has sleeping space for six, a bathroom, a trash compactor, and computer stations.

Electrical cables and tubes connect the *Aquarius* to a buoy on the ocean's surface. The tubes carry fresh air to the *Aquarius*, and the cables supply electricity.

The work the aquanauts are doing is expected to help NASA. NASA scientists say that living and working on the *Aquarius* is similar to what it will be like to live and work in a space station. They hope to better prepare astronauts for space by studying how the aquanauts live and work underwater.

Find out more! Log on to **www.hspscience.com**

SC.H.2.2.1.4.2
patterns in nature

Meet a Young CONSERVATIONIST

Fourth grader Blake Wichtowski told people at last year's Kids' Summit that wild blue lupine flowers would help the endangered Karner blue butterfly. Officials from New York are turning this idea into a reality.

Blue lupine is the only food that Karner caterpillars will eat.

With the help of the Seneca Park Zoo in Rochester and other officials, Blake's fourth-grade class and a class at another elementary school will plant seeds for a blue lupine garden near the local airport.

You Can Do It!

Materials

- plastic funnel
- gravel
- sand
- bowl
- water with some soil and leaves in it

Quick and Easy Project

Getting Out the Dirt

Procedure

1. Fill the bottom of a funnel with gravel. Then add a thick layer of sand.
2. Hold the funnel over a bowl. Pour the "dirty" water into it. The water will run out the bottom of the funnel, into the bowl.
3. Observe the water in the bowl. See if you can find the soil and leaves.

Draw Conclusions

How did your funnel filter affect the dirty water? Where might you find this kind of natural filter? How might soil and other substances get into a water supply?

Design Your Own Investigation

Checking for Air Pollution

Is the air in your school or neighborhood polluted? Air pollution often includes bits of ash and dust. If you smear petroleum jelly on the inside of baby-food jars and put them somewhere for several days, bits of pollution may stick to the jelly. Which areas of your school or neighborhood do you think might have this kind of pollution? Write a hypothesis. Then design an experiment, and carry it out to see whether your hypothesis is supported.

Vocabulary Review

Use the terms below to complete the sentences. The page numbers tell you where to look in the chapter if you need help.

> **environment** p. 456
> **ecosystem** p. 456
> **population** p. 458
> **community** p. 460
> **biotic** p. 464
> **diversity** p. 470
> **adaptation** p. 476
> **pollution** p. 484

1. A group of maple trees is an example of a _____.

2. The living parts of an ecosystem are _____.

3. All the living and nonliving things in an area interact to form an _____.

4. An ecosystem that includes many kinds of living things has _____.

5. Several kinds of plants and animals living in the same place form a _____.

6. Trash in a stream is one kind of _____.

7. Many animals have an _____ that helps them meet their needs.

8. An _____ includes all the living things and nonliving things in an area.

Check Understanding

Write the letter of the best choice.

9. Which of these is an abiotic factor?
   A. lack of food
   B. disease
   C. cold temperatures
   D. introduction of a new plant

10. Which of these is **not** a basic need?
    F. air   **H.** soil
    G. shelter   **I.** water

11. **MAIN IDEA AND DETAILS** What is the main idea behind planting trees in an area that has been logged?
    A. adaptation
    B. habitat restoration
    C. meeting basic needs
    D. preserving an ecosystem

12. **CAUSE AND EFFECT** Which statement is true about an ecosystem?
    F. Biotic factors are the climate.
    G. The climate affects biotic factors.
    H. Biotic factors cause abiotic factors.
    I. Adaptations change abiotic factors.

13. What does the picture show?

    A. adaptation   **C.** habitat restoration

    B. diversity   **D.** pollution

14. Which of these has the greatest effect on an ecosystem?

    F. adaptation   **H.** climate

    G. biotic factors   **I.** population

15. Which of these is **never** a result of human actions?

    A. adaptations

    B. changes in abiotic factors

    C. natural increase in diversity

    D. pollution

16. Which climate zone is probably shown in the photo?

    F. savanna   **H.** temperate forest

    G. taiga   **I.** tundra

Inquiry Skills

17. Compare an environment and an ecosystem.

18. A scientist has tracked the migration route of a Yellowstone elk herd every winter for 10 years. The table shows how far south the elk herd has traveled each year. **Draw conclusions** about the elk herd's migration pattern over the 10-year period.

Year	Kilometers Migrated
1990	122
1991	122
1992	130
1993	126
1994	130
1995	133
1996	132
1997	133
1998	133
1999	136

Read/Inquire/Explain

19. Imagine that a new kind of animal has suddenly appeared. What will determine where on Earth this kind of animal can live?

20. A builder has bought land that includes a forest. The builder is planning to put in a housing development.

Part A Name two possible negative effects the builder and other humans might have on this forest.

Part B Now name two possible positive effects the builder and other humans might have on this ecosystem.

14 Energy Transfer in Ecosystems

Lesson 1 What Are the Roles of Living Things?

Lesson 2 How Do Living Things Get Energy?

Lesson 3 How Do Living Things of the Past Compare with Those of Today?

Vocabulary

FCAT-Tested	predator
producer	food web
consumer	energy pyramid
herbivore	fossil
carnivore	**Other Terms**
decomposer	omnivore
habitat	niche
food chain	extinction
prey	

What do YOU wonder?

This lynx must catch and eat hares and many other small animals in order to live. This hare may provide energy for the lynx. Where do hares get the energy they need to live?

1

What Are the Roles of Living Things?

Fast Fact

Nothing Fishy About Eating This archer fish is leaping for its prey. It eats insects to get energy for living. Archer fish also hunt by spitting at insects to knock them into the water. Some archer fish are eaten by other animals or die and then decay in the water. In the Investigate, you will find out how decomposers (dee•kuhm•POHZ•erz) help once-living matter decay.

Decomposing Bananas

Materials
- 2 slices of banana
- 2 zip-top plastic bags
- spoon
- package of dry yeast
- marker

Procedure

1. Put a banana slice in each bag.

2. Sprinkle $\frac{2}{3}$ spoonful of dry yeast on one banana slice. Yeast is a decomposer, so use the marker to label this bag *D.*

3. Close both bags. Put the bags in the same place.

4. Check both bags every day for a week. Observe and record the changes you see in each bag.

Draw Conclusions

1. Which banana slice shows more changes? What is the cause of these changes?

2. **Inquiry Skill** Scientists use time relationships to measure progress. How long did it take for your banana slices to begin showing signs of decomposition? How long do you think it would take for your banana slices to completely decompose?

Step 2

Step 4

Investigate Further

What will happen if you put flour, instead of yeast, on one banana slice? Write down your prediction, and then try it.

SC.G.1.2.4.4.1 decomposers
SC.H.1.2.2.4.1 experimental design

497

VOCABULARY
producer p. 498
consumer p. 498
herbivore p. 500
carnivore p. 500
omnivore p. 500
decomposer p. 502

SCIENCE CONCEPTS
▶ how living things use the energy from sunlight
▶ how living things get energy from other living things

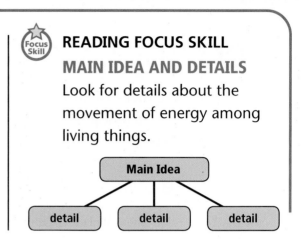

READING FOCUS SKILL

MAIN IDEA AND DETAILS
Look for details about the movement of energy among living things.

Producers and Consumers

Most living things on Earth get the energy to live from sunlight. Green plants and algae (AL•jee) use energy in sunlight, plus water and carbon dioxide, to make their own food. Any living thing that can make its own food is called a **producer**. Producers can be as small as a tiny moss or as large as a huge redwood tree.

Some animals, such as deer and cattle, get the energy they need to live by eating plants. When these animals eat, the energy stored in the plants moves into the animals' bodies.

Not all animals eat plants. Lions and hawks, for example, get the energy they need by eating other animals.

An animal that eats plants or other animals is called a **consumer**. Consumers can't make their own food, so they must eat other living things.

These plants are using energy in sunlight to produce food. Without sunlight, the plants would die.

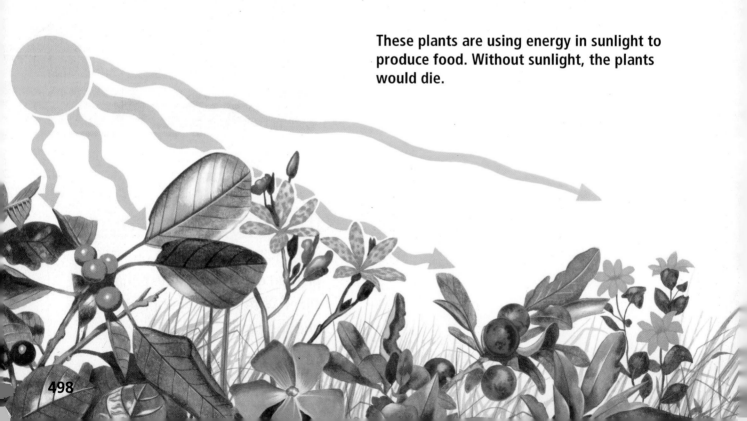

Horse

Which animal gets its energy directly from producers? Which one gets its energy from other consumers? Which one gets its energy from both?

Florida panther

Some consumers eat the same kind of food all year. Horses, for example, eat grass during warm weather. During winter, they eat hay, a kind of dried grass.

Other consumers eat different things in different seasons. For example, black bears eat grass in spring. Later on, they might eat birds' eggs. Bears might also dig up tasty roots or eat fish from streams. In fall, bears eat ripe berries.

Florida panthers eat other consumers, but their diet varies. Mostly, panthers consume wild hogs, which are easy for them to catch. Another favorite meal is deer. Panthers also eat rabbits, raccoons, rats, birds, and sometimes even alligators.

 MAIN IDEA AND DETAILS What is a producer? What is a consumer? Give two examples of each.

Black bear

49

Kinds of Consumers

Consumers are not all the same. In fact, there are three kinds—herbivores, carnivores, and omnivores.

A **herbivore** is an animal that eats only plants, or producers. Horses are herbivores. So are giraffes, squirrels, and rabbits.

A **carnivore** is an animal that eats only other animals. The Florida panther and the lion are carnivores. A carnivore can be as large as a whale or as small as a frog.

An **omnivore** is an animal that eats both plants and other animals. That is, omnivores eat both producers and other consumers. Bears and hyenas are omnivores. Do any omnivores live in your home?

Producers and all three kinds of consumers can be found living in water. Algae are producers that live in water. They use sunlight to make their own food. Tadpoles, small fish, and other small herbivores eat algae. Larger fish that are carnivores eat the tadpoles. Some animals, including green sea turtles, are omnivores. Green sea turtles eat seaweed, algae, and fish. In fact, algae make the flesh of the green sea turtle green!

 MAIN IDEA AND DETAILS Name the three kinds of consumers. Give two examples of each.

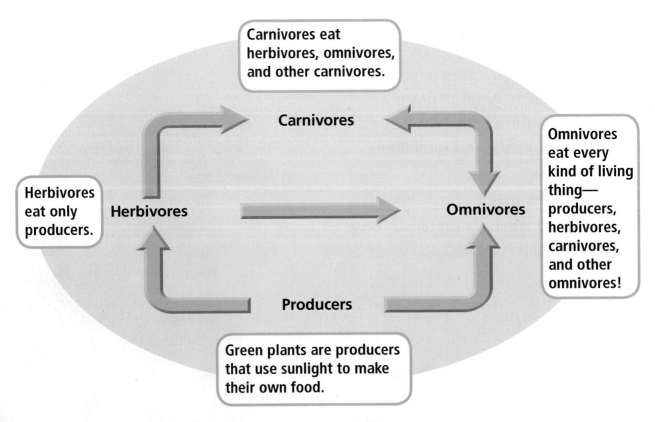

This diagram shows how kinds of consumers get energy to live. The arrows show the direction of energy flow.

Carnivores eat herbivores, omnivores, and other carnivores.

Carnivores

Omnivores eat every kind of living thing—producers, herbivores, carnivores, and other omnivores!

Herbivores eat only producers.

Herbivores

Omnivores

Producers

Green plants are producers that use sunlight to make their own food.

◄ The jaguar, a carnivore, eats tapirs, river hogs, and other consumers.

Jaguar

River hog

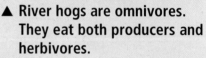

Tapir

▲ River hogs are omnivores. They eat both producers and herbivores.

▲ The tapir, a herbivore, eats only producers. It eats tender buds and twigs.

Jungle bush

▲ This plant is a producer. It makes its own food and provides stored energy for consumers.

Insta-Lab

Who's an Omnivore?

Read the nutrition labels on several food containers.

Think about the source of each kind of food. What does the food's source tell about consumers who eat it?

Decomposers

A **decomposer** is a living thing that feeds on wastes and on the remains of dead plants and animals. Decomposers break down wastes into nutrients, substances that are taken in by living things to help them grow. These nutrients become part of the soil. Next, plants take up the nutrients through their roots. Animals eat the plants. When plants and animals die, decomposers break down their bodies into nutrients. This cycle is repeated again and again.

Decomposers come in many shapes and sizes. Some are tiny bacteria that you can see only with a microscope. Other decomposers are as big as mushrooms and earthworms.

Without decomposers, Earth would be covered with dead plants and animals. Instead, decomposers turn wastes into nutrients. They allow living things to recycle nutrients.

 MAIN IDEA AND DETAILS Name two kinds of decomposers, and describe their role in nature.

Sow bugs

Sow bugs are related to lobsters. They help plant matter decay faster than it would without them.

Millipede

In the forest, millipedes chew up dead plant material. Like sow bugs, millipedes aren't insects.

Bracket fungus

The bracket fungus is one of a group of fungi (FUN•jy) that includes mushrooms. Bracket fungi often grow on dead tree trunks and help them decay quickly.

1. MAIN IDEA AND DETAILS Copy and complete this graphic organizer.

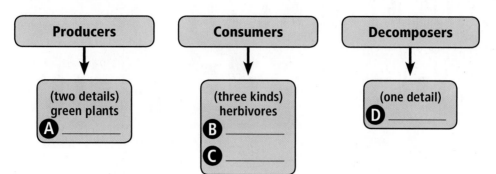

Producers	Consumers	Decomposers
(two details) green plants **A** _____	(three kinds) herbivores **B** _____ **C** _____	(one detail) **D** _____

2. SUMMARIZE Write two sentences that tell what this lesson is mainly about.

3. DRAW CONCLUSIONS How are decomposers consumers?

4. VOCABULARY Construct a crossword puzzle, using this lesson's vocabulary words.

FCAT Prep

5. Read/Inquire/Explain How do eagles depend on sunlight for their energy?

6. Which term describes a hyena?
A. carnivore   C. omnivore
B. herbivore   D. producer

Links

Writing

Narrative Writing
Write a **science fiction story**. Tell about a time when all the producers on Earth disappear. Describe what happens to the consumers.

Math

Solve a Problem
A shrew eats about $\frac{2}{3}$ of its body weight daily. Suppose a child who weighed 30 kilograms (66 lb) could eat $\frac{2}{3}$ of his or her body weight. How many kilograms of food is that?

Health

Eating Decomposers
Find out what vitamins and minerals are in mushrooms. Find healthful recipes that have mushrooms as one of the ingredients.

 For more links and activities, go to www.hspscience.com

How Do Living Things Get Energy?

Make a Food Chain

Materials • 8 to 10 blank index cards
• colored pencils or markers
• reference books about animals

Procedure

1. Choose a place where animals live. Some examples are pine forest, rain forest, desert, wetland, and ocean.

2. On an index card, draw a living thing that lives in the place you have chosen. Draw more living things, one kind on each card. Include large animals, small animals, and producers. Look up information about plants and animals if you need help.

3. Put your cards in an order that shows what eats what. You might have more than one set of cards. If one of your animals doesn't fit anywhere, trade cards with someone. You can also draw another animal to link two of your cards. For example, you could draw a rabbit to link a grass card and a hawk card.

Draw Conclusions

1. Could the same animal fit into more than one set of cards? Explain your answer.

2. **Inquiry Skill** Scientists communicate their ideas in many ways. What do your cards communicate about the relationships of these living things to one another?

Step 2

Step 3

Investigate Further

Draw a series of cards in order, with yourself as the last consumer. Compare your role with the roles of other consumers.

SC.G.1.2.1.4.2 food chains
SC.H.2.2.1.4.2 patterns in nature **505**

VOCABULARY
habitat p. 506
niche p. 507
food chain p. 508
prey p. 508
predator p. 508
food web p. 510
energy pyramid p. 512

SCIENCE CONCEPTS
▶ how consumers depend on other living things
▶ how energy moves through food chains and food webs

READING FOCUS SKILL

SEQUENCE Look for the order in which things happen.

Habitats

You probably wouldn't see a heron in a desert or a penguin in a swamp. Animals must live in places that meet their needs. A **habitat** is an environment that meets the needs of a living thing. An insect's habitat can be as small as the space under a rock. A migrating bird's habitat can cross a continent.

Many habitats can overlap. For example, the three living things pictured on this page all live in a desert habitat. This desert habitat meets all their needs. Sagebrush grows well here. Sidewinders and tarantulas find many small consumers to eat.

These living things thrive in the desert habitat, even though it's hot and has little water.

The venomous sidewinder eats mice, rats, lizards, and birds. ▶

Sidewinder

◀ Tarantulas are venomous, too. They eat insects, other spiders, and small lizards.

Tarantula

Sagebrush can grow where other plants can't. Sheep and cattle often eat sagebrush in the winter. ▶

Sagebrush

Each living thing in a habitat has a role, or **niche** (NICH). The term *niche* describes how a living thing interacts with its habitat. Part of a living thing's niche is how it gets food and shelter. Its niche also includes how it reproduces, cares for its young, and avoids danger. Each animal has body parts that help it carry out its role. For example, a cat's pointed claws and sharp eyes help it catch its food.

Part of the sidewinder's niche is to eat small animals in its habitat. If all these snakes died, the desert would have too many mice, birds, and lizards. These small animals would eat all the available food and would soon starve. The sidewinder's niche helps keep the number of small desert animals in balance.

 SEQUENCE **What would happen next if all the sagebrush disappeared from a desert?**

Crab

Lion-fish

Anemone

This coral reef habitat has a balance of producers and consumers. Everything in this picture is a consumer.

507

Food Chains

Living things depend on one another to live. A **food chain** is the movement of food energy in a sequence of living things. Every food chain starts with producers. Some consumers, such as deer, eat these producers. Then the deer are eaten by other consumers, such as mountain lions. Consumers that are eaten are called **prey**. A consumer that eats prey is a **predator**. Prey are what is hunted. Predators are the hunters.

Some animals in a habitat are prey, while other animals are predators. Predators limit the number of prey animals in a habitat. Wolves are predators of antelope. They keep the population of antelope from increasing too much, so the antelope don't eat all of the producers. Predators often compete for the same prey. This limits the number of predators in a habitat.

 SEQUENCE What would happen next if the number of predators in a habitat increased too much?

A mangrove swamp is one kind of habitat. Special prop roots hold mangrove trees in the muddy soil. Fresh water and salt water mix in this habitat.

Many organisms live in and around the mangrove roots.

Mullets are fish that can live in fresh water or salt water.

Without hawks, the chipmunk population would get very large. The chipmunks would eat all the acorns and then starve.

Acorns provide energy for the chipmunk, which in turn provides energy for the hawk.

An alligator is just one of the predators in a mangrove swamp. Alligators dig burrows for themselves that also provide shelter for other animals during dry times.

Insta-Lab

Chain of Life

Cut white paper into strips that are 2.5 cm (1 in.) by 12.5 cm (5 in.) On each strip, write the name of a producer or a consumer. Then use glue or tape to combine the strips into paper food chains. Which food chains end with you?

Food Webs

A food chain shows how an animal gets energy from one food source. But food chains can overlap. One kind of producer may be food for different kinds of consumers. Some consumers may eat different kinds of food. For example, hawks eat sparrows, mice, and snakes.

Several food chains that overlap form a **food web**. There are food webs in water habitats, too. For example, herons eat snails, fish, and other birds.

On the next page, you can see an ocean food web. It shows that energy moves from plankton, small producers in the ocean, to small shrimp. These shrimp are called *first-level consumers.*

These shrimp then become prey for fish and other *second-level consumers.* They, in turn, are eaten by the biggest fish and mammals in the ocean, called *top-level consumers.*

 SEQUENCE What happens after a first-level consumer eats a producer?

Follow several paths in this food web. Begin at the bottom, with a producer, and trace the movement of energy through the web.

Antarctic Ocean Food Web

This food web begins with energy from the sun. The producers are tiny plants called phytoplankton (FYT•oh•plangk•tuhn). They float near the water's surface because sunlight can't reach deep underwater. No plants grow at the bottom of the ocean. Where would decomposers fit in this food web?

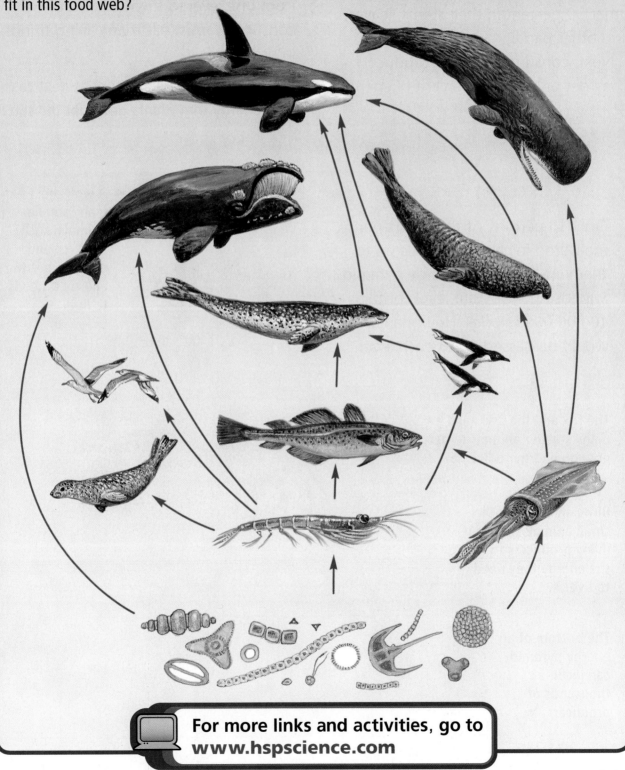

For more links and activities, go to www.hspscience.com

Energy Pyramids

An **energy pyramid** shows how much energy is passed from one living thing to another along a food chain. Producers form the base of the pyramid. They use about 90 percent of the energy they get from the sun to grow. They store the other 10 percent in their stems, leaves, and other parts.

Next, consumers eat the producers. They get only the 10 percent of energy that the plants stored. These consumers use about 90 percent of the energy they get from the producers to grow and then store the other 10 percent in their bodies. That 10 percent is passed on to the consumers that eat them.

You can see how little energy is passed from one level to the next. That's why consumers must eat many living things in order to live.

 SEQUENCE What happens next to the energy that plants get from the sun?

Math in Science
Interpret Data

Only 10 percent of the food energy, measured in calories, passes up to the next level in an energy pyramid. Suppose the bottom level contains 10,000,000 calories. How many would be passed up to each level?

The fox and the owl must eat many smaller animals to get enough energy to live. ▶

Birds, mice, and other small animals must eat many producers to get the energy they need to live. ▶

The bottom of an energy pyramid can include thousands of producers. ▶

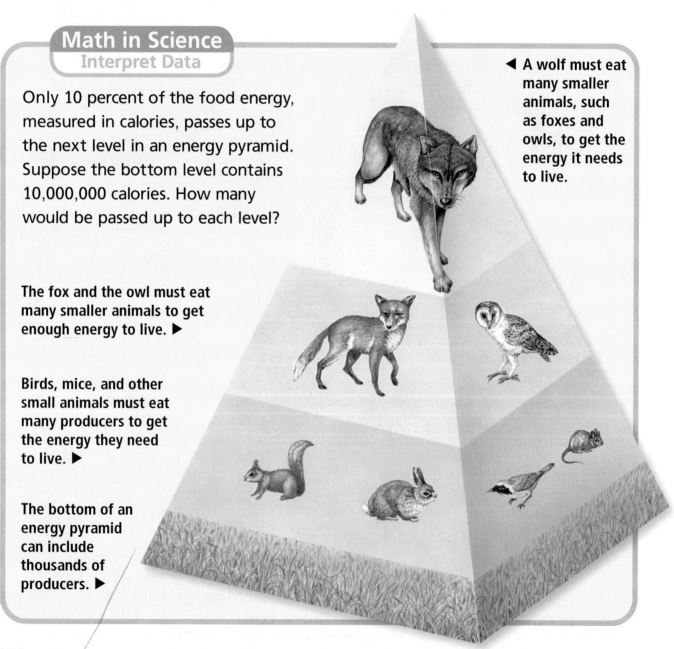

◀ A wolf must eat many smaller animals, such as foxes and owls, to get the energy it needs to live.

512

1. SEQUENCE Copy and complete this graphic organizer. Put the living things in order to create a food chain.

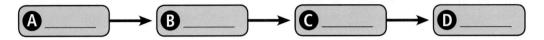

| woodpecker | hawk | leaves | insect |

A _____ → B _____ → C _____ → D _____

2. SUMMARIZE Write a summary of this lesson by using the lesson vocabulary terms in a paragraph.

3. DRAW CONCLUSIONS How are predators good for prey?

4. VOCABULARY Use the vocabulary terms to make a quiz. Then trade quizzes with a partner.

FCAT Prep

5. Read/Inquire/Explain How would the deaths of all of one kind of consumer affect a food web?

6. Which of these best shows why deer must eat grass all day long?

A. diagram   **C.** food chain

B. energy pyramid   **D.** food web

Links

Writing

Expository Writing

Write a **description** of ways humans might affect a food web and what would then change. For example, people might clear trees for a housing development or feed the deer in a park.

Math

Solve a Problem

Producers in a field have stored 20,000 calories. Herbivores get 2000 calories by eating the producers. How much energy is available to the next level of the energy pyramid?

Art

Food Chains

Choose any art medium, such as watercolor, charcoal, collage, or torn paper, and show the living things in a food web. (You don't have to show them eating one another!)

 For more links and activities, go to **www.hspscience.com**

How Do Living Things of the Past Compare with Those of Today?

Make a Fossil

Materials
- white glue
- 8 sugar cubes
- strainer
- sink or large bowl
- warm water

Procedure

1. Use the glue to put together 4 sugar cubes, making a 2 x 2 layer.

2. Glue the other 4 cubes together to make a second layer. Let both layers dry separately for 5 minutes.

3. Spread glue in the shape of a shell on one layer, and place the other layer on top. Let them dry overnight.

4. Put the two-layer structure in the strainer. Hold the strainer over a sink or bowl.

5. Pour warm water over the structure. Observe what happens to the sugar and the glue. Record your observations.

Draw Conclusions

1. You made a model of a fossil. What parts of a plant or an animal did the sugar cubes stand for? What parts did the dried glue stand for?

2. **Inquiry Skill** Scientists infer, or explain, based on what they observe. Based on your observations, what can you infer about how fossils form?

Step 1

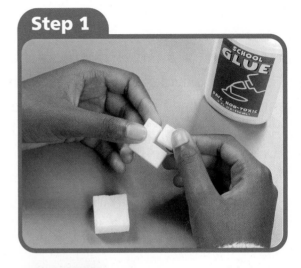

Step 5

Investigate Further

Why might fossil skeletons break apart? Hypothesize what will happen if you put your fossil in a bag with rocks and shake it. Try it. Record your results.

Reading in Science

VOCABULARY
fossil p. 516
extinction p. 520

SCIENCE CONCEPTS
► how living things of long ago compare with those of today

Focus Skill
READING FOCUS SKILL
COMPARE AND CONTRAST
Look for ways animals of long ago are like those of today.

[alike]———[different]

Animals Then and Now

A **fossil** is evidence of a plant or an animal that lived long ago. Footprints that formed when an animal stepped in mud are one kind of fossil. Over a long time, the mud hardened into rock. Footprints tell us about an animal's size. They also can tell how it moved.

Many fossils are bones that became buried before they could decay. Minerals replaced the bones, but the shapes remain.

Scientists compare these fossils with the footprints and bones of animals that are alive today. Using the comparisons, they can infer how animals have changed.

Although they are completely unrelated, fossils show that the triceratops (try•SAIR•uh•tahps) and today's rhinoceros (ry•NAHS•er•uhs) share the same body shape and a horned nose. Dinosaurs were reptiles, while rhinos are mammals.

Triceratops fossil skeleton

Modern-day rhinoceros

Triceratops

Camels lived in North America many years ago. Fossils tell us that some ancient camels were about the size of a rabbit. Others were about 4.5 meters (15 ft) tall at their shoulders!

Modern-day camel

Florida camel

Florida camel fossil

A few animals, such as turtles, are much like ones from long ago. Others are very different now. By a careful study of their fossils, scientists can link animals of long ago with those of today. However, many ancient animals are now gone.

COMPARE AND CONTRAST How is the study of ancient animals different from the study of animals that live today?

Modern-day coelacanth

By the early part of the twentieth century, the coelacanth (SEE•luh•kanth) fish shown in this fossil was thought to exist no longer. But a live coelacanth was caught near South Africa in 1938. ▶

Plants Then and Now

You might have found a plant fossil on a flat rock in a park or in your own back yard. Some of these fossils were formed when plant leaves fell on muddy ground millions of years ago. The leaves made an impression in the mud. When the mud dried, the imprint of the leaf was still there. This imprint shows the size, shape, and details of the leaf.

Have you ever held a piece of wood that felt like a rock? Petrified wood is another kind of plant fossil. It formed when a tree fell on the ground and was buried in mud before it could decay.

Minerals slowly replaced the wood. In time, the wood became rock.

Like some animals of long ago, many plants of long ago disappeared. Scientists know about them only because of fossils. You can also find fossils that look much like some plants that still grow today.

Many other plants have survived, but they have changed over time. In fact, plants are still changing. For example, farmers are now growing new kinds of corn that resist insects.

COMPARE AND CONTRAST How are plants of long ago like animals of long ago?

About 300 million years ago, most of the plants on Earth were ferns. These plants and others died and were buried under many layers of soil. ▼

Insta-Lab

Fossil Quiz

Flatten some clay, and lightly press an object into it. Don't let anyone see the object you used. Then challenge others to identify the object you used by looking only at the imprint. How is your imprint like a fossil imprint?

Fern fossil

Modern-day fern

Ginkgo trees are often called living fossils because they have not changed much in 100 million years. Some types of ginkgo trees growing in China have existed more than 3000 years.

Ginkgo leaf fossil

Ginkgo leaves

Modern-day ginkgo tree

Bristlecone pine trees were growing 100 million years ago. The oldest tree living today is almost 5000 years old! Fossils show that these trees have changed very little.

Bristlecone pine

Pine cones

Fossilized pine cones

531

Extinction

Many plants and animals are now extinct (ek•STINGKT). **Extinction** means that all the members of a certain kind of living thing have died. Extinction can happen when a habitat changes. For example, a habitat may become drier. Then the habitat may no longer meet the needs of some living things. Plants in these places die. Animals must find new places to live or they will die, too.

Extinction can also happen for other reasons. One reason is an increase in predators. Another is a decrease in the food supply. About 65 million years ago, 70 percent of all living things became extinct. It is possible that an asteroid hit Earth, changing the environment and reducing the food supply.

Extinction is still happening. People may cause extinction when they cut forests or fill in wetlands. This change in the environment can cause living things to lose their habitats.

COMPARE AND CONTRAST How might a change in the environment affect plants differently than it would animals?

The last woolly mammoth died about 30,000 years ago. ▼

◀ The last great auk died in 1844. These birds, which could not fly, were killed for food and to be used as bait.

Fossils of saber-toothed cats have been found in California's La Brea (BRAY•uh) tar pits. The last saber-toothed cat died about 10,000 years ago.

1. COMPARE AND CONTRAST Copy and complete this graphic organizer. Show how a rhinoceros and a triceratops are the same and different.

Alike One way a rhinoceros and a triceratops are the same **A** _____	**Different** One way a rhinoceros and a triceratops are different **B** _____

2. SUMMARIZE Write two sentences to tell the most important information in this lesson.

3. DRAW CONCLUSIONS Suppose you have found a fossil. Why should you be careful with it?

4. VOCABULARY Write a paragraph, leaving spaces for this lesson's two vocabulary words. Have a partner fill in the words.

FCAT Prep

5. Read/Inquire/Explain Why are fossils important?

6. Which of these could be called a living fossil?

A. woolly mammoth   **C.** camel

B. rhinoceros   **D.** bristlecone pine

Links

Writing

Persuasive Writing

Suppose you find an unusual fossil. Write a **letter** to a scientist, describing your fossil. Try to persuade him or her to come to see it. Explain why the fossil might be important.

Math

Make a Bar Graph

Make a bar graph to show how many plants and animals are close to extinction in these states: Hawai'i, 317; California, 299; Florida, 111; Tennessee, 96; Texas, 91.

Social Studies

Then and Now

Research what your region may have looked like 65 million years ago. What kinds of plants and animals lived in your neighborhood then?

 For more links and activities, go to **www.hspscience.com**

On the Prowl

Cameras are helping scientists count jaguars.

A sleek, spotted jaguar sneaks along the thick forest floor. As it passes a fig tree, there is a whirring noise. A flashing light and click follow. A camera has just snapped the cat's photograph.

No person was behind the camera's lens. The camera was triggered by motion and heat from the passing cat.

A Narrowing Range

Scientists from the Wildlife Conservation Society in New York have placed about 30 such cameras in trees throughout the tropical forest of Belize (beh•LEEZ). That is a country in Central America.

The forest is also the site of the world's first jaguar reserve. A reserve is an area set apart for a special purpose. At the reserve in Belize, jaguars are protected and can safely roam.

Belize has a healthy number of jaguars. The wildlife group estimates that about 14 jaguars live within a 143-square-km (55-square-mile) area there. The cameras are helping researchers count the jaguars within certain areas of Belize and in other places where jaguars roam.

"Camera trapping" will help scientists because jaguars are hard to study. Despite the cats' hefty size, their mysterious nature and the thick jungle where they live make them difficult to spot.

A camera snaps a photograph of a passing jaguar.

The map shows how the range of jaguars has changed.

KEY

Where jaguars live now

Where jaguars used to live

"The cameras help researchers determine how many cats are out there and where they make their homes," jaguar expert Kathleen Conforti told WR.

The researchers will use that information to help protect the endangered animals. They want to conserve, or save, the jaguars' habitat. A habitat is the area where the animal naturally lives.

The actions of people have caused a decline in the animal's range. The cutting down of trees has destroyed some of the jaguar's habitat.

THINK ABOUT IT

1. How might the loss of trees affect how jaguars live?
2. How might equipment such as cameras help protect endangered animals around the world?

What a Roar

- Jaguars, which are carnivorous, can grow up to 1.8 meters (6 ft) long and weigh up to 136 kilograms (300 pounds).
- Jaguars are the third-largest cats, after tigers and lions.
- The cats usually live alone and are very territorial. That means they protect their habitat from other jaguars.
- In Spanish, this cat's name is *el tigre,* which means "the tiger."

Find out more! Log on to
www.hspscience.com

WORKING WITH ELEPHANTS

In India, adult Asian elephants have no natural enemies. However, humans have killed many elephants. Now elephants are close to dying out. Raman Sukumar wants to save them.

Sukumar studied how building changes elephant habitats. New dams, roads, and railways force elephants closer to towns. He also studied elephant deaths. He found that illegal hunting has killed many elephants.

Sukumar has found ways to help humans and elephants live together. Areas of the wild are being linked. Elephants can move safely from one area to the next. They don't have to go through farms or towns. Farmers now use different types of fences so that elephants will not eat crops.

Career   Paleontologist

If you like digging, then you may want to become a paleontologist. These scientists study the fossils of ancient animals and plants. As a result, paleontologists can figure out why some species disappeared long ago while other species still exist today.

Materials

- scrap paper
- ruler
- large sheet of white paper
- colored pencils

Quick and Easy Project

Energy Pyramid

Procedure

1. Identify producers, herbivores, carnivores, and omnivores that live in your area. List them on scrap paper.

2. Use the ruler to draw a large pyramid on the white paper. Divide the pyramid into three or four levels, depending on the kinds of living things you have identified.

3. Arrange some or all of these living things on your energy pyramid. Draw only one animal at the top level, ten at the next level, and so on.

Draw Conclusions

Do all the things from your list fit into your pyramid? If not, why not? If you lived in a different kind of habitat—for example, a desert or a seashore—how would your energy pyramid change?

Design Your Own Investigation

Carnivore or Herbivore?

Identify several insects of the same kind, such as caterpillars or ants, from your area. Design an experiment to determine if this kind of insect is a herbivore, a carnivore, or an omnivore. For example, you might give the insects a choice of foods and see which foods they eat. Be sure to use safety precautions. Release the insects when the experiment is over.

Vocabulary Review

Use the terms below to complete the sentences. The page numbers tell you where to look in the chapter if you need help.

producers p. 498   predators p. 508
omnivores p. 500   energy pyramid
decomposers p. 502   p. 512
niche p. 507   extinction p. 520
food chain p. 508

1. Animals that eat both plants and other animals are _____.

2. Nutrients would be lost without _____.

3. The animals at the top of a food chain are always _____.

4. The kind of food that an animal eats is part of its _____.

5. Actions of people that harm the environment can cause the _____ of plants and animals.

6. Herbivores and omnivores both eat _____.

7. A food web shows relationships among living things more accurately than a _____.

8. The loss of energy along a food chain is shown in an _____.

Check Understanding

Write the letter of the best choice.

9. Which of these must a pond food chain have?
   A. algae   C. tiny fish
   B. sunlight   D. whales

10. **MAIN IDEA AND DETAILS** Which term includes herbivores, carnivores, and omnivores?
    F. consumers   H. prey
    G. predators   I. producers

11. How much energy is used at each level of the energy pyramid and not passed on?
    A. 10 percent   C. 80 percent
    B. 20 percent   D. 90 percent

12. Which of the following do herbivores eat?
    F. consumers   H. predators
    G. omnivores   I. producers

13. What is shown below?

    A. extinction   C. habitat
    B. food chain   D. food web

14. What are robins, which eat worms and insects?

   F. carnivores   **H.** omnivores

   G. herbivores   **I.** prey

15. Antelopes are herbivores. What other term describes them?

   A. omnivores   **C.** prey

   B. predators   **D.** producers

16. SEQUENCE Fossils form in different ways. Examine the fossil below.

What happened before this fossil appeared?

   F. Mud hardened.

   G. Minerals replaced wood.

   H. An animal was buried in mud.

   I. A heavy animal walked across a rock.

Inquiry Skills

17. Compare a carnivore and a predator. How are these living things the same? How are they different?

18. While hiking with your family, you follow a trail that has been cut into a mountainside. In the rocky wall next to the trail, you see the fossils of two different plants beside each other. What can you **infer** about when and where these two plants lived?

Read/Inquire/Explain

19. Which of these could survive without being part of a food chain— a strawberry plant, a chicken, or a dog? Explain your answer.

20. Different types of diagrams are used to show the relationships among living things. Study the diagram below.

Part A Would this diagram be correct if there were two snakes at the top? Explain your answer.

Part B How is this diagram different from a food chain?

References

Contents

Your Skin

Your skin is your body's largest organ. It provides your body with a tough protective covering. It protects you from disease. It provides your sense of touch, which allows you to feel pressure, textures, temperature, and pain. Your skin also produces sweat to help control your body temperature. When you play hard or exercise, your body produces sweat, which cools you as it evaporates. The sweat from your skin also helps your body get rid of extra salt and other wastes.

▼ The skin is the body's largest organ.

Epidermis
Many layers of dead skin cells form the top of the epidermis. Cells in the lower part of the epidermis are always making new cells.

Oil Gland
Oil glands produce oil that keeps your skin soft and smooth.

Hair Follicle
Each hair follicle has a muscle that can contract and make the hair "stand on end."

Pore
These tiny holes on the surface of your skin lead to your dermis.

Sweat Gland
Sweat glands produce sweat, which contains water, salt, and various wastes.

Dermis
The dermis is much thicker than the epidermis. It is made up of tough, flexible fibers.

Fatty Tissue
This tissue layer beneath the dermis stores food, provides warmth, and attaches your skin to the bone and muscle below.

Caring for Your Skin

- To protect your skin and to keep it healthy, you should wash your body, including your hair and your nails, every day. This helps remove germs, excess oils and sweat, and dead cells from the epidermis, the outer layer of your skin. Because you touch many things during the day, you should wash your hands with soap and water frequently.

- If you get a cut or scratch, you should wash it right away and cover it with a sterile bandage to prevent infection and promote healing.

- Protect your skin from cuts and scrapes by wearing proper safety equipment when you play sports or skate, or when you're riding your bike or scooter.

Your Digestive System

Your digestive system is made up of connected organs. It breaks down the food you eat and disposes of the leftover wastes your body does not need.

Mouth to Stomach

Digestion begins when you chew your food. Chewing your food breaks it up and mixes it with saliva. When you swallow, the softened food travels down your esophagus to your stomach, where it is mixed with digestive juices. These are strong acids that continue the process of breaking your food down into the nutrients your body needs to stay healthy. Your stomach squeezes your food and turns it into a thick liquid.

Small Intestine and Liver

Your food leaves your stomach and goes into your small intestine. This organ is a long tube just below your stomach. Your liver is an organ that sends bile into your small intestine to continue the process of digesting fats in the food. The walls of the small intestine are lined with millions of small, finger-shaped bumps called villi. Tiny blood vessels in these bumps absorb nutrients from the food as it moves through the small intestine.

Large Intestine

When the food has traveled all the way through your small intestine, it passes into your large intestine. This last organ of your digestive system absorbs water from the food. The remaining wastes are held there until you go to the bathroom.

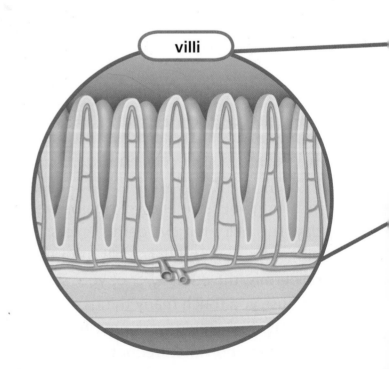

villi

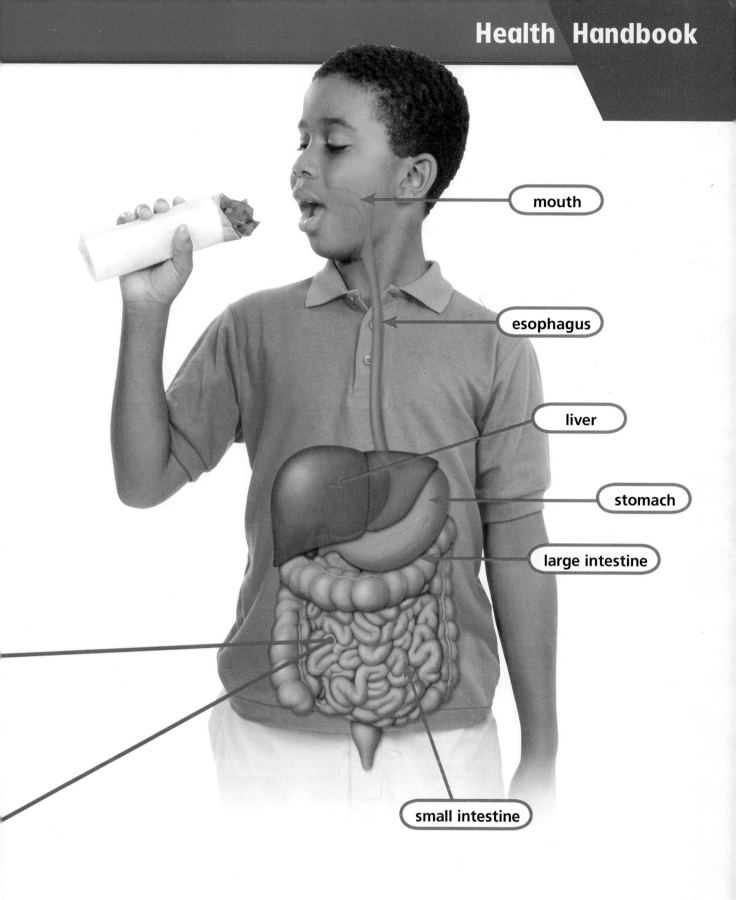

mouth

esophagus

liver

stomach

large intestine

small intestine

Your Circulatory System

Your circulatory system carries to every cell in your body the nutrients your digestive system takes from food and the oxygen your lungs take from the air you breathe. As your blood moves throughout your body, it also helps your body fight infections, control your temperature, and remove wastes from your cells.

vein

heart

artery

Your Heart and Blood Vessels

Your heart is the organ that pumps your blood through your circulatory system. Your heart is a strong muscle that beats continuously. As you exercise, your heart adjusts itself to beat faster to deliver the energy and oxygen your muscles need to work harder.

Blood from your heart is pumped through veins into your lungs, where it releases carbon dioxide and picks up oxygen. Your blood then travels back to your heart to be pumped through your arteries to every part of your body.

Your Blood

The blood in your circulatory system is a mixture of fluids and specialized cells. The watery liquid part of your blood is called plasma. Plasma allows the cells in your blood to move through your blood vessels to every part of your body. It also plays an important role in helping your body control your temperature.

Blood Cells

There are three main types of cells in your blood. Each type of cell in your circulatory system plays a special part in keeping your body healthy and fit.

Red Blood Cells are the most numerous cells in your blood. They carry oxygen from your lungs throughout your body. They also carry carbon dioxide back to your lungs from your cells, so you can breathe it out.

White Blood Cells help your body fight infections when you become ill.

Platelets help your body stop bleeding when you get a cut or other wound. Platelets clump together as soon as you start to bleed. The sticky clump of platelets traps red blood cells and forms a blood clot. The blood clot hardens to make a scab that seals the cut and lets your body begin healing the wound.

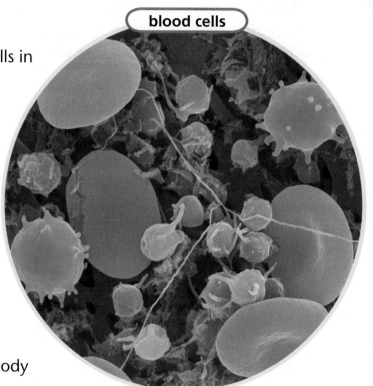

blood cells

Caring for Your Circulatory System

• Eat foods that are low in fat and high in fiber. Fiber helps take away substances that can lead to fatty buildup in your blood vessels.

• Eat foods high in iron to help your red blood cells carry oxygen.

• Drink plenty of water to help your body replenish your blood.

• Avoid contact with another person's blood.

• Exercise regularly to keep your heart strong.

• Never smoke or use tobacco.

Your Skeletal System

Your skeletal system includes all of the bones in your body. These strong, hard parts of your body protect your internal organs, help you move, and allow you to sit and to stand up straight.

Your skeletal system works with your muscular system to hold your body up and to give it shape.

Your skeletal system includes more than 200 bones. These bones come in many different shapes and sizes.

Your Skull

The wide flat bones of your skull fit tightly together to protect your brain. The bones in the front of your skull give your face its shape and allow the muscles in your face to express your thoughts and feelings.

Your Spine

Your spine, or backbone, is made up of nearly two dozen small, round bones. These bones fit together and connect your head to your pelvis. Each of these bones, or vertebrae (VUHR•tuh•bree), is shaped like a doughnut with a small round hole in the center. Your spinal cord is a bundle of nerves that carries information to and from your brain and the rest of your body. Your spinal cord runs from your brain down your back to your hips through the holes in your vertebrae. There are soft, flexible disks of cartilage between your vertebrae. This allows you to bend and twist your spine. Your spine, pelvis, and leg bones work together to allow you to stand, sit, or move.

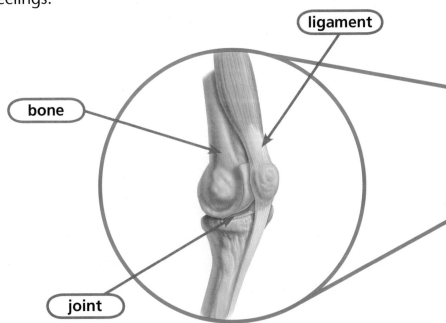

ligament

bone

joint

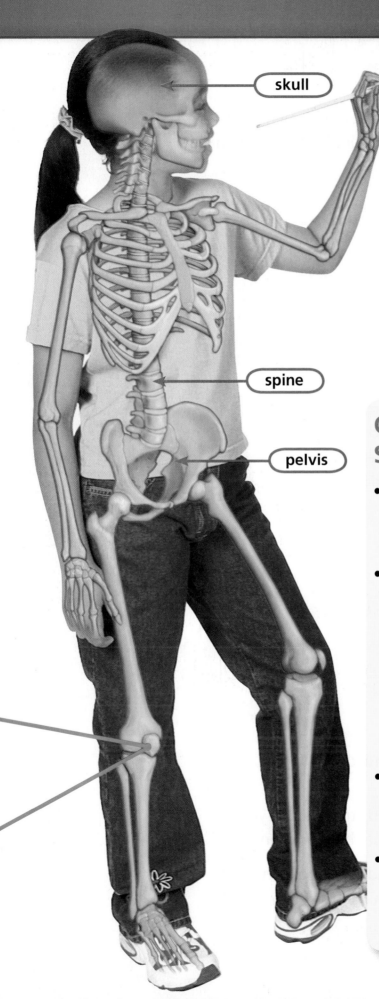

skull

spine

pelvis

Caring for Your Skeletal System

• Always wear a helmet and proper safety gear when you play sports, skate, or ride a bike or a scooter.

• Your bones are made mostly of calcium and other minerals. To keep your skeletal system strong and to help it grow, you should eat foods that are high in calcium like milk, cheese, and yogurt. Dark green, leafy vegetables like broccoli, spinach, and collard greens are also good sources of calcium.

• Exercise to help your bones stay strong and healthy. Get plenty of rest to help your bones grow.

• Stand and sit with good posture. Sitting slumped over puts strain on your muscles and on your bones.

Your Muscular System

A muscle is a body part that produces movement by contracting and relaxing. All of the muscles in your body make up the muscular system.

Voluntary and Involuntary Muscles

Voluntary Muscles are the muscles you use to move your arms and legs, your face, head, and fingers. You can make these muscles contract or relax to control the way your body moves.

Involuntary Muscles are responsible for movements you usually don't see or control. These muscles make up your heart, your stomach and digestive system, your diaphragm, and the muscles that control your eyelids. Your heart beats and your diaphragm powers your breathing without your thinking about them. You cannot stop the action of these muscles.

How Muscles Help You Move

All muscles pull when they contract. Moving your body in more than one direction takes more than one muscle. To reach out with your arm or to pull it back, you use a pair of muscles. As one muscle contracts to extend your arm, the other relaxes and stretches. As you pull your arm back, the muscles reverse their functions.

Your muscles let you do many kinds of things. The large muscles in your legs allow you to walk and run. Tiny muscles in your face allow you to smile.

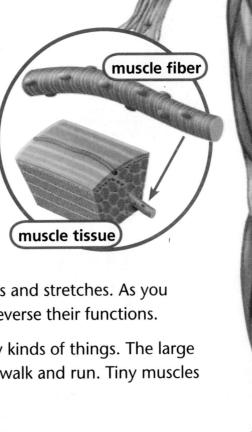

muscle fiber

muscle tissue

arm muscle

Your Muscles and Your Bones

The muscles that allow you to move your body work with your skeletal system. Muscles in your legs that allow you to kick a ball or ride a bicycle pull on the bones and joints of your legs and lower body. Your muscles are connected to your skeletal system by strong, cordlike tissues called tendons.

Your Achilles tendon just above your heel connects your calf muscles to your heel bone. When you contract those muscles, the tendon pulls on the heel bone and allows you to stand on your toes, jump, or push hard on your bicycle's pedals.

Caring for Your Muscular System

- Always stretch and warm your muscles up before exercising or playing sports. Do this by jogging or walking for at least ten minutes. This brings fresh blood and oxygen into your muscles and helps prevent injury or pain.

- Eat a balanced diet of foods to be sure your muscles have the nutrients they need to grow and remain strong.

- Drink plenty of water when you exercise or play sports. This helps your blood remove wastes from your muscles and helps you build endurance.

- Always cool down after you exercise. Walk or jog slowly for five or ten minutes to let your heartbeat slow and your breathing return to normal. This helps you avoid pain and stiffness after your muscles work hard.

- Stop exercising if you feel pain in your muscles.

- Get plenty of rest before and after you work your muscles hard. They need time to repair themselves and recover from working hard.

Your Eyes and Vision

Your eyes allow you to see light reflected by the things around you. This diagram shows how an eye works. Light enters through the clear outer surface called the cornea. It passes through the pupil. The lens bends the incoming light to focus it on the retina. The retina sends nerve signals along the optic nerve. Your brain uses the signals to form an image. This is what you "see."

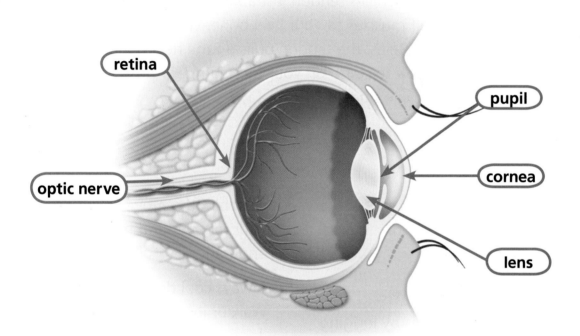

Caring for Your Eyes

- You should have a doctor check your eyesight every year. Tell your parents or your doctor if your vision becomes blurry or if you are having headaches or pain in your eyes.

- Never touch or rub your eyes.

- Protect your eyes by wearing safety goggles when you use tools or play sports.

- Wear swim goggles to protect your eyes from chlorine or other substances in the water.

- Wear sunglasses to protect your eyes from very bright light. Looking directly at bright light or at the sun can damage your eyes permanently.

Your Ears and Hearing

Sounds travel through the air in waves. When some of those waves enter your ear you hear a sound. This diagram shows the inside of your ear.

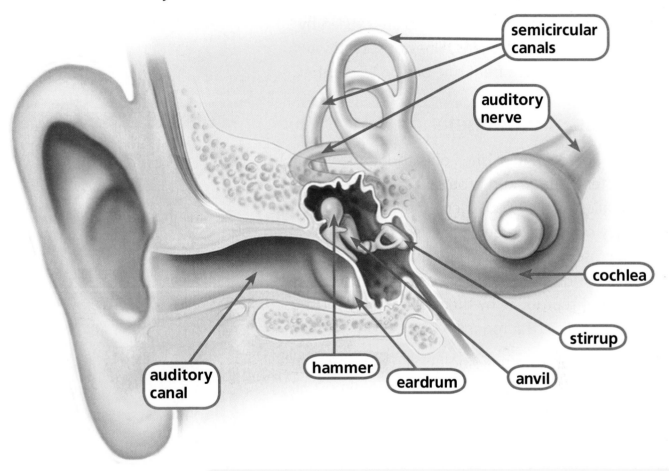

semicircular canals

auditory nerve

cochlea

stirrup

anvil

eardrum

hammer

auditory canal

Caring for Your Ears

- Never put anything in your ears.

- Wear a helmet that covers your ears when you play sports.

- Keep your ears warm in winter.

- Avoid loud sounds and listening to loud music.

- Have your ears checked by a doctor if they hurt or leak fluid or if you have any loss of hearing.

- Wear earplugs when you swim. Water in your ears can lead to infection.

Your Immune System

Pathogens and Illness

You may know someone who had a cold or the flu this year. These illnesses are caused by germs called pathogens. Illnesses spread when pathogens move from one person to another.

Types of Pathogens

There are four kinds of pathogens—viruses, bacteria, fungi, and protozoans. Viruses are the smallest kind of pathogen. They are so small that they can be seen only with very powerful electron microscopes. Viruses cause many types of illness, including colds, the flu, and chicken pox. Viruses cannot reproduce by themselves. They must use living cells to reproduce.

Bacteria are tiny single-cell organisms that live in water, in the soil, and on almost all surfaces. Most bacteria can be seen only with a microscope. Not all bacteria cause illness. Your body needs some types of bacteria to work well.

The most common type of fungus infection is athlete's foot. This is a burning, itchy infection of the skin between your toes. Ringworm is another skin infection caused by a fungus. It causes itchy round patches to develop on the skin.

Protozoans are the fourth type of pathogen. They are single-cell organisms that are slightly larger than bacteria. They can cause disease when they grow in food or drinking water.

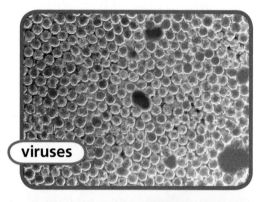
viruses

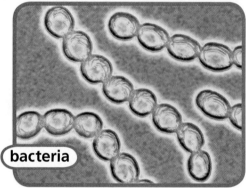
bacteria

fungi

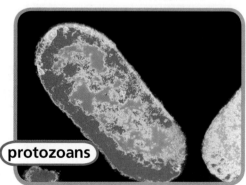
protozoans

Fighting Illness

Pathogens that can make you ill are everywhere. When you become ill, a doctor may be able to treat you. You also can practice healthful habits to protect yourself and others from the spread of pathogens and the illnesses they can cause.

The best way to avoid spreading pathogens is to wash your hands with warm water and soap. This floats germs off of your skin. You should wash your hands often. Always wash them before and after eating, after handling animals, and after using the bathroom. Avoid touching your mouth, eyes, and nose. Never share hats, combs, cups, or drinking straws. If you get a cut or scrape, pathogens can enter your body. It is important to wash cuts and scrapes carefully with soap and water. Then cover the injury with a sterile bandage.

When you are ill, you should avoid spreading pathogens to others. Cover your nose and mouth when you sneeze or cough.

Don't share anything that has touched your mouth or nose. Stay home from school until an adult or your doctor tells you that you are well enough to go back.

Even though pathogens are all around, most people become ill only once in a while because the body has systems that protect it from pathogens. These defenses keep pathogens from entering your body.

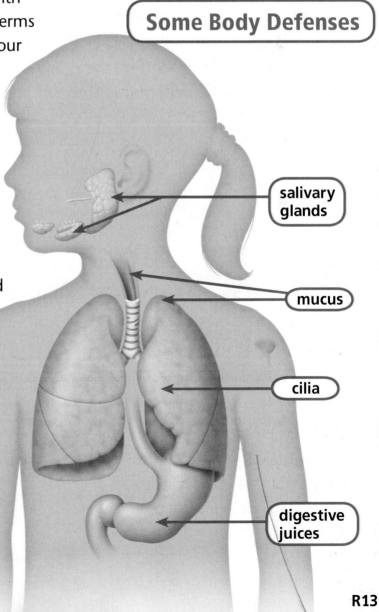

Some Body Defenses

salivary glands

mucus

cilia

digestive juices

Eat a Balanced Diet

Eating the foods that your body needs to grow and fight illness is the most important thing you can do to stay healthy. A balanced diet of healthful foods gives your body energy. Your body's systems need nutrients to function properly and work together.

Choosing unhealthful foods can cause you to gain excess weight and to lack energy. Inactivity and poor food choices can lead to your becoming ill more frequently. Unhealthful foods can also cause you to develop noncommunicable diseases. Unlike communicable diseases, which are caused by germs, these illnesses occur because your body systems are not working right.

Exercise Regularly

Exercise keeps your body healthy. Regular exercise helps your heart, lungs, and muscles stay strong. It helps your body digest food. It also helps your body fight disease. Exercising to keep your body strong also helps prevent injury when you play sports.

Exercise allows your body to rest more effectively. Getting enough sleep prepares your body for the next day. It allows your muscles and bones to grow and recover from exercise. Resting also helps keep your mind alert so you can learn and play well.

Identify the Main Idea and Details

Many of the lessons in this science book are written so that you can understand main ideas and the details that support them. You can use a graphic organizer like this one to show a main idea and details.

Main Idea: The most important idea of a selection

| **Detail:** Information that tells more about the main idea | **Detail:** Information that tells more about the main idea | **Detail:** Information that tells more about the main idea |

Tips for Identifying the Main Idea and Details

• To find the main idea, ask *What is this mostly about?*

• Remember that the main idea is not always stated in the first sentence of a passage.

• Look for details that answer questions such as *who, what, where, when, why,* and *how.* Use pictures as clues to help you.

Here is an example.

Main Idea

An environment that meets the needs of a living thing is called its habitat. Some habitats are as big as a whole forest. This is often true for birds that fly from place to place. Some habitats are very small. For example, fungi might grow only in certain places on a forest floor.

Detail

Here is what you could record in the graphic organizer.

Main Idea: An environment that meets the needs of a living thing is called its habitat.

| **Detail:** Some habitats are as big as a whole forest. | **Detail:** A bird's habitat might be a whole forest. | **Detail:** Fungi might grow only in certain places on a forest floor. |

More About Main Idea and Details

Sometimes the main idea is not at the beginning of a passage. If the main idea is not stated, it can be understood from the details. Look at the graphic organizer. What do you think the main idea is?

Main Idea:		
Detail: Green plants are the producers in a food chain. They make their own food.	**Detail:** Consumers make up the next level of a food chain. They eat plants and other living things for energy.	**Detail:** Decomposers are the next level. They feed on the wastes of consumers or on their remains.

A paragraph's main idea may be supported by details of different types. In this paragraph, identify whether the details give reasons, examples, facts, steps, or descriptions.

A group of the same species living in the same place at the same time is called a population. A forest may have populations of several different kinds of trees. Trout may be one of several populations of fish in a stream. Deer may be one population among many in a meadow.

Skill Practice

Read the following paragraph. Use the Tips for Identifying the Main Idea and Details to answer the questions.

Animals do not get their energy directly from the sun. Many eat plants. The plants use sunlight to make food. Animals that don't eat plants still depend on the energy of sunlight. They eat animals that eat plants. The sun is the main source of energy for all living things.

1. What is the main idea of the paragraph?

2. What supporting details give more information about the main idea?

3. What details answer any of the questions *who, what, where, when, why,* and *how*?

Compare and Contrast

Some lessons are written to help you see how things are alike or different. You can use a graphic organizer like this one to compare and contrast.

> **Topic:** Name the two things you are comparing and contrasting.

> **Alike**
> List ways the things are alike.

> **Different**
> List ways the things are different.

Tips for Comparing and Contrasting

- To compare, ask *How are the people, places, objects, ideas, or events alike?*

- To contrast, ask *How are the people, places, objects, ideas, or events different?*

- When you compare, look for signal words and phrases such as *similar, alike, both, the same as, too,* and *also.*

- When you contrast, look for signal words and phrases such as *unlike, different, however, yet,* and *but.*

Here is an example.

> **Compare**

> Mars and Venus are the two planets closest to Earth. They are known as inner planets. Venus and Earth are about the same size, but Mars is a little smaller. Venus does not have any moons. However, Mars has two moons.

> **Contrast**

Here is what you could record in the graphic organizer.

> **Topic:** Mars and Venus

> **Alike**
> Both are inner planets.
> Are the planets closest to Earth.

> **Different**
> Mars is smaller than Venus.
> Mars has two moons.

More About Compare and Contrast

You can better understand new information about things when you know how they are alike and how they are different. Use the graphic organizer from page R18 to sort the following items of information about Mars and Venus.

Mars	Venus
Mars is the fourth planet from the sun.	Venus is the second planet from the sun.
A year on Mars is 687 Earth days.	A year on Venus is 225 Earth days.
Mars has a diameter of 6794 kilometers.	Venus has a diameter of 12,104 kilometers.
The soil on Mars is a dark reddish brown.	Venus is dry and has a thick atmosphere.

Sometimes a paragraph compares and contrasts more than one topic. In the following paragraph, one topic being compared and contrasted is underlined. Find the second topic being compared and contrasted.

Radio telescopes and optical telescopes are two types of telescopes that are used to observe objects in space. A radio telescope collects radio waves with a large, bowl-shaped antenna. Optical telescopes use light. There are two types of optical telescopes. A refracting telescope uses lenses to magnify an object and a reflecting telescope uses a curved mirror to magnify an object.

Skill Practice

Read the following paragraph. Use the Tips for Comparing and Contrasting to answer the questions.

Radio telescopes and optical telescopes work in the same way. However, optical telescopes collect and focus light, while radio telescopes collect and focus invisible radio waves. Radio waves are not affected by clouds and poor weather. Computers can make pictures from data collected by radio telescopes.

1. How are radio and optical telescopes alike? Different?

2. What are two compare and contrast signal words in the paragraph?

Identify Cause and Effect

Some of the lessons in this science book are written to help you understand why things happen. You can use a graphic organizer like this one to show cause and effect.

Cause		Effect
A cause is an action or event that makes something happen.	→	An effect is what happens as a result of an action or event.

Tips for Identifying Cause and Effect

• To find an effect, ask *What happened?*

• To find a cause, ask *Why did this happen?*

• Remember that actions and events can have more than one cause or effect.

• Look for signal words and phrases such as *because* and *as a result* to help you identify causes and effects.

Here is an example.

Cause

Effect

A pulley is a simple machine. It helps us do work. It is made up of a rope or chain and a wheel around which the rope fits. When you pull down on one rope end, the wheel turns and the other rope end moves up.

Here is what you could record in the graphic organizer.

Cause		Effect
One rope end is pulled down on a pulley.	→	The wheel of the pulley turns and the other rope end moves up.

More About Cause and Effect

Actions and events can have more than one cause or effect. For example, suppose the paragraph on page R20 included a sentence that said *The pulley can be used to raise or lower something that is light in weight.* You could then identify two effects of operating a pulley.

Cause One rope end is pulled down on a pulley.	→	**Effect** The wheel of the pulley turns and the other rope end moves up.
		Effect Something light in weight is raised or lowered.

Some paragraphs contain more than one cause and effect. In the following paragraph, one cause and its effect are underlined. Find the second cause and its effect.

> A fixed pulley and a movable pulley can be put together to make a compound machine. The movable pulley increases your force. As more movable pulleys are added to a system, the force is increased. The fixed pulley changes the direction of your force.

Skill Practice

Read the following paragraph. Use the Tips for Identifying Cause and Effect to help you answer the questions.

> A lever can be used to open a paint can. The outer rim of the can is used as the fulcrum. Your hand supplies the effort force. The force put out by the end under the lid is greater than the effort force. As a result, the can is opened.

1. What causes the paint can to open?

2. What is the effect when an effort force is applied?

3. What signal phrase helped you identify the cause and effect in this paragraph?

Sequence

Some lessons in this science book are written to help you understand the order in which things happen. You can use a graphic organizer like this one to show a sequence.

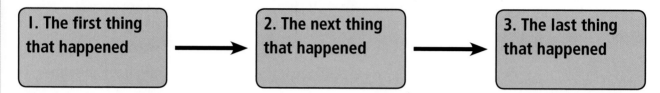

| 1. The first thing that happened | → | 2. The next thing that happened | → | 3. The last thing that happened |

Tips for Understanding a Sequence

• Pay attention to the order in which events happen.

• Recall dates and times to help you understand the sequence.

• Look for signal words such as *first, next, then, last,* and *finally.*

• Sometimes it is helpful to add your own time-order words to help you understand a sequence.

Here is an example.

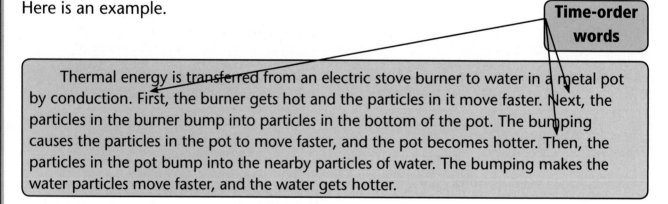

Time-order words

Thermal energy is transferred from an electric stove burner to water in a metal pot by conduction. First, the burner gets hot and the particles in it move faster. Next, the particles in the burner bump into particles in the bottom of the pot. The bumping causes the particles in the pot to move faster, and the pot becomes hotter. Then, the particles in the pot bump into the nearby particles of water. The bumping makes the water particles move faster, and the water gets hotter.

Here is what you could record in the graphic organizer.

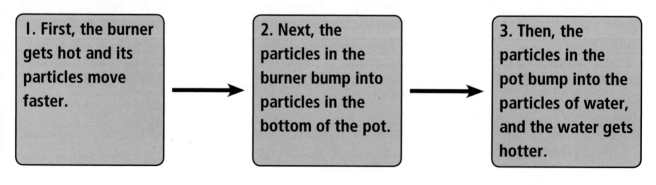

| 1. First, the burner gets hot and its particles move faster. | → | 2. Next, the particles in the burner bump into particles in the bottom of the pot. | → | 3. Then, the particles in the pot bump into the particles of water, and the water gets hotter. |

More About Sequence

Sometimes information is sequenced by time. For example, an experiment might be done to measure temperature change over time. Use the graphic organizer to sequence the experiment.

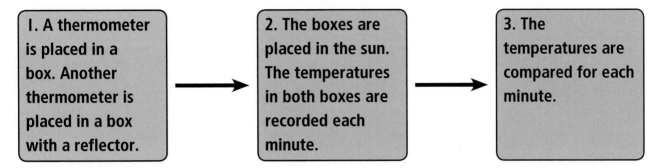

When time-order words are not given, add your own words to help you understand the sequence. In the paragraph below, one time-order word has been included and underlined. How many more time-order words can you add to understand the paragraph's sequence?

> Convection is the transfer of thermal energy in a fluid, a liquid or gas. As the fluid near a hot object gets hot, it expands. The hot fluid is forced up by the cooler, denser fluid around it. As the hot fluid is forced up, it warms the fluid around it. <u>Then</u>, as it slowly cools, it sinks.

Skill Practice

Read the following paragraph. Use the Tips for Understanding a Sequence to answer the questions.

> Solar energy can be used to heat water in a home. First, solar panels are placed on the roof of a house. Next, the panels absorb infrared radiation from the sun. Then, the radiation heats the water as it flows through the panels.

1. What is the first thing that happens in the sequence?

2. How many steps are involved in the process?

3. What three signal words helped you identify the sequence in this paragraph?

⭐ Focus Skill Summarize

At the end of every lesson in this science book, you are asked to summarize. When you summarize, you use your own words to tell what something is about. In the lesson, you will find ideas for writing your summary. You can also use a graphic organizer like this one to summarize.

| **Main Idea:** Tell about the most important information you have read. | + | **Details:** Add details that answer important questions such as *who, what, where, when, why,* **and** *how.* | = | **Summary:** Retell what you have just read, including only the most important details. |

Tips for Summarizing

• To write a summary, first ask *What is the most important idea of the paragraph?*

• To add details, ask *who, what, when, where, why,* and *how.*

• Remember to use fewer words than the original.

• Tell the information in your own words.

Here and on the next page is an example.

Main Idea

Details

The water cycle is the constant recycling of water. As the sun warms the ocean, water particles leave the water and enter the air as water vapor. This is evaporation, the process of a liquid changing to a gas. Clouds form when water vapor condenses high in the atmosphere. Condensation occurs when the water vapor rises, cools, and changes from a gas to liquid. When the drops of water are too large to stay up in the air, precipitation occurs.

Here is what you could record in the graphic organizer.

Main Idea:		Details:		Summary:
The water cycle is the constant recycling of water.	+	Evaporation is the change from a liquid to a gas. Condensation is the change from a gas to a liquid. Precipitation is water that falls to Earth.	=	The constant recycling of water is the water cycle. It includes evaporation, condensation, and precipitation.

More About Summarizing

Sometimes a paragraph has details that are not important enough to be included in a summary. The graphic organizer remains the same because those details are not important to understanding the paragraph's main idea.

Skill Practice

Read the following paragraph. Use the Tips for Summarizing to answer the questions.

Tides are the changes in the ocean's water level each day. At high tide, much of the beach is covered with water. At low tide, waves break farther away from the shore and less of the beach is under water. Every day most shorelines have two high tides and two low tides. High tides and low tides occur at regular times and are usually a little more than 6 hours apart.

1. If a friend asked you what this paragraph was about, what information would you include? What would you leave out?

2. What is the main idea of the paragraph?

3. Which two details would you include in a summary of the paragraph?

Draw Conclusions

At the end of each lesson in this science book, you are asked to draw conclusions. To draw conclusions, use the information that you have read and what you already know. Drawing conclusions can help you understand what you read. You can use a graphic organizer like this.

What I Read Use facts from the text to help you understand.	+	**What I Know** Use your own experience to help you understand.	=	**Conclusion:** Combine facts and details in the text with personal knowledge or experience.

Tips for Drawing Conclusions

• To draw conclusions, first ask *What information from the text do I need to think about?*

• Then ask *What do I know from my own experience that could help me draw a conclusion?*

• Ask yourself whether the conclusion you have drawn is valid, or makes sense.

Here is an example.

Plants need air, nutrients, water, and light to live. A plant makes its own food by a process called photosynthesis. Photosynthesis takes place in the plant's leaves. In an experiment, a plant is placed in a dark room without any light. It is watered every day.

Text information

Here is what you could record in the graphic organizer.

What I Read A plant needs air, nutrients, water, and light to live.	+	**What I Know** Plants use light to make the food they need to live and grow.	=	**Conclusion:** The plant will die since it is not getting any light.

More About Drawing Conclusions

Sensible conclusions based on your experience and the facts you read are valid. For example, suppose the paragraph on page R26 included a sentence that said *After a day, the plant is removed from the dark room and placed in the sunlight.* You could then draw a different conclusion about the life of the plant.

What I Read A plant needs air, nutrients, water, and light to live.	**What I Know** Plants use light to make the food they need to live and grow.	**Conclusion:** The plant will live.

+ between first two, = before last.

Sometimes a paragraph might not contain enough information to draw a valid conclusion. Read the following paragraph. Think of one valid conclusion you could draw. Then think of one conclusion that would be invalid or wouldn't make sense.

> Cacti are plants that are found in the desert. Sometimes it does not rain in the desert for months or even years. Cacti have thick stems. The roots of cactus plants grow just below the surface of the ground.

Skill Practice

Read the following paragraph. Use the Tips for Drawing Conclusions to answer the questions.

> Animals behave in ways that help them meet their needs. Some animal behaviors are instincts, and some are learned. Tiger cubs learn to hunt by watching their mothers hunt and by playing with other tiger cubs. They are not born knowing exactly how to hunt.

1. What conclusion can you draw about a tiger cub that is separated from its mother?

2. What information from your own experience helped you draw the conclusion?

3. What text information did you use to draw the conclusion?

Using Tables, Charts, and Graphs

As you do investigations in science, you collect, organize, display, and interpret data. Tables, charts, and graphs are good ways to organize and display data so that others can understand and interpret your data.

The tables, charts, and graphs in this Handbook will help you read and understand data. The Handbook will also help you choose the best ways to display data so that you can draw conclusions and make predictions.

Reading a Table

A scientist is studying the rainfall in Bangladesh. She wants to know when the monsoon season is, or the months in which the area receives the greatest amounts of rainfall. The table shows the data she has collected.

Monthly Rainfall in Chittagong, Bangladesh	
Month	Rainfall (inches)
January	1
February	2
March	3
April	6
May	10
June	21
July	23
August	10
September	13
October	7
November	2
December	1

Title

Headings

Data

How to Read a Table

1. **Read the title** to find out what the table is about.

2. **Read the headings** to find out what information is given.

3. **Study** the data. Look for patterns.

4. **Draw conclusions.** If you display the data in a graph, you might be able to see patterns easily.

By studying the table, you can see how much rain fell during each month. If the scientist wanted to look for patterns, she might display the data in a graph.

Reading a Bar Graph

The data in this bar graph is the same as that in the table. A bar graph can be used to compare the data about different events or groups.

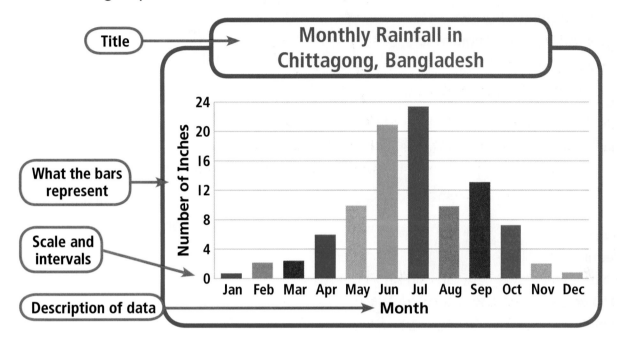

Title → **Monthly Rainfall in Chittagong, Bangladesh**

What the bars represent →

Scale and intervals →

Description of data →

How to Read a Bar Graph

1. **Look** at the graph to determine what kind of graph it is.

2. **Read** the graph. Use the numbers and labels to guide you.

3. **Analyze** the data. Study the bars to compare the measurements. Look for patterns.

4. **Draw conclusions.** Ask yourself questions like the ones under Skills Practice.

Skills Practice

1. In which two months does Chittagong receive the most rainfall?

2. Which months have the same amounts of rainfall?

3. **Predict** During which months are the roads likely to be flooded?

4. How does the bar graph help you identify the monsoon season and the rainfall amounts?

5. Was the bar graph a good choice for displaying this data?

Reading a Line Graph

A scientist collected this data about temperatures in Pittsburgh, Pennsylvania.

Average Temperatures in Pittsburgh	
Month	Temperature (degrees Fahrenheit)
January	28
February	29
March	39
April	50
May	60
June	68
July	74
August	72
September	63
October	52
November	43
December	32

How to Read a Line Graph

1. **Look** at the graph to determine what kind of graph it is.

2. **Read** the graph. Use the numbers and labels to guide you.

3. **Analyze** the data. Study the points along the lines. Look for patterns.

4. **Draw conclusions.** Ask yourself questions like the ones under Skills Practice.

Here is the same data displayed in a line graph. A line graph is used to show changes over time.

Title

What the points represent

Scale and intervals

Description of data

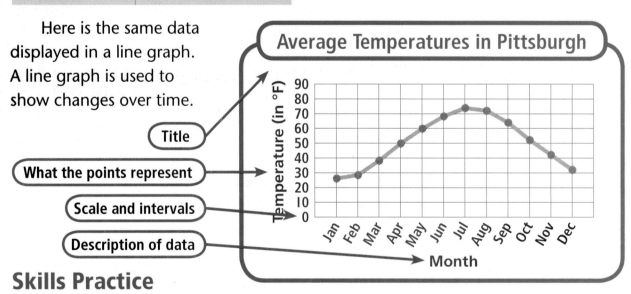

Skills Practice

1. In which three months are the temperatures the warmest in Pittsburgh?

2. **Predict** During which months are ponds in Pittsburgh likely to freeze?

3. Was the line graph a good choice for displaying this data? Explain why.

Reading a Circle Graph

Some scientists counted 100 animals at a park. The scientists wanted to know which animal group had the most animals. They classified the animals by making a table. Here is their data.

Animal Groups at the Park

Animal Group	Number Observed
Mammals	7
Insects	63
Birds	22
Reptiles	5
Amphibians	3

The circle graph shows the same data as the table. A circle graph can be used to show data as a whole made up of parts.

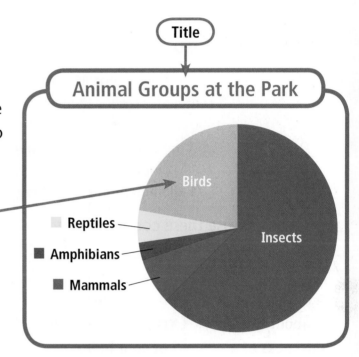

How to Read a Circle Graph

1. **Look** at the title of the graph to learn what kind of information is shown.

2. **Read** the graph. Look at the label of each section to find out what information is shown.

3. **Analyze** the data. Compare the sizes of the sections to determine how they are related.

4. **Draw conclusions.** Ask yourself questions like the ones under Skills Practice.

Skills Practice

1. Which animal group had the most members? Which one had the fewest?

2. **Predict** If you visited a nearby park, would you expect to see more reptiles or more insects?

3. Was the circle graph a good choice for displaying this data? Explain.

Measurements

When you measure, you compare an object to a standard unit of measure. Scientists almost always use the units of the metric system.

Measuring Length and Capacity in Metric Units

When you measure length, you find the distance between two points. The table shows the metric units of **length** and how they are related.

Equivalent Measures
1 centimeter (cm) = 10 millimeters (mm)
1 decimeter (dm) = 10 centimeters (cm)
1 meter (m) = 1000 millimeters
1 meter = 10 decimeters
1 kilometer (km) = 1000 meters

You can use these comparisons to help you learn the size of each metric unit of length:

A **millimeter (mm)** is about the thickness of a dime.

A **centimeter (cm)** is about the width of your index finger.

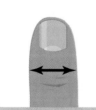

A **decimeter (dm)** is about the width of an adult's hand.

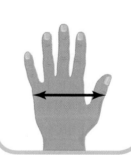

A **meter (m)** is about the width of a door.

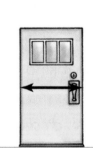

The following diagram shows how to multiply and divide to change to larger and smaller units.

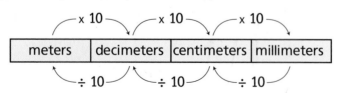

When you measure capacity, you find the amount a container can hold when it is filled. The images show the metric units of **capacity** and how they are related.

A **milliliter (mL)** is the amount of liquid that can fill one part of a dropper.

A **liter (L)** is the amount of liquid that can fill a plastic water bottle.

1 L = 1000 mL

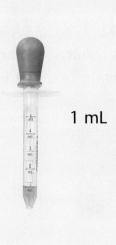

1 mL

You can use multiplication to change liters to milliliters.

You can use division to change milliliters to liters.

2 L = _____ mL

Think: There are 1000 mL in 1 L.

2 L = 2 x 1000 = 2000 mL

So, 2 L = 2000 mL.

4000 mL = _____ L

Think: There are 1000 mL in 1 L.

4000 ÷ 1000 = 4

So, 4000 mL = 4 L.

Skills Practice

Complete. Tell whether you multiply or divide.

1. 3 L = _____ mL

2. 5000 mL = _____ L

3. 7000 mL = _____ L

4. 6 L = _____ mL

5. 500 dm = _____ cm

6. 4 m = _____ mm

7. 8 _____ = 80 cm

8. _____ m = 1400 cm

Measuring Mass

Matter is what all objects are made of. **Mass** is the amount of matter that is in an object. The metric units of mass are the gram (g) and the kilogram (kg). You can use these comparisons to help you understand the masses of some everyday objects:

A paper clip is about **1 gram** (g).

A slice of wheat bread is about **20 grams.**

A box of 12 crayons is about **100 grams.**

A large wedge of cheese is about **1 kilogram** (kg).

You can use multiplication to change kilograms to grams.

You can use division to change grams to kilograms.

2 kg = ____ g	4000 g = ____ kg
Think: There are 1000 g in 1 kg.	Think: There are 1000 g in 1 kg.
2 kg = 2 x 1000 = 2000 g	4000 ÷ 1000 = 4
So, 2 kg = 2000 g.	So, 4000 g = 4 kg.

Skills Practice

Complete. Tell whether you multiply or divide by 1000.

1. 5000 g = ____ kg

2. 3000 g = ____ kg

3. 4 kg = ____ g

4. 7 kg = ____ g

Measurement Systems

SI Measures (Metric)

Temperature
Ice melts at 0 degrees Celsius (°C).
Water freezes at 0°C.
Water boils at 100°C.

Length and Distance
1000 meters (m) =
                    1 kilometer (km)
100 centimeters (cm) = 1 m
10 millimeters (mm) = 1 cm

Force
1 newton (N) = 1 kilogram x
    1 meter/second/second (kg-m/s^2)

Volume
1 cubic meter (m^3) =
                    1 m x 1 m x 1 m
1 cubic centimeter (cm^3) =
                    1 cm x 1 cm x 1 cm
1 liter (L) = 1000 millimeters (mL)
1 cm^3 = 1 mL

Area
1 square kilometer (km^2) =
                    1 km x 1 km
1 hectare = 10,000 m^2

Mass
1000 grams (g) = 1 kilogram (kg)
1000 milligrams (mg) = 1 g
1000 kilograms = 1 metric ton

Rates
km/hr = kilometers per hour
m/sec = meters per second

Customary Measures

Temperature
Ice melts at 32 degrees
    Fahrenheit (°F).
Water freezes at 32°F.
Water boils at 212°F.

Length and Distance
12 inches (in.) = 1 foot (ft)
3 ft = 1 yard (yd)
5280 ft = 1 mile (mi)

Force
16 ounces (oz) = 1 pound (lb)
2000 pounds = 1 ton (T)

Volume of Fluids
2 cups (c) = 1 pint (pt)
2 pt = 1 quart (qt)
4 qt = 1 gallon (gal)

Area
1 square mile (mi^2) = 1 mi x 1 mi
1 acre = 4840 sq ft

Rates
mph = miles per hour
ft/sec = feet per second

Safety in Science

Doing investigations in science can be fun, but you need to be sure you do them safely. Here are some rules to follow.

1. **Think ahead.** Study the steps of the investigation so you know what to expect. If you have any questions, ask your teacher. Be sure you understand any caution statements or safety reminders.

2. **Be neat.** Keep your work area clean. If you have long hair, pull it back so it doesn't get in the way. Roll or push up long sleeves to keep them away from your activity.

3. **Oops!** If you should spill or break something, or get cut, tell your teacher right away.

4. **Watch your eyes.** Wear safety goggles anytime you are directed to do so. If you get anything in your eyes, tell your teacher right away.

5. **Yuck!** Never eat or drink anything during a science activity.

6. **Don't get shocked.** Be especially careful if an electric appliance is used. Be sure that electric cords are in a safe place where you can't trip over them. Don't ever pull a plug out of an outlet by pulling on the cord.

7. **Keep it clean.** Always clean up when you have finished. Put everything away and wipe your work area. Wash your hands.

Visit the Multimedia Science Glossary to see illustrations of these terms and to hear them pronounced.
www.hspscience.com

Glossary

As you read your science book, you will notice that new or unfamiliar terms have been respelled to help you pronounce them while you are reading. Those respellings are called *phonetic respellings.* In this Glossary you will see the same kind of respellings.

In phonetic respellings, syllables are separated by a bullet (•). Small uppercase letters show stressed syllables.

The boldfaced letters in the examples in the Pronunciation Key below show which letters and combinations of letters are pronounced in the respellings.

The page number (in parentheses) at the end of a definition tells you where to find the term, defined in context, in your book. Depending on the context in which it is used, a term may have more than one definition.

Pronunciation Key

Sound	As in	Phonetic Respelling	Sound	As in	Phonetic Respelling
a	bat	(BAT)	oh	over	(OH•ver)
ah	lock	(LAHK)	oo	pool	(POOL)
air	rare	(RAIR)	ow	out	(OWT)
ar	argue	(AR•gyoo)	oy	foil	(FOYL)
aw	law	(LAW)	s	cell	(SEL)
ay	face	(FAYS)		sit	(SIT)
ch	chapel	(CHAP•uhl)	sh	sheep	(SHEEP)
e	test	(TEST)	th	that	(THAT)
	metric	(MEH•trik)		thin	(THIN)
ee	eat	(EET)	u	pull	(PUL)
	feet	(FEET)	uh	medal	(MED•uhl)
	ski	(SKEE)		talent	(TAL•uhnt)
er	paper	(PAY•per)		pencil	(PEN•suhl)
	fern	(FERN)		onion	(UHN•yuhn)
eye	idea	(eye•DEE•uh)		playful	(PLAY•fuhl)
i	bit	(BIT)		dull	(DUHL)
ing	going	(GOH•ing)	y	yes	(YES)
k	card	(KARD)		ripe	(RYP)
	kite	(KYT)	z	bags	(BAGZ)
ngk	bank	(BANGK)	zh	treasure	(TREZH•er)

A

abiotic [ay•by•AHT•ik] Describes a nonliving part of an ecosystem **(466)**

absorption [ab•ZAWRP•shuhn] The taking in of light or sound energy by an object **(83)**

acceleration [ak•sel•er•AY•shuhn] Any change in the speed or direction of an object's motion **(187)**

adaptation [ad•uhp•TAY•shuhn] A characteristic of a living thing that helps it survive in its environment **(476)**

air mass [AIR MAS] A large body of air that has a similar temperature and moisture level **(304)**

amplitude [AM•pluh•tood] A measure of the amount of energy in a wave **(73)**

anemometer [an•uh•MAHM•uht•er] A weather instrument that measures wind speed **(310)**

artery [ART•er•ee] A blood vessel that carries blood away from the heart **(432)**

axis [AK•sis] The imaginary line around which Earth spins as it rotates **(356)**

B

barometer [buh•RAHM•uh•ter] A weather instrument used to measure air pressure **(310)**

basic needs [BAY•sik NEEDZ] The things a living thing needs to survive and grow **(474)**

bedrock [BED•rahk] The solid rock that forms Earth's surface **(267)**

biotic [by•AHT•ik] Describes a living part of an ecosystem **(464)**

bone [BOHN] A hard organ made of a hard outer covering tissue and a softer inside tissue **(422)**

C

capillary [KAP•uh•lair•ee] A blood vessel with very thin walls that allows oxygen and carbon dioxide to pass through **(432)**

carnivore [KAHR•nuh•vawr] An animal that eats only other animals **(500)**

cell [SEL] The smallest unit of a living thing **(390)**

cell membrane [SEL MEM•brayn] The thin covering that controls what enters and leaves a cell **(391)**

cell wall [CEL WAWL] The stiff outer layer of a plant cell **(392)**

change of state [CHAYNJ uhv STAYT] The change from a solid to a liquid or from a liquid to a gas **(48)**

chemical energy [KEM•ih•kuhl EN•er•jee] Energy that can be released by a chemical reaction **(162)**

clay [KLAY] The smallest particles that make up soil **(268)**

cold front [KOHLD FRUHNT] The boundary where a cold air mass moves under a warm air mass **(306)**

comet [KAHM•it] A ball of rock, ice, and frozen gases in space **(368)**

community [kuh•MYOO•nuh•tee] All the populations of organisms living together in an environment **(460)**

Multimedia Science Glossary: www.hspscience.com

condensation [kahn•duhn•SAY•shuhn] The process by which a gas changes into a liquid **(285)**

conduction [kuhn•DUK•shuhn] The movement of heat between two materials that are touching **(106)**

conductor [kuhn•DUK•ter] Materials that let electric charges travel through them easily **(134)**

conservation [kahn•ser•VAY•shuhn] The careful use and protection of natural resources **(342)**

constellation [kahn•stuh•LAY•shuhn] A pattern of stars that form an imaginary picture or design in the sky **(374)**

consumer [kuhn•SOOM•er] A living thing that can't make its own food and must eat other living things **(496)**

convection [kuhn•VEK•shuhn] The movement of heat in liquids and gases from a warmer area to a cooler area **(107)**

current electricity [KUR•uhnt ee•lek•TRIS•uh•tee] A steady movement of charges through certain materials **(130)**

D

decomposer [dee•kuhm•POHZ•er] A living thing that feeds on the wastes of plants and animals **(502)**

density [DEN•suh•tee] The mass of one unit of volume of a substance **(40)**

diaphragm [DY•uh•fram] The muscle in your body that allows you to inhale and exhale **(430)**

diversity [duh•VER•suh•tee] A great variety of living things **(470)**

E

ecosystem [EE•koh•sis•tuhm] A community and its physical environment together **(456)**

electric motor [uh•LEK•trik MOHT•er] A device that changes electrical energy to energy of motion **(147)**

electromagnet [ee•lek•troh•MAG•nit] A temporary magnet caused by an electric current **(144)**

energy pyramid [EN•er•jee PIR•uh•mid] A diagram showing how much energy is passed from one organism to the next in a food chain **(512)**

energy resource [EN•er•jee REE•sawrs] A resource that is used to produce electricity, heat, or light **(323)**

energy transfer [EN•er•jee TRANS•fer] A change of energy from one form to another **(113)**

environment [en•VY•ruhn•muhnt] All of the living and nonliving things surrounding an organism **(456)**

erosion [uh•ROH•zhuhn] The process of moving sediment from one place to another **(262)**

esophagus [ih•SAHF•uh•guhs] A muscular tube that connects your mouth with your stomach **(440)**

evaporation [ee•vap•uh•RAY•shuhn] The process by which a liquid changes into a gas **(284)**

experiment [ek•SPAIR•uh•muhnt] A test of a hypothesis **(15)**

extinction [ek•STINGK•shuhn] The death of all the members of a certain kind of organism **(520)**

food chain [FOOD CHAYN] A series of organisms that depend on one another for food **(508)**

food web [FOOD WEB] A group of food chains that overlap **(510)**

force [FAWRS] A pull or push of any kind **(188)**

fossil [FAHS•uhl] Physical evidence of a plant or an animal that lived long ago **(516)**

fossil fuel [FAHS•uhl FYOO•uhl] A natural resource that formed from the remains of plants and animals that lived millions of years ago **(324)**

frequency [FREE•kwuhn•see] A measure of the number of waves that pass in a second **(73)**

friction [FRIK•shuhn] A force that resists motion between objects that are touching **(197)**

fulcrum [FUHL•kruhm] The fixed point on a lever **(212)**

galaxy [GAL•uhk•see] A huge system of many stars, gases, and dust **(374)**

gas [GAS] The state of matter that does not have a definite shape and does not take up a definite amount of space **(34)**

generator [JEN•er•ayt•er] A device that produces an electric current **(146)**

geothermal energy [jee•oh•THER•muhl EN•er•jee] Heat that comes from the inside of Earth **(155)**

gravitation [grav•ih•TAY•shuhn] A force that acts between any two objects and pulls them together **(195)**

gravity [GRAV•ih•tee] The force of attraction between Earth and other objects, an expression of gravitation **(195)**

habitat [HAB•ih•tat] An environment that meets the needs of an organism **(506)**

habitat restoration [HAB•ih•tat res•tuh•RAY•shuhn] Returning a natural environment to its original condition **(485)**

hail [HAYL] Round pieces of ice formed when frozen rain is coated with water and refreezes **(291)**

heat [HEET] The flow of thermal energy from a warmer object to a cooler object **(47, 105)**

herbivore [HER•buh•vawr] An animal that eats only plants, or producers **(500)**

horizon [huh•RY•zuhn] A layer in the soil **(267)**

humus [HYOO•muhs] The remains of decayed plants or animals in the soil **(266)**

hurricane [HER•ih•kayn] A large tropical storm with wind speeds of at least 74 miles per hour **(292)**

hydroelectric power [hy•droh•ee•LEK•trik POW•er] Electrical energy made by using the kinetic energy of falling water **(154)**

hypothesis [hy•PAHTH•uh•sis] A statement of what you think will happen and why **(15)**

igneous rock [IG•nee•uhs RAHK] A type of rock that forms from melted rock that cools and hardens **(246)**

inclined plane [in•KLYND PLAYN] A simple machine that is a slanted surface **(226)**

inertia [in•ER•shuh] The property of matter that keeps an object at rest or keeps it moving in a straight line **(190)**

inference [IN•fer•uhns] An untested conclusion based on your observations **(12)**

insulator [IN•suh•layt•er] A material that does not let current electricity move through it easily **(134)**

intensity [in•TEN•suh•tee] A measure of how loud or soft a sound is **(67)**

joint [JOYNT] A place in the body where two bones meet **(422)**

kinetic energy [kih•NET•ik EN•er•jee] The energy of motion **(153)**

land breeze [LAND BREEZ] A breeze that moves from the land to the water **(298)**

lever [LEV•er] A simple machine made of a bar that pivots on a fixed point **(212)**

light [LYT] A form of energy that can travel through space and lies partly within the visible range **(96)**

liquid [LIK•wid] The state of matter that takes up the shape of its container and takes up a definite amount of space **(33)**

magnet [MAG•nit] An object that attracts iron and a few other (but not all) metals **(140)**

magnetic field [mag•NET•ik FEELD] The space around a magnet in which the force of the magnet acts **(143)**

magnetic poles [mag•NET•ik POHLZ] The parts of a magnet at which its force is strongest **(142)**

mass [MAS] The amount of matter in an object **(38)**

mechanical energy [muh•KAN•ih•kuhl EN•er•jee] The total potential and kinetic energy of an object **(163)**

metamorphic rock [met•uh•MAWR•fik RAHK] A type of rock that forms when heat or pressure change an existing rock **(248)**

microscope [MY•kruh•skohp] A tool that makes an object look several times bigger than it is **(6)**

mineral [MIN•er•uhl] A solid nonliving substance that occurs naturally in rocks or in the ground **(244)**

mineral resource [MIN•er•uhl REE•sawrs] A natural resource that comes from minerals found on or beneath Earth's surface **(326)**

moon [MOON] A natural body that revolves around a planet **(358)**

motion [MOH•shuhn] A change of position of an object **(178)**

muscle [MUHS•uhl] An organ that is made of bundles of long fibers and works with bones to help you move **(424)**

natural resource [NACH•er•uhl REE•sawrs] A resource that is found in nature and not made by people **(322)**

neuron [NUR•ahn] A cell of the nervous system **(402)**

niche [NICH] The role of an organism in its habitat **(507)**

nonrenewable resource [nahn•rih•NOO•uh•buhl REE•sawrs] A resource, such as a fossil fuel, that can't be replaced within a human lifetime **(340)**

nucleus [NOO•klee•uhs] The control center of a cell **(391)**

observation [ahb•zer•VAY•shuhn] Information from your senses **(12)**

omnivore [AHM•nih•vawr] An animal that eats both plants and other animals **(500)**

orbit [AWR•bit] The path of one object in space around another object **(356)**

organ [AWR•guhn] A body part made of different kinds of tissues that work together to perform a particular job **(408)**

pan balance [PAN BAL•uhns] A tool that measures mass **(8)**

parallel circuit [PAIR•uh•lel SER•kit] A circuit that has more than one path for an electric current to follow **(132)**

phases [FAYZ•uhz] The different shapes that Earth's moon seems to have **(358)**

physical property [FIZ•ih•kuhl PRAHP•er•tee] Information about matter that you can observe without changing the matter **(40)**

pitch [PICH] A measure of how high or low a sound is **(66)**

planet [PLAN•it] A large object that moves around a star **(364)**

pollution [puh•LOO•shuhn] Waste products that damage an ecosystem **(484)**

population [pahp•yuh•LAY•shuhn] All the individuals of the same kind living in the same ecosystem **(458)**

position [puh•ZISH•uhn] The location of an object **(178)**

potential energy [poh•TEN•shuhl EN•er•jee] Energy that an object has because of its position or its condition **(153)**

precipitation [pree•sip•uh•TAY•shuhn] Water that falls to Earth **(282)**

predator [PRED•uh•ter] A consumer that eats prey **(508)**

preservation [prez•er•VAY•shuhn] The protection of resources **(334)**

prey [PRAY] Consumers that are eaten by predators **(508)**

producer [pruh•DOOS•er] A living thing, such as a plant, that can make its own food **(498)**

pulley [PUHL•ee] A simple machine made of a wheel with a line around it (218)

radiation [ray•dee•AY•shuhn] The movement of heat without matter to carry it (108)

rain [RAYN] Precipitation that is liquid water (290)

rain shadow [RAYN SHAD•oh] The area on the side of a mountain range that gets little or no rain or cloud cover (300)

red blood cell [RED BLUHD SEL] A type of cell that carries oxygen to all other cells in the body (398)

reflection [rih•FLEK•shuhn] The bouncing of light, sound, or heat off an object (82, 97)

refraction [rih•FRAK•shuhn] The bending of light when it moves from one kind of matter to another (99)

renewable resource [rih•NOO•uh•buhl REE•sawrs] A resource that can be replaced within a human lifetime (338)

resource [REE•sawrs] Any material or energy that people use to satisfy a need (322)

rock [RAHK] A solid substance made of one or more minerals (244)

rock cycle [RAHK SY•kuhl] The sequence of processes that change rocks from one type to another over long periods (252)

sand [SAND] The largest particles that make up soil (268)

scientific method [sy•uhn•TIF•ik METH•uhd] A way that scientists find out how things work and affect each other (20)

screw [SKROO] A simple machine made of a post with an inclined plane wrapped around it (228)

sea breeze [SEE BREEZ] A breeze that moves from the water to the land (298)

sedimentary rock [sed•uh•MEN•ter•ee RAHK] A type of rock that forms when layers of sediment are pressed together (247)

series circuit [SIR•eez SER•kit] A circuit that has only one path for an electric current to follow (132)

simple machine [SIM•puhl muh•SHEEN] A machine with few or no moving parts that you apply just one force to (211)

sleet [SLEET] Precipitation made when rain falls through freezing-cold air and turns to ice (290)

snow [SNOH] Precipitation made when water vapor turns directly into ice and forms ice crystals (291)

solar energy [SOH•ler EN•er•jee] The energy of the sun (156)

solar system [SOH•ler SIS•tuhm] A group of objects in space that revolve around a central star (364)

solid [SAHL•id] The state of matter that has a definite shape and takes up a definite amount of space (32)

speed [SPEED] The measure of an object's change in position during a unit of time (180)

spinal cord [SPY•nuhl KAWRD] A tube of nerves that runs through your backbone to your brain (438)

spring scale [SPRING SKAYL] A tool that measures forces, such as weight **(8)**

standard measure [STAN•derd MEZH•er] An accepted measurement **(4)**

star [STAR] A huge ball of superheated gases **(372)**

static electricity [STAT•ik ee•lek•TRIS•uh•tee] An electrical charge that builds up on an object **(128)**

stomach [STUHM•uhk] A baglike organ in which food is mixed with digestive juices and squeezed by muscles **(440)**

sun [SUHN] The star at the center of our solar system **(372)**

temperature [TEM•per•uh•cher] A measure of the average energy of motion of particles of matter **(47)**

tissue [TISH•oo] A group of cells of the same type that work together to perform a certain job **(406)**

tornado [tawr•NAY•doh] A fast-spinning spiral of wind that touches the ground **(292)**

transmission [tranz•MISH•uhn] The passing of light or sound waves through a material **(84)**

universe [YOO•nuh•vers] Everything that exists in space **(374)**

vein [VAYN] A blood vessel that carries blood back to the heart from another part of the body **(432)**

velocity [vuh•LAHS•uh•tee] The measure of the speed and direction of motion of an object **(186)**

vibration [vy•BRAY•shuhn] A quick back-and-forth motion **(64)**

volume [VAHL•yoom] The amount of space an object takes up **(39)**

warm front [WAWRM FRUHNT] The boundary where a warm air mass moves over a cold air mass **(306)**

waste heat [WAYST HEET] Heat that can't be used to do useful work **(116)**

water cycle [WAW•ter SY•kuhl] The movement of water from the surface of Earth into the air and back again **(282)**

wavelength [WAYV•length] The distance between a point on one wave and the identical point on the next wave **(73)**

weathering [WETH•er•ing] The breaking down of rocks on Earth's surface into smaller pieces **(258)**

wedge [WEJ] A simple machine made of two inclined planes placed back to back **(230)**

weight [WAYT] A measure of the gravitational force acting on an object **(196)**

wheel-and-axle [weel•and•AK•suhl] A simple machine made of a wheel and an axle that turn together **(220)**

white blood cell [WYT BLUHD SEL] A type of cell that helps you heal after an injury and protects you from illness **(400)**

work [WERK] The use of force to move an object over a distance **(210)**

Index

Rain shadows, 300

Ramps. *See* Inclined planes

Recording data, 16
  flood modeling, 289
  lighting a bulb, 127

Recycling, 342

Red blood cells, 398–399, 434

Red stars, 373

Reduce (conservation), 342

Red-winged blackbirds, 459

Reflection
  light, 97
  by minerals, 245
  of sound, 82

Refraction, light, 99

Renewable resources, 338–339, 482

Reservoirs, 330

Resources
  conservation of, 334, 342
  definition of, 322
  energy, 323
  mineral, 326
  misuse of, 332–333
  natural, 322–323
  nonrenewable, 340–341, 482
  preserving, 334
  renewable, 338–339, 482
  use of, 330–331

Respiratory system, 430–431

Reuse (conservation), 342
  in art, 336

Rhyolite, 246

River hogs, 501

Robotics, 233

Robots, DNA, 446

Rock(s)
  definition of, 244
  igneous, 246, 254
  metamorphic, 248, 254
  minerals in, 244, 248
  sedimentary, 247, 254
  in soil horizons, 267
  weathering of, 258–260
  See also Rock cycle

Rock climbing, 216

Rock cycle, 252–254

Roebling, Emily, 54

Roller coasters, 195

Ross, 154, 373

Rovers (spacecraft), 2

Rulers, 4

Runoff, 286

S

Saber-toothed cats, 520

Safety
  in science investigations, R36
  during severe weather, 294

Sagebrush, 506

Sailboats, 218–219

Saliva, 440, 441

Sand, 268

Sandstone, 242, 247, 254

Sandwiches, long-lasting, 52–53

Saturn, 362, 366

Savanna climate, 468, 469

Scales, 8

Science projects
  book balancing, 235
  carnivores vs. herbivores, 525
  changing density, 55
  checking for air pollution, 491
  conductors, 121
  deep freeze, 275
  energy pyramid, 525
  filtering dirt, 491
  frame of reference, 203
  generating electricity, 169
  insulators and conductors, 169
  intestine model, 447
  long-distance listening, 89
  making it float, 55
  making rain gauges, 315
  motion and frames of reference, 203
  pulleys, 235
  reduce, reuse, recycle, 347

rock cycle signs, 275
  seeing around corners, 121
  skin's oil glands, 415
  small intestine model, 447
  solar cooker, 347
  sound over distance, 89
  spiral galaxies, 381
  sundials, 381
  sweat glands model, 415
  weather and seasons, 315

Scientific inquiries. *See* Inquiries

Scientific method, 20–22

Screws, 224, 228–229

Sea breezes, 298

Seasons, Earth's tilt and, 356–357

Second-level consumers, 510

Sediment, 262
  erosion of, 262
  in soil, 266

Sedimentary rocks, 247, 254

Seeman, Nadrian, 446

Seesaws, 208, 212

Segway Human Transporter, 232

Sense organ, taste, 442

Senses, R10–11

Sensory receptors, 402

Sequence, R22–23

Series circuits, 132, 133

Shadows, 96
  rain shadows, 300

Shale, 247, 248

Shape, 40

Shelter, need for, 475

SI. *See* International System

Sidewinders, 506, 507

Silt, 247, 268

Simple machines, 211
  inclined planes, 226–227
  levers, 212–214
  pulleys, 218–219
  screws, 224, 228–229
  wedges, 230
  wheel-and-axles, 220–221

Sinkholes, 259

Getty Images; **462** Karl Kummels/SuperStock; **464** (*c*) Jerome Wexler/Visuals Unlimited; (*bl*) Adam Jones/Visuals Unlimited; (*br*) Rob Simpson/Visuals Unlimited; **465** David L. Shirk/Animals Animals; **469** (*tr*) Greg Neise/Visuals Unlimited; (*cl*) Adam Jones/Visuals Unlimited; (*tl*) Julie Eggers/Bruce Coleman, Inc.; (*br*) Eastcott-Momatiuk/The Image Works; (*bl*) Patrick Endres/Visuals Unlimited; (*cr*) Richard Thom/Visuals Unlimited; **472** Peter Arnold/Peter Arnold, Inc.; **474** Peter Arnold/Peter Arnold, Inc.; **475** (*br*) Gil Lopez Espina/Visuals Unlimited; (*cr*) E & P Bauer/Bruce Coleman, Inc.; **475** (*cl*) Masa Ushioda/Bruce Coleman, Inc.; **476** (*bl*) Michael & Patricia Fogden/Minden Pictures; (*br*) David Moore/Alamy Images; (*cl*) Jean Paul Ferrero/Ardea London; (*cr*) Lynn Stone/Animals Animals; **477** (*t*) Chase Swift/CORBIS; (*tcr*) Alan G. Nelson/Animals Animals; **478** (*cl*) Brad Mitchell/Alamy Images; (*b*) Robert W. Domm/Visuals Unlimited; **480** Jim Richardson/CORBIS; **482** (*bl*) Dennis Brack/IPN; (*b*) Joel Sartore/Getty Images; **483** (*cl*) CORBIS; (*tr*) Stuart Westmorland/CORBIS; (*cr*) Masterfile; (*tl*) Micheal Rose/Photo Researchers; **484** (*r*) Mark Richards/PhotoEdit; (*bcr*) Steve Maslowski/Visuals Unlimited; (*tcr*) Susan Van Etten/Photo Edit; (*br*) Rick Poley/Visuals Unlimited; **485** (*tl*) Cary Wolinsky/IPN; (*tr*) Nancy Richmond/The Image Works; **486** (*bl*) CORBIS; (*cr*) Frank Ordonez/Syracuse Newspapers/The Image Works; **488–489** NOAA; **490** (*bg*) Index Stock; (*inset*) Courtesy Mutual of Omaha; **491** (*bg*) Dennis MacDonald/Alamy Images; **493** (*tl*) Image Source/Inmagine; (*bl*) Eastcott-Momatiuk/The Image Works; **494** Tom and Pat Leeson; **496** Kim Taylor/Bruce Coleman, Inc.; **499** (*br*) D. Robert & Lorri Franz/CORBIS; (*tr*) Lynn Stone/Animals Animals; (*tl*) Darrell Gulin/CORBIS; **501** (*bl*) Michael Fogden/Animals Animals; (*cr*) Bob Barber/Barber Nature Photography; (*tc*) Lynn Stone/Animals Animals; (*cl*) Kevin Schafer/CORBIS; **502** (*cr*) Wolfgang Kaehler/CORBIS; (*b*) Jim Brandenburg/Minden Pictures; (*cl*) Ken Lucas/Visuals Unlimited; **503** (*br*) D.Hurst/Alamy Images; **504** CDC/PHIL/CORBIS; **506** (*b*) Royalty-Free/CORBIS; (*cr*) Gerry Ellis / Minden Pictures; (*br*) Darrell Gulin/CORBIS; **506** (*tr*) ZSSD/MINDEN PICTURES; **507** (*br*) Dale Sanders/ Masterfile; (*tl*) CORBIS; (*c*) Andrew J. Martinez/Photo Researchers; (*tr*) Dale Sanders/Masterfile; **508** (*bl*) M. Timothy O'Keefe/Bruce Coleman, Inc.; (*bg*) Wolfgang Kaehler/CORBIS; (*br*) Doug Perrine/SeaPics.com; **509** (*bl*) Joe McDonald/CORBIS; (*tc*) Bill Brooks/Masterfile; (*cr*) Barry Runk/Stan/Grant Heilman Photography; (*tl*) Jim Zipp/Photo Researchers; **514** Tammy L. Johnson/Florida Museum of Natural History; **516** (*bg*) Mitsuaki Iwago/Minden Images; (*bcr*) Paul A. Souders/CORBIS; (*br*) Roger Harris/Science Photo Library; **517** (*bcr*) Peter Scoones/Science Photo Library; (*br*) Dr. Schwimmer/Bruce Coleman, Inc.; (*bg*) SuperStock; (*cl*) Jeff Gage/Florida Museum of Natural History; **518** (*bg*) Carol Havens/Corbis; (*br*) Kevin Schafer/CORBIS; **519** (*tr*) Ken Lucas/Visuals Unlimited; (*bcl*) D. Robert & Lorri Franz/CORBIS; (*bl*) Patti Murray/Animals Animals; (*br*) David Cavagnaro/Visuals Unlimited; (*tc*) Barry Runk/Stan/Grant Heilman Photography; **520** (*cl*) Gianni Dagli Orti/CORBIS; (*cr*) Hulton Archive/Getty Images; (*b*) Ron Testa/The Field Museum; **522** (*bl*) Animals Animals; **523** (*t*) Wildlife Conservation Society; (*b*) Animals Animals; **524** (*t*) Assign Nature Conservation Foundation; (*b*) Corbis; **525** (*bg*) Mark Mattock/Getty Images

Health Handbook

R5 Dennis Kunkel/Phototake; **R12** (*t*) CNRI/Science Photo Library/Photo Researchers; **R12** (*tc*) A. Pasieka/Photo Researchers; **R12** (*bc*) CNRI/Science Photo Library/Photo Researchers; **R12** (*b*) Custom Medical Stock Photo; **R15** (*inset*) David Young-Wolff/PhotoEdit; **R15** (*b*) Bill O'Connor/Peter Arnold, Inc.

All other photos © Harcourt School Publishers. Harcourt Photos provided by the Harcourt Index, Harcourt IPR, and Harcourt photographers; Weronica Ankarorn, Victoria Bowen, Eric Camden, Doug Dukane, Ken Kinzie, April Riehm, and Steve Williams.

BEHAVIOR Playing helps wolf cubs develop strength and hunting skills.

HOWLING Wolves howl to communicate with other wolves or sometimes just for fun.

BEHAVIOR Wolves bare their teeth when they are angry.

SPEED Wolves can run up to 56 kilometers per hour.

SENSES Wolves can hear prey up to 12 km away, can smell prey up to 3 km away, and have excellent eyesight.